THE BEDFORD BIBLIOGRAPHY FOR TEACHERS OF WRITING

Sixth Edition

THE BEDFORD BIBLIOGRAPHY FOR TEACHERS OF WRITING

Sixth Edition

Nedra Reynolds
University of Rhode Island

Patricia Bizzell
College of the Holy Cross

Bruce Herzberg
Bentley College

Bedford/St. Martin's   Boston ◆ New York

For Bedford/St. Martin's

Developmental Editor: Amanda Bristow
Production Editor: Kerri Cardone
Production Supervisor: Jennifer L. Wetzel
Copyeditor: Jeannine Thibodeau
Cover Design: Donna Lee Dennison

President: Joan E. Feinberg
Editorial Director: Denise B. Wydra
Editor in Chief: Karen S. Henry
Director of Marketing: Karen Melton
Director of Editing, Design, and Production: Marcia Cohen
Managing Editor: Elizabeth M. Schaaf

Manufactured in the United States of America.

9 8 7
f   e

For information, write: Bedford/St. Martin's, 75 Arlington Street, Boston, MA 02116 (617-399-4000)

ISBN-10: 0–312–40501–4
ISBN-13: 978–0–312–40501–4

Publisher's Note

Bedford/St. Martin's is pleased to make available this reorganized and expanded sixth edition of *The Bedford Bibliography for Teachers of Writing*. We are gratified by the response to the first five editions. Not only have they proved a useful addition to the professional libraries of thousands of individual instructors, but they have also found a place on the reading lists for many graduate courses on the teaching of writing.

Since first appearing in 1984, both the *Bibliography* and the list of books in the back have expanded — the *Bibliography* to reflect the growth in the body of literature in composition studies and the list to reflect the growth of our composition program. Bedford Books was founded in 1981 as an independent editorial arm of the St. Martin's Press college division. The two publishing programs were combined in 1998 under a single imprint — Bedford/St. Martin's. Today we are the largest publisher of college composition texts in the country. We are immensely proud of the authors we have attracted to this list and of the books they have worked with us to produce. We continue to believe that any publisher ultimately must be judged by the quality of the books it publishes. As we enter our third decade, we continue to invite such judgment.

Joan E. Feinberg
President
Bedford/St. Martin's

Preface

The opening sentence of the preface to the first edition of *The Bedford Bibliography* in 1984 stated that "The study of composition is well established as a specialization in English, a serious discipline worthy of advanced graduate work." The former claim was based on the growing quantity and sophistication of scholarship in the field, on the rising numbers of composition specialists being hired and tenured, and on the appearance of more and more courses on composition theory and pedagogy in graduate school offerings. Still, the claim that the field was "well established" may have been just a little tendentious — a statement of confidence and hope rather than a clear fact. Today, though, the study of composition seems unequivocally well established. The latter claim in the opening sentence, that the discipline was worthy of graduate work, was true then as now. Then, however, we had vanishingly few colleagues with degrees in composition.

More scholars means more scholarship: Extraordinary growth in the quantity of scholarship in the discipline has been particularly evident to us in the time since the fifth edition of the *Bibliography* in 2000. Most notable is the proliferation of books, both edited collections and monographs. Relatively few books appeared in the 1984 edition — a half dozen collections of previously published articles and a couple of pedagogical books by single authors. In subsequent editions of the *Bibliography*, those numbers increased, to be sure, but preparing for the current edition, we faced hundreds of books in history, theory, literacy, communication, administration, and every branch of pedagogy. In addition, new journals have arisen and established ones have flourished. Each year since the late 1980s, the comprehensive CCCC *Bibliography* has recorded between sixteen hundred and two thousand items. Reviewing and selecting from this mass of material would have been impossible for the three of us alone. While we have benefited from suggestions offered by many readers and reviewers, for the current edition we have also formally enlisted nineteen consultants (identified and thanked in the Acknowledgments below) to sift through the materials in particular categories and suggest which books and essays should be considered for inclusion in the *Bibliography*. This task was not easy for any of us and making selections was very difficult.

For the most part, we have attempted to adhere to the same guidelines in the sixth edition that shaped the first: selecting materials that represent the theoretical and pedagogical concerns in composition studies today and those that will be useful to the working teacher of composition. We recognize, however, that the *Bibliography* has been used in graduate courses in composition and that there are now many teachers who are specialists in the field. Although we continue to believe that the job of the *Bibliography* is to introduce the wide range of valuable scholarship in the field to the many writing teachers who are not specialists, we have now included citations for works of history, theory, and research that are not, strictly speaking, "immediately applicable to classroom practice" but that engage pressing issues for the discipline. We have had nonetheless to make some uncomfortable decisions about what theoretical issues, scholarly disputes, and research findings might or might not be of interest to this audience and about which of the older pedagogical materials included in past editions of the *Bibliography* have retained or lost their usefulness. Some pieces that should be on the reading lists of courses in composition theory or cited as milestones in the development of the field will not be found here.

In this sixth edition of the *Bibliography*, we have grouped the 704 entries under five major headings and thirty subheadings (see the table of contents).

First, under the heading "Resources" appears information on basic tools for research in the field, in sections on "Periodicals" and "General Bibliographies." (Bibliographies on specific topics appear in the appropriate sections.) Under the second major heading, "History and Theory," we have three subheads. "The Rhetorical Tradition" cites primary texts from classical to modern times. "History of Rhetoric and Education" selects secondary texts covering the same time period. "Rhetoric and Composition Theory" collects important work done in recent years on discourse, argument, genre, ideology, approaches to composition pedagogy and research, and other theoretical concerns.

The third major heading has been renamed for this edition; "Composing, Literacy, and Rhetorics of Writing" introduces "The Process Movement," which includes entries that range over a period of nearly thirty years. "Literacy," the second section, includes works on literacy theory, cultural literacy, literacy programs, diversity, and teaching issues associated with these concerns. The following sections follow roughly the classical model of rhetoric, beginning with "Invention and Pre-Writing," and followed by "Arrangement" and "Argument." Works cited in "Arrangement" discuss systems for classifying the structures of paragraphs and essays, structures that can be used to teach patterns for composing. "Argument" treats arrangement issues affecting the entire structure of a text, such as the enthymeme or the Toulmin model. "Audience," the next section, groups works defining audience and its uses in teaching writing. The following section, "Revision," includes works on the place of revision in the composing process, especially as a way of developing ideas. Under "Style, Grammar, and Usage," corresponding to the third classical canon, "style," we have grouped works on sentence combining, other methods of increasing syntactic fluency in student writing, and prose style; we have also placed here works on teaching Standard English usage and grammar. Finally, "Response and Evaluation" includes works on responding to student writing, conference teaching, grading, portfolios, and assessment.

The fourth major heading, "Curriculum Development," begins with the section "Course Development," which includes works on writing course design and teaching. Then special topics are addressed: "Collaborative Learning" lists works on the theory and practice of writing groups and peer response. "Essay and Personal Writing" highlights works on the genre of the essay, on voice in writing, and on pedagogical techniques for helping students write more honestly and less pompously. "Literature and Composition" includes works on the theoretical connections between the two and on the use of literature in composition classes. "Advanced Composition" cites works on history and theory as well as pedagogical techniques for teaching advanced writing courses. "Basic Writing" features works that help teachers to understand the circumstances of underprepared writers, the conditions of multicultural basic writing classrooms, the kinds of errors beginning college writers make, and the effects on their writing of cultural and political considerations. The intersections of "Gender, Race, and Class" are represented in a section that addresses the influence of socially constructed gender roles and sexual orientation on writing, and techniques for feminist teaching. The implications for writing pedagogy of "Cultural Studies" appears next, followed by "Teaching English as a Second Language," which includes works analyzing the writing for students whose first language is not English. Issues concerning writing in the workplace are divided into two sections, "Technical Communication" and "Business Communication," and both categories evince new interest in visual communication.

The fifth major heading, "Writing Programs," provides introductory material on administrative concerns. "Writing Program Administration" addresses program design and evaluation, teacher training, and working conditions; "Writing Centers" cites theoretical and practical works on setting up and managing tutorial workshops, including tutor training; "Writing across the Curriculum" provides material on cross-disciplinary course design and on faculty development in interdisciplinary writing programs; "Electronic Writing Technologies" cites recent work on using computers, hypertext, and networks in writing instruction; and "Service Learning" cites resources for developing writing courses and programs that include a community-based component.

In the annotations of articles and single-author books, we attempt to summarize the thesis and main points of the work. In annotations of edited collections, of which there are now a great many, we characterize the central theme of the collection and then list several of the authors and essays included, choosing titles that give a sense of the contents of the collection. In collections of previously published articles, we include cross-references if the article has been cited separately. For edited collections of new essays, however, we have as a matter of policy not cited articles separately when the entire collection is cited. We have been partial to edited collections whose themes are carefully articulated and whose contributors have adhered to the volumes' stated purposes.

The entries in *The Bedford Bibliography* are numbered consecutively. Numbers in brackets, used for citations in "A Brief History of Rhetoric and Composition" and for cross-references in the bibliographic listings, refer to these entry numbers and can also be used to locate items in the index.

In selecting works for *The Bedford Bibliography*, our chief concern has been to provide access to materials that would be helpful to practicing writing teachers. Even so, we have undoubtedly left out much that is important, despite our efforts — and the efforts of our consultants — to be fair if not exhaustive. We welcome, as always, suggestions for revision.

Acknowledgments

We are particularly indebted to our consultants, without whom a daunting task would have been inconceivable. Thanks to Linda Adler-Kassner, Eastern Michigan University; Beth Boquet, Fairfield University; John Brereton, University of Massachusetts-Boston; Lorie Goodman, Pepperdine University; Jim Henry, George Mason University; Rebecca Moore Howard, Syracuse University; Daphne Jameson, Cornell University; Susan Jarratt, University of Miami, Ohio; Johndan Johnson-Eilola, Clarkson University; Min-Zhan Lu, University of Wisconsin-Milwaukee; Paul Kei Matsuda, University of New Hampshire; Roxanne Mountford, University of Arizona; Patricia Webb Peterson, Arizona State University; Stuart Selber, Pennsylvania State University; Ruth Spack, Bentley College; Peter Vandenberg, DePaul University; Irwin Weiser, Purdue University; Robert Yagelski, SUNY-Albany

Thanks also to Amanda Bristow at Bedford/St. Martin's, who worked with us on the project, Karin Halbert, who diligently and steadfastly located journals and articles, and Caryn O'Connell for manuscript preparation. We are also indebted to the graduate assistant Mary Gormley, who helped with reading and annotation. John Amburg, with the assistance of Kerri Cardone, expertly guided the book through production, and Jeannine Thibodeau copyedited the manuscript . We can never forget that *The Bedford Bibliography* was the brainchild of Chuck Christensen, the guiding force behind all of Bedford's work. Finally, we warmly thank those who have used the *Bibliography* and told us that they found it helpful. They have made the project worthwhile.

Contents

A Brief History of Rhetoric and Composition

Classical Rhetoric: Stages of Composing, Functions of Discourse

The formal study of rhetoric in the West began in Greece in the fifth century B.C.E. with the Sophists [42], followed by Isocrates [44], Plato [45], and Aristotle [46]. The main line of Greek rhetoric was extended by Roman rhetoricians, notably Cicero [47, 49] and Quintilian [51, 52]. Classical rhetoric, although concerned with oratory, still influences writing instruction. For example, by Roman times a five-stage model of the process of composing a speech had evolved. Three of these stages — invention, or discovering ideas; arrangement, or organizing ideas; and style, or putting ideas into words — have been modified into elements in modern models of writing processes. Memory and delivery, the last two classical stages, dwindled in postclassical times into mechanical techniques before being revived for serious study in modern departments of speech.

Scholars traditionally regarded classical rhetoric as a system with the built-in assumption that one first finds knowledge and then puts it into words. In our own day, in the context of a renewed interest in the Sophists, this view has been challenged by a number of historians of rhetoric, who argue that knowledge is actually created by words (see Jarratt [105] and Swearingen [138]). But the strongest influence on rhetoric has undoubtedly been the Aristotelian model. Aristotle described a number of *topoi*, or topics, for discovering ideas and arguments. These topics — ways of analyzing, evaluating, and extending virtually any subject — constitute a heuristic, or method of systematic inquiry.

Scholars have also emphasized classical rhetoric's sorting of discourse forms according to social function. Many classical rhetorics divide oratory into three categories. Deliberative speeches, primarily devoted to political purposes, aim to persuade hearers to choose or avoid some future course of action. Forensic speeches, used primarily in legal situations, aim to accuse or defend someone involved in a disputed past action. Epideictic speeches, produced in classical times on ceremonial occasions, aim to help hearers see some present event or person as worthy of praise or blame. Epideictic orations may make more use than others of literary ornaments and vocal pyrotechnics.

Although these classical categories for oral discourse have been reshaped by later rhetoricians, the premise that discourse can be classified according to

1

social function has been persistently influential. In eighteenth-century American colleges, for example, discourse was classified according to its use by clergymen, lawyers, or politicians. Contemporary composition scholars have redirected the interest in social function to analyses of the ways in which audience or social context affects the interpretation of written text.

Medieval and Renaissance Rhetoric

We often think of the Middle Ages as a time when many classical sources were not accessible: Quintilian and much of Cicero, for example, were lost until the Renaissance. But it is more accurate to see medieval rhetoricians selecting and reshaping the classical heritage in light of Augustine's reinterpretation of rhetoric to suit Christian purposes [53]. One important emphasis in medieval rhetoric following Augustine was the redirection of deliberative discourse from political to religious ends. The goal became saving souls, not leading the state. Another important emphasis was the desire to codify authoritative classical precepts on good composition. Classical rhetoric texts had often been prescriptive, providing rules for achieving effective speeches. In the Middle Ages, this prescriptive impulse so intensified that many medieval rhetoric texts consist entirely of lists of rules and examples illustrating them.

Medieval university students studied grammar, rhetoric, and dialectic — the "trivium." As exemplified in the popular classical textbooks of Donatus, grammar means not simply the study of correct constructions but also the analysis of style. The study of grammar thereby shaded over into the medieval study of rhetoric, which emphasized style. Grammar and rhetoric merely prepared the beginning student for the serious business of the university, the study of dialectic, which offered practice in oral argumentation on historical, religious, or legal issues. Bishop Isidore of Seville wrote an important summary of the arts of grammar, rhetoric, and dialectic.

Dialectic was regarded as a preparation for logic, the oral arguments of which became opportunities for stylistic display, but the subject was still not considered closely allied with rhetoric. The study of rhetoric was manifested, however, in techniques for adult practitioners, for example, in ars dictaminis, the art of composing official letters through which church and state business was conducted, and ars praedicandi, the art of preaching. Medieval theorists of poetry also drew on rhetorical studies of style.

In the early Renaissance, major texts by Cicero and Quintilian were recovered. In the sixteenth century, a proliferation of rhetorics following classical models but written in the vernacular appeared, such as those in English by Leonard Cox, Richard Sherry, Thomas Wilson, and George Puttenham. Most of these rhetoricians emphasized the study of style, sometimes linking their practice explicitly with poetic. The generally acknowledged master of stylistic rhetoric in the Renaissance was Erasmus, whose Copia (1512) [56] was originally conceived as a textbook.

Another source of change for Renaissance rhetoric was the influential work of Peter Ramus (Pierre de la Ramée), whose ideas were recorded in

Institutiones Oratoriae (1545) by his colleague Talaeus (Omer Talon). Ramus wished to reform the medieval trivium by reemphasizing the classical division of the stages of composing. Ramist rhetoric intensifies the separation between these stages and the importance of their sequence, at the same time divorcing invention and arrangement from rhetoric and assigning them to logic. Ramists hoped to define a logical, scientific discourse, untainted by nonlogical appeals, that would win assent from the rational audience by virtue of rationality alone. Ramus's fellow Puritans widely adopted this plain style for all serious matters.

Rhetoric under the Ramist scheme is left to deal only with style, memory, and delivery. Memory had figured importantly in some early Renaissance hermetic precursors of modern science, and delivery would give rise in the eighteenth century to elaborate elocutionary techniques for public speakers and actors. Still, memory and delivery tended to continue their decline in importance as the Renaissance dissemination of printing made written texts ever more important to academic, religious, and political life. Rhetoricians, then, came increasingly to focus upon the study of language as the dress of ideas that were generated elsewhere. The goal of rhetorical study was to clothe one's ideas in the most elegant dress possible, and rhetoric thus came to be seen as the finishing refinement of an upper-class education.

Rhetoric in the Eighteenth Century: The Scottish Influence

Seeing rhetoric as the study of the dress of thought rather than the study of thought itself threatened to trivialize it. Rhetoricians from the University of Edinburgh sought to stop this trend by arguing that the study of correct and persuasive style produced not only competent public speakers but virtuous people. This was a strong defense, for the study of rhetoric in American colleges focused on oratory that would be useful to clergy, lawyers, and politicians. In addition, the Edinburgh rhetoricians connected the study of persuasion with the more prestigious scientific discipline of psychology. And these rhetoricians adapted ornamentation from Cicero to correct the emphasis on plain style that the Puritans had kept alive from Ramism.

Perhaps the most influential book to come from Edinburgh to America was Hugh Blair's Lectures on Rhetoric and Belles-Lettres [66], published in 1783 and adopted as the standard text at Yale in 1785 and Harvard in 1788. Blair's text was widely used in American colleges and secondary schools until the end of the nineteenth century. Americans found Blair's emphasis on the moral qualities of belletristic taste particularly important, since his approach justified the social leadership of the well-trained orator.

Less popular in the schools but perhaps more important for modern rhetoric was another Scottish rhetorician, George Campbell, whose Philosophy of Rhetoric (1776) [65] professes to validate its principles by relating them to the working of the human mind. More innovative than his contemporaries, Campbell extended the purpose of rhetoric beyond persuasion, defining eloquence as the "art or talent by which discourse is adapted to its end."

A later rhetorician in the Scottish tradition was Alexander Bain, who showed the importance of psychology for achieving goals of persuasion in *English Composition and Rhetoric: A Manual* (1866) [71]. Bain argued that persuasive discourse is organized by associating ideas in a way that produces the desired emotion in the audience. From Bain's work comes the now familiar taxonomy of essay structures, or modes of discourse: narration, description, exposition, and argumentation.

In America, the Scottish revision of classical rhetoric had special significance. A nascent democracy, so the argument went, needed people of refinement who could direct the vulgar taste into virtuous channels; the psychology of persuasion could help these leaders consolidate their control. Hence, the study of rhetoric both conferred and garnered prestige. Long before American colleges had English departments, they had distinguished professors of rhetoric.

Rhetoric in Nineteenth-Century America: The Harvard Influence

In 1806 Harvard College established the Boylston Professorship of Rhetoric and Oratory and became, thereafter, the dominant influence on the development of rhetoric at other American colleges. Edward T. Channing, who held the chair for thirty-two years (1819–1851), continued the Scottish emphasis on belletristic taste and the psychology of persuasion but shifted the emphasis in practice from speaking to writing and increased attention to literary exempla. From the literary models, Channing derived rules for correct grammar, style, and organization, which were taught more and more prescriptively as the century went on.

Francis J. Child, who held the Boylston Professorship after Channing (1851–1876), had studied philology at a German university before taking the chair and came to Harvard determined to turn the study of English from rhetoric to literature. Child bitterly resented the time he had to spend correcting student compositions. He delegated as much of this work as he could to faculty underlings and concentrated on enlarging Harvard's offerings in literature. In 1876, to keep Child from moving to Johns Hopkins (the first American university to be organized in departments on the German model), Harvard created the first Professorship of English for him, and Child spent the next twenty years developing the English literature curriculum. His successor in the Boylston Professorship, A. S. Hill, continued the rule-bound focus on written composition begun by Channing, but it was now clear that composition was a second-class subject and that rhetoric was hardly mentioned in the English department.

These changes are neatly encapsulated in Harvard's 1874 entrance requirement in English composition:

> Each candidate will be required to write a short English composition, correct in spelling, punctuation, grammar, and expression, the subject to be taken from such works of standard authors as shall be announced from

time to time. The subject for 1874 will be taken from one of the following works: Shakespeare's *Tempest, Julius Caesar,* and *Merchant of Venice;* Goldsmith's *Vicar of Wakefield;* Scott's *Ivanhoe* and *Lay of the Last Minstrel.*

The Harvard model of freshman composition began to spread, particularly with the publication in 1890 of Harvard Professor Barrett Wendell's *English Composition: Eight Lectures.* Blair and Bain had used literary exempla to illustrate rhetorical principles. In the Harvard course, this belletristic tradition culminated in rules derived from the exempla and rigidly applied to student essays. Furthermore, the works of literature to be studied were strictly specified in lists of standard authors, such as the one given in the entrance requirements. These lists soon came to dictate secondary-school curricula, since one needed to know the listed works to perform well on admissions tests at prestigious colleges. And the prestige of those colleges that regulated their admissions according to the lists made it hard for other colleges to avoid similar requirements.

Progressive Education in Twentieth-Century America

In the early twentieth century, more and more secondary-school and college teachers came to oppose the domination of college admissions by the standard lists of works generated at Harvard and other elite eastern schools. The National Council of Teachers of English (NCTE) was formed in 1911 largely to consolidate resistance to the lists and to the conception of English studies they represented. To further this cause, the NCTE began to publish *English Journal* in 1912 [8]. The first president of the NCTE was Fred Newton Scott of the University of Michigan. A past president of the Modern Language Association (MLA), Scott possessed impeccable credentials in literary scholarship; nevertheless, he deplored the demotion of rhetoric and promoted an understanding of writing that reemphasized self-expression and the adaptation of prose to its social purposes.

At the same time, departments of speech were growing more numerous in American colleges, taking over the study of historical rhetoric and many of its traditional concerns, such as response to audience. Speech teachers broke away from the NCTE in 1914 to form their own professional organization, the National Association for Academic Teachers of Public Speaking — now the Speech Communication Association.

English teachers' dissatisfaction with the reading lists soon became caught up in the larger progressive reform movement, which directly challenged the idea that the goal of higher education in America should be to empower an elite. The progressives believed that the purpose of education is to integrate a diverse population into a community of productive citizens. Progressive education sought to equip students with intellectual and social skills they would need as adults and to give attention to the needs of each individual student. John Dewey was an important leader of this movement. He became chair in 1894 of the Department of Philosophy, Psychology, and Pedagogy at the University of Chicago, and his *School and Society* was published in 1899.

Progressive education sought to free writing instruction from the service of canonical literary study. Correctness remained a goal of writing instruction, justified not by some authoritative set of rules but by its usefulness in the world beyond school. While respectful of the diverse cultural backgrounds of a school population that included record numbers of immigrants, progressive education stressed the communicative function of writing to help draw diverse groups together and integrate them into the mainstream of American society. A class writing project, for example, might collect data about some local social problem and prepare a report to be sent to the appropriate public official.

The progressives were not very often successful, at least on the college level, in separating composition and literature. In progressive hands, however, writing about literature became a way to understand one's own responses to the text. Such an approach can be found in Louise Rosenblatt's *Literature as Exploration* (1938) and in early issues of *College English,* which the NCTE began to publish in 1939 [4]. As progressive education moved into the 1930s and 1940s, its social agenda became more modest, but the main goal was still life adjustment — helping adolescents pass through their difficult developmental period and emerge as productive citizens.

Progressive education was also innovative in its interest in the social sciences as a source of information for English studies. Of course, progressives were not the first to look in this direction; rhetoric in the eighteenth and nineteenth centuries had incorporated some study of psychology. But with the demotion of rhetoric in the late nineteenth century, contacts between English and the social sciences were downplayed. Progressive education, in contrast, aimed to study students' abilities, needs, and achievements scientifically and to redesign curricula accordingly. These efforts had very little effect on college writing instruction, however.

Freshman English courses were rarely devoted only to writing instruction. Their main goal was to introduce students to literary study and in the process to correct the writing in students' literary essays according to long-established standards of grammatical, stylistic, and formal correctness. Where writing courses did exist, they usually patterned their syllabi after Bain's modes of discourse and justified their existence with arguments similar to Blair's for the good writer as a virtuous person. Widespread changes did not begin to occur until after World War II.

Beginnings of Modern Composition Studies: New Criticism

In the 1930s, New Criticism began to supplant biographical and philological criticism as the dominant mode of academic literary study. New Criticism put its emphasis on the close analysis of literary texts and appeared to have no common ground with the current forms of rhetorical study or composition pedagogy. By the 1940s, at any rate, the separation in English departments between literary study and the teaching of writing was so complete that academics committed to literary study could easily ignore the writing program.

New Criticism ultimately had a profound effect on writing instruction, however, because it approached literary texts as complex structures of meaning. In its view, changing a word in a poem changed the poem's meaning — it did not simply select an alternative dress for an idea that remained unchanged. New Criticism therefore made it possible to see the relation between thought and language as fundamental rather than superficial. The freshman English course patterned on a nineteenth century model (the current-traditional model, as it is often called), treated the relation between thought and language too mechanically. What could be taken for granted in the writing class quickly became problematic.

Recognizing the need for serious reconsideration of the freshman writing course, the NCTE mandated the Conference on College Composition and Communication (CCCC) in 1949. The journal *College Composition and Communication* appeared in 1950 [3]. In the 1950s, the CCCC did much to lay the foundations for the modern discipline of composition studies. On the practical side, the CCCC worked to improve conditions for the graduate assistants who taught almost all college writing courses and to exchange ideas among college writing program administrators. The conference also championed the cause of semanticists and linguists looking for a home in college English departments and urged that the Ph.D. in English literature include coursework in linguistics as preparation for teaching writing.

Reinforcing these efforts pertaining to college composition was the post-Sputnik concern in the early 1960s to encourage excellence in all areas of American education. To make the college writing course more rigorous, ways were sought to expand its focus beyond socialization or linguistics to the full traditional range of rhetorical concerns. Distinguished literary critics such as Wayne Booth began to write on rhetoric. In 1963, the NCTE published a survey of research to date in composition, compiled by Richard Braddock, Richard Lloyd-Jones, and Lowell Schoer. Little valuable work was found, but the study itself encouraged high standards for new research in the field. To give such research an outlet, the NCTE began publishing the journal *Research in the Teaching of English* in 1967 [19].

The 1960s: Classical Rhetoric, Writing Processes, and Authentic Voice

With the encouragement of the CCCC in the early 1960s, composition specialists looked to the classical texts that had rarely been studied in English departments (although speech departments had preserved an interest in them) and to transformations of the classical heritage by later rhetoricians. Several important collections of premodern documents on rhetoric and discussions of classical rhetoric's value to the modern student were published. This renewed attention to classical sources helped to foster an increased interest in stages of the writing process and in style as an expression of personal ethos.

The classical model is a five-stage process, consisting of invention, arrangement, style, memory, and delivery. After the Ramists excluded invention and arrangement, and memory and delivery dwindled into elocution,

American writing courses, in their focus on one stage, style, had lost a sense of writing as a process. Now writing as a process was reemphasized in the study of what Gordon Rohman called the pre-writing stages, those that precede production of a finished piece of work. Invention and arrangement began to be reclaimed for composition studies as preliminary stages in the writing process. Style, too, was seen as a process of developing ideas by recasting sentences, not merely pouring ideas into preset sentence forms.

Interest in the writing process and in writing as self-expression prompted the MLA and the NCTE to sponsor the 1966 conference at Dartmouth College on the teaching of English (see John Dixon [373]). Attended by American and British educators from the elementary, secondary, and college levels, the conference helped spread the conviction that writing instruction should emphasize self-expressive uses of language and assist students in shaping their ideas through writing. Unlike the Harvard-model course, which imposed standards on passive students, the new Dartmouth-model writing course encouraged more interaction among teacher and students, more dramatic and collaborative activities. One influential process-oriented pedagogy appeared in James Moffett's *Teaching the Universe of Discourse* (1968) [381].

The Dartmouth Conference called for writing instruction that takes more notice of students' needs for self-expression as opposed to their adjustment to social demands. Now composition studies searched for a pedagogy to help students find personal writing styles that were honest and unconstrained by conventions. Such a style came to be termed the writer's authentic voice — an important concept in the work of Ken Macrorie [411] and Peter Elbow [397, 408]. The need for such pedagogy seemed especially poignant in the late 1960s and early 1970s, when many writing teachers sought some critical response to the opaque, impersonal prose that dominates politics. Authentic-voice pedagogy contributed techniques, such as Elbow's freewriting, that became part of every writing teacher's repertoire.

The 1970s: Cognitive Processes, Basic Writing, and Writing across the Curriculum

In the 1970s, interest in the writing process prompted inquiry into what cognitive psychology and psycholinguistics might discover about it. Composition scholars began to refer not to the "writing" process but to the "composing" process, as in the pioneering work of Janet Emig [176, 228]. The significance of this shift in terminology was its emphasis on the cognitive activities involved in writing. "Composing," in other words, is what goes on in the writer's head and is then recorded in writing. This interest in composing processes first focused on what had been the initial stages in the classical process, invention and arrangement. Theorists developed structured invention techniques that would guide the student through an optimal composing process. The particle-wave-field heuristic devised by Richard Young, Alton Becker, and Kenneth Pike was one influential modern invention technique [294].

Progressive educators before World War II had urged researchers to use social-scientific methods for investigating students' real needs. These urgings were rarely heeded in college English departments. Now empirical studies based on observations of working writers began, such as those of Nancy Sommers [320] and Sondra Perl [239]. The whole composing process came under study. Research indicated that there might be more than one successful composing process. Furthermore, the process no longer seemed to be neatly linear, as described in the classical model, but appeared recursive and hierarchical, as developed in the model of Linda Flower and cognitive psychologist John R. Hayes [232].

In comprehensive theoretical works, the philosophical and psychological bases for the study of composing were explored. Some authors argued that the forms of discourse are structurally similar to the forms of cognitive processes and perhaps even to the brain itself. To teach the forms of discourse, then, is not merely to teach conventional modes of arrangement but to provide students with models of actual cognitive processes. If the forms of discourse parallel cognitive processes, they should be equally accessible to every student, regardless of cultural background.

In the 1970s, the increasing number of college freshmen whose home language was not Standard English severely tested the applicability of cognitive theories of writing. The work of William Labov [460] and other sociolinguists on dialectal variation helped writing teachers see that this new classroom population, in need of so much help with the requirements of academic writing, was not cognitively deficient but, rather, linguistically and culturally diverse. One immediate result of this new understanding was a 1974 resolution by the CCCC on students' right to their own languages. This resolution argued that students would learn Standard English more easily if they were allowed to write some school assignments in their home languages, whether or not these were Standard. The document also called for teacher education to include work in dialectal variation.

Later in the decade, studies of basic writing explored the pedagogical problems posed by dialectal variation in the classroom. Mina Shaughnessy's important work, *Errors and Expectations* (1977) [472], argues for respect for students' home languages but also advises teachers on how to help these students become more comfortable with academic writing. Many student errors with Standard forms are actually regular, if not rule-governed, attempts to achieve academic correctness. A student whose home language is Black English, for example, might write her school papers in neither Black English nor Standard English but in an idiosyncratic blend of the two. Furthermore, socialization to school is a problem for many basic writers. If students' home cultures place little value on the intellectual abstractions of academic work, for example, a typical research paper assignment might seem pointless. The study of error, therefore, as Shaughnessy argues, must consider students' cultural background and how this may affect their relation to the social contexts of school as well as what appears on the page when they write.

With so many students seeming to need extra help in mastering college-level writing, many composition scholars came to feel that professors in all disciplines must be enlisted in the effort of teaching writing or, rather, helped to see that they were already contributing to students' introduction to academic discourse. They could learn to make this contribution in better ways, which would improve both students' writing and their learning of disciplinary content. To address these needs, cross-disciplinary writing programs, or programs in "writing across the curriculum," to use James Britton's phrase, began to develop. The first American writing-across-the-curriculum program was started at Carleton College in Minnesota in 1974, and Elaine Maimon directed an influential program at Beaver College in Pennsylvania [662, 663].

These programs typically attempt to educate students and faculty from all disciplines about the conventions of academic discourse and about the range of activities that constitute mature composing processes. Maimon argues that the literary training most composition scholars have received makes them uniquely suited to analyze the conventions of discourse for writers who are not aware of the conventions' function in the generation of knowledge [662]. Toby Fulwiler stresses the importance of journal keeping in the composing processes of all academic disciplines. Fulwiler finds that writing-across-the-curriculum programs encourage students and teachers alike to become more confident writers and eager collaborators in a literate community of scholars [657]. James Kinneavy suggests that a further outcome may be wider participation in a literate community beyond the academy, in which important public issues can be discussed [660].

The 1980s: Social and Historical Approaches to Rhetoric

In the 1980s, composition scholars focused on the social nature of writing, building upon previous work in both basic writing and writing across the curriculum. Research into the cognitive processes of writers continued, but it was informed by new interest in how these processes are conditioned by social circumstances. For example, Mike Rose shows that writer's block may be as much a result of bad writing instruction as of individual cognitive disabilities [240]. Moreover, ethnographic studies, such as that by Shirley Brice Heath [264], which focus on writers at various school levels and beyond school, became increasingly important.

James Kinneavy's early work on the modes of discourse (1971) [194] returned to Aristotle for a revitalized sense of the decisive role of social function in determining the form of discourse. Kinneavy classifies rhetorical situations according to their emphasis on the writer (expressive), audience (persuasive), subject matter (referential), or verbal medium (aesthetic). Kinneavy's theory allows for the literary analysis of a wide variety of texts, thus laying the groundwork for studies in writing across the curriculum. His work became more influential in the 1980s as these studies proliferated.

The search for a social theory of writing became broadly interdisciplinary. Composition scholars studied not only writing but all aspects of language use, which they regarded as actually creating knowledge, not merely disseminating it. These interests have been shared with scholars in history, literary criticism, philosophy, psychology, sociology, and speech communication. Scholars in all these fields sought an account of discourse — language in use — that acknowledges the power of rhetoric to help create a community's worldview, knowledge, and interpretive practices.

If rhetoric is epistemic, then there can be no language that does not require interpretation. As Richard Rorty shows, modern philosophers have failed to define a value-neutral language in which purely objective and rational arguments can be conducted (see 204). Chaim Perelman describes the ways a community united by discourse establishes its interpretive practices [209, 210]. His "universal audience" is the audience that is presumed to adhere perfectly to a given community's interpretive practices and hence to serve as that community's standard of the purely objective and rational audience. Different communities can be expected to hold different conceptions of their universal audience.

Literary-critical theories of the role of the reader in making meaning also discuss the establishment of interpretive practices. Stanley Fish describes readers as participants in interpretive communities, which are defined by their agreement on the conventions of discourse. Fish's work suggests a method for analyzing the conventions a writer must learn to enter the academic discourse community. No taxonomy of such conventions has appeared, although studies of a number of fields have exposed much about disciplinary conventions. More recently, studies of writing in various disciplines have revealed and analyzed the social creation of disciplinary knowledge through discourse.

Historical studies of rhetoric have been another resource for a social theory of discourse. Andrea Lunsford and Lisa Ede drew on Aristotle for a theory of argument that legitimates ethical and pathetic as well as logical appeals. This theory supports the idea that cultural assumptions have more to do with persuasion than the "universal" rationality of a proposition [196]. S. Michael Halloran shows that when the classical emphasis on socially rooted appeals disappeared from nineteenth-century colleges, public debate on important national issues diminished [82, 96]. James Berlin describes the reduction of rhetoric to stylistic prescriptions [74]. He suggests that the roots of a more socially responsive rhetoric may be found in Emersonian romanticism.

The field of composition studies grew in professional respectability during the 1980s. By the end of the decade, graduate degrees in composition and rhetoric — not simply one introductory survey or teaching practicum — had come to be offered by departments of English in many prestigious universities. Under the auspices of the NCTE, the CCCC began publishing comprehensive bibliographies in the field [39]. The U.S. Department of Education funded an empirical research institute, the Center for the Study of Writing, at the University of California at Berkeley and Carnegie Mellon University. Series of bibliographic anthologies, collections, reprints, and monographs began to appear regularly from a number of research and university presses.

Part of the field's coming-of-age process was increased interest in the history of rhetoric and composition, now an extensive area of scholarly work and a regular curricular offering. Composition work was not to be seen as a temporary response to unusual gaps in college-bound students' preparation. Rather, writing teachers and researchers came to view themselves as the most recent generation of serious thinkers about language in use, heirs of the rhetorical tradition. Many of our classroom practices were recast in light of historical traditions. For example, personal writing was connected with the genre of the personal essay stretching back at least to the Renaissance, as traced variously by William Covino [89] and Kurt Spellmeyer [414].

Although historical studies of rhetoric and poetic suggested theoretical bases for the location of composition studies in English departments, the relationship between composition studies and literary studies was (and is still to some extent) uneasy. Some composition scholars called for the formation of departments of composition and rhetoric, separate from departments of English. Some worked to redress the professional inequities that prompted the impulse to separate through, for example, the Wyoming Resolution and ensuing professional policy work by both the CCCC and the MLA [619]. Greatly increased self-consciousness about the institutional structures in which we work gave rise not only to more scholarship on writing-program administration but also to more ideologically sensitive criticism of our institutional functions, for example, in James Berlin's work on the history of twentieth century writing [74, 149].

Analyses of the political problems within the profession extended to efforts to connect our profession with political problems in society at large, to a degree not seen, perhaps, since the late 1960s. An important intersection of personal work life and national political life emerged in the analyses of inequity and redress offered by feminist critics within composition studies. In 1988, Elizabeth Flynn [491] could lament that issues of feminism were rarely raised at our annual conventions, but this situation changed dramatically the very next year.

The late 1980s also saw a rise in awareness of the degree to which race and social class affect the situation of basic writers. Linda Brodkey analyzes teacher-student class differences in "The Literacy Letters" [444], and Mike Rose provides an autobiographical account of how such barriers may be negotiated in *Lives on the Boundary* [467]. "Politics" became a key concept for understanding the educational difficulties of all writers: witness Richard Bullock and John Trimbur's collection, *The Politics of Writing Instruction* [165]. Composition scholars gave increased attention to pedagogical innovations with an explicitly liberatory political agenda, drawing once again on the work of Brazilian literacy educator Paulo Freire [258] (see Cooper and Holzman [446]) and learning from education theorists like Henry Giroux [185]. The desire to trace the influences of class, race, and gender to their roots also seemed to generate a great deal of attention among college-level writing teachers to work in the acquisition of literacy and its cognitive and cultural implications, as the works in the "Literacy" section of the *Bibliography* attest.

By the end of the 1980s, seeing writing in social and cultural contexts was the prevailing tendency in the field. Concern for writing in communal contexts appeared in the work of many theorists. Linda Flower, in a variation on the theme, argued for a sociocognitive theory of writing, according to which, writer, text, and context are mutually constitutive [231]. Studying writing in context means more than assessing the immediate audience. Rather, as Marilyn Cooper argues, we must consider a complex "ecology of writing" that comprises not only immediate personal relationships and social purposes but also larger generic and cultural constraints on composing [227]. To study this rich network, we need to look not only at the individual writer but at the collaborative situation of his or her classroom, personal and institutional histories, and writers' and teachers' political hopes.

Rhetoric and Composition Studies in the 1990s: The Challenge of Diversity

The powerful themes of the 1980s — social construction, politics, literacy, and gender issues — extended in the 1990s to work that related composition to postmodernism and cultural studies. Social construction was widely accepted as a theoretical basis for understanding language use, as can be seen in the research directions of technical and business communication, English as a second language, and writing centers. The history of composition, too, received generous and fruitful attention in the 1990s, a time of stocktaking in the discipline, some of which was motivated by the challenge of diversity in all areas of the field.

A number of scholars explored the connections among social construction, postmodernism, politics, and cultural studies and their implications for composition. The contributors to Patricia Harkin and John Schilb's *Contending with Words* explored the sources of postmodern ideas in the works of influential theorists [188], and Lester Faigley analyzed the relationship of computer technologies and postmodern consciousness [179]. James Berlin drew upon cultural studies to argue for a reform of English studies [515], while others used these theories to complicate our notions of student subjectivity and to promote interdisciplinary research.

The impulse to write the field's history appears in such collections as *Taking Stock: The Writing Process Movement in the '90s* [243] as well as in a series of landmark essays on the writing process [239], invention [295], voice [408], writing centers [618], and writing across the curriculum [653], published by Hermagoras Press. In addition, a number of scholars have shone light on the teaching of rhetoric in nineteenth-century American colleges, finding there the stories of how the field of composition was positioned — and in some ways compromised — for the next century and beyond. Revisionist histories of writing and rhetoric such as those written by Robert J. Connors [84], Thomas P. Miller [119], and Robin Varnum [140] situate the role of composition in the development of English studies while recent books in the history of rhetoric focus very specifically on the rhetorical practices of women speakers and writers. Cheryl Glenn studies the rhetorical contributions of women from antiquity through the Renaissance [95] while Shirley Wilson Logan [115] and Carol Mattingly [118] document the work of nineteenth century women rhetors. Influenced by feminist theory, these histories attempt to recover lost or neglected voices in the rhetorical tradition, fill in disturbing gaps in our understanding of the history of rhetoric, and remind us of the wealth of archival research.

In response to the growing cultural diversity of student populations, composition now has its first longitudinal studies of college writers. Marilyn Sternglass's *Time to Know Them* follows nine City College students through their academic careers [477], and Ruth Spack reports on a three-year study of a second-language student [543]. At the same time, composition also now has its first critique of process pedagogy; Lisa Delpit criticizes the writing process movement for its tendency to restrict minority students' access to linguistic codes [488]. In 1991, Mary Louise Pratt called upon educators to think of the curriculum and the classroom as "contact zones" in which cultural groups of unequal power can interact under conditions that enable sharing and understanding [212]. Composition teachers and scholars were quick to respond to Pratt's challenge (see, e.g., Bizzell [158]) in ways that confirm the richness of the contact zone metaphor and its potential for pedagogy; for example, while A. Suresh Canagarajah finds the concept of "safe houses" important for his students [485], Joseph Harris finds it problematic if those "houses" serve only as retreats where differences need not be negotiated [455].

The attraction of spatial metaphors to describe diverse classrooms continues with Gloria Anzaldúa's "borderlands" (la frontera), places of cultural, spiritual, geographical, and linguistic difference, where the reward for discomfort and conflict is a satisfying sense of shifting and multiple identities. Along with Pratt's contact zones, Anzaldúa's borderlands give teachers and writers more ways to think about the space of the classroom and the curriculum, but more important, her "mestiza rhetoric" invites writers to blend genres, to occupy multiple identities, and to refuse to enclose discourses within well-defined parameters.

Such border crossing occurs in extracurricular studies of literacy. Beverly Moss's collection Literacy across Communities [272], and Brian Street's collection Cross-Cultural Approaches to Literacy [280] extend the work of Labov and Heath in sociolinguistic and anthropological studies of literacy outside the academy; these scholars help composition teachers to understand the cultural histories and languages from which our students increasingly come. With a growing recognition that literacy does not mean school literacy, Deborah Brandt and Anne Ruggles Gere, among others, focus on extracurricular reading, writing, and communicative practices. Also interested in community literacy are those teachers pursuing service learning, an effort to expand the awareness of cultural difference beyond classrooms and campuses and to introduce students to the rhetoric of citizenship.

With more understanding of the complexities of students' literacies and identities, composition continues to respond to issues of diversity in our classrooms, institutions, and communities. Writing in Multicultural Settings, edited by Carol Severino, Juan C. Guerra, and Johnnella E. Butler [511], attempts to describe, without prescribing answers, the conflicts, tensions, and struggles of both students and teachers in classrooms defined by difference. Mary Soliday describes a program at City College designed to mainstream at-risk students — a program supported across the institution but also determined by the complex institutional politics of remediation [474]. And Vivian Zamel reminds us that ESL students' language use is too often equated with their intellectual ability [546]. Writing centers, similarly, are responding to the challenge of diversity. Anne DiPardo, for example, connects the difficulties of center clients from diverse cultures to campus tensions aroused by diversity and shows how tutors can help [625].

The last few years have also seen an emerging critical discourse on race in composition studies, a discourse that does not embrace multiculturalism, necessarily, but that tries to confront institutionalized racism through analyzing images, discourses, and practices. Keith Gilyard's edited collection, *Race, Rhetoric, and Composition* [495], as well as articles by Catherine Prendergast [508] and David Wallace and Annissa Bell [513] interrogate constructions of race in composition and in the academy. Feminist teaching and gender issues in the classroom continued to be important scholarly concerns in rhetoric and composition in the 1990s [499]. A variety of other women's concerns are reflected in studies of autobiographical writing [410], of academic women's sense of authority [500], and of the history of gender-coded texts [80]. At the same time, the typical categories of difference — race, class, and gender — are beginning to be complicated by other, overlapping identities or subject positions. Harriet Malinowitz, for example, casts light on the writing problems of gay and lesbian students [505].

An important "contact zone" for composition scholars is electronic writing technologies. Still intrigued by the new frontiers of networking and hypertext and other online writing technologies, compositionists continue to explore these regions for their pedagogical implications. Their initial enthusiasm tempered by critical accounts of technology's exclusions, scholars approach computers armed with an awareness of, for example, how computer interfaces show effects of domination and colonialism [684]. Theoretical interpretations of technology range from Jay David Bolter's explanation of how electronic text radically changes the relationship between writer and reader and revives features of oral literature [671] to a dialogic, experimental essay about e-mail as a genre [686]. Studies of online writing are more likely to focus on the rhetoric and politics of exchanges [674, 681], and to question the implications of adding technology to classrooms or writing centers [620].

As composition studies moves into a new century, there are many signs of its scholarly maturity. The profession has celebrated the fiftieth anniversary of the Conference on College Composition and Communication, and there are other signs, too, that composition has come of age. Expanding forums for publishing — print as well as electronic — have enabled more voices and views to be heard while also encouraging the rise of specialized, focused studies.

However, despite composition's maturity as a discipline and its rapid adoptions of new technologies, the inequities and injustices for low-status composition instructors, well-documented in books by Eileen Schell and Theresa Enos, remain, in part, Sharon Crowley argues, because composition remains a requirement [172]. Composition's characteristic commitment to exploring the relationship between theory and practice [180], however, would seem to indicate its continued productivity. While it remains to be seen if composition can construct new theories in a new century, the field continues to be defined by a blend of interest in pedagogy, research, and theory, and scholarship in composition continues to be richly interdisciplinary.

Into the Twenty-First Century:
Post-Process Perspectives and Concerns

At the turn of the century, responding to diversity remains one of the most significant issues in writing studies, as evidenced by more attention to disability studies [484], sexual identity [494], and whiteness [509], welcome complications to the category of gender, race, and class. Scholars' and researchers' efforts to rewrite composition history, to formulate new theoretical perspectives, and to analyze new media and technologies provide signs that responding to diversity requires not only an examination of student identities but also a full accounting of diverse histories, theories, and curricula.

Recent historical scholarship refuses to demonize nineteenth century current-traditional rhetoric and paints a much fuller picture of the cultural issues and conditions that inform both writing instruction and conceptions of literacy. Charles Paine's *The Resistant Writer: Rhetoric as Immunity, 1850 to the Present* [127], for example, reads composition history through competing cultural institutions, a move that complicates historiography and questions the dominant portrayal of nineteenth century composition instruction as being in league with capitalism and business. Paine traces how larger cultural issues have actually transformed composition theory and practice. Composition's canonical histories and primary texts can blind us to seeing other patterns, namely the long-standing presence of African Americans in arenas of higher education and their successes as insiders (see Royster and Williams [129]).

Historians continue to mine archives and introduce teachers and rhetorical theorists, previously neglected or unrecognized, to a twenty-first century audience [108]. Accompanying these efforts to locate historical materials is a burgeoning interest in writing's materiality, an attention to the spaces, places, bodies, and tools that characterize, shape, or determine acts of writing, or to the ways in which writing is embodied [219, 688, 670, and 572]. Some scholars examine the parlors or pulpits in which speakers and writers are constructed by those surroundings (see Johnson [106], and Mountford [201]) while others look to a larger context; for example, John Trimbur traces writing's materiality through circulation — a system of production and delivery [220], and Bruce McComiskey bases his social-process rhetorical inquiry on the cycle of production, distribution, and consumption [236].

The influence of materiality can also be seen in the proliferation of in-depth qualitative studies of everyday literacies — home, school, public, and multiple [281, 245]. A blurring of literacy and orality characterizes the literate forms of African American women (Royster [130]), and the task of the literacy educator is to enable learners to understand how literacy — even in its blurred forms — functions (Yagelski [286]). For literacy and other areas of rhetoric and composition, ethnographic research — from full-scale ethnographies to some use of qualitative methods — increasingly constitute one of the most important ways of making new knowledge in the field (see Henry [588], and Cintron [168]). The importance of self-reflection, learned in part from qualitative research, has influenced many areas; for example, service learning scholarship, where recognition of community expertise, reciprocity and sustainability are central concerns (see, for example, Deans [696]).

While interdisciplinary borrowings continue to inform much of composition studies, if there is one theorist who seems to be guiding recent directions in rhetoric and composition scholarship, it would be Bakhtin [187, 585]. Anis Bawarshi, for example, relies on Baktinian theory to demonstrate how the genre function makes possible and meaningful many kinds of relations and identities [146], and Kay Halasek uses Bakhtin to reimagine the rhetorical situation as a site where centripetal and centrifugal discourses battle and where essays are utterances rather than organic wholes [187].

Genre studies and activity theory may prove to be two of the most fruitful pursuits of post-process theories of writing, which currently co-exist with writing process theories even though debate still continues about the relationship between the two and the definition of post-process [193]. In the post-process era, if we are there yet, what remains vividly clear is that pedagogical and programmatic concerns cannot be separated from political contexts: Mary Soliday argues, for example, that remediation exists to serve institutional needs [475], and Tom Fox identifies lack of access, not a crisis of standards, as the most pressing problem in higher education [451]. In addition, if composition's interest in critical pedagogy continues, Chris Gallagher warns that it cannot result in empowered students *unless* pedagogy is cast as shared knowledge-building — not as the opposite of theory [183].

With widening contexts for understanding genres and discourses, writing programs now turn their attention to expanding their curriculums beyond first-year composition, and they prepare, too, for the political battles of expansion (Ramage [436]). However, this curriculum reform takes place at the same time as long-held assumptions about what composition courses should do, and whom they should serve, become the subject of strong critiques: first, of the composition requirement, and most recently, of the "first worldist" ideology, in both language and culture, of composition courses (Trimbur [439]). One of the central challenges facing program design is to imagine writing instruction and curriculum from an internationalist perspective, beyond mastery of English-Only.

Looking beyond the classroom and the academy has long been at the root of research in such areas as technical communication, business communication, and electronic writing technologies, where addressing both workplace and classroom demands continues to be the focus. Despite the specialized nature of some of this work, narrative theory [596, 590], ethics [590], and analysis of IText [586] offer *all* writing instructors a greater understanding of critical technology literacy [682], feminist rhetorics of technology [564], online discourse [689], or new media [672].

New collections of essays on topics of writing program administration [602, 605, 610, 612], new editions of important anthologies [41, 182], and the size and scope of this sixth edition of *The Bedford Bibliography* testify to the twenty-first century status of rhetoric and composition and indicate a continued development of subfields and secondary specializations.

Along with the obvious signs of expansion, however, many recent publications in rhetoric and composition studies show a diminished concern with the status of the field and a deliberate effort to outline future research and commitments. Ryoko Kubota, for example, analyzes how conceptions of culture tend to dichotomize Western culture and Eastern culture and to essentialize Japanese culture as exotic Other [533]. An alternative model, that of critical multiculturalism, supports both cultural pluralism and critical acquisition of the dominant language. Kubota's research suggests that a deep and complex understanding of cultural difference remains an important goal, unachieved until all constituencies of rhetoric and composition have been accounted for, their voices heard.

Bibliography

Resources

Periodicals

1   *ADE Bulletin*. New York: Association of Departments of English. Three times a year, beginning 1964. Submissions and subscriptions: ADE Bulletin, 26 Broadway, 3rd floor, New York, NY 10004-1789.

       The journal of the Association of Departments of English. Articles on writing program and English department administration and the relationships between composition and literature. Ed. Stephen Olsen.

2   *The CEA Forum*. Lewisburg, Pa.: The College English Association. Semiannually, beginning 1970. Now published exclusively online. Submissions, CEA members only: Dr. Bege Bowers, Dept. of English, Youngstown State University, Youngstown, OH 44555.

       The journal of the College English Association. Most articles concern the teaching of literature and composition. Ed. Bege Bowers.

3   *College Composition and Communication*. Urbana, Ill.: NCTE/CCCC. Quarterly, beginning 1950. Subscriptions: 1111 Kenyon Rd., Urbana, IL 61801. Submissions: Marilyn Cooper, CCC Editor, Humanities Dept., Michigan Technological Univ., 1400 Townsend Dr., Houghton, MI 49931.

CCC   The principal journal of the Conference on College Composition and Communication. Most articles explore pedagogical applications of composition theory and research. Ed. Marilyn Cooper.

4   *College English*. Urbana, Ill.: NCTE College Section. Bimonthly, beginning 1939. Subscriptions: 1111 Kenyon Rd., Urbana, IL 61801. Submissions: *College English*, Dept. of English, Santa Clara Univ., Santa Clara, CA 95053.

CE   The principal journal of the NCTE College Section. Articles on teaching literature, literary theory, the history of the discipline, and teaching writing. Ed. Jeanne Gunner.

5   *Composition Studies* (formerly *Freshman English News*). Chicago: DePaul Univ. Twice a year, beginning 1972. Subscriptions and submissions: Editor, *Composition Studies*, DePaul Univ., Dept. of English, 802 W. Belden Ave., Chicago, IL 60614-3214.

Short articles on the theory and practice of teaching and writing and, occasionally, longer theoretical essays. Ed. Peter Vandenberg.

6   *Computers and Composition*. Norwood, N.J.: Ablex Publishing Co. Three times a year, beginning 1984. Subscriptions: Elsevier Science Inc., 655 Avenue of the Americas, New York, NY 10010-5107. Submissions: Kris Blair, Acquisitions Editor: kblair@bgnet.bgsu.edu. Contributions must be submitted in electronic form.

Articles on the uses of computers in teaching writing. Ed. Cynthia Selfe and Gail Hawisher.

7   *English for Specific Purposes: An International Journal*. Oxford, England: Elsevier Science Ltd. Three times a year, beginning 1980. Subscriptions: Elsevier Science Ltd., Regional Sales Customer Support Dept., P.O. Box 945, New York, NY 10159-0945. Submissions: Diane Belcher, ESL Programs, Ohio State University, 60 Arps Hall, 1945 N. High Street, Columbus, OH 43210-1172, USA, or Martin Hewings, Dept. of English, School of Humanities, The University of Birmingham, Edgbaston, Birmingham B15 2TT, United Kingdom.

Articles analyze the discourse conventions of writing in particular professions and disciplines. Eds. Diane Belcher and Martin Hewings.

8   *English Journal*. Urbana, Ill.: NCTE Secondary Section. Bimonthly, beginning 1912. Subscriptions: 1111 Kenyon Rd., Urbana, IL 61801. Submissions: Louann Reid, Editor; Dept. of English; 359 Eddy Hall, Colorado State University, Fort Collins, CO 80523-1773. The principal journal of the NCTE Secondary Section. Articles on teaching literature and writing and on pedagogical research in the secondary schools. Ed. Louann Reid.

9   *JAC: A Journal of Composition Theory* (formerly *Journal of Advanced Composition*). Logan, UT: Council of Editors of Learned Journals, with support from the Univ. of South Florida, Georgia State University, and Eckerd College. Annually, beginning 1980; twice a year, beginning 1990. Subscriptions and submissions: Lynn Worsham, Dept. of English, Univ. of South Florida, Tampa, FL 33620.

Articles on rhetorical theory, interviews with scholars, and pedagogical articles on expository, technical, creative, and other advanced writing courses. Ed. Lynn Worsham.

10   *Journal of Basic Writing*. New York: City Univ. of New York Instructional Resource Center. Twice a year, beginning 1978. Subscriptions and submissions: City University of New York, 555 West 57 Street, Room 1601, New York, New York 10019.

From the Instructional Resource Center, previously directed by Mina Shaughnessy. Articles on literacy, teaching grammar and basic writing, English as a second language (ESL), and theoretical issues in basic writing. Eds. George Otte and Bonne August.

11   *Journal of Business and Technical Communication*. Ames: Iowa State Univ. Four times a year, beginning 1987. Subscriptions: Sage Periodicals Press, 2455 Teller Rd., Thousand Oaks, CA 91320. Submissions: Rebecca E. Burnett, Dept. of English, Iowa State Univ., Ames, IA 50011.

    Articles on business and technical writing practice and teaching. Ed. Dorothy Winsor.

12   *Journal of Second Language Writing*. Norwood, N.J.: Ablex Publishing Co. Quarterly, beginning 1992. Subscriptions: Elsevier Science, Regional Sales Office, Customer Support Dept., P.O. Box 945, New York, NY 10159-0945. Submissions: Ilona Leki, Department of English, 301 McClung Tower, University of Tennessee, Knoxville, TN 37996-0430.

    Full-length articles on theories of ESL composition. Selected bibliographies of recent scholarship. Eds. Ilona Leki and Tony Silva.

13   *Journal of Teaching Writing*. Indianapolis: Indiana Teachers of Writing and Indiana Univ./Purdue Univ. at Indianapolis. Twice a year, beginning 1981. Subscriptions and submissions: IUPUI, 425 University Blvd., Indianapolis, IN 46202.

    Articles cover composition theory and the relation of composition to other fields, as well as pedagogical concerns. Ed. Barbara Cambridge.

14   *Journal of Technical Writing and Communication*. Amityville, N.Y.: Baywood Publications. Four times a year, beginning 1971. Subscriptions: Baywood Publishing Company, Inc., 26 Austin Avenue, Box 337, Amityville, NY 11701. Submissions: Charles H. Sides, P.O. Box 546, Westminster, MA 01473.

    Articles on research and teaching in technical and professional writing. Ed. Charles H. Sides.

15   *Philosophy and Rhetoric*. State College: Pennsylvania State Univ. Press. Quarterly, beginning 1968. Subscriptions and submissions: The Pennsylvania State University Press, USB-1, Suite C, 820 North University Drive, University Park, PA 16802.

    Articles on classical rhetoric, rhetorical theory, and language theory from the perspectives of English, speech, and philosophy. Eds. Stephen H. Browne, Richard Doyle, and Richard Lee.

16   *PRE/TEXT*. Arlington: Univ. of Texas. Quarterly, beginning 1979. Subscriptions and submissions: Victor Vitanza, *PRE/TEXT*, P.O. Box 14621, Arlington, TX 76094-1621.

    Long essays on rhetorical theory and pedagogical philosophy. Ed. Victor Vitanza.

17   *Quarterly Journal of Speech*. Washington, D.C.: National Communcation Association. Subscriptions: NCA, 1765 N Street, NW, Washington, DC 20036. Submissions: Karlyn Kohrs Campbell,

Department of Speech-Communication, 225 Ford Hall, 224 Church St. S.E., University of Minnesota, Minneapolis, MN 55455-0427.

The principal theoretical journal of the National Communication Association. Articles on rhetorical theory and the history of rhetoric, and analyses of texts and speeches. Contributors from English and philosophy as well as speech. Ed. Andrew King.

18   *Radical Teacher*. Cambridge, Mass.: Center for Critical Education, Inc. Subscriptions: *Radical Teacher*, P.O. Box 382616, Cambridge, Ma 02238. Submissions: Marjorie Feld, 100 Walnut Street, Watertown, MA 02472. Submissions: Louis Kampf, 14 Glenwood Ave., Cambridge, MA 02139.

Articles on the political concerns of teachers and students; perspectives on progressive pedagogy, feminism, and Marxism in teaching in all disciplines.

19   *Research in the Teaching of English*. Urbana, Ill.: NCTE. Four times a year, beginning 1967. Subscriptions: 1111 Kenyon Rd., Urbana, IL 61801. Submissions: *RTE*, Peter Smagorinsky, Univ. of Georgia, College of Education, Dept. of Language Education, 125 Aderhold Hall, Athens, GA 30602-7123.

Research reports on teaching English at all school levels, cognitive development and language skills, and the composing process. Eds. Peter Smagorinsky and Michael W. Smith.

20   *Rhetoric Review*. Tucson, Ariz.: Rhetoric Review Association of America. Quarterly, beginning 1982. Subscriptions and submissions: Theresa Enos, Dept. of English, Univ. of Arizona, Tucson, AZ 85721.

Both theoretical and practical articles emphasizing the importance of rhetoric to composition instruction. Ed. Theresa Enos.

21   *Rhetoric Society Quarterly*. St. Cloud, Minn.: Rhetoric Society of America. Quarterly, beginning 1968. Submissions: *RSQ*, Gregory Clark, Dept. of English, Brigham Young Univ., Provo, UT 84602.

Articles on rhetorical theory, history, and professional concerns. Contributors from both English and speech. Ed. Gregory Clark.

22   *Rhetorica*. Berkeley: Univ. of California Press, International Society for the History of Rhetoric. Quarterly, beginning 1983. Subscriptions: Univ. of California Press, Journals Division, 2000 Center St., Suite 303, Berkeley, CA 94720. Submissions: Peter Mack, Dept. of English and Comparative Literary Studies, Univ. of Warwick, Coventry, CV4 7AL, United Kingdom.

The journal of the International Society for the History of Rhetoric. Articles on premodern rhetoric by contributors from English, speech, philosophy, and history. Ed. Harvey Yunis.

23   *TESOL Quarterly*. Alexandria, Va.: TESOL. Four times a year, beginning 1967. Subscriptions: TESOL, 700 South Washington St.,

Suite 200, Alexandria, VA 22314. Submissions: Carol A. Chapelle, 203 Ross Hall, Dept. of English, Iowa State Univ., Ames, IA 50011-1201.

Articles on teaching and research in English as a second language. Ed. Carol A. Chapelle.

24   *Teaching English in the Two-Year College.* Urbana, Ill.: NCTE. Quarterly, beginning 1974. Subscriptions: 1111 Kenyon Rd., Urbana, IL 61801. Submissions: Howard Tinberg, Dept. of English, Bristol Community College, 777 Elsbree St., Fall River, MA 02720.

Summaries and reviews of composition theory, as well as teaching suggestions for teachers of freshman and sophomore writing courses. Ed. Howard Tinberg.

25   *Technical Communication Quarterly.* St. Paul: Univ. of Minnesota for the Association of Teachers of Technical Writing. Four times a year, beginning 1991. Subscriptions: membership in ATTW, Billie J. Wahlstrom, TCQ, Dept. of Rhetoric, 64 Classroom Office Building, 1994 Buford Avenue, Univ. of Minnesota, St. Paul, MN 55108-6122. Submissions: Mary M. Lay, same address.

Articles on pedagogy, research, theory, applications, software, and book reviews for teachers of technical communication. Eds. Mary M. Lay and Billie J. Wahlstrom.

26   *The Writing Center Journal.* Fairfield, CT: International Writing Centers Association. Twice a year, beginning 1980. Milwaukee, WI: International Writing Centers Association. Subscriptions: Neal Lerner/ WCJ, Massachusetts Institute of Technology, Rm. 14E-303, 77 Mass. Ave., Cambridge, MA 02139. Submissions: Email to eboquet@mail.fairfield.edu and nlerner@mit.edu. Ed. Neal Lerner and Elizabeth Boquet.

Full-length articles on writing center administration and practices. Eds. Joan Mullin and Albert C. De Ciccio.

27   *The Writing Instructor.* San Marcos: California State University. Quarterly, beginning 1981. Subscriptions: now an online publication. Submissions: *The Writing Instructor,* c/o Dawn Formo, Literature & Writing Studies Program, California State University, San Marcos, San Marcos, CA 92096-0001.

A journal from the University of Southern California Freshman Writing Program. Articles on teaching college writing, writing program administration, and curriculum development. Ed. David Blakesly and Dawn Formo.

28   *Writing Lab Newsletter.* West Lafayette, Ind.: National Writing Centers Association of the NCTE. Monthly, beginning 1976. Subscriptions and submissions: Muriel Harris, Dept. of English, Purdue Univ., 1356 Heavilon Hall, West Lafayette, IN 47907-1356.

Short articles by lab directors and tutors, including student tutors, on writing-lab theory, problems, and techniques. Ed. Muriel Harris.

29   *Writing on the Edge.* Campus Writing Center, Univ. of California at Davis. Twice a year, beginning 1989. Subscriptions and submissions: John Boe, Campus Writing Center, Univ. of California, Davis, CA 95616.

Shorter articles on all facets of composition and rhetoric: history, theory, pedagogy, writing centers, and politics. Ed. John Boe.

30   *Written Communication.* Beverly Hills, Calif.: Sage Publications. Quarterly, beginning 1984. Subscriptions: Customer Service, Sage Publications, 2455 Teller Rd., Thousand Oaks, CA 91320. Submissions: Editors, *Written Communication,* Univ. of Wisconsin at Madison, Dept. of English, 6185 Helen C. White Hall, 600 N. Park St., Madison, WI 53706-1475.

Research reports on social and cognitive factors in discourse production for young and adult writers. Eds. Martin Nystrand and Stephen Witte.

31   *WPA: Writing Program Administration.* Normal: Illinois State Univ., Council of Writing Program Administrators. Twice a year, beginning 1979. Subscriptions: Jennie Dautermann, Secretary, WPA, Dept. of English, Miami Univ., Oxford, OH 45056. Submissions: Dennis Lynch, Humanities Dept., Michigan Technological Univ., 1400 Townsend Ave., Houghton, MI 49931.

Articles on writing program administration and writing instruction; textbook bibliographies. Eds. Marguerite Helmers and Dennis Lynch.

General Bibliographies

32   "Annotated Bibliography of Research in the Teaching of English." *Research in the Teaching of English* (Spring and Fall, 1967–present).

Items focusing on empirical work are divided into sections on literature, humanities, and media; written and oral communication; language and verbal learning; bilingual and dialectal programs; and general English curriculum. Subdivided by educational level. Items are annotated beginning Spring 1973.

33   Enos, Theresa, ed. *Encyclopedia of Rhetoric and Composition: Communication from Ancient Times to the Information Age.* New York: Garland, 1995.

467 entries by 288 scholars of rhetoric, composition, speech communication, and philosophy, covering the history, theory, concepts, and major figures in the field of rhetoric. Entries are arranged alphabetically and range from brief identifications of terms and minor figures to essays on major figures and topics. A selected bibliography follows each entry. Includes an index.

34   ERIC: Educational Resources Information Center. Operated by the
      National Institute of Education, U.S. Department of Education.
      There are sixteen ERIC clearinghouses, each responsible for a par-
      ticular area of education. ERIC/RCS, the Clearinghouse on Reading
      and Communication Skills, is sponsored by the NCTE. Abstracts of
      articles available through ERIC are published in *Resources in Educa-
      tion*. Microfiche and paper copies may be ordered through the ERIC
      Document Reproduction Service, Box 190, Arlington, VA 22210.
      ERIC materials since 1982 are available on CD-ROM; materials since
      1966 are on OCLC.

35   Haswell, Richard. CompPile. http://comppile.tamucc.edu/.
      An ongoing inventory of publications in post-secondary composi-
      tion, rhetoric, ESL, and technical writing: 1939–1999. Includes 63
      journals, all major publishing houses, over 800 volumes of edited col-
      lections, over 50 edited series, and 6,231 dissertations from 1939–93.

36   Heilker, Paul, and Peter Vandenberg, eds. *Keywords in Composition
      Studies*. Portsmouth, N.H.: Heinemann-Boynton/Cook, 1996.
      Fifty-four brief essays by twenty-seven scholars in composition stud-
      ies, arranged alphabetically and accompanied by brief bibliographies
      of important works, introduce the field of composition studies by iden-
      tifying the issues that cluster around its key terms.

37   Kennedy, Mary Lynch, ed. *Theorizing Composition: A Critical
      Sourcebook of Theory and Scholarship in Contemporary Composition Stud-
      ies*. Westport, Conn.: Greenwood Press, 1998.
      Sixty-six brief essays by seventy-three authors, arranged alphabeti-
      cally, summarize various theoretical schools in composition studies,
      as well as those in literature, philosophy, and rhetoric that are rel-
      evant to composition studies. The theoretical school's main ideas are
      given and its significance to composition studies treated. Extensive
      bibliographies accompany the entries.

38   Lindemann, Erika. *Longman Bibliography of Composition and Rhetoric:
      1984–1985* (1987) and *1986* (1988). New York: Longman.
      The 1984–1985 volume contains 3,853 entries; the 1986 volume con-
      tains 2,724. Nearly all the entries have twenty-five- to fifty-word de-
      scriptive annotations. Includes journals, books, dissertations,
      textbooks, ERIC entries, and computer programs in the following
      categories: theory and research (in rhetoric, history of rhetoric, types
      of rhetoric, reading, linguistics, education, and psychology), teacher
      education and administration, curriculum (preschool through col-
      lege, business and technical writing, adult education, and ESL), text-
      books and instructional materials, and testing and evaluation.

39   Lindemann, Erika. CCCC *Bibliography of Composition and Rhetoric,
      1987*. Carbondale: Southern Illinois Univ. Press, 1990. Succeeding
      editions: *1988* (1991), *1989* (1992), *1990* (1993).

Hawisher, Gail E., and Cynthia L. Selfe. CCCC *Bibliography of Composition and Rhetoric, 1991*. Carbondale: Southern Illinois Univ. Press, 1993. Succeeding editions: *1992* (1994), *1993* (1995).

Successor to the *Longman Bibliography of Composition and Rhetoric* [38], which covers elementary and secondary as well as college materials, the CCCC *Bibliography* focuses on work related to college and university teaching and research. Categories are Bibliographies and Checklists; Theory and Research (in fourteen subcategories); Teacher Education, Administration, and Social Roles (four subcategories); Curriculum (thirteen subcategories); and Testing, Measurement, and Evaluation (four subcategories). Each item is briefly annotated.

40   Tate, Gary, ed. *Teaching Composition: Twelve Bibliographic Essays*. Fort Worth: Texas Christian Univ. Press, 1987.

A substantially revised and enlarged edition of the important *Teaching Composition: Ten Bibliographic Essays* (1976). Includes Richard E. Young on invention (supplements the 1976 essay); Richard L. Larson on nonnarrative prose (summarizes and updates the 1976 essay); Edward P. J. Corbett on style (1976 essay reprinted with an update) [325]; Frank J. D'Angelo on the modes of discourse (substantially revised and updated); Richard Lloyd-Jones on testing (new essay); Mina P. Shaughnessy, "Basic Writing" [471]; Andrea A. Lunsford, "Basic Writing Update"; Jenefer M. Giannasi on language varieties (substantially revised) [452]; W. Ross Winterowd, "Literacy, Linguistics, and Rhetoric" (substantially revised and updated); Joseph Comprone, "Literary Theory and Composition" (new essay); Jim Corder, "Studying Rhetoric and Literature" (substantially revised); James L. Kinneavy on writing across the curriculum (new essay — surveys textbooks and programs as well as scholarship); and Hugh Burns on computers and composition (new essay). The first edition essays on media (by Joseph Comprone) and "Composition and Related Fields" (by James L. Kinneavy and C. Robert Kline) are not in the new edition.

History and Theory

The Rhetorical Tradition

Listed in chronological order by date of composition.

41 Bizzell, Patricia, and Bruce Herzberg. *The Rhetorical Tradition: Readings from Classical Times to the Present.* 2nd edition. Boston: Bedford / St. Martin's, 2001.

A new and enlarged edition focused on rhetorical theory. Substantial excerpts and some complete works from classical rhetoric (Gorgias, Aspasia, Isocrates, Plato, Aristotle, Cicero, Quintilian, *Rhetorica ad Herennium*, others); medieval rhetoric (Augustine, Boethius, Christine de Pizan, others); Renaissance rhetoric (Erasmus, Ramus, Wilson, Bacon, Margaret Fell, others); Enlightenment rhetoric (Mary Astell, Vico, Sheridan, Campbell, Blair); nineteenth century rhetoric (Whately, Maria W. Stewart, Sarah Grimké, Frederick Douglass, Frances Willard, Bain and Hill, Nietzsche, others); modern and postmodern rhetoric (Bakhtin, Virginia Woolf, Richards, Burke, Weaver, Perelman, Toulmin, Foucault, Cixous, Gates, Gloria Anzaldúa, others). Includes a general introduction, period and author introductions, and annotated bibliographies.

42 Sprague, Rosamond Kent. *The Older Sophists.* Columbia: Univ. of South Carolina Press, 1972, 1990.

43 *Contrasting Arguments: An Edition of the* Dissoi Logoi (ca. 400 B.C.E.). Ed. and trans. R. M. Robinson. New York: Arno Press, 1979.

44 Isocrates. *Against the Sophists and Antidosis* (ca. 390 B.C.E., 353 B.C.E.). *Isocrates,* II. Ed. and trans. George Norlin. Loeb Classical Library. Cambridge: Harvard Univ. Press, 1982.

45 Plato. *Apology, Menexenus, Gorgias, Protagoras, Phaedrus, Symposium, Republic* (ca. 370 B.C.E.). *The Collected Dialogues of Plato.* Ed. Edith Hamilton and Huntington Cairns. Princeton: Princeton Univ. Press, 1961.

46 Aristotle. *Aristotle on Rhetoric: A Theory of Civic Discourse* (ca. 333 B.C.E.). Ed. and trans. George A. Kennedy. New York: Oxford Univ. Press, 1991.

47 Cicero. *De Inventione* (ca. 88 B.C.E.). Trans. H. M. Hubbell. Cambridge: Harvard Univ. Press, 1949.

48 *Rhetorica ad Herennium* (ca. 86 B.C.E.). Trans. Harry Caplan. Cambridge: Harvard Univ. Press, 1954.

49   Cicero. *De Oratore* (55 B.C.E.). *Books I–II.* Trans. E. W. Sutton and H. Rackham. Cambridge: Harvard Univ. Press, 1942. *Book III.* Trans. H. Rackham. Cambridge: Harvard Univ. Press, 1942.

50   Longinus. *On the Sublime* (ca. 40 C.E.). *Aristotle, The Poetics, and Longinus, On the Sublime.* Trans. W. Hamilton Fyfe. Includes *Demetrius, On Style.* Trans. W. Rhys Roberts. Cambridge: Harvard Univ. Press, 1932.

51   Quintilian. *Institutio Oratoria* (ca. 88 C.E.). Trans. H. E. Butler. 4 vols. Cambridge: Harvard Univ. Press, 1922.

52   Murphy, James J., ed. *Quintilian on the Teaching of Speaking and Writing: Translations from Books One, Two and Ten of the Institutio Oratoria.* Trans. J. S. Watson; rev. by J. J. Murphy. Carbondale: Southern Illinois Univ. Press, 1987.

These selections from the *Institutio* concern Quintilian's ideas about child development and the relationships among reading, writing, and speaking. Murphy's helpful introduction sets Quintilian's life and work in the context of Roman times and traces the reception of his ideas through the Renaissance and to the present.

53   Augustine. *On Christian Doctrine* (426 C.E.). Trans. D. W. Robertson. New York: Library of Liberal Arts, 1958.

54   Murphy, James J. *Three Medieval Rhetorical Arts.* Berkeley: Univ. of California Press, 1971.

Contains medieval manuals on letter writing and on preaching, excerpts from textbooks on Aristotelian dialectic, and Geoffrey of Vinsauf's *Poetria Nova.*

55   Christine de Pisan. *The Treasure of the City of Ladies, or the Book of the Three Virtues.* (1405). Ed. and trans. Sarah Lawson. New York: Viking Penguin Classics, 1985.

56   Erasmus, Desiderius. *Copia: Foundations of the Abundant Style* (1512). Trans. Betty I. Knott. *Collected Works of Erasmus.* Ed. Craig R. Thompson. 42 vols. Toronto: Univ. of Toronto Press, 1978.

57   Erasmus, Desiderius. *On the Writing of Letters/De conscribendis epistolis.* *Collected Works of Erasmus, Volumes 25–26.* (1522). Ed. and trans. Charles Fantozzi. Toronto: Univ. of Toronto Press, 1985.

58   Castiglione, Baldesar. *The Book of the Courtier* (1527). Trans. Charles Singleton. New York: Charles Scribner's Sons, 1959.

59   Ramus, Peter. *Peter Ramus's Attack on Cicero: Text and Translation of Ramus's Brutinae Quaestiones.* (1547). Ed. and intro. James J. Murphy. Trans. Carole Newlands. Davis, Calif.: Hermagoras Press, 1992.

60   Ramus, Peter. *Arguments in Rhetoric against Quintilian* (1549). Trans. Carole Newlands and James J. Murphy. De Kalb: Univ. of Northern Illinois Press, 1983.

61   Fell, Margaret. *Women's Speaking Justified by the Scriptures.* (1666.) Ed. David J. Latt. Los Angeles: William Andrews Clark Memorial Library, Augustan Reprint Society Publication #194, 1979.

62   de la Cruz, Sor Juana. *The Answer/La Respuesta, Including a Selection of Poems.* (1691.) Ed. and trans. Electa Arenal and Amanda Powell. New York: Feminist Press, 1994.

63   Astell, Mary. *A Serious Proposal to the Ladies, Parts I and II.* (1694, 1697.) Ed. Patricia Springborg. London: Pickering and Chatto, 1997.

64   Burke, Edmund. *A Philosophical Enquiry into the Origin of Our Ideas of the Sublime and the Beautiful.* (1757.) Ed. James T. Boulton. Notre Dame: Univ. of Notre Dame Press, 1968.

65   Campbell, George. *The Philosophy of Rhetoric.* (1776.) Ed. Lloyd Bitzer. Carbondale: Southern Illinois Univ. Press, 1963.

66   Blair, Hugh. *Lectures on Rhetoric and Belles-Lettres.* (1783.) Ed. Harold Harding. Carbondale: Southern Illinois Univ. Press, 1966.

67   Witherspoon, John. *The Selected Writings of John Witherspoon.* (1810.) Ed. Thomas Miller. Carbondale: Southern Illinois Univ. Press, 1990.

68   Golden, James L., and Edward P. J. Corbett, eds. *The Rhetoric of Blair, Campbell, and Whately.* 1968. New York: Holt, Rinehart and Winston, 1980.

69   Whately, Richard. *Elements of Rhetoric.* (1828.) Ed. Douglas Ehninger. Carbondale: Southern Illinois Univ. Press, 1963.

70   Grimké, Sarah. *Letters on the Equality of the Sexes and Other Essays.* (1838.) Ed. Elizabeth Ann Bartlett. New Haven: Yale Univ. Press, 1988.

71   Bain, Alexander. *English Composition and Rhetoric: A Manual.* (1866; American ed., rev. 1888.) New York: Appleton, 1980.

72   Willard, Frances E. *Woman in the Pulpit.* Boston: D. Lothrop Company, 1888 (other 1888 editions published regionally).

History of Rhetoric and Education

73   Applebee, Arthur N. *Tradition and Reform in the Teaching of English: A History.* Urbana, Ill.: NCTE, 1974.

Since the 1600s, English curriculum design in America has reflected a struggle between traditional goals of preserving high literary culture and a standard language and progressive goals of democratic social reform. European cultural and institutional models dominated the curriculum until the late 1800s, when the first English departments appeared in American colleges. Applebee discusses English studies, in both literature and language arts, at the elementary, high school, and college levels. He also discusses the work of professional organizations in shaping curriculum. An excellent short history of American English education.

74   Berlin, James A. *Rhetoric and Reality: Writing Instruction in American Colleges, 1900–1985*. Carbondale: Southern Illinois Univ. Press, 1987.

Discussions of writing pedagogy in textbooks and essays during the twentieth century can be divided into three groups, based on their theoretical assumptions about the nature of reality and the purpose of rhetoric. Objective theories regard external reality as empirically knowable and treat rhetoric as the medium (ideally transparent) for conveying this knowledge. Subjective theories regard truth as attainable only through inner vision and value a rhetoric that uses emotionally charged language to stimulate subjective knowing as well as to communicate one's vision to others. Transactional theories see truth as at least partly provisional, arrived at by argument and interpretation. Transactional theories, then, see rhetoric as a means of persuasion and of negotiating different interpretations of reality. Objective theories dominated writing instruction in the early years of the century, challenged only by progressive education and the communications movement. In recent years, though, subjective and transactional theories have increased in importance. See Berlin [75].

75   Berlin, James A. *Writing Instruction in Nineteenth-Century American Colleges*. Carbondale: Southern Illinois Univ. Press, 1984.

Three rhetorics shaped nineteenth century writing instruction. The first, classical rhetoric, was concerned with conveying universal truths to rational beings with the aid of emotional and ethical appeals. Early in the nineteenth century, classical rhetoric was replaced by the rhetoric of the eighteenth century Scottish Common Sense philosophers, which emphasized conveying facts derived from sensory experience to beings possessing normal faculties of perception, with the aid of forms of discourse suited to divergent kinds of experience. This rhetoric dominated nineteenth century writing instruction and remains influential in the form of so-called current-traditional rhetoric. A third rhetoric, derived from Emersonian romanticism, emphasized the individual writer's vision, which creates knowledge of reality by an interpretive insight into its underlying ideal structure, and which evokes a similarly holistic response from the audience. Romantic rhetoric did not challenge eighteenth century rhetoric's dominance until the end of the nineteenth century, but it has recently inspired some of the most cogent critiques of current-traditional rhetoric.

76   Bolgar, R. R. *The Classical Heritage and Its Beneficiaries*. Cambridge: Cambridge Univ. Press, 1958.

A history of education from late Roman times to the fourteenth century in Byzantium, and in the West, to early medieval education in Ireland, England, and France, Scholasticism, and classical education in the Renaissance. Bolgar points out the ways scholars selected and interpreted classical texts and analyzes the political motives for their choices and views.

77   Brereton, John C., ed. *The Origins of Composition Studies in the American College, 1875–1925: A Documentary History*. Pittsburgh: Univ. of Pittsburgh Press, 1995.

A number of histories of composition have focused on the formative years of the discipline, around the turn of the twentieth century. The major original documents from this critical period have, however, been difficult to access. Having many of them together in this volume makes it possible to see their self-consciousness about theoretical choices, their rhetorical sophistication, and their diversity. The documents are in five sets: Harvard's program from 1870–1900, with course descriptions, reports from the composition committee, and reflections by Adams Sherman Hill and Barrett Wendell; the new writing curriculum from 1895–1915, with essays by John Genung, program descriptions from a dozen representative institutions, and reports from the MLA's pedagogical section; the attack on Harvard, with essays on teaching composition by Gertrude Buck, Lane Cooper, Thomas Lounsbury, and others; textbooks, with excerpts from sixteen texts by Hill, Genung, Wendell, Scott, Cooper, Strunk, and others; and essay writing, with a wide selection of articles, textbook extracts, sample admission essays, and course materials. Includes a substantial introductory history by Brereton and, as a concluding chapter, Warner Taylor's *National Survey of Conditions in Freshman English* of 1929.

78   Brereton, John, ed. *Traditions of Inquiry*. New York: Oxford Univ. Press, 1985.

Eight essays assess the contributions of important teachers of writing: Wallace Douglas, "Barrett Wendell"; Donald C. Stewart, "Fred Newton Scott"; Ann E. Berthoff, "I. A. Richards"; John Brereton, "Sterling Andrus Leonard"; William F. Irmscher, "Kenneth Burke"; Walker Gibson, "Theodore Baird"; Richard Lloyd-Jones, "Richard Braddock"; and Robert Lyons, "Mina Shaughnessy."

79   Bridenthal, Renate, Claudia Koonz, and Susan Stuard, eds. *Becoming Visible: Women in European History*. 2nd ed. Boston: Houghton Mifflin, 1987.

Twenty essays debunk myths about women's nonparticipation in history and consider how these myths arose and shaped European culture. An excellent introduction to women's history and education from the times of European tribal peoples, ancient Egypt, Greece, and Rome to the present day.

80   Brody, Miriam. *Manly Writing: Gender, Rhetoric, and the Rise of Composition*. Carbondale and Edwardsville: Southern Illinois Univ. Press, 1993.

In the Western rhetorical tradition, good writing has typically been described in terms of masculine virtues: it is coherent, clear, forceful, trustworthy, and true. Bad writing has been characterized in terms of vices usually associated with women: it is confused, overly ornamented, timid, and obscure or deliberately deceitful. Good writing has often openly been called "manly," while bad writing has been labeled "effeminate." Yet scholarship has left this gendering of evaluative terms largely unexamined. Brody traces its origins to Quintilian and argues that its status was assured by the condemnation of elaborate rhetoric promulgated by the British Royal Society in the late 1600s. Eighteenth century theorists of rhetoric such as Adam Smith and Hugh Blair made these gendered distinctions into pedagogical commonplaces. Brody tracks them into nineteenth century American composition texts and finally into the work of twentieth century composition scholar Peter Elbow.

81   Campbell, Karlyn Kohrs. *Man Cannot Speak for Her, Volume I: A Critical Study of Early Feminist Rhetoric*. Westport, Conn., and New York: Praeger/Greenwood Press, 1989.

Nineteenth century women had to struggle for their very right to speak in public against age-old prohibitions, largely religiously based. They argued for one moral law governing both men and women, a law that compelled their activism on behalf of abolition and African American rights, women's suffrage, temperance, and more. They learned how to address male audiences, emphasizing either that men and women were essentially morally and intellectually equal or that women possessed superior spiritual insight that required they benefit society with their political participation. In the latter part of the century, women's efforts concentrated on winning the vote — not without increasing tensions between white and black activists. Among the women rhetors with whom Campbell illustrates this groundbreaking study are Sarah and Angelina Grimké, Elizabeth Cady Stanton, Susan B. Anthony, Frances Willard, Ida B. Wells, and Mary Church Terrell. Volume II of Campbell's study collects representative speeches by these and other nineteenth century women rhetors.

82   Clark, Gregory, and S. Michael Halloran, eds. *Oratorical Culture in Nineteenth-Century America: Transformations in the Theory and Practice of Rhetoric*. Carbondale: Southern Illinois Univ. Press, 1993.

Eleven original essays trace and analyze the development of American rhetoric from neoclassical oratorical forms that focused on civic matters to rhetorics that reflected a growing individualism and professionalism. Essays include an introduction by Clark and Halloran; Ronald F. Reid on Edward Everett and neoclassical oratory; Gregory Clark on Timothy Dwight; P. Joy Rouse on Margaret Fuller; Nan Johnson on elocution and the private learner; Nicole Tonkovich on *Godey's Lady's Book*; and Catherine Peaden on Jane Addams.

83   Conley, Thomas M. *Rhetoric in the European Tradition*. New York: Longman, 1990.

Rhetoric has been defined somewhat differently in different ages, reflecting the needs — and particularly the crises — of the times. Greek notions of rhetoric reflect several different views of nature and beliefs about the ends of rhetoric. The four basic Greek models, which see rhetoric as variously manipulative or consensus seeking (the Sophistic versions) or dialectical (in Plato) or problematic (in Aristotle) persist throughout the history of rhetoric, one or another dominating at different times. Conley traces the dominant theories from Greek to modern times, focusing on schools and individual rhetorical theorists, giving most attention to those who exerted the greatest influence on their own contemporaries and on later thinkers, and setting each in the historical and political context that seems to account for the nature of the rhetorical model. Conley's purpose is to provide the background material needed to comprehend the major texts themselves, as well as to reorder our idea of which texts and figures are truly the major ones.

84   Connors, Robert J. *Composition-Rhetoric: Backgrounds, Theory, and Pedagogy*. Pittsburgh: Univ. of Pittsburgh Press, 1997.

The period from about 1760 to 1960 was significant in the history of rhetoric for the growth of theory and pedagogy that focused on written rhetoric to be used by newly expanding professional and managerial classes, a kind of rhetoric once called "current-traditional." Before the Civil War, it tended to combine instruction in oral and written rhetoric and to be taught in small classes or by tutorial. After the Civil War, as new state universities and new opportunities for higher education for women greatly enlarged and diversified the school population, class size grew and textbooks became increasingly important in defining the curriculum. By the early twentieth century, instruction in composition-rhetoric was largely institutionalized in the required multisection first-year programs known today and dominated by textbooks that inculcated formal and mechanical correctness. Composition-rhetoric had lost status as a discipline, courses were taught by academic underlings, and research on writing had virtually ceased. Connors organizes his analysis of these developments thematically, focusing on the influences of changing gender roles and increasing coeducation, textbooks and the emphasis on mechanical correctness, new standards of professionalism and licensure, and the teaching of discourse taxonomies, theories of style, types of assignments, and invention procedures.

85   Connors, Robert J. "The Erasure of the Sentence." CCC 52 (September 2001): 96–128.

Sentence-based pedagogies of the 1960s and 1970s have been completely elided within contemporary composition studies despite the evidence that they did work to improve student writing. Three sentence-based rhetorics of the New Rhetoric were the generative rhetoric of Francis Christensen, imitation exercises, and sentence-combining. The first full-scale empirical study of the Christensen system did demonstrate statistically significant classroom results; imitation was also tested and determined successful in helping writers to internalize sentence structures and design. Kellogg Hunt's work on syntactic maturity and his concept of the T-unit paved the way for important experiments on sentence-combining, with confident results that sentence-combining exercises improved both syntactic maturity as well as perceived quality of writing in general. Reasons for the erasure of the sentence and the devaluation of sentence rhetorics can be linked to anti-formalism, anti-behaviorism, and anti-empiricism, and to the changing demographics of composition studies as it became a subfield of English.

86   Connors, Robert J. "The Rise and Fall of the Modes of Discourse." CCC 32 (December 1981): 444–63.

This survey of the most popular rhetoric textbooks used in American colleges since the early 1800s shows that, until the 1950s, the dominant method of writing instruction was imitation of models of the modes of discourse — narration, description, exposition, and argument. In the 1950s, self-expression and audience models challenged the older method. Connors traces the influence of Bain, Hill, Scott, Genung, the CCCC, and others. Braddock Award winner.

87   Connors, Robert J., Lisa S. Ede, and Andrea A. Lunsford, eds. *Essays on Classical Rhetoric and Modern Discourse*. Carbondale and Edwardsville: Southern Illinois Univ. Press, 1984.

In this festschrift for Edward P.J. Corbett, seventeen contributors discuss the importance of classical rhetoric to modern composition studies. Essays include Robert J. Connors, Lisa S. Ede, and Andrea A. Lunsford, "The Revival of Rhetoric in America"; James L. Golden, "Plato Revisited: A Theory of Discourse for All Seasons"; James L. Kinneavy, "Translating Theory into Practice in Teaching Composition: A Historical View and a Contemporary View"; James C. Raymond, "Enthymemes, Examples, and Rhetorical Method"; John T. Gage, "An Adequate Epistemology for Composition: Classical and Modern Perspectives"; and S. Michael Halloran and Annette Norris Bradford, "Figures of Speech in the Rhetoric of Science and Technology." Also includes a bibliography of works by Corbett. Mina P. Shaughnessy Prize cowinner.

88   Corbett, Edward P.J., and Robert J. Connors. *Classical Rhetoric for the Modern Student*. 1965; 4th ed. New York: Oxford Univ. Press, 1999.

Training in classical rhetoric can help modern students understand public persuasive discourse while they discover the educational tradition that has shaped Western culture for two thousand years. Chapters on discovery of arguments, arrangement of material, and style explain logic, the types of appeal, the topics, resources for invention, types of refutation, schemes, and tropes, illustrated by modern essays and speeches. The final chapter is a brief history of rhetoric. A comprehensive introduction to classical rhetorical theory and practice. For the fourth edition, Corbett is joined by Connors, who expands and updates the chapter on the history of rhetoric and contributes a new chapter on the progymnasmata, the sequence of prose composition exercises employed in classical Greek rhetorical education.

89   Covino, William A. *The Art of Wondering: A Revisionist Return to the History of Rhetoric*. Portsmouth, N.H.: Heinemann-Boynton/Cook, 1988.

Conventional histories of rhetoric depict its major texts as sets of prescriptions for constructing sentences, organizing speeches, and (amorally) manipulating audiences. In contrast, a revisionist history could see Plato, Aristotle, and Cicero as describing and performing a rhetoric that explores ambiguities. From this perspective, an alternative tradition might be traced through Montaigne, Vico, Hume, Byron, and De Quincey, a tradition of rhetoric used to inquire into uncertain questions from multiple viewpoints while remaining open to any stylistic innovations that facilitate such explorations. This rhetoric, an "art of wondering," is particularly appropriate to the postmodern epistemological orientation of Burke, Derrida, Feyerabend, and Geertz. It fosters tolerance and interdependence by keeping the exploratory conversation going.

90   Covino, William A., and David A. Jolliffe. *Rhetoric: Concepts, Definitions, Boundaries*. Boston: Allyn and Bacon, 1995.

An anthology offering information and selections in nearly every area of rhetoric. "Part I: An Introduction to Rhetoric" defines the field in a few brief chapters. "Part II: Glossary of Major Concepts, Historical Periods, and Rhetors" is a small encyclopedia with sixty-eight one-page entries. "Part III: Perspectives on the History and Theory of Rhetoric" is an anthology of fifteen essays by well-known scholars chiefly on major themes in the history of the field. "Part IV: The Contents of Rhetoric" is an anthology of essays by authors in a wide range of fields, with three to five essays in each of the following categories: Rhetoric and Cultural Studies; Rhetoric and Non-Western Culture; Rhetoric, Feminism, and Gender Studies; Rhetoric and Philosophy; Rhetoric and the Arts; Rhetoric and Literary Criticism; Rhetoric and Science; Rhetoric and Linguistics; Rhetoric and Education; Rhetoric and Literacy; Rhetoric and Composition; Rhetoric and Technology; and Rhetoric and Oratory. Includes an index.

91   Crowley, Sharon. *The Methodical Memory: Invention in Current-Traditional Rhetoric*. Carbondale: Southern Illinois Univ. Press, 1990.

Current-traditional rhetoric, until recently the dominant approach in American schools, developed in the late eighteenth and nineteenth centuries when rhetoricians like George Campbell and Richard Whately rejected classical rhetoric's invention schemes. To discover arguments, they claimed, the writer had merely to investigate the workings of his or her own mind, for all minds worked alike. In this model of invention, the individual authorial mind was privileged over community wisdom, and the written text was regarded as a record of the mind's operations. Clarity and logic were the goal. Pedagogy based on this model emphasized the formal features of texts — correctness and logical organization, for example — that presumably reflected the well-ordered mind at work. The metaphysical principles, supposedly universal, on which this pedagogy is based make it inherently conservative and insensitive to cultural difference. A preferable rhetoric and pedagogy is one that values difference and the diversity of communal treasures as archives for invention.

92   de Romilly, Jacqueline. *Great Sophists in Periclean Athens.* 1988. Trans. Janet Lloyd. Oxford: Clarendon Press, 1992.

The greatest Sophists were Protagoras, Gorgias, Prodicus, Hippias, and Thrasymachus. Before their advent in the fifth century B.C.E., Athenian education focused on athletics and music, and aimed to cultivate only the well-born. The Sophists became famous as teachers of public speaking, who would impart successful techniques to anyone who could pay their fees, and they emphasized intellectual development. Under their influence, the scientific study of nature began, and philosophy turned its attention from cosmogony to human action, which likewise became the focus of history, drama, and art. The gods, oracles, and the supernatural generally diminished in importance. The Sophists promoted cultural toleration and Panhellenism. They argued that human societies were held together by man-made laws that people could choose to break, rather than by divine decrees of justice that compelled obedience. Although this view could lead (as in Protagoras) to a sort of social contract theory of human society, the Sophists were attacked for encouraging impiety and lawless behavior. Nevertheless, their ideas formed the foundation of Western philosophy and education.

93   Donawerth, Jane. "Conversation and the Boundaries of Public Discourse in Rhetorical Theory by Renaissance Women." *Rhetorica* 16 (Spring 1998): 181–99.

Madeleine de Scudéry, Margaret Cavendish, Margaret Fell, and Mary Astell appropriated classical rhetorical theory for their own purposes. Barred by their sex from the public practice of rhetoric and from exercising verbal power openly, each in her own way developed the supposedly private genre of conversation as a women's rhetorical venue, where influence on public events could be exercised indirectly. Donawerth argues that although recommending conversation to women as an appropriate rhetorical sphere paid lip service to existing restrictions on women's public action, it did not relegate women to a realm of powerlessness. They had the opportunity to influence public events, however indirectly — indeed, these women were so influential that their conversation, with its public implications, can hardly be considered a "private" genre. De Scudéry, Cavendish, and Astell were well connected among the ruling nobility of France (de Scudéry) and England — Cavendish herself was a duchess — and Fell was a noted Protestant reformer, one of the founders of the Society of Friends (Quakers).

94   Donawerth, Jane, ed. *Rhetorical Theory by Women before 1900: An Anthology*. Lanham, Md.: Rowman & Littlefield, 2002.

Presents a broad selection of women rhetorical theorists before 1900. Following an introduction that outlines a history of rhetorical theory by women, chapters offer biographical information and excerpts from women who wrote conduct books, composition and rhetoric textbooks, or about a variety of communication arts: conversation, letter writing, elocution, public speaking, or the Delsarte method. Included are Aspasia, Pan Chao, Sei Shonagon, Bathsua Makin, Mary Astell, Maria Edgeworth, Lydia Sigourney, Hallie Quinn Brown, Genevieve Stebbins, Jennie Willing, Sara Lockwood, Anna Morgan, Mary Augusta Jordan, and ten others.

95   Glenn, Cheryl. *Rhetoric Retold: Regendering the Tradition from Antiquity through the Renaissance*. Carbondale and Edwardsville: Southern Illinois Univ. Press, 1997.

The traditional image of rhetorical practice depicts men speaking in public while women remain silent at home. Recent feminist scholarship has disrupted this traditional image by arguing that it does not represent all possible instances of rhetoric in use. Thus traditional historiography has been undermined, while female rhetorical figures have been recovered for study and new venues of rhetorical practice, where women participate actively, have been explored. Efforts to understand why and how women have been excluded from the rhetorical tradition must proceed in tandem with work that studies their rhetorical contributions. This scholarly process defines Glenn's project here. Areas of study include Sappho, Aspasia, and Diotima of classical Greece; ancient Roman women such as Cornelia; medieval mystics Julian of Norwich and Margery Kempe; and Renaissance women including Elizabeth I, Protestant intellectual Margaret More Roper, and Protestant martyr Anne Askew. Glenn situates these women in the political and cultural climate of their times, and critically analyzes previous scholarship that has highlighted, or more likely, neglected their rhetorical contributions.

96   Halloran, S. Michael. "Rhetoric in the American College Curriculum: The Decline of Public Discourse." *PRE/TEXT* 3 (Fall 1983). Rpt. in Vitanza [222].

Classical rhetoric emphasizes effective communication about public problems. Seventeenth century theories of rhetoric in American colleges led away from such public discourse by assigning argument to the realm of logic and retaining only "pleasing expression" in rhetoric, as well as by ignoring vernacular English in favor of Greek and Latin. In the eighteenth century, a more "classical" conception of rhetoric recovered invention, arrangement, and audience, and English became the language of formal academic disputation, which dealt more often with public concerns. In the nineteenth century, emphasis shifted to written products, to the "modes" of discourse, and to correctness, and away from invention and public discourse. These changes were closely related to the dominance of belletristic aesthetics, to the specialization of the curriculum that presented knowledge in small course-units, and to a shift in the function of education from preparation for public service to preparation for personal advancement. Many aspects of classical rhetoric are being revived, but public discourse has not yet reemerged.

97   Hauser, Gerard A. "Aristotle on Epideictic: The Formation of Public Morality." *Rhetoric Society Quarterly* 29 (Winter 1999): 5–23.

Democracy is plagued by tension between the majority of people, who may not have a clear grasp of moral issues, and the privileged minority, who see themselves as the guardians of virtue. When no strong, experienced leader can mediate this tension, the merely clever who can manipulate people's emotions may gain political influence while the community fragments. This is what happened in Athens with the rise of Demosthenes, after the rule of Pericles. Aristotle wished to rectify the situation by creating an art of rhetoric that the good person can learn so as to use it in teaching the majority what good values are, thus mitigating tension and creating political consensus. Aristotle saw, according to Hauser, that while deliberative and forensic rhetoric may teach values incidentally, by implying them as the bases for judgment, epideictic rhetoric is the most important means of teaching values. In the epideictic speech, the rhetor does not merely tell about the values that he (or she) deems most central to the community, but attempts to demonstrate them in his (or her) performance. Audiences thus witness the very possibility of virtue enacted before their eyes. Hauser closes with brief discussions of a few contemporary examples of speeches that serve this epideictic function.

98   Havelock, Eric A. *The Literate Revolution in Greece and Its Cultural Consequences*. Princeton: Princeton Univ. Press, 1982.

A revolutionary development in human thought was the Greek alphabet, around 700 B.C.E. It was the first to assign symbols to individual sounds rather than to whole words or syllables, thus greatly reducing the number of symbols to memorize, which democratized the new technology and helped it spread. Literacy, in turn, encouraged dramatic changes in human thought processes. In the earlier world of orality, both verbal style and thought processes are characterized by parataxis, the simple juxtaposition of ideas; by concrete imagery that appeals to the senses and the emotions; by ritualized

references to authority — for example, in proverbs; and by an agonistic posture in disputation. In contrast, literate verbal style and
thought processes are marked by hypotaxis, the subordination of one
idea to another in logical hierarchies; by generalizations that appeal
to reason and text-assisted memory for validation; and by a questioning attitude toward authority that encourages the disinterested criticism of ideas. These literate modes, treating language as an artifact
that can be examined and molded, enabled philosophical discourse.

99   Hawhee, Debra. "Composition History and the *Harbrace College Hand-
      book.*" CCC 50.3 (February 1999): 504–23
      First published in 1941 and in its twelfth edition, *The Harbrace Col-
      lege Handbook* has helped to "write" the discipline of composition
      and has shaped teacher and student subjectivities. Other than a few
      minor changes, the *Harbrace* has functioned as a stable force in an
      otherwise unstable field. The original goal of John C. Hodges' hand-
      book was to make paper marking an easier task, determined by what
      errors students made in an extensive study at the University of Ten-
      nessee in the late 1920s and early 1930s. An analysis of 20,000 essays
      determined a need for 35 rules, in a volume small enough to fit into
      a coat pocket but systematic enough to liberate instructors. The stu-
      dent subject is defined in terms of lack or deficiency, with overt in-
      stances of infantilization and no room for experimentation. Current
      editions of the *Harbrace* continue to illustrate the disciplinary func-
      tion of current-traditional rhetoric.

100   Hobbs, Catherine, ed. *Nineteenth-Century Women Learn to Write.*
      Charlottesville: Univ. Press of Virginia, 1995.
      The thirteen essays in this collection focus on women's education:
      the contexts in which women acquired advanced literacy in the nine-
      teenth century and the practices they developed as they put their
      literacy to use. Essays include Jane E. Rose, "Conduct Books for
      Women, 1830–1860: A Rationale for Women's Conduct and Do-
      mestic Role in America"; Devon A. Mihesuah, "'Let Us Strive Ear-
      nestly to Value Education Aright': Cherokee Female Seminarians as
      Leaders of a Changing Culture"; June Hadden Hobbs, "His Religion
      and Hers in Nineteenth-Century Hymnody"; Nicole Tonkovich,
      "Writing in Circles: Harriet Beecher Stowe, the Semi-Colon Club,
      and the Construction of Women's Authorship"; Shirley Wilson Lo-
      gan, "Literacy as a Tool for Social Action among Nineteenth-
      Century African American Women"; P. Joy Rouse, "Cultural Models
      of Womanhood and Female Education: Practices of Colonization and
      Resistance"; and Sue Carter Simmons, "Radcliffe Responses to
      Harvard Rhetoric: 'An Absurdly Stiff Way of Thinking.'"

101   Horner, Winifred Bryan, ed. *Historical Rhetoric: An Annotated Bibli-
      ography of Selected Sources in English.* Boston: G. K. Hall, 1980.
      Selected primary and secondary sources, divided into five areas: the
      classical period, the Middle Ages, the Renaissance, the eighteenth

century, and the nineteenth century. Each chapter has an introduction, primary sources listed chronologically, and secondary sources listed alphabetically. Most entries are annotated.

102   Horner, Winifred Bryan, ed. *The Present State of Scholarship in Historical and Contemporary Rhetoric*. Rev. ed. Columbia: Univ. of Missouri Press, 1990.

An indispensable collection of six bibliographic essays by eminent scholars in each period: Richard Leo Enos and Ann M. Blakeslee, "The Classical Period"; James J. Murphy and Martin Camargo, "The Middle Ages"; Don Paul Abbott, "The Renaissance"; Winifred Bryan Horner and Kerri Morris Barton, "The Eighteenth Century"; Donald C. Stewart, "The Nineteenth Century"; and James L. Kinneavy, "Contemporary Rhetoric." The authors also identify areas where further study is needed.

103   Howell, Wilbur Samuel. *Eighteenth-Century British Logic and Rhetoric*. Princeton: Princeton Univ. Press, 1971.

Classical rhetoric and logic remained influential throughout the eighteenth century, though challenged by the new rhetoric and logic of science. Classical logic, which came from Aristotle, aimed to deduce new truths from those already known and to communicate them to a learned audience. Classical rhetoric was of three kinds: Ciceronian rhetoric aimed to communicate truths to a popular audience; stylistic rhetoric analyzed orations and literary works; and elocutionary rhetoric, a new form, prescribed methods of delivery for public speaking, stage acting, and polite conversation. In contrast, the new logic propounded by Francis Bacon and John Locke worked inductively, testing ideas against perceived reality. The new rhetoric claimed to be a general theory of communication, learned as well as popular, advocating inductive reasoning and plain style. Adam Smith and George Campbell were its chief proponents.

104   Howell, Wilbur Samuel. *Logic and Rhetoric in England, 1500–1700*. Princeton: Princeton Univ. Press, 1956.

In Renaissance England, a persistent metaphor likened logic, the discourse of science, to a closed fist (tight and rigorous) and rhetoric, the discourse of popularized knowledge, to an open hand (loose and popular). In the early sixteenth century, rhetorical study had three patterns: the Ciceronian pattern focused on the five rhetorical arts; the stylistic pattern concerned the study of tropes and figures; and the formulary pattern was the study of models for imitation. Later in the sixteenth century, Ramism reformed dialectic and rhetoric (see "A Brief History of Rhetoric and Composition"). At the end of the seventeenth century, the *Port-Royal Logic* popularized Cartesian logic. Bacon's logic and rhetoric paralleled this development and led to the Royal Society's project for language reform. Howell's work is the standard history of this important period in the history of rhetoric.

105   Jarratt, Susan. *Rereading the Sophists: Classical Rhetoric Refigured.*
        Carbondale: Southern Illinois Univ. Press, 1991.

        The Greek Sophists of the fifth century B.C.E. developed a theory and
        practice of socially constructed discourse, focused on the historical
        contingency and democratic usefulness of strategies of persuasion,
        and delighted in the play of language. Recovered from its denigra-
        tion by Plato and Aristotle, sophism provides a good model for un-
        derstanding the political effects and goals of feminist discourse and
        critical-education discourse today.

106   Johnson, Nan. *Gender and Rhetorical Space in American Life, 1866–
        1910.* Carbondale: Southern Illinois Univ. Press, 2002.

        Thousands of readers in postbellum America had the opportunity to
        study rhetoric only through the parlor curriculum: conduct litera-
        ture, advice and etiquette manuals, and (parlor) encyclopedias, all
        designed to offer instruction in elocution, oratory, and composition.
        The influence of the parlor-rhetoric movement appears in a range of
        nineteenth century texts and artifacts — newspaper advertisements,
        letters, biographies, and autobiographies. The nineteenth century
        middle class parlor was a rhetorical space devoted to improving and
        enlarging the discourse practices and possibilities of middle class
        women, yet successfully marketed parlor instruction, including a com-
        mon "separate-desks" motif, served to keep women in the home and
        to restrict their access to public rhetorical activities. Cultural inter-
        ests combined to silence women in spite of their access to prestige
        discourses: parlor rhetorics performed ideological work in a culture
        desperate to restrict public rhetorical space. Women orators were
        judged in an era defined by cultural anxiety about women's increas-
        ing appearances at the podium. Performing gender, then, was an ex-
        plicit criterion by which women orators were judged; they had to be
        persuasive that they had not really left the parlor at all.

107   Johnson, Nan. *Nineteenth-Century Rhetoric in North America.*
        Carbondale: Southern Illinois Univ. Press, 1991.

        Nineteenth century rhetoric was a synthesis of classical elements (the
        canons of invention, arrangement, and style), belletrism (focusing
        on criticism and literary taste), and epistemological ideas about the
        relation of language and persuasion to the mental "faculties" (will,
        imagination, understanding, and passions). All three of these ap-
        proaches developed in the eighteenth century and found a solid place
        in the discipline of rhetoric, in theoretical treatises as well as text-
        books. The civic and cultural status of rhetoric was as yet secure in
        the nineteenth century: It was still seen as a significant factor in
        maintaining social and political order, as well as in formulating the
        conventions for scientific and philosophical communication. Both
        oratory and composition were firmly within its purview. "Nineteenth-
        century rhetoricians claimed for rhetoric the status of science, prac-
        tical art, and civil servant. In laying this claim, they addressed and

confirmed the dominant intellectual and cultural values of their era"
(246).

See: James L. Kastely, *Rethinking the Rhetorical Tradition* [191].

108   Kates, Susan. *Activist Rhetorics and American Higher Education, 1885–
       1937*. Carbondale: Southern Illinois Univ. Press, 2001.

       Rhetoric curricula designed for specific student constituencies served
       the needs of disenfranchised students by making their marginalization
       in the larger culture a focus of course content. Educators Mary Au-
       gusta Jordan of Smith College, Hallie Quinn Brown of Wilberforce
       University, and Josephine Colby, Helen Norton, and Louis Budenz
       of Brookwood Labor College were concerned more with language
       and ideology than with correctness. A variety of archival materials
       and pedagogical artifacts distinguish activist rhetorical education from
       more traditional forms and demonstrate the ways in which activist
       rhetoric instruction has a long history in the United States — char-
       acterized by an emphasis on writing and speaking, language and iden-
       tity, and service and social responsibility. Because the prospect of
       confronting difference in the rhetoric classroom is a more complex
       endeavor than most educational theorists realize, the pedagogical lega-
       cies of these activist educators should inform current controversies
       in composition studies.

109   Kennedy, George A. *The Art of Persuasion in Greece*. Princeton:
       Princeton Univ. Press, 1963.

       Volume 1 of Kennedy's history of classical rhetoric (see [110]), the
       standard work on the period, treats individual rhetoricians and their
       works and supplies historical background. Kennedy emphasizes that
       Greek rhetoric was overwhelmingly an art of oral discourse. He dis-
       cusses the conflict between rhetoric and philosophy, and traces the
       development of the great central theory of rhetoric to which all clas-
       sical rhetoricians contributed, foreshadowing Greek influence on the
       Romans.

110   Kennedy, George A. *The Art of Rhetoric in the Roman World 300* B.C.–
       A.D. *300*. Princeton: Princeton Univ. Press, 1972.

       This is volume 2 of Kennedy's history of classical rhetoric (see [109]),
       the standard work on the period. It treats individual rhetoricians and
       their works in detail, supplies much historical background, and traces
       the fall and rise of persuasion as the main focus of rhetoric under
       Roman influence. Kennedy has two chapters on Cicero, two on Au-
       gustan rhetoric, one on Quintilian, and two on later Greek rhetoric.

111   Kennedy, George A. *Classical Rhetoric and Its Christian and Secular
       Tradition from Ancient to Modern Times*. Chapel Hill: Univ. of North
       Carolina Press, 1980.

       Originally formulated in ancient Greece as an art, rhetoric later de-
       veloped into three types. Technical rhetoric prescribed the correct
       forms for invention, organization of speeches, and style. Sophistic

rhetoric, taught by imitation, emphasized the speaker's ethos and the magical powers of stylistic display, whereas philosophical rhetoric sought to discover truth and convey it to audiences for their good. Kennedy traces these lines of rhetorical study up to the 1700s, chiefly through summaries of the contributions of important rhetoricians.

112   Kimball, Bruce A. *Orators and Philosophers: A History of the Idea of Liberal Education*. New York: Teachers College Press, 1986.

The history of liberal education from the Middle Ages to the present can be seen as a struggle between two kinds of teacher-scholars. *Orators* stressed citizenship education, emphasized commonly held ("liberal") notions of the good, and valued rhetoric as a method of creating consensus on public issues. *Philosophers* stressed education for the pursuit of pure truth, supported education for the elite by defining "liberal" as liberation from worldly cares (hence, freedom to pursue the truth), and denigrated rhetoric in their search for a language transparent to the truth. Philosophers have come to dominate Western education through the force of science and technology, but the influence of the Orators ought to be restored.

113   Levin, Carole, and Patricia A. Sullivan, eds. *Political Rhetoric, Power, and Renaissance Women*. Albany: State Univ. of New York Press, 1995.

The Renaissance was a time of powerful queens and also of violent invective against women in political life, much of it religiously motivated. This collection examines the political rhetoric of powerful Renaissance women, men's rhetoric directed against them, literature by male and female authors of the time that considers women as political agents, and historical evaluations of powerful Renaissance women from their own time to the present. Fifteen essays include Carole Levin and Patricia A. Sullivan, "Politics, Women's Voices, and the Renaissance: Questions and Context"; Daniel Kempton, "Christine de Pisan's *Cité des Dames* and *Trésor de la Cité*: Toward a Feminist Scriptural Practice"; Ilona Bell, "Elizabeth I — Always Her Own Free Woman"; Elizabeth Mazzola, "Expert Witnesses and Secret Subjects: Anne Askew's *Examinations* and Renaissance Self-Incrimination"; Arlen Feldwick, "Wits, Whigs, and Women: Domestic Politics as Anti-Whig Rhetoric in Aphra Behn's Town Comedies"; and Jane Donawerth, "The Politics of Renaissance Rhetorical Theory by Women."

114   Logan, Shirley Wilson. *"We Are Coming": The Persuasive Discourse of Nineteenth-Century Black Women*. Carbondale: Southern Illinois Univ. Press, 1999.

Although the public discourse of prominent black women was not always recorded or preserved, much was produced in the last two decades of the nineteenth century — in the nadir — when club women, church women, and educators addressed concerns of all classes. Largely trained in speaking skills in the black church and despite resistance to their activities, black women chose to participate in public discourse in ways grounded in African origins but adapted to multiple audiences and multilayered exigencies, arguing for, for example, common communities of interest. The speeches of Maria Stewart, Frances Harper, Ida Wells, Fannie Barrier Williams, Anna Julia Cooper, Victoria Earle Matthews, and others, analyzed through the new rhetorics of Perelman and Olbrechts-Tyteca, Burke, and Bitzer, reveal strategic shifts, audience adaptations, and tactics of arrangement that achieved particular communicative aims, molded and constrained by prevailing conventions and traditions. The discourse of racial uplift, in particular, induced social action by representing it as work, and black women created, organized, and publicized a large number of public forums, firmly establishing a tradition of political activism among black women.

115   Logan, Shirley Wilson. *With Pen and Voice: A Critical Anthology of Nineteenth-Century African-American Women*. Carbondale and Edwardsville: Southern Illinois Univ. Press, 1995.

In unprecedented numbers, African American women entered public rhetorical fora in the nineteenth century to agitate for African American rights, women's rights, higher education for African Americans of both sexes, temperance, and more. They developed distinctive rhetorical strategies that responded to traditional prohibitions against their public activism on grounds of race and sex. Logan collects representative works by seven women: Maria W. Stewart, Sojourner Truth, Frances Ellen Watkins Harper, Anna Julia Haywood Cooper, Ida B. Wells, Fannie Barrier Williams, and Victoria Earle Matthews. Logan provides a critical summary of each woman's career, and introduces the volume with an essay that sets these rhetors in their political and cultural contexts.

116   Lunsford, Andrea A., ed. *Reclaiming Rhetorica: Women in the Rhetorical Tradition*. Pittsburgh: Univ. of Pittsburgh Press, 1995.

Sixteen original essays examine the contribution to rhetorical theory of women such as Aspasia (Susan Jarratt and Rory Ong), Diotima (C. Jan Swearingen), Christine de Pisan (Jenny Refern), Mary Astell (Christine Mason Sutherland), Margaret Fuller (Annette Kolodny), Ida B. Wells (Jacqueline Jones Royster), Sojourner Truth (Drema R. Lipscomb), Suzanne K. Langer (Arabella Lyon), and Louise Rosenblatt (Annika Hallin).

See: Andrea A. Lunsford and Lisa S. Ede, "Classical Rhetoric, Modern Rhetoric, and Contemporary Discourse Studies" [196].

117   Marrou, H. I. *A History of Education in Antiquity*. Trans. George Lamb. New York: Sheed & Ward, 1956.

The standard introduction to the subject. Marrou describes the origins of classical education from Homer to Isocrates and traces primary, secondary, and postsecondary education from Greek and Roman times to early Christian schooling and Byzantine and monastic education.

118   Mattingly, Carol. *Well-Tempered Women: Nineteenth-Century Temperance Rhetoric*. Carbondale and Edwardsville: Southern Illinois Univ. Press, 1998.

The temperance movement was the largest political movement of women in the nineteenth century. It began as a struggle against the sale of alcohol, which was heavily implicated in the impoverishment and physical abuse of women and children by addicted men. Under the leadership of Frances Willard, president of the Women's Christian Temperance Union (WCTU) in the latter part of the century, temperance activism enlarged to embrace other social reform issues, such as improved treatment of prostitutes and women criminals, improved availability of day care for working mothers, unionized labor contracts for both women and men, and women's suffrage. In this mass movement, women took the speaker's platform and published their opinions in unprecedented numbers, in part due to the WCTU's deliberate policy of encouraging women to find their public voices. Mattingly argues that the temperance movement did more than any other force to educate nineteenth century women in rhetorical practices. She provides richly detailed documentation of women's temperance rhetoric, studies temperance fiction, and explores racial tensions within the movement.

119   Miller, Thomas P. *The Formation of College English: Rhetoric and Belles Lettres in the British Cultural Provinces*. Pittsburgh: Univ. of Pittsburgh Press, 1997.

In the middle of the eighteenth century, the first professorships to teach composition, rhetoric, and literature in English were founded in British universities, primarily in schools in the cultural provinces of Scotland and Ireland and in Dissenters' academies in England. The whole discipline of English studies has developed from these professorships, which were originally established to focus on a new kind of instruction in rhetoric. While Ciceronian rhetoric, deductive logic, and prescriptive grammar — essentially a classicist approach — persisted at Oxford and Cambridge, a utilitarian plain style of rhetoric was taught at these schools, along with inductive logic and grammar based in usage. The new approaches emerged where they did because these were the schools in which previously excluded groups were entering the academy and seeking language training that would facilitate their upward mobility. Parallel to this trend was an unprecedented effort to codify the English that they would learn, through the publication of record numbers of dictionaries and grammar books. Instruction in rhetoric and in moral philosophy were linked by the aim of both to direct people's actions. The new professors of rhetoric sought to make moral philosophy more empirical by developing the social sciences, such as economics and political science;

they sought to make rhetoric similarly scientific with an emphasis on psychology. Eventually, the curriculum of higher education was divided between the arts and the sciences. Rhetoric was still too engaged in the contingencies of persuasion to become either fully scientific or aesthetically focused. Hence it tended to fall out of the new curriculum, while English studies was reduced to the aesthetic appreciation of nonutilitarian texts, or what is now called "literature."

See: Roxanne Mountford, "On Gender and Rhetorical Space" [201].

120   Murphy, James J., ed. *Renaissance Eloquence: Studies in the Theory and Practice of Renaissance Rhetoric*. Berkeley: Univ. of California Press, 1983.

Many leading scholars in Renaissance rhetoric are represented in this collection of twenty-three essays that surveys the field, including Paul Oskar Kristeller, "Rhetoric in Medieval and Renaissance Culture"; James J. Murphy, "One Thousand Neglected Authors: The Scope and Importance of Renaissance Rhetoric"; John Monfasani, "The Byzantine Rhetorical Tradition and the Renaissance"; Nancy Struever, "Lorenzo Valla: Humanist Rhetoric and the Critique of the Classical Languages of Morality"; John W. O'Malley, "Content and Rhetorical Forms in Sixteenth-Century Treatises on Preaching"; Richard J. Schoeck, "Lawyers and Rhetoric in Sixteenth-Century England"; Judith Rice Henderson, "Erasmus on the Art of Letter-Writing"; Thomas O. Sloane, "Reading Milton Rhetorically"; and Brian Vickers, "'The Power of Persuasion': Images of the Orator, Elyot to Shakespeare."

121   Murphy, James J. *Rhetoric in the Middle Ages*. Berkeley: Univ. of California Press, 1974.

Saint Augustine turned the prescriptive Aristotelian and Ciceronian rhetorics to Christian use by arguing that rhetoric is neither empty nor merely ornamental if it is filled with religious truth and dedicated to saving souls. Medieval rhetoricians, following Augustine, made the art of preaching one of the three chief rhetorical genres. The others were letter writing, devoted to political ends, and prescriptive grammar, which was studied by writing and analyzing poetry. Prescriptive rhetoric, based on fragmentary knowledge of classical texts, declined after the rediscovery in the 1400s of complete copies of Quintilian's *Institutio* and Cicero's *De Oratore*.

122   Murphy, James J., ed. *The Rhetorical Tradition and Modern Writing*. New York: MLA, 1982.

Twelve essays treat the place of classical, eighteenth century, and nineteenth century rhetoric in the modern curriculum and analyze the work of Cicero, John Locke, Alexander Bain, and other premodern rhetoricians. Essays include James J. Murphy, "Rhetorical History as a Guide to the Salvation of American Reading and Writing: A Plea for Curricular Courage"; James L. Kinneavy, "Restoring the Humanities: The Return of Rhetoric from Exile"; Susan Miller, "Classical Practice and Contemporary Basics"; S. Michael Halloran and Merrill D. Whitburn, "Ciceronian Rhetoric and the Rise of Science: The Plain Style Reconsidered"; Winifred Bryan Horner, "Rhetoric in the Liberal Arts: Nineteenth-Century Scottish Universities"; and Donald C. Stewart, "Two Model Teachers and the Harvardization of English Departments."

123   Murphy, James J., ed. *A Short History of Writing Instruction from Ancient Greece to Twentieth Century America*. Davis, Calif.: Hermagoras Press, 1990.

Seven essays focus on the contributions of rhetoricians to writing instruction: Kathleen Welch, "Writing Instruction in Ancient Athens After 450 B.C."; James J. Murphy, "Roman Writing Instruction as Described in Quintilian"; Marjorie Woods, "The Teaching of Writing in Medieval Europe"; Don Paul Abbott, "Rhetoric and Writing in Renaissance Europe and England"; Winifred Bryan Horner, "Writing Instruction in Great Britain: Eighteenth and Nineteenth Centuries"; S. Michael Halloran, "From Rhetoric to Composition: The Teaching of Writing in America to 1900"; and James A. Berlin, "Writing Instruction in School and College English, 1890–1985." Includes glossary and bibliography.

124   Murphy, James J., ed. *A Synoptic History of Classical Rhetoric*. Davis, Calif.: Hermagoras Press, 1983.

Six essays provide an introductory overview of rhetoric in Greek and Roman culture and include summaries of major works: James J. Murphy, "The Origins and Early Development of Rhetoric"; Forbes I. Hill, "The *Rhetoric* of Aristotle"; James J. Murphy, "The Age of Codification: Hermagoras and the Pseudo-Ciceronian *Rhetorica ad Herennium*"; Donovan J. Ochs, "Cicero's Rhetorical Theory"; Prentice A. Meador, Jr., "Quintilian and the *Institutio Oratoria*"; James J. Murphy, "The End of the Ancient World: The Second Sophistic and Saint Augustine." Also includes a basic bibliography on classical rhetoric compiled by Michael C. Leff.

See: Jasper Neel, *Plato, Derrida, and Writing* [202].

125   North, Stephen M. *The Making of Knowledge in Composition: Portrait of an Emerging Field*. Upper Montclair, N.J.: Boynton/Cook, 1987.

Composition is an interdisciplinary field comprising three methodological communities: first, the practitioners, who generate lore about writing instruction through classroom experience; second, the scholars, whose research produces histories and philosophical works; and third, the researchers, whose empirical methods include protocol analysis and ethnography. At present, scholars and researchers are battling for control of the field and for the allegiance of the practitioners — whose status has been downgraded by the implication that they should adopt one or the other of these ways of making knowledge. North summarizes and critiques examples of work in each of the communities.

126   Ong, Walter J., S.J. *Ramus, Method, and the Decay of Dialogue*. 1958. Rpt. New York: Farrar, Straus and Giroux, 1974.

Although the works of Peter Ramus decisively changed rhetoric, he was heavily influenced by his scholastic predecessors. Like them, he attempted to describe a universal method for systematizing knowledge into academic disciplines that could be easily taught to the young boys who attended the university. Unlike them, Ramus lived in a world in which printed texts were increasingly available. He came to conceive of knowledge as broken up into "fields" (like the visual field of the printed page), composed of discrete bits of information (like printed letters), and hence susceptible to quantification. Ramus "reformed" classical rhetoric by moving invention and arrangement to the realm of dialectic and by treating dialectic as the arranging of bits of information in dichotomies, which presumably convince by virtue of their logical structure alone. Ramus dropped memory and delivery because they are not necessary for print communication. Rhetoric itself has to do only with style, and, because the dichotomies of Ramist dialectic convey rational truth, rhetoric need be used only when a recalcitrant audience required ornamentation of the truth to induce belief. Ramus's view of the quantifiable nature of knowledge contributed to the development of empirical scientific method, and his plain style seemed the appropriately neutral medium for scientific study. Ong argues that Ramus himself cared little about advancing knowledge of the external world or rescuing language from the "distortions" of rhetorical ornamentation.

127   Paine, Charles. *The Resistant Writer: Rhetoric as Immunity, 1850 to the Present*. Albany: State Univ. of New York Press, 1999.

An inoculation and resistance model of education, particularly strong in the nineteenth century and today, serves to maintain individuality and the status quo. While most composition histories have focused on villainous forebears and our inheritance of current traditional practices, reading composition history through competing cultural institutions complicates historiography and questions the dominant portrayal of nineteenth century composition instruction as being in league with capitalism and business. Rather than demonstrating that connections exist between composition instruction and larger cultural issues, work must be done to investigate how larger cultural issues have actually *transformed* composition theory and practice. The rhetorical theories of Edward T. Channing and Adams Sherman Hill responded to cultural imperatives similar to those today. Channing tried to help students distance themselves from mainstream culture while indoctrinating them into the university. Hill produced his rhetorical theory during an era of intense animosity between intellectuals and the powerful rise of mass culture, particularly the newspaper industry. Hill's easy-to-manage rhetorical assignments allowed the construction of a stable self — critical and aloof and able to resist cultural norms. Rather than designing writing courses to shore up students' defenses, composition instructors should teach students to live *in* conflict, not overcome it.

See: Krista Ratcliffe, *Anglo-American Feminist Challenges to the Rhetorical Traditions* [213].

128   Peterson, Carla. *"Doers of the Word": African-American Women Speakers and Writers in the North (1830–1880)*. New York: Oxford Univ. Press, 1995.

The cultural work of nineteenth century black women activists was produced from social, psychological, and geographical positions of marginality that shifted as these women diversified their rhetorical approaches. They had to contend with silencing and exploitation of the body that emerged not only from the dominant white culture but also from their home communities. Often fortified by a sense of divine mission, they persevered and accomplished much for racial uplift. Among the speakers and writers Peterson studies are Sojourner Truth, Maria Stewart, Jarena Lee, Harriet A. Jacobs, and Frances Ellen Watkins Harper.

129   Royster, Jacqueline Jones and Jean C. Williams. "History in the Spaces Left: African American Presence and Narratives of Composition Studies." CCC 50.4 (June 1999): 563–84.

Several historical accounts of composition studies have established national parameters for the field but none accounts for the seventeen historically African American colleges and universities established in the 1890s. Historians have not typically been pushed to specify their own ideological locations and the resulting limitations to their gaze; their reliance on primary texts can block their perception of the simultaneous existence of multiple viewpoints. Student-centered narratives of composition often ignore the long-standing presence of African Americans in arenas of higher education and their successes as insiders, resulting in a conflation of ethnicity, otherness, and basic writing, and making race a rare focal point for scholars' analyses. Setting the gaze toward the nineteenth century allows for a fuller understanding of African American students as active participants in higher education. Several historical moments, such as the establishment of Howard University in 1867, created academic spaces for intellectual work in the African American community; recovering the contributions of African American teachers and scholars begins by acknowledging the achievements of Alain Locke, Hallie Quinn Brown, and Hugh M. Gloster. As official narratives take on social, political, and cultural consequences, resisting these narratives invites a search for better interpretive frames and different method-

ologies that will account more richly for the participation of historically suppressed groups.

130   Royster, Jacqueline Jones. *Traces of a Stream: Literacy and Social Change
Among African American Women*. Pittsburgh: Univ. of Pittsburgh Press,
2000.

Acts of literacy are rhetorical events that embody an individual vision and voice but are also culturally produced and often enacted in
the interest of social change, as illustrated by the essaying practices
of African American women writers. Tracing the development of rhetorical prowess in public domains and analyzing essays of social change
begins at the intersections of context, ethos formation, and rhetorical action — and requires the tools of advocacy and activism. Although they are not monolithic in personhood or in literate practices,
African American women use language and literacy as a tool to authorize, entitle, and empower themselves and others, with characteristic reliance upon cooperative practices and commitment to social
responsibility. Separated from their original homelands, these women
brought a sense of ancestral connection, one that translated into their
uses of written language. Best analyzed in a kaleidoscopic view of the
rhetorical process, the literate forms of African American women
show evidence of a blurring of literacy and orality, with features that
are inclusive, healing, and generative. Despite a litany of obstacles,
these women persevered to achieve higher education at such institutions as Oberlin College, where they received formal rhetorical training, participated in literary clubs, and went on to organize cooperative
community activities or reform movements. African American
women wrote for the periodical press, critical mechanisms for par-
ticipating in public discourse, and spoke before varied audiences; they
operated in *both* religious and secular contexts. Organized by three
views, rhetorical, historical, and ideological, Royster outlines a paradigm for Afrafeminist scholarship and argues, in part, "people who
do intellectual work need to understand their intellectual ancestry"
(265). Includes a photographic essay and a thematic bibliography.

131   Rudolph, Frederick. *Curriculum: A History of the American Undergraduate Course of Study since 1636*. San Francisco: Jossey-Bass, 1977.

An invaluable history of the establishment and development of colleges in the United States, their curricula, student populations, purposes for education and certification, and the rationale in each period and at key colleges for determining what counts as knowledge.

132   Russell, David R. "Romantics on Writing: Liberal Culture and the
Abolition of Composition Courses." *Rhetoric Review* 6 (Spring 1988):
132–48.

The required composition course has, during its hundred-year history, frequently been attacked by proponents of Arnoldian "liberal
culture," who advocate an elitist view of education and oppose the

democratic, professional, and scientific character of the modern university. In the view of Thomas Lounsbury, Oscar James Campbell, and others, writing is a creative act that cannot be taught; the required composition course is stultifying to students, instructors, and the English department as a whole; and writing ability should therefore be regarded as an admission criterion, not a college course. The combination of composition with an introduction to literature in many programs reflects the influence of the liberal-culture argument. In recent times, the assumptions underlying calls for abolition of the composition course persist in conflicts over the status of composition in English departments, in expressivist composition theories, and in policy decisions about admissions standards.

133   Russell, David R. *Writing in the Academic Disciplines, 1870–1990: A Curricular History*. Carbondale: Southern Illinois Univ. Press, 1991.

In a long flirtation with writing instruction in the disciplines, universities have begun hundreds of programs to teach writing across the curriculum in the twentieth century, all of which became marginalized. Writing was not integrated in content learning, and professors continued to resist teaching writing and reading papers. These failures reflect the persistent attitude that writing is a skill, a form of recorded speech, that writing instruction is remediation, and that the academy is a single discourse community. They also reflect the myth of transcience, the belief that students' inability to write is a problem that will soon, or eventually, be solved. The structure of the university makes cross-disciplinary conversation unproductive, hence the fantasy that the academy is a single discourse community, for to acknowledge the diversity of discourse conventions would require more attention to one's own conventions and present a clear necessity to teach them. General education reforms reinforced this delusion, as well as the myth of transcience, by calling for a unified society and explicitly remedial writing courses. Writing in the disciplines is much more difficult to learn under these conditions, which contributes to the perceived high status of the disciplines, but also opposes social equity by creating a hurdle that many students cannot vault. Writing across the curriculum has been more influential since 1970, but the same forces of resistance are still at work.

134   Salvatori, Mariolina Rizzi, ed. *Pedagogy: Disturbing History, 1819–1929*. Pittsburgh: Univ. of Pittsburgh Press, 1996.

"Pedagogy" was a disputed term throughout the nineteenth century in Europe and the United States. Its meaning moved along a spectrum defining it, at one extreme, as useless pedantry and, at the other, as the crucial knowledge required of responsible teachers. But often, as the concept of pedagogy was rehabilitated, it also had to be renamed "education." Often at issue was whether pedagogy was an art, proceeding primarily by inspiration, or a science, subject to empirical investigation and codification in rules. Important sites of this struggle were the new normal schools for teachers that emerged in the 1840s and the university departments of education that came of age in the 1880s and 1890s. Among the disputants of these contested meanings were the authors of dictionaries and encyclopedias, women's conduct book writers, philosophers of education, professors of education, and teachers. In this volume, Salvatori collects primary documents from all these sources and provides historical analysis of the nuances of their arguments. Ultimately, she aims to show that pedagogy does have a history and that it does not deserve the lack of respect it often incurs in the academy today.

135   Schultz, Lucille M. *The Young Composers: Composition's Beginnings in Nineteenth-Century Schools.* Studies in Writing and Rhetoric Series. Carbondale: Southern Illinois Univ. Press, 1999.

Composition historians have overlooked the importance of nineteenth century first books, or those written for children in the primary grades, and the pedagogical innovation that these books suggest. As the concept of childhood changed, so did the role of writing in a child's education; most significantly, students practiced writing from lived experience. Major changes in school-based language instruction can be traced to reform educator Johann Pestalozzi, whose object-centered teaching influenced Frost's *Easy Exercises*. Illustrations in these first books served both as writing prompts and as moral lessons. Evidence of extracurricular writing, such as letters and memoirs, suggests that current-traditional pedagogy did not rule all literacy instruction in the mid- and late century. Schultz considers the experience-based essay as the most significant innovation of these nineteenth century writing classrooms.

136   Sloane, Thomas O. *On the Contrary: The Protocol of Traditional Rhetoric.* Washington, D.C.: Catholic Univ. of America Press, 1997.

Practice in arguing both sides of a question, traced here to recommendations in Cicero's *De oratore*, has been a mainstay of traditional rhetorical education in the West since classical times. It has been the basic method of rhetorical invention, the process whereby one finds ideas for one's discourse. Familiarity with this pedagogy aids in understanding two great Renaissance texts, the *De copia* of Desiderius Erasmus and the *Discourse on Usury* of Thomas Wilson. Sloane argues that what he calls a "contrarian" pedagogy would also assist modern students to learn critical thinking and rhetorical invention. He urges that this method not be dismissed as too agonistic and masculine in orientation. While the process does require putting ideas into opposition with each other, Sloane argues that it is in fact "maieutic," a sort of mental midwifery that assists at the birth of well-examined ideas in the minds of one's readers or hearers. Sloane announces that his scholarly method here is "antiquarian," devoted to digging up details from the past that are entertaining as well as relevant to his argument but that have as their ultimate purpose the

revelation of the intellectual poverty and lack of humanity in education today, when compared with traditional instruction in rhetoric.

137   Sutherland, Christine Mason, and Rebecca Sutcliffe, eds. *The Changing Tradition: Women in the History of Rhetoric*. Calgary: Univ. of
Calgary Press, 1999.

Seventeen essays (one printed in French with a translation) by scholars from seven countries who attended the 1997 annual conference
of the International Society for the History of Rhetoric expand traditional definitions of rhetoric by considering the rhetorical activities of women who have been excluded from the tradition or who
have developed practices parallel to it. The essays look at images of
rhetorical women in myth and fiction as well as historical figures,
treat women's reception as well as production of rhetoric, and more.
They include Christine Mason Sutherland, "Women in the History
of Rhetoric: The Past and the Future"; C. Jan Swearingen, "Plato's
Women: Alternative Embodiments of Rhetoric"; Vicki Collins, "Account of the Experience of Hester Ann Rogers: Rhetorical Functions
of a Methodist Mystic's Journal"; John Ward, "Women and Latin
Rhetoric from Hrotsvit to Hildegard"; Erin Herberg, "Mary Astell's
Rhetorical Theory: A Woman's Viewpoint"; Suzanne Bordelon, "Resisting Decline Stories: Gertrude Buck's Democratic Theory of Rhetoric"; and Lynette Hunter, "Feminist Thoughts on Rhetoric."

138   Swearingen, C. Jan. *Rhetoric and Irony: Western Literacy and Western
Lies*. New York: Oxford Univ. Press, 1991.

Is language a lie, a fiction capable of creating only fictive meanings
and identities? Pre-Platonic philosophers resisted the idea that language was deceptive and began to develop a writing-based technical
rhetoric to anatomize arguments and cast them in forms reflecting
truth. Plato tried to scuttle this movement, proposing instead that
only honest dialogue could attain truth. Plato condemned the self-
consciously manipulative rhetor as an "eiron," regarding the manipu-
lator as a liar. Technical rhetoric nevertheless triumphed with
Aristotle, progenitor of the "linear-monological-grammatical-logical
systems" that have dominated rhetoric in the West. Cicero tried, too,
to combat technical rhetoric in favor of dialogue, an effort blocked
and obscured by the loss of his mature works. Augustine criticized
mendacity in language, also connected, for him, to the deceptive techniques of rhetoric, which were to be corrected by sermonic teaching
and inner dialogues between self and soul. The dialogic rhetorics of
Plato, Cicero, and Augustine are pertinent to our own age, when
textual literacy is being challenged by new technologies and linear-
logical argument forms are regarded as too restrictive and abstract.

139   Tuana, Nancy, ed. *Feminist Interpretations of Plato*. University Park:
Pennsylvania State Univ. Press, 1994.

In this collection of work by philosophers and classicists, six essays
look at Plato's explicit views on women, and six consider Plato's use

of feminine imagery in his philosophy. The first group includes Gregory Vlastos, "Was Plato a Feminist?"; Elizabeth V. Spelman, "Hairy Cobblers and Philosopher-Queens"; and Natalie Harris Bluestone, "Why Women Cannot Rule: Sexism in Plato Scholarship." Among the second group are Page duBois, "The Platonic Appropriation of Reproduction"; Andrea Nye, "Irigaray and Diotima at Plato's Symposium"; and Nancy Tuana and William Cowling, "The Presence and Absence of the Feminine in Plato's Philosophy."

140   Varnum, Robin. *Fencing with Words: A History of Writing Instruction at Amherst College during the Era of Theodore Baird, 1938–1966*. Urbana, Ill: NCTE, 1996.

In Theodore Baird's two-semester first-year writing course, he and the instructors together designed a common sequence of assignments that called on students to write from experience and to bring their work to class for discussion. Students and instructors found themselves engaged in stiff competition for the cachet of intellectual excellence, a dynamic that was intended to make students independent and reliant on only their own imaginative resources. Varnum sees this course as reflecting American ideologies of masculinity, particularly a combat-oriented ideal valorized by World War II. Although Baird never attempted to promote his approach in the profession, it has been widely influential through the teachers he trained, among them Walker Gibson, Roger Sale, and William Coles.

141   Wertheimer, Molly Meijer, ed. *Listening to Their Voices: The Rhetorical Activities of Historical Women*. Columbia: Univ. of South Carolina Press, 1997.

Nineteen essays both analyze and exemplify feminist rhetorical scholarship on topics ranging from classical times to the present including: Cheryl Glenn, "Locating Aspasia on the Rhetorical Map"; Barbara Warnick, "Lucie Olbrechts-Tyteca's Contribution to *The New Rhetoric*"; Robert W. Cape, Jr., "Roman Women in the History of Rhetoric and Oratory"; Shirley Wilson Logan, "Black Women on the Speaker's Platform (1832–1899)"; Julia Dietrich, "The Visionary Rhetoric of Hildegard of Bingen"; Vicki Tolar Collins, "Women's Voices and Women's Silence in the Tradition of Early Methodism"; Jane Donawerth, "'As Becomes a Rational Woman to Speak': Madeleine de Scudéry's Rhetoric of Conversation" and "Textbooks for New Audiences: Women's Revisions of Rhetorical Theory at the Turn of the Century."

142   Woodward, William Harrison. *Studies in Education during the Age of the Renaissance, 1400–1600*. Cambridge: Cambridge Univ. Press, 1906.

In what is still an authoritative source for the period, Woodward describes the Quattrocento beginnings of humanist education, traces its influence in Europe by examining the careers of important educators (including Guarino, Agricola, Erasmus, Vives, and Melanchthon), examines Italian and English doctrines of courtesy, and reviews the humanist education of Elizabethan aristocrats.

143   Wozniak, John Michael. *English Composition in Eastern Colleges, 1850–1940*. Washington, D.C.: Univ. Press of America, 1978.

A detailed history of composition courses, textbooks, methods, rationales, and instructors, interwoven with an analysis of theories and purposes and a general history of institutional development.

Rhetoric and Composition Theory

144   Bartholomae, David. "Inventing the University." In *When a Writer Can't Write*. Ed. Mike Rose [240].

Students must learn to sound like experts when they write, and they thus adopt personae that seem to them authoritative and academic. The errors of inexperienced writers should be seen as the result of this effort to approximate and finally to control a complex and alien discourse. Students "extend themselves, by successive approximations, into the commonplaces, set phrases, rituals and gestures, habits of mind, tricks of persuasion, obligatory conclusions and necessary connections" that constitute knowledge in academic communities. Writer, audience, and subject are all located in discourses that exist outside the individual, and it requires an act of courage to penetrate such discourses and earn the right to speak in them.

145   Bartholomae, David. "Writing with Teachers: A Conversation with Peter Elbow." CCC 46 (February 1995), 62–71.

Academic writing — writing done in the shadow of others — is the real work of the academy and therefore the key term for teaching writing. To pretend otherwise is to withhold from students knowledge of the politics of discursive practice. Student writing is situated in a heavily populated textual space in an institution where power is unequally distributed. The image of a free space for expression, found in Peter Elbow's work, reflects a desire to be outside of history and culture, a desire for a common language, free of jargon and full of presence; a desire for an autonomous author and a democratic classroom. If we wish to help students become aware of the forces at work in producing knowledge, we need, rather, to invoke the reality of the classroom as a substation in the cultural network, not disguise it as a utopian space. Critical knowledge requires working with texts, understanding the possibilities beyond quotation, and not pretending that writing is purely one's own. Composition should not foster the genre of sentimental realism and pretend it is transcendent, but preside over critical writing, academic writing. See Elbow [174].

146   Bawarshi, Anis. "The Genre Function." *College English* 62.3 (2000): 335–60.

Genre plays a role not only in the constitution of texts but also in the *contexts*; genres are the rhetorical environments within which situations and practices are recognized, enacted, and reproduced. Because genres constitute all communicative action, genre provides an alternative to Foucault's author-function, which cannot account for how *all* discourses function, only privileged ones. How do we recognize the situations within which we function? Through genres, which are rhetorically constitutive of our social actions. Genres function on conceptual, discursive, and ideological levels, and they carry with them social motives. For genre theorists in literary studies, literary genres constitute and regulate literary activities or literary textual relations rather than being seen as constituting social reality. Building from Bakhtin, genre theorists in several fields are beginning to synthesize how the genre function makes possible and meaningful many kinds of relations and identities. Halliday defines genre through register; however, genre has a more constitutive role, an integral part of genre as social semiotic, part of an activity system. Giddens's theory of structuration has much to offer genre studies, as an extended example of a medical history form makes clear. The genre function accounts for all discursive activities, not just those endowed with a certain literary value.

147   Bazerman, Charles. "What Written Knowledge Does: Three Examples of Academic Discourse." *Philosophy of the Social Sciences* 11 (September 1981): 361–87. Rpt. in Bazerman, *Shaping Written Knowledge*. Madison: Univ. of Wisconsin Press, 1988.

We can study the way written knowledge contributes to a discipline by analyzing how writers in different disciplines use specialized lexicons, citations, tacit knowledge, and personae. Examples from biochemistry, sociology of science, and literary criticism illustrate the ways in which discourse constitutes knowledge in each field.

148   Berlin, James A. "Poststructuralism, Cultural Studies, and the Composition Classroom." *Rhetoric Review* 11 (Fall 1992): 16–33.

The postmodern critique of traditional liberal-humanist epistemology has been useful to social-epistemic rhetoricians. In place of the traditional view of the individual as a unified consciousness unencumbered by historical circumstances, postmodernism posits a subject shaped by history and conflicting discourses, making individual consciousness contradictory and mutable. In place of the view of language as a neutral device for conveying truth, postmodernism sees language as constructing reality and deriving its meaning from differences among the signs themselves. Postmodernism critiques master narratives of human experience as part of, not external to, experience, and locates their meanings in what they exclude. These views mesh with the social-epistemic treatment of the writer as a construct, the audience as an unstable repertoire of constructed selves, and language as the constructive medium — hence as the site of the struggle to define reality in one's best interests. All texts are thus ideological. In studying texts, rhetoric cannot accept claims of transcendence. The writing course, then, should study many ways of using language, emphasizing the need to negotiate among textual and contextual meanings. This approach fosters democratic values by enabling students to analyze claims made on them by competing discourses.

149   Berlin, James A. "Rhetoric and Ideology in the Writing Class." CE 50 (September 1988): 477–94.

Rhetoric has generally been seen as the arbiter of ideological claims, but rhetorical theories are themselves ideological constructs. Three rhetorics that have had significant influence in composition classrooms — cognitive psychology, expressionism, and the social-epistemic — have distinctive ideological bases. Cognitive psychology claims to be scientific and ideologically neutral. Moreover, it offers no critique of epistemology, the formation of values, or the arrangements of power. In this way, it accepts and therefore advances the current hegemonic political and social order. Its rationalization of the writing process is an extension of rationalized economic activity. Expressionism begins with a critique of oppressive social and political constraints, positing that writing is liberating for the individual. But its critical position is vitiated by the romantic and individualistic approach that fends off collective opposition to oppression. If individualism modulates into entrepreneurship, expressivism becomes a capitalist tool. The social-epistemic approach attempts to keep ideological analysis at its center, to recognize that the self, the community, and the material conditions of existence are in dialectical tension. In this view, rhetoric is the study of how knowledge comes into existence: it asks how the perception of reality is structured, how values are formed, and how change is constrained or enabled.

See: James A. Berlin, *Rhetoric, Poetics, and Cultures: Refiguring English Studies* [515].

150   Bernard-Donals, Michael, and Richard R. Glejzer, eds. *Rhetoric in an Antifoundational World: Language, Culture, and Pedagogy*. New Haven: Yale Univ. Press, 1998.

The eighteen essays in this volume, some previously published, address antifoundationalism, the philosophical position that all standards of judgment are historically and culturally contingent, never universally applicable or value-free. This position has been regarded as enhancing the importance of rhetoric when rhetoric is seen as a process of helping people arrive at decisions in situations in which absolute standards or certain knowledge cannot be used. Three major essays connecting rhetoric and antifoundationalism are reprinted here: Stanley Fish, "Rhetoric"; Richard Rorty, "The Contingency of Language"; and Terry Eagleton, "A Short History of Rhetoric." Following are essays that address the extent to which language constructs people's understanding of reality, among them: Michael Hill, "Toward a 'Materialist' Rhetoric: Contingency, Constraint, and the Eighteenth-Century Crowd"; Linda Frost, "The Decentered Subject of Feminism: Postfeminism and *Thelma and Louise*"; and Patricia Roberts, "Habermas's Rational-Critical Sphere and the Problem of Criteria." Also, essays address new configurations of rhetoric in relation to antifoundationalism, including: Robert E. Smith III, "Hymes, Rorty, and the Social-Rhetorical Construction of Meaning," and Kurt Spellmeyer, "'Too Little Care': Language, Politics, and Embodiment in the Life-World." Finally, essays that address implications for teachers include Patricia Bizzell, "Beyond Antifoundationalism to Rhetorical Authority: Problems Defining 'Cultural Literacy,'" and James A. Berlin, "Composition Studies and Cultural Studies: Collapsing Boundaries."

151   Berthoff, Ann E. *The Sense of Learning*. Portsmouth, N.H.: Heinemann-Boynton/Cook, 1990.

"The sense of learning" is an innate human ability to make sense of experience with the aid of signs. It is variously explored in the eleven essays in this volume, including: "Is Teaching Still Possible?" [152]; "Is Reading Still Possible?" [418]; "'Reading the World . . . Reading the Word': Paulo Freire's Pedagogy of Knowing"; "Democratic Practice, Pragmatic Vistas: Louise Rosenblatt and the Reader's Response"; and "I. A. Richards and the Concept of Literacy." An epilogue imagines that "Ramus Meets Schleiermacher and They Go Off for a Triadic Lunch with Peirce; Vico Drops By."

152   Berthoff, Ann E. "Is Teaching Still Possible? Writing, Meaning, and Higher Order Reasoning." *CE* 46 (December 1984): 743–55. Rpt. in Berthoff [151].

The human capacity for thinking about thinking is "the ground of hope in the enterprise of teaching reading and writing." A positivist view of language as a medium cannot account for meaning and leads to models of cognitive stages and composing processes that misapply psychology, overestimate empirical research, and rely on shaky analogies. Positivist research leads to teaching by exhortation and away from the consciousness of consciousness that allows us to make meaning. A pedagogy of knowing, on the other hand, works from the premise that language can both name (hypostatize) the world and allow us to reflect on it in discourse: to abstract and then to generalize. Teaching can develop this ability when it does not run aground on spurious developmental concepts. See also Berthoff [153, 287].

153   Berthoff, Ann E. *The Making of Meaning: Metaphors, Models and Maxims for Writing Teachers*. Upper Montclair, N.J.: Boynton/Cook, 1981.

Teachers should see composing as the active formation of understanding by the imagination, an act of sorting and selecting experiences according to our needs and purposes. To study composing is to study how we use language to interpret and know the world. In this collection of essays, Berthoff connects the theories of Richards [215],

Vygotsky, and Tolstoy and the pedagogies of Paulo Freire [258], Sylvia Ashton-Warner, Jane Addams, and others. A useful book for teachers at all levels.

154   Bitzer, Lloyd F. "The Rhetorical Situation." *Philosophy and Rhetoric* 1 (Winter 1968): 1–14.

Rhetorical discourse is determined by its situation, which has three constituent elements: exigence, the complex of people, events, and objects that create a need that rhetorical discourse attempts to satisfy; audience, the people who, if persuaded, will act on the exigence; and constraints, the audience's beliefs, traditions, and interests and the rhetor's ethos, style, and logic, all of which bear on the persuasive power of the discourse. Some discourse, such as scientific and poetic discourse, is not rhetorical.

155   Bitzer, Lloyd F., and Edwin Black, eds. *The Prospect of Rhetoric*. Englewood Cliffs, N.J.: Prentice-Hall, 1971.

Proceedings of the Wingspread Conference, at which leading figures from speech communication and English addressed common theoretical concerns about rhetoric. Fourteen essays include Richard McKeon, "The Uses of Rhetoric in a Technological Age: Architectonic Productive Arts"; Henry W. Johnstone, Jr., "Some Trends in Rhetorical Theory"; Wayne C. Booth, "The Scope of Rhetoric Today: A Polemical Excursion"; Chaim Perelman, "The New Rhetoric"; and Wayne E. Brockriede, "Trends in the Study of Rhetoric: Toward a Blending of Criticism and Science."

156   Bizzell, Patricia. *Academic Discourse and Critical Consciousness*. Pittsburgh: Univ. of Pittsburgh Press, 1992.

Bizzell traces the development of her thought about discourse communities, basic writers, and education for critical consciousness in this collection of eleven previously published and two new essays, with a lengthy introduction. Includes "The Ethos of Academic Discourse," "Thomas Kuhn, Scientism, and English Studies" [159], "Cognition, Convention, and Certainty: What We Need to Know about Writing" [157], "Academic Discourse and Critical Consciousness: An Application of Paulo Freire," "What Happens When Basic Writers Come to College?" [443], "Composing Processes: An Overview," "Foundationalism and Anti-Foundationalism in Composition Studies" [443], "What Is a Discourse Community?" and "Beyond Anti-Foundationalism to Rhetorical Authority: Problems Defining 'Cultural Literacy.'"

157   Bizzell, Patricia. "Cognition, Convention, and Certainty: What We Need to Know about Writing." *PRE/TEXT* 3 (Fall 1982): 213–43. Rpt. in Bizzell [157] and in Vitanza [222].

Composition research has proceeded along two theoretical lines: inner-directed research that looks at the writer's cognitive processes, and outer-directed research that looks at the social context of language use. Inner-directed researchers look for innate processes and mental structures, but they regard these processes as teachable. Linda Flower and John Hayes, for example, claim to have described a set of thought processes that produce writing. They assert that the process followed by good writers should be taught to students. Their model separates thought ("planning") from writing ("translating") and fails to account for the writer's knowledge or sense of context. Outer-directed research examines the dialectical relationship between thought and language by describing the intentions, genres, communal expectations, and knowledge that shape language use. In the Flower and Hayes model, basic writers are cognitively deficient, whereas in the sociolinguistic model, they are simply alien to the community in which they are being judged. Inner-directed models seek scientific certainty, while outer-directed models examine political, ethical, and social dynamics. What we need to know about writing will emerge from the debate between these two camps.

158   Bizzell, Patricia. "Contact Zones and English Studies." CE 56 (February 1994): 163–69.

Multiculturalism is stalled by the outdated national and chronological structure of English studies. Adding new materials to the old categories will not suffice. New categories like feminism continue to essentialize and separate. But the contact-zone notion conceptualized by Mary Louise Pratt provides a way of seeing how diverse literatures may come into productive dialogue with each other. A contact zone is an historical time and space in which a cultural struggle occurs. Instead of seeing literature as a monolingual exchange, the contact zone casts it as a negotiation among people with different languages attempting to represent themselves each to the others. America has always been a congeries of overlapping contact zones, and the growing diversity of our classrooms brings this out. Contact-zone categories release us from evaluating the literary goodness of a text: Instead, we look at the rhetorical effectiveness of a writer in dealing with the matter at hand. This approach reconnects literature with composition and rhetoric, not only through rhetorical criticism but also by casting student writing as contending in contact zones and engaging in the arts of cultural mediation.

159   Bizzell, Patricia. "Thomas Kuhn, Scientism, and English Studies." CE 40 (March 1979): 764–71. Rpt. in Bizzell [156].

Kuhn's description of paradigms and paradigm shifts in the sciences has led to speculation about an impending paradigm shift in the field of composition. Presumably, this shift, based on empirical research, will put composition studies on a scientific basis. But such speculations betray a desire to escape into scientific "certainty" and fundamentally misread Kuhn's thesis that knowledge in all disciplines develops by a rhetorical process of debate. Thus, Kuhn teaches us to study the ways in which rhetoric constitutes knowledge. Cf. Bazerman [147].

160   Bloom, Lynn Z., Donald A. Daiker, and Edward M. White. *Composition in the 21st Century: Crisis and Change*. Carbondale: Southern Illinois Univ. Press, 1995.

Sixteen paired essays and a response to each pair, on issues that face the profession in this century. Originally papers presented at the Conference on Composition in the 21st Century, most offer challenges and warnings. Selections include: David Bartholomae, "What Is Composition and (if you know what that is) Why Do We Teach It?"; Sylvia Holladay, "Order Out of Chaos: Voices from the Community College"; Robert Connors, "The New Abolition Debate in Composition: A Short History"; Peter Elbow, "Writing Assessment in the 21st Century: A Utopian View"; Anne Ruggles Gere, "The Long Revolution in Composition"; John Trimbur, "Writing Instruction and the Politics of Professionalization"; Stephen North, "The Death of Paradigm Hope, the End of Paradigm Guilt, and the Future of (Research in) Composition"; James Berlin, "English Studies, Work, and Politics in the New Economy"; Shirley Brice Heath, "Work, Class, and Categories: Dilemmas in Identity"; Linda Flower, "Literate Action"; and Andrea Lunsford, "Intellectual Property in an Age of Information."

161   Booth, Wayne C. "The Rhetorical Stance." CCC 14 (October 1963): 139–45. Rpt. in Young and Liu [295].

Good writing takes a "rhetorical stance," a conscious balance between subject, audience, and the writer's persona. Writing, as traditionally taught, overvalues the subject, fostering the "pedant's stance," which produces dry, obscure work. In reaction, some newer writing pedagogies have overvalued the audience-persona relationship, fostering the "entertainer's stance," which produces charming vacuities.

See: Doug Brent, *Reading as Rhetorical Invention* [288].

162   Brodkey, Linda. "Modernism and the Scene(s) of Writing." *Writing Permitted in Designated Areas Only* [163].

Scholars in English studies usually picture the scene of writing as "a solitary writer alone in a cold garret" working late at night by the light of one candle. This is a modernist image, akin to themes of alienation in modern art and atomism in modern science. The image presents the act of transcribing as a synecdoche for the entire composing process. The image removes all responsibility for what is written from the writer, since it does not suggest that there will be consequences when the text being written in the garret is read. The image also allows readers to treat the text as an autonomous entity, ignoring not only these consequences but also the text's provenance — the author's personality, cultural background, and historical circumstances. Thus the prevailing image of a writer becomes one of a person who is ignored, isolated, a victim or prisoner of writing. Also, this writer is always male — as can be inferred from the struggle chronicled in Virginia Woolf's work for women to find (a) room in which to write. Perhaps because they are aware of this struggle, Woolf and other women writers generally reject the modernist alienated victim position and take a more pragmatic view of the world and how to change it. Brodkey critiques the modernist imagery at length because she fears its influence on writing teachers, most of whom have much more professional training in modernist-influenced literary study than in composition. Ironically, too, if these teachers do know recent cognitive research on writing, they only see again the solitary writer — in this case, artificially isolated by the research situation. To effectively teach a richly collaborative and recursive writing process, teachers must experience their own writing this way, as well as encounter the composition research that explores writing's social contexts.

163   Brodkey, Linda. *Writing Permitted in Designated Areas Only.* Minneapolis: Univ. of Minnesota Press, 1996.

This volume collects seventeen of Brodkey's published and previously unpublished works on literacy, ethnography, cultural studies, and composition pedagogy, including "Modernism and the Scene(s) of Writing." [162], "On the Subjects of Class and Gender in 'The Literacy Letters'" [444], "On the Intersection of Feminism and Cultural Studies," and "Writing about Difference: 'Hard Cases' for Cultural Studies," coauthored with Richard Penticoff. Several essays discuss the innovative composition curriculum that Brodkey designed for the University of Texas and the controversy that engulfed it. A concluding section presents five essays by students in a graduate seminar of Brodkey's, demonstrating her pedagogy by way of its results. Brodkey provides introductions to the volume and to each of the four sections in which the pieces are organized.

164   Bruffee, Kenneth A. "Collaborative Learning and the 'Conversation of Mankind.'" CE 46 (November 1984): 635–52.

Psychologists contend that the ability to think is not innate but is developed socially. As children converse with those around them, they learn how to think in ways the community sanctions. Children internalize this conversation, which becomes reflective thought, and finally, when learning to write, externalize their thought in a social medium. Thus both thought and writing are transformations of oral conversation. William Perry, Stanley Fish, and Richard Rorty argue that knowledge, like thought, is socially generated and authorized. They describe a process of "conversation," spoken and written, which constitutes knowledge for participants in a discourse community. If students are to think and write according to academic standards, they must have opportunities for academic talk, as they have in collaborative learning — in a writing workshop, for example, with peer tutors. If students lack academic knowledge, teachers can structure collaborative tasks to generate this knowledge. Teachers should emphasize that academic discourse is not intended to stifle creativity: It is only one of many available discourses the student can choose. Mastery of any community's discourse, however, should be understood as acculturation, which may change the student profoundly. See also Olson [644].

165   Bullock, Richard, and John Trimbur. *The Politics of Writing Instruction, Postsecondary*. Portsmouth, N.H.: Heinemann-Boynton/Cook, 1991.

Eighteen original essays (and a Foreword by Richard Ohmann) that develop a political critique of writing instruction and demonstrate the inseparability of teaching writing from social, cultural, and economic forces. Essays include James S. Slevin, "Depoliticizing and Politicizing Composition Studies"; James A. Berlin, "Rhetoric, Poetic, and Culture: Contested Boundaries in English Studies"; Susan Miller, "The Feminization of Composition"; Robert Connors, "Rhetoric in the Modern University: The Creation of an Underclass"; Bruce Herzberg, "Composition and the Politics of the Curriculum"; Elizabeth Flynn, "Composition Studies from a Feminist Perspective"; Richard Bullock, "Autonomy and Community in the Evaluation of Writing"; Robert Schwegler, "The Politics of Reading Student Papers"; Victor Villanueva, Jr., "Considerations of American Freireistas"; and John Trimbur, "Literacy and the Discourse of Crisis." Winner of the CCCC Outstanding Book Award for 1993.

166   Burke, Kenneth. *A Grammar of Motives*. Englewood Cliffs, N.J.: Prentice-Hall, 1945.

The "basic forms of thought . . . are exemplified in the attributing of motives." Thought and language are modes of action, and all action can be regarded as dramatic. The dramatistic method analyzes motives by dividing motivated action into a dramatic pentad: act, scene, agent, agency, and purpose. Composition specialists have extracted Burke's pentad from this rich book of philosophy and literary criticism and have used it as a heuristic (see Comprone [290]). For Burke's comments on this use of the pentad, see "Questions and Answers About the Pentad," CCC 29 (December 1978): 330–35.

167   Burke, Kenneth. *A Rhetoric of Motives*. Englewood Cliffs, N.J.: Prentice-Hall, 1950.

The persuasive power of rhetoric lies in "identification": The persuader convinces the audience that they share traditions, experiences, and values, all embodied in their shared language. The use of identification for persuasion need not be deliberate, nor acquiescence to identification conscious, except for the desire to identify. Thus, rhetoric is an instrument of socialization, and all social interactions are rhetorical.

168   Cintron, Ralph. *Angels' Town: Chero Ways, Gang Life, and Rhetorics of the Everyday*. Boston: Beacon Press, 1997.

An ethnography of a Latino community called Angelstown studies rhetorics of everyday life through the *tekhne* of making and the *topos* of order. A variety of scenarios and participants contribute to the theme of distinct semiotic systems and the tension of order versus disorder. First, maps and texts are used as practical tools that help to fix a place; in this case, the field site bordered by a railroad levee. A ward map of the town serves to reflect on the discourses of measurement — the city grid a synecdoche for social controls. Other dominant social controls occur in the form of paperwork and official documents: Mexican immigrants refer to *arreglar sus papeles*, to fix your papers, and Don Angel's false documents "parodied and manipulated bureaucratic discourse," allowing him to hide behind the representations. Similarly, Valerio's bedroom walls demonstrate the effort to create respect under conditions of little or no respect. The ideology and guiding ethos that circulate through Angelstown become embodied as felt truths, evidenced in part by the language of violence. Graffiti and the use of gang colors illustrate the possibilities for appropriating mainstream symbols and recontextualizing them into new meanings. Cintron reflects on writing as the making of an order, raises questions about the ordered worlds that texts give rise to, and critiques the making of ethnographic texts.

169   Clark, Gregory. *Dialogue, Dialectic, and Conversation: A Social Perspective on the Function of Writing*. Carbondale: Southern Illinois Univ. Press, 1990.

Through collaborative textual exchange, readers and writers construct their collectivity, negotiating beliefs, values, and actions. Dialogue, as defined by Bakhtin and others, is the conscious cooperative exchange of discourse in this process of social construction. Dialectic, in both classical and modern definitions, is the process of constructing knowledge collaboratively. Conversation, as social science research confirms, is the actual experience of persuading and compromising through which dialogue and dialectic are enacted. Many disciplines today share and develop this perspective on the creation of knowledge in communities, suggesting that social life is essentially a rhetorical process. The social theory of discourse entails an ethics of reading that places the responsibility for a text's social force and function on its readers, whose criticism should be public. We should teach composition students to read and write as a democratic practice, as an exercise in public discourse that collaboratively constructs and sustains the community.

170   Clifford, John, and John Schilb, eds. *Writing Theory and Critical Theory*. New York: MLA, 1994.

Historiography, cultural studies, rhetoric, social construction, politics, discourse communities, social construction, narrative, postmodernism, and the move to theory itself — the dominant concerns of composition theory today — are analyzed and criticized in these essays. Fourteen essays comprise the three main sections of the book. Essays include Susan Miller, "Composition as a Cultural Artifact: Rethinking History as Theory"; James Slevin, "Reading and Writing in the Classroom and the Profession"; Kurt Spellmeyer, "On Conventions and Collaboration: The Open Road and the Iron Cage"; Suzanne Clark, "Rhetoric, Social Construction, and Gender: Is It Bad to Be Sentimental?"; Susan Wells, "The Doubleness of Writing and Permission to Lie"; Beth Daniell, "Theory, Theory Talk, and Composition"; Joseph Harris, "The Rhetoric of Theory"; Judith Summerfield, "Is There a Life in This Text? Reimagining Narrative"; Lester Faigley, "Street Fights over the Impossibility of Theory: A Report of a Seminar"; and Linda Brodkey, "Making a Federal Case out of Difference: The Politics of Pedagogy, Publicity, and Postponement." These are followed by three responses to Brodkey and a symposium, "Looking Backward and Forward," with Louise Rosenblatt, Robert Scholes, W. Ross Winterowd, Elizabeth Flynn, Sharon Crowley, and Victor Villanueva.

171   Corbett, Edward P. J., Nancy Myers, and Gary Tate. *The Writing Teacher's Sourcebook*. 4th ed. New York: Oxford Univ. Press, 2000.

Thirty-six previously published essays (twenty-five of which appeared in the third edition) on immediate pedagogical concerns of writing teachers, divided into ten sections: Perspectives, Teachers, Students, Locations, Approaches, Assigning, Responding and Assessing, Composing and Revising, Audiences, and Styles. Essays include Richard Fulkerson, "Four Philosophies of Composition"; James Berlin, "Contemporary Composition: The Major Pedagogical Theories"; Peter Elbow, "Embracing Contraries in the Teaching Process"; Dan Morgan, "Ethical Issues Raised by Students' Personal Writing" [412]; Vivian Zamel, "Strangers in Academia: The Experiences of Faculty and ESL Students across the Curriculum" [547]; Gary Tate, "A Place for Literature in Freshman Composition" [424]; Hephzibah Roskelly, "The Risky Business of Group Work"; Sondra Perl, "Understanding Composing"; Nancy Sommers, "Between the Drafts"; Jeanne Fahnestock and Marie Secor, "Teaching Argument: A Theory of Types" [303]; Brooke Horvath, "The Components of Written Response: A Practical Synthesis of Current Views" [358]; Douglas Park, "The Meanings of 'Audience'" [313]; Lisa Ede and Andrea Lunsford, "Audience Addressed/Audience Invoked: The Role of Audience in Composition Theory and Pedagogy" [308]; Peter Elbow, "Closing My Eyes as I Speak: An Argument for Ignoring Audience" [309]; Richard Ohmann, "Use Definite, Specific, Concrete Language" [340]; Winston Weathers, "Teaching Style: A Possible Anatomy" [341]; David Bartholomae, "The Study of Error" [441]; and Mike Rose, "Remedial Writing Courses: A Critique and a Proposal" [469].

See: William A. Covino and David Jolliffe, *Rhetoric: Concepts, Definitions, Boundaries* [90].

172   Crowley, Sharon. *Composition in the University: Historical and Polemical Essays*. Pittsburgh: Univ. of Pittsburgh Press, 1998.

The first-year composition requirement is motivated by institutional and disciplinary functions, leaving the course with no rhetorical purpose and questionable reasons for its persistence. As rhetorical education shifted toward the bourgeois project of self-improvement, civic virtue was replaced by a pedagogy of taste, signaling the end of rhetorical instruction and ushering in the study of literature and the belief that correctness constitutes character. Using literature to replace rhetoric in freshman English courses enabled the creation of English studies and made composition from its inception a service course, taught by those with low status. Various movements — basic skills, communication skills, process pedagogy — have not changed the policing mechanism of the first-year requirement or the focus on students' identities, and the staying power of the requirement results from composition specialists' middle-class affiliations and the reluctance to tamper with hard-won prestige. Marshaling historical and ideological evidence, Crowley argues that English departments have colonized composition and that writing in the university need not depend upon freshman English.

173   Dillon, George L. *Constructing Texts*. Bloomington: Indiana Univ. Press, 1981.

Psycholinguists, deconstructionists, and reader-response critics agree that to read is to create meaning, not merely to decode what the text encodes. The reader is enabled to create meaning by prior knowledge of the conventions governing text formation in a given discourse community and of patterns of concepts, or schemata, familiar within the discourse community. Conventions and schemata are cognitive in function, but they are not cognitively determined according to fixed, innate rules: They change gradually as the community itself changes. Writing instruction should reflect this flexible definition of conventions and schemata rather than persist in treating writing as encoding information. Dillon criticizes Hirsch's Philosophy of Composition for such cognitive determinism.

174   Elbow, Peter. "Being a Writer vs. Being an Academic: A Conflict in Goals." CCC 46 (February 1995): 72–83.

While it would be best if students could be comfortable in both the role of the writer and of the academic, freshman composition cannot aim at both. The role of the writer is preferable. Writing should be the predominant course activity, with reading secondary. Academics are chiefly readers and their courses privilege reading — input — over writing. Academic readers exercise control over the text by nullifying the author, while writers seek a reader who believes in them. Similarly, academics get to be readers of student texts and decide what they mean. Writers must be free to insist that readers cannot ignore intentions and searches for meaning; they must be free to ignore readers. Writing teachers who wish to foster the writer's role should primarily *understand* what writers are saying and only secondarily point out where that understanding is difficult to attain. The writing course need not situate writers in the ongoing intellectual conversation, but cannot pretend that no authorities have written on students' topics before. Students should see themselves at the center, not the periphery, of discourse. See Bartholomae [145].

175   Elbow, Peter. *Embracing Contraries: Explorations in Learning and Teaching*. New York: Oxford Univ. Press, 1986.

Twelve essays trace Elbow's thinking since the late 1960s about the complexity — even messiness — of the learning process, the conflicts raised by assumptions about teaching and its goals, the authority of teachers, the mystifications of evaluating students, and the philosophical basis for embracing contraries through dialectical thinking. Includes "Cooking" (from *Writing without Teachers* [397]), "The Pedagogy of the Bamboozled" (on American attempts to use Freire [258]), "Trying to Teach While Thinking about the End" (on competency-based teaching), "Evaluating Students More Accurately," "The Value of Dialectic," and "Methodological Doubting and Believing." Also includes a bibliography of Elbow's works on writing and teaching.

176   Emig, Janet. *The Web of Meaning: Essays on Writing, Teaching, Learning, and Thinking*. Ed. Dixie Goswami and Maureen Butler. Upper Montclair, N.J.: Boynton/Cook, 1983.

Eleven selections trace the development of Emig's thought from 1963 to 1982, including Chapters 4, 6, and 7 from *The Composing Processes of Twelfth Graders* [228]; "Hand, Eye, Brain: Some 'Basics' in the Writing Process"; "Writing as a Mode of Learning" [291]; and "Non-Magical Thinking: Presenting Writing Developmentally in Schools." Mina P. Shaughnessy Prize winner.

177   Enos, Theresa, and Stuart C. Brown. *Defining the New Rhetorics*. Newbury Park, Calif.: Sage Publications, 1993.

This collection of fifteen essays characterizes twentieth-century rhetoric as pluralistic. Essays include Richard Leo Enos, "Viewing the Dawns of Our Past Days Again: Classical Rhetoric as Reconstructive Literacy"; Carolyn Miller, "Rhetoric and Community: The Problem of the One and the Many"; S. Michael Halloran, "Further Thoughts on the End of Rhetoric"; Robert Scott, "Rhetoric Is Epistemic: What Difference Does That Make?"; James Berlin, "Poststructuralism, Semiotics, and Social-Epistemic Rhetoric: Convergence Agendas"; Christopher Burnham, "Expressive Rhetoric: A Source Study"; Linda Flower, "Cognitive Rhetoric: Inquiry into the Art of Inquiry"; and James Porter, "Developing a Postmodern Ethics of Rhetoric and Composition."

178   Enos, Theresa, and Stuart C. Brown. *Professing the New Rhetorics*. Englewood Cliffs, N.J.: Blair Press, 1994.

Fourteen selections from major figures in the development of twenti-eth century rhetorical theories, followed by thirteen essays of "com-mentary and application" by scholars in composition and speech com-munication. Theorists represented are Ferdinand de Saussure, I. A. Richards, Kenneth Burke, Mikhail Bakhtin, Richard Weaver, Ernesto Grassi, Stephen Toulmin, Richard McKeon, Chaim Perelman, Michel Foucault, Michael Polanyi, Jürgen Habermas, Roland Barthes, and Wayne Booth. Scholars are Donald Bryant; Richard Ohmann; Rob-ert Scott; Douglas Ehninger; S. Michael Halloran; Terry Eagleton; E.D. Hirsch, Jr.; Walter Fisher; Andrea Lunsford and Lisa Ede; Jim Corder; Paulo Freire and Donaldo Macedo; Patricia Bizzell; and James Berlin.

179   Faigley, Lester. *Fragments of Rationality*. Pittsburgh: Univ. of Pitts-burgh Press, 1992.

The postmodern era is characterized by randomness of experience, unopposed by any transcendent terms, a randomness that terrifies with the prospect of total dissolution while exhilarating with the pos-sibility of free play of identities and social locations — that is, of sub-ject positions. Composition pedagogy is often unresponsive to postmodernity, continuing to assume that unitary selves compose pur-poseful, linearly structured, generically recognizable texts. While this focus is often promoted by academic institutions as serving the prac-tical ends of efficient communication, composition scholars increas-ingly resist it as oppressive to diverse students. A more postmodern composition study entails looking at how discourses, and the unequal power relations among them, are historically produced. Yet the field is still reluctant to abandon a unitary notion of students' subjectivities. The field needs the kind of destabilized, decentered view that char-acterizes the networked classroom, where online discussion allows free play with different personae and even "forbidden" discourses (e.g., homophobic, racist, sexist). The problem that remains is how to es-tablish an ethics of engagement for social action against the oppres-sive economic and discursive structures that postmodern analysis pur-ports to reveal. Winner of CCCC Outstanding Book Award for 1994.

180   Farris, Christine, and Chris M. Anson, eds. *Under Construction: Work-ing at the Intersections of Composition Theory, Research, and Practice*. Logan: Utah State Univ. Press, 1998.

The authors of eighteen chapters seek to complicate composition by reconsidering the relationship among theory, research, and practice — an issue that largely defines our discipline. Essays include Peter Vandenberg, "Composing Composition Studies: Scholarly Publica-tion and the Practice of Discipline"; James Zebroski, "Toward a Theory of Theory for Composition Studies"; David Seitz, "Keeping Honest: Working-Class Students, Difference, and Rethinking the Critical Agenda in Composition"; Susan Peck MacDonald, "Voices of Re-search: Methodological Choices of a Disciplinary Community"; Yuet-

Sum Chiang, "Insider/Outsider/Other?: Confronting the Centeredness of Race, Class, Color, and Ethnicity in Composition Research"; Ruth Ray and Ellen Barton, "Farther Afield: Rethinking the Contributions of Research"; and Gail Y. Okawa, "Coming (in)to Consciousness: One Asian American Teacher's Journey into Activist Teaching and Research."

181   Fishman, Stephen M., and Lucille McCarthy. *John Dewey and the Challenge of Classroom Practice*. New York: Teachers College Press, 1998.

A key theme in John Dewey's philosophy is to refuse either-or choices and to attempt to integrate dualisms. Dewey sees a person's growth as involving not only formal education, in which oppositions between student and curriculum must be reconciled, but also morality, requiring individual and group to be mutually dependent; art, where creativity and appreciation must balance; and day-to-day practice, in which action should induce reflection that conditions further action. In general, Dewey urges uncovering the conflicting forces at work in any problem and attempting to integrate them. Learning occurs when problems are engaged, which is why Dewey favors curricula that involve students in interesting problems and show them how to use academic knowledge to address these problems. Dewey emphasizes that emotional and moral engagement in problem-solving is essential to learning. Fishman details the nested dualisms underlying student-curriculum integration and how this integration should work to develop students' moral character. In the second half of the book, McCarthy reports on her research in Fishman's classroom where he experimented with Deweyan methods of collaborative learning. Deweyan approaches are especially needed now, Fishman and McCarthy argue, to replace destructive classroom competition with a new sense of community.

182   Foss, Sonja K., Karen A. Foss, and Robert Trapp. *Contemporary Perspectives on Rhetoric*. 3rd edition. Prospect Heights, Ill.: Waveland Press, 2002.

The diversity of contemporary rhetoric and the continual expansion of rhetorical theory are demonstrated through the work of eleven rhetorical theorists, arranged by the breadth of their theories about rhetoric: I. A. Richards, Ernesto Grassi, Chaim Perelman and Lucie Olbrechts-Tyteca, Stephen Toulmin, Richard M. Weaver, Kenneth Burke, Jürgen Habermas, bell hooks, Jean Baudrillard, and Michel Foucault. Following an introduction to rhetoric in Chapter One, each chapter features a theorist by presenting biographical information, an overview of their ideas, analysis of their contributions to rhetoric, and commentary on their theories. Extensive bibliographies complete each chapter.

183   Gallagher, Chris W. *Radical Departures: Composition and Progressive Pedagogy*. Urbana: NCTE, 2002.

Composition and Rhetoric is uniquely positioned to participate in a reclamation of pedagogical progressivism — if pedagogy is cast as shared knowledge-building rather than as the binary opposite of theory. Pedagogy, a form of collective action and reflexive inquiry, is necessarily a collaboration between teachers and learners. Two distinct groups of progressives — pedagogical and administrative — developed in the same years as the new NCTE. Administrative progressivism became more dominant, as evidenced by current educational reforms. A new strand of progressivism, now the mainstream discourse of critical pedagogy, has, ironically, drawn composition away from pedagogical progressivism; critical pedagogy positions students and teachers in disempowering ways. Placing pedagogy at the center of our work in the academy works against disciplinary and administrative constraints, both historical and contemporary. Rather than debating abolitionism, composition needs to rethink disciplinarity altogether, particularly replacing "service" with outreach. Six intraludes offer narrative representations of the issues.

184   Gere, Anne Ruggles. *Into the Field*. New York: MLA, 1993.

Twelve essays explore the connections between composition and other disciplines as forms of *restructuring* — the idea that interaction between fields is not simply borrowing but reconceptualizing, repositioning on disappearing, contested, or negotiated boundaries. Essays include Kurt Spellmeyer, "Being Philosophical about Composition: Hermeneutics and the Teaching of Writing"; Brenda Deen Schildgen, "Reconnecting Rhetoric and Philosophy in the Composition Class"; George Disson, "Argumentation and Critique: College Composition and Enlightenment Ideals"; James Berlin, "Composition Studies and Cultural Studies: Collapsing Boundaries"; John Trimbur, "Composition Studies: Postmodern or Popular"; Irene Papoulis, "Subjectivity and Its Role in 'Constructed' Knowledge: Composition, Feminist Theory, and Psychoanalysis"; and David Bleich, "Ethnography and the Study of Literacy: Prospects for Socially Generous Research."

185   Giroux, Henry A. *Schooling and the Struggle for Public Life: Critical Pedagogy in the Modern Age*. Minneapolis: Univ. of Minnesota Press, 1988.

The discourse of democracy and citizenship must be reclaimed by progressive educators to counteract the historical amnesia promoted by the New Right. A critical theory of citizenship reveals the ideological conflicts in American history, opposes chauvinism (especially in media images), and envisions a public philosophy that truly honors equality, liberty, and human life. Questions about the student's voice, literacy, and teacher authority are central to this project.

186   Hairston, Maxine. "Diversity, Ideology, and Teaching Writing." CCC 43 (May 1992): 179–93. Rpt. in Corbett, Myers, and Tate [171].

Making ideology and social goals the center of a writing course or program, as many theorists have advocated, threatens the low-risk, student-centered classroom in which writing is not about anything other than itself. The leftward political move is the result of critical theories in English departments trickling down to the freshman English floors below. Composition theorists who are part of English departments naturally seek approval from the power structure, which favors political theories. But writing classes should focus on student writing, and writing teachers are not qualified to teach complex issues such as racial discrimination and class or gender inequities. Moreover, no classroom should be the forum for the professor's political agenda. Students learn to write by writing about what they care about, not by conforming to a political position and stifling their creative impulses. A diverse student body writing about and sharing their own experiences will produce real cultural diversity. [Responses appear in CCC 42 (May 1993).]

187   Halasek, Kay. A *Pedagogy of Possibility: Bakhtinian Perspectives on Composition Studies*. Southern Illinois Univ. Press, 1999.

The complexity of dialogue as Bakhtin characterizes it is often overlooked in composition practices. A dialogic paradigm serves as a model for a conversation among competing pedagogies, their points of contact and conflict. Recognizing the inherent dialogism within the word and among utterances demands that students and teachers *enact* the intertextual nature of discourse. Bakhtinian discourse theory reimagines the rhetorical situation as a site where centripetal and centrifugal discourses battle; the writer, audience, and subject must all be reimagined by analyzing the implications of metaphors for describing writing and writers and by characterizing both the audience and subject as co-authors and co-participants in the discourse — the subject as hero. Understanding essays as utterances rather than as organic wholes situates students in a process of ideological becoming. A pedagogy of possibility engages with critical literacy, authoritative and internally persuasive discourses, and, for example, the politics of reported speech. Halasek readily takes on all of the tensions between Bakhtinian theories and their application in the classroom and provides a model of scholarship that strives to maintain a dialogic balance between practice and theory. Winner of 2001 CCCC Outstanding Book Award.

188   Harkin, Patricia, and John Schilb, eds. *Contending with Words: Composition and Rhetoric in a Postmodern Age*. New York: MLA, 1991.

"A collection of essays for college and university teachers of English who believe that the study of composition and rhetoric is not merely the service component of the English department, but also an inquiry into cultural values" (3). Twelve essays on the general theme of the discursive formation of knowledge contend with the many current attempts to formulate the aims of composition programs and courses: Don Bialostosky, "Liberal Education, Writing, and the Dialogic Self"; William A. Covino, "Magic, Literacy, and the *National*

Enquirer"; John Clifford, "The Subject in Discourse"; Patricia Bizzell, "Marxist Ideas in Composition Studies"; Bruce Herzberg, "Michel Foucault's Rhetorical Theory"; Lynn Worsham, "Writing against Writing: The Predicament of *Ecriture Feminine* in Composition Studies"; Susan Jarratt, "Feminism and Composition: The Case for Conflict"; Patricia Harkin, "The Postdisciplinary Politics of Lore"; Victor Vitanza, "Three Countertheses: Or, A Critical In(ter)vention into Composition Theories and Pedagogies"; John Schilb, "Cultural Studies, Postmodernism, and Composition"; and two reflections on the collection itself by Sharon Crowley and James Sosnoski.

189   Harris, Joseph. *A Teaching Subject: Composition Since 1966.* Upper Saddle River, N.J.: Prentice-Hall, 1997.

The 1966 Dartmouth conference serves as a starting point for this account of the conflicts and tensions that continue to shape the teaching of writing. Five keywords — growth, voice, process, error, and community — have served to make composition an academic enterprise but not an intellectual endeavor. The process movement, for example, sacrifices content to method and asks teachers to be composing coaches rather than *readers*. Even seemingly revolutionary views of error completely ignore revision and position students as academics-in-training rather than as critics and intellectuals. Harris offers the keyword "public" as a counter to the metaphor of the contact zone and as an invitation to "wrangle" with the ways in which differences get negotiated.

190   Harris, Joseph. "The Idea of Community in the Study of Writing." CCC 40 (February 1989): 11–22.

The concept of discourse community has helped reveal the ways that writers' intentions emerge not from within but through interaction with communal projects. The image of "community," notably, is entirely positive and unified. Thus, David Bartholomae [144, 371, 441] and Patricia Bizzell [157, 158, 159, 234] suggest that students must completely abandon other discourse communities in order to fully enter the academic community. The idea of community should instead acknowledge the normal presence of internal conflict and competing voices. Braddock Award winner.

191   Kastely, James L. *Rethinking the Rhetorical Tradition: From Plato to Postmodernism.* New Haven: Yale Univ. Press, 1997.

Using language requires that one betray one's morality because it provides an inevitably partial view of the world — that is, both incomplete and biased, conditions under which morality cannot be consistently applied. Thus, using language inevitably implicates one in injustice: the most serious problem with language use, for the ancient Greeks. Rhetoric is designed to deal with this human condition, in which people must make decisions based on limited knowledge, which cannot be fair to everyone. Rhetoric's chief method for dealing with this condition is a kind of skepticism that requires one to doubt and question every assertion. By doubting — that is, by attempting to ensure that all possible views will be considered — rhetoric provides the best chance of arriving at admittedly provisional but collective agreements. This was Plato's view of rhetoric. But this function of rhetoric was destroyed by Aristotle when he schematized rhetoric so that it could make assertions. Postmodern theorists are either too concerned with the limitations on human knowledge or not concerned enough with the problem of injustice. Plato's view of rhetoric, then, is needed now more than ever, to restore public discourse. Kastely illustrates the evolution of these ideas through analyzing Plato, Greek tragedy, Jane Austen, Jean-Paul Sartre, Paul de Man, Richard Rorty, and other thinkers.

192   Kent, Thomas. *Paralogic Rhetoric: A Theory of Communicative Interaction*. Lewisburg, Pa.: Bucknell Univ. Press, 1993.

Expressivism, cognitivism, and social constructionism all construe the mind and external reality as completely separate, with contact mediated by transcendent mental forms, cognitive processes, or discourse conventions, respectively. The mind is thus unable to get in touch with other minds — the mediating structure is always in the way. The mind is also unable to verify the structure it must use. Relativism is the inescapable conclusion of such views. Philosopher Donald Davidson suggests a better model of communication as a triangulated process in which two people compare their impressions of a shared sensory stimulus, each guessing what the other has in mind. To the extent that they are able to communicate, they may ascertain whether these guesses are correct. This process is paralogical, not logical, because it is not reducible to rules. It follows that the communication process cannot be taught as there are no rules to teach. Communication can only be practiced, collaboratively. Winner of CCCC Outstanding Book Award for 1995.

193   Kent, Thomas, ed. *Post-Process Theory: Beyond the Writing-Process Paradigm*. Carbondale: Southern Illinois Univ. Press, 1999.

Most post-process theorists assume that writing is public, interpretive, and situated. Thirteen chapters define post-process theory, its pedagogical ramifications, and its possibilities for reforming practices. Essays include Gary Olson, "Toward a Post-Process Composition: Abandoning the Rhetoric of Assertion"; Barbara Couture, "Modeling and Emulating: Rethinking Agency in the Writing Process"; Nancy Blyler, "Research in Professional Communication: A Post-Process Perspective"; David Russell, "Activity Theory and Process Approaches: Writing (Power) in School and Society"; John Clifford and Elizabeth Ervin, "The Ethics of Process"; and John Schilb, "Reprocessing the Essay."

194   Kinneavy, James L. *A Theory of Discourse*. Englewood Cliffs, N.J.: Prentice-Hall, 1971. New York: Norton, 1980.

Discourse can be divided into four main types: reference, persuasive, literary, and expressive, each emphasizing a particular element in the exchange between writer and audience about the subject of the discourse. Reference discourse emphasizes the subject, which it presents with as little interference as possible from writer, reader, or language itself. In persuasive discourse, the aim is to move the reader, and the other elements — writer, subject, and language — are subordinated to that end. Literary discourse focuses on language itself: writer, reader, and subject are incidental. Expressive discourse emphasizes the writer, suiting subject and language to the writer's need for self-expression. A complex and influential work in the study of discourse. See also James L. Kinneavy, "The Basic Aims of Discourse," CCC 20 (December 1969): 297–304. Rpt. in Corbett, Myers, and Tate [171].

195   Lunsford, Andrea A. "Toward a Mestiza Rhetoric: Gloria Anzaldúa on Composition and Postcoloniality." *Journal of Advanced Composition* 18.1 (1998): 1–27.

A mestiza lives in geographical and cultural borderlands and must learn to tolerate contradiction and ambiguity, to juggle cultures, and to imagine spaces not limited by dichotomies. For writing, this means using a rich variety of genres, languages, and registers, while also engaging in collaboration. In this interview, Anzaldúa discusses her earliest writings and drawings, her composing rituals, and issues that range from internal censorship to precolonial histories and activism. In addition to her poetry and children's books, one of Anzaldúa's current book projects is about composition and postcolonial issues of identity, based on the theme of *compustura*, or seaming together fragments to make a garment that represents oneself.

196   Lunsford, Andrea A., and Lisa S. Ede. "Classical Rhetoric, Modern Rhetoric, and Contemporary Discourse Studies." *Written Communication* 1 (January 1984): 78–100.

Some proponents of the "new rhetoric" claim that in classical rhetoric humans are regarded as rational beings moved chiefly by logic but subject to the coercion of rhetors. Grimaldi shows, however, that for Aristotle, both inductive argument (by example) and deductive argument (by enthymeme) rely on all three appeals (logos, pathos, and ethos) in order to discover contingent truths. Thus, classical rhetoric is similar to modern rhetoric as a cross-disciplinary enterprise. But unlike modern rhetoric, classical rhetoric relied on oral language and searched for stable truths in the world.

197   Mailloux, Steven. *Reception Histories: Rhetoric, Pragmatism, and American Cultural Politics*. Ithaca: Cornell Univ. Press, 1998.

Rhetoric is the study of how textual effects are produced and received. Thus, rhetoric has affinities with hermeneutics and is particularly helpful to interpretation in cross-cultural situations. This view of rhetoric is found in the work of the Greek Sophists, and its connection to contemporary pragmatism can be traced through the history of the Sophist Protagoras's reception by founding pragmatists William James, John Dewey, and F. C. S. Schiller. Mailloux illustrates his concept of "rhetorical hermeneutics" by analyzing three reception histories: Margaret Fuller's review of Frederick Douglass's *Narrative*; 1970s reader-response critics' readings of John Bunyan's *Pilgrim's Progress*; and the function of the metaphor of reading as eating in nineteenth century debates over adolescent education and juvenile delinquency. Mailloux concludes by calling for increased attention to rhetoric in English studies and by describing what happened when he attempted to persuade his colleagues to structure the major around his approach at Syracuse University.

198   Miller, Richard E. "Fault Lines in the Contact Zone." *CE* (April 1994): 389–408.

How should teachers handle student work that attacks the institution of schooling or that expresses virulently prejudiced views? This question was posed dramatically by a student paper submitted to openly gay teacher Scott Lankford, which he first shared at an MLA workshop in 1991. The writer describes an evening out with drunken friends during which they harass gay men on the street and severely beat a homeless man. Should such a student writer be reported to the police or referred for psychological counseling? That response risks treating as fact an account that may be fictional. On the other hand, responding to the paper solely as a work of fiction and commenting only on its structural and stylistic features, as Lankford did, ignores content that the student may have meant to be provocative and thus silences this kind of resistance to the classroom agenda. A third approach might ask Lankford's student to write another version of the evening from the perspective of one of the victims, but this risks eliciting work that insincerely reproduces the teacher's views. Needed, instead, is a pedagogy that responds to the kinds of parodic, oppositional, and/or inflammatory texts that are likely to be produced in a course that emphasizes addressing cultural differences, as often recommended in work that builds on Mary Louise Pratt's concept of the "contact zone" [see 212]. Needed is a pedagogy that examines the cultural forces that produce papers like Lankford's, and that encourages students to evaluate a range of written responses to situations of cultural conflict, including some that may be hateful to the teacher or to some class members.

199   Miller, Susan. *Rescuing the Subject: A Critical Introduction to Rhetoric and the Writer.* Carbondale: Southern Illinois Univ. Press, 1989.

The story of instruction in language use must be liberated from the traditional major-texts approach. Premodern rhetoric cannot provide an adequate theoretical base for modern composition studies, first, because it focuses on oratory and neglects intertextuality, and second, because it focuses on officially sanctioned forms of language use and neglects adventitious and popular uses. We need a textual rhetoric that highlights intertextuality while avoiding the social and historical decontextualization of writing that besets contemporary literary studies. This approach includes a complex view of the writing subject that avoids both the naive classical definition of the rhetor as a "good man speaking well" and the postmodern reduction of the person to a discursive position.

200   Miller, Susan. *Textual Carnivals: The Politics of Composition.* Carbondale: Southern Illinois Univ. Press, 1991.

Composition teachers submit to the continuing subordination of composition to literature and even unwittingly reinforce the perception of composition as a merely practical art without disciplinary status or intellectual rigor. Like other groups marginalized by race, gender, or class, composition teachers have created self-images of sacrifice and rebellion that actually maintain their inequality, reproduce the received history of composition's inferiority, and hide the institutional agendas that stigmatize it. To change the story told about composition requires a close examination of the connections between it and literature, a critique of received history, and an effort to "endow agency and dignity" on the protagonists of the story: students, teachers (like the "sad women in the basement"), and program administrators. Includes an appendix, "The Status of Composition: A Survey of How Its Professionals See It." Winner of the CCCC Outstanding Book Award for 1992.

201   Mountford, Roxanne. "On Gender and Rhetorical Space." *Rhetoric Society Quarterly* 31.1 (2001): 41–71.

Rhetorical space becomes a useful concept if it accounts for the effect of physical spaces on a communicative event, including the cultural and material arrangement of space. The pulpit, an embodiment of clerical authority, is a gendered location so constructed as to make women's presence "metonymically problematic." Literary images of the pulpit have located women preachers in natural settings (meadows or front porches), where the sermons develop from the setting, and women preachers must continually reimagine the space of the traditional pulpit because, as architecture, pulpits participate in the "social imaginary" or the cultural dimension of space. Gender hierarchies, persistently associated with geography, emphasize that status in the social imaginary must be marked by geographical exclusions, sometimes resulting in symbolic trespasses upon sacred ground. Rhetorical spaces carry the residue of history and the physical representation of relationships and ideas; thus, the complex relationship of gender and rhetorical space in the art of preaching can be traced through the history of church architecture and its functions in producing meaning.

202   Neel, Jasper. *Plato, Derrida, and Writing.* Carbondale: Southern Illinois Univ. Press, 1988.

Plato and Derrida launch much the same attack on writing, denying that the process of writing can generate transcendent truth. Plato argued that the rhetor must find truth by philosophical means before attempting to convey it and should convey it by speech rather than writing, because interlocutors cannot interrogate a text about its method. Derrida denies Plato's contentions that philosophy can attain transcendent truth and that dialogue gives access to the philosophical method. Instead, says Derrida, we have only the fictions constructed by writing, a web of texts accumulating over time, allusively linked. Derrida argues correctly that transcendent truth does not exist (or at least that such truth is unknowable), but he is mistaken when he concludes that no *usable* truth exists. There is sufficient truth to serve as a basis for decisions about social action in the "strong discourse" of Sophists — be they Isocrates and Gorgias or the leaders of modern democracies. The strong discourse of probabilistic rhetoric is not mere propaganda, as Plato argued, if only because such discourse tends to generate competing discourses that test its claims. Composition studies can work to free rhetoric from the strictures of philosophy so that it can fulfill its political mission.

203   Ohmann, Richard. *English in America*. New York: Oxford Univ. Press, 1976.

The professional, institutional, and economic structures within which we teach severely constrain the efficacy of liberalizing curricular reforms. Universities continue to serve the needs of government and industry for efficient, docile communicators, while teachers resist acknowledging the political implications of their control of knowledge. This book includes a chapter by Wallace Douglas on English education in America in the 1800s, focusing on the influence of Channing of Harvard.

204   Olson, Gary A., ed. *Philosophy, Rhetoric, Literary Criticism: (Inter)views*. Carbondale: Southern Illinois Univ. Press, 1994.

Six interviews with scholars outside of composition — philosopher Donald Davidson, literary theorists Stanley Fish, bell hooks, J. Hillis Miller, and Jane Tompkins, and philosopher Stephen Toulmin — are each followed by two response essays by composition scholars. The responses explore the applications of "outside" theories to composition and sometimes react contentiously to them. Response essays are by Susan Wells, Reed Way Dasenbrock, Patricia Bizzell, John Trimbur, Joyce Irene Middleton, Tom Fox, Patricia Harkin, Jasper Neel, Susan Jarratt, Elizabeth Flynn, Arabella Lyon, and C. Jan Swearingen. Includes a foreword by Clifford Geertz, introduction by Patricia Bizzell, and commentary by David Bleich.

205   Olson, Gary A., ed. *Rhetoric and Composition as Intellectual Work*. Carbondale: Southern Illinois Univ. Press, 2002.

Rhetoric and composition is engaged in an ongoing disciplinary debate about whether it should be an intellectual as well as a service discipline. Organized in five parts (Disciplinary Concerns, Historical Inquiry, Ideological Inquiry, Philosophical Inquiry, and New Directions), nineteen chapters include Jasper Neel, "Reclaiming Our Theoretical Heritage: A Big Fish Tale"; Charles Bazerman, "The Case for Writing Studies as an Intellectual Discipline"; Susan Wells, "Claiming the Archive for Rhetoric and Composition"; Gary A. Olson, "Ideological Critique in Rhetoric and Composition"; Keith Gilyard, "Holdin It Down: Students' Right and the Struggle over Language Diversity"; Steven Mailloux, "From Segregated Schools to Dimpled Chads: Rhetorical Hermeneutics and the Suasive Work of Theory"; Victor J. Vitanza, "Seeing in Third Sophistic Ways"; Sharon Crowley, "Body Studies in Rhetoric and Composition"; John Trimbur, "Delivering the Message: Typography and the Materiality of Writing"; and Cynthia L. Selfe and Richard J. Selfe, "The Intellectual Work of Computers and Composition Studies."

206   Olson, Gary A., and Sidney I. Dobrin, eds. *Composition Theory for the Postmodern Classroom*. Albany: State Univ. of New York Press, 1995.

Twenty-two essays originally published in the *Journal of Advanced Composition* [9], including James Kinneavy, "The Process of Writing: A Philosophical Base in Hermeneutics"; Jasper Neel, "Dichotomy, Consubstantiality, Technical Writing, Literary Theory: The Double Orthodox Curse"; Patricia Sullivan, "Writing in the Graduate Curriculum: Literary Criticism as Composition"; David Smit, "Some Difficulties with Collaborative Writing"; Thomas Fox, "Repositioning the Profession: Teaching Writing to African American Students"; W. Ross Winterowd, "Rediscovering the Essay"; Robert Wood, "The Dialectic Suppression of Feminist Thought in Radical Pedagogy"; Henry Giroux, "Paulo Freire and the Politics of Postcolonialism"; Joseph Harris, "The Other Reader"; John Trimbur, "Articulation Theory and the Problem of Determination: A Reading of *Lives on the Boundary*"; J. Hillis Miller, "Nietzsche in Basel: Writing Reading"; and Richard Coe, "Defining Rhetoric — and Us: A Meditation on Burke's Definitions."

207   Olson, Gary A., and Irene Gale, eds. (Inter)views: Cross-Disciplinary Perspectives on Rhetoric and Literacy. Carbondale: Southern Illinois Univ. Press, 1991.

Seven interviews with scholars outside of composition — Mary Field Belenky, Noam Chomsky, Jacques Derrida, Paulo Freire, Clifford Geertz, Richard Rorty, and Gayatri Spivak — each followed by two response essays by composition scholars. The responses explore and criticize the applications of their theories to composition. Response essays are by Elizabeth Flynn, Marilyn Cooper, James Sledd, Sharon Crowley, Jasper Neel, James Berlin, C. H. Knoblauch, Linda Brodkey, Kenneth Bruffee, and Thomas Kent. Includes a foreword by David Bleich and an afterword by Andrea Lunsford.

208   Owens, Derek. *Resisting Writings (and the Boundaries of Composition)*. Dallas: Southern Methodist Univ. Press, 1994.

Composition courses that teach only academic discourse or the personal essay are ethnocentric. Rather, the introductory course should survey kinds of writing produced in different cultures, in feminist work, and in experimental writing inspired by electronic media in which fiction and nonfiction are often blurred. Upper-division courses could be devoted to each of these kinds. Additionally, academics should push for a wider variety of writing to be acceptable in all undergraduate and graduate courses and in scholarly publications. Only this way will American education's "process of rigid mechanization and self-effacement" be resisted creatively by students and teachers alike, with healthy results for social justice.

209   Perelman, Chaim. *The Realm of Rhetoric*. Trans. William Kluback. Notre Dame, Ind.: Univ. of Notre Dame Press, 1982. Trans. of *L'Empire Rhetorique*. 1977.

A summary of *The New Rhetoric* [210].

210   Perelman, Chaim, and L. Olbrechts-Tyteca. *The New Rhetoric: A Treatise on Argumentation*. Trans. John Wilkinson and Purcell Weaver. 1958. Rpt. Notre Dame, Ind.: Univ. of Notre Dame Press, 1969. Excerpted in Bizzell and Herzberg [41].

Rhetoric is the art of gaining adherents to propositions that cannot be verified through calculations. All rhetorical discourse, then, is argumentation. Some arguments aim to convince only a particular audience, whereas others try to persuade all rational people — the imagined "universal audience." Arguments can be evaluated rationally and good reasons given for or against adherence to them, both for particular and for "universal" audiences. Such evaluations, though rational, are conditioned by the culture of the evaluator's discourse community — its traditions, language-using conventions, and beliefs. This book exhaustively catalogs the kinds of arguments that can be used in most Western discourse communities, with numerous examples from canonical works in philosophy, literature, history, and other fields. A seminal work in discourse theory.

211   Petraglia, Joseph, ed. *Reconceiving Writing, Rethinking Writing Instruction*. Mahwah, N.J.: Lawrence Erlbaum Associates, 1995.

Should general-skills first-year writing programs be abolished? Most programs claim to inculcate a set of abilities that can be transferred to any other writing situation. The idea that such skills could be taught, however, flies in the face of much current research on writing. Yet the profession has ignored this contradiction and diverted scholarly attention to areas not directly relevant to the classroom. The thirteen essays included here address the "abolition" question: by looking at the history of attempts to abolish first-year general-skills courses (e.g., Robert Connors, "The New Abolitionism: Toward a Historical Background," and Maureen Daly Goggin, "The

Disciplinary Instability of Composition"); by exploring the mismatches between pedagogical practices in such courses and current theories of composing (e.g., Joseph Petraglia, "Writing as an Unnatural Act," and Cheryl Geisler, "Writing and Learning at Cross Purposes in the Academy"); and by analyzing the theoretical inadequacies undergirding such courses (e.g., David Jolliffe, "Discourse, Interdiscursivity, and Composition Instruction").

212   Pratt, Mary Louise. "Arts of the Contact Zone." *Profession 91* (1991): 33–40.

Contact zones are social spaces where cultures meet and clash, often in contexts of highly asymmetrical power relations, such as colonialism or its aftermath. In such situations we find examples of texts that subordinate groups produce to describe themselves to the dominant group and engage with representations others have made of them. Such texts selectively use the forms and idioms of the other group (a part of the process of transculturation) and may, as in the case of Inca Guaman Poma's Andean text addressed to the king of Spain, be a marginalized group's entry into literacy. Such texts seem chaotic unless read as expressions of those who live in a contact zone. The utopian image of a unified speech community with shared norms is challenged by such texts. What are we to do when the classroom community, another imagined utopia, is challenged by unsolicited oppositional discourse, as is happening more frequently? Multicultural curricula can and should create contact zones in which all interests are represented, where multiple cultural histories intersect, where there are ground rules for communication across lines of difference and hierarchy, and where there is a systematic approach to cultural mediation.

213   Ratcliffe, Krista. *Anglo-American Feminist Challenges to the Rhetorical Traditions: Virginia Woolf, Mary Daly, Adrienne Rich.* Carbondale: Southern Illinois Univ. Press, 1996.

Because of different material and cultural circumstances, women relate to language differently from men. Because these circumstances have usually been oppressive, women need to find ways to liberate their potential for creative language use. Woolf is especially alert to how women's limiting material circumstances are conditioned by social class as well as gender. She advocates both borrowing freely from male traditions of language use, when these can be adapted for women's purposes, and creating new ways of using language that are expressly feminine. She looks for a "woman's sentence" in literature. Daly rejects completely patriarchal ways of using language. Even more aggressively than Woolf, she indicts traditional ways of using language as designed to silence women. She devises her own argumentative forms and polemically punning vocabulary to advance her radical theology and, more, the possibilities of a whole new women's culture. Rich struggles in her poetry to escape the stifling hand of the male tradition and to find ways of using language that speak to and for women's, and especially lesbians', experiences. She advocates a "politics of location" in which the literary artist attempts to account for the complexity of her material and cultural circumstances and to take a stand for social reform in the interests of white women and of people of color. Ratcliffe critically juxtaposes these writers' ideas about language with themes in traditional rhetorical theory, showing both resonances and redefinitions.

214   Reynolds, Nedra. "Composition's Imagined Geographies: The Politics of Space in the Frontier, City, and Cyberspace." *College Composition and Communication* 50 (1998): 12–35.

A geographic study of composition asks us to confront many of our assumptions about place and space as they influence our conceptions of classrooms, those who occupy them, and ways to control textual space. Socially produced through discourse, the politics of space are often enacted through spatial metaphors and the most powerful of these metaphors tend to mask material conditions or deny material reality. Geographers and spatial theorists demonstrate the impact of time-space compression and transparent space. Both concepts are a result of changing conceptions of space in a late-capitalist economy and both are problematic. Three imagined geographies in the discourses of composition — the frontier, city, and cyberspace — have given composition vision and a sense of mission but also leave unexamined the consequences of the politics of space; in giving composition a sense of disciplinary identity, imagined geographies ignore worn urban classrooms or the increased workloads from electronic technologies. A spatial politics of writing instruction calls for a paradoxical sense of space, resists notions of transparent space, and examines the impact of time-space compression on composition's workers.

215   Richards, I. A. *The Philosophy of Rhetoric*. New York: Oxford Univ. Press, 1936. Excerpted in Bizzell and Herzberg [41].

All discourse allows multiple meanings, but most interpretations of discourse are based on cultural conventions and the widespread idea that words have single determinate meanings. Rhetoric is the study of the misunderstandings that arise from such interpretations. Rhetoric looks at the "context" of disputed passages — the surrounding text, which constrains the meaning of the passage. Because meaning is determined by context, usage must be based on appropriateness to context rather than on fixed standards. Rhetoric must rely on Coleridge's idea that all language is metaphor and that we understand the world through the resemblances offered by language. See also Berthoff [153].

216   Roskelly, Hephzibah, and Kate Ronald. *Reason to Believe: Romanticism, Pragmatism, and the Teaching of Writing*. Albany: State Univ. of New York Press, 1998.

The "social turn" in composition and the influence of postmodern theory in literary studies have undercut teachers' belief in students' abilities to produce powerful language, without which belief teaching is hardly possible. Composition studies must recover "romantic/pragmatic rhetoric," rather than treating "romantic" and "pragmatic" as opposites. American romanticism, best exemplified in the work of Emerson, develops a sustaining vision of human possibility. American pragmatism applies romanticism to action in the world. C. S. Pierce, William James, and others encourage a pragmatic method that inquires into human experience by testing hypotheses, using as varied a range of inquirers and sites of inquiry as possible, and tending to show the relations between opposing ideas and to arrive at contingent truths. Major proponents of a pedagogy devised from romantic/pragmatic thinking are John Dewey and Paulo Freire. Roskelly and Ronald trace the development of romantic/pragmatic ideas from Puritan times, analyze how these ideas became occulted in current theory, and provide accounts of classrooms in which romantic/pragmatic pedagogy functions successfully.

See: Thomas Rosteck, ed., *At the Intersection: Cultural Studies and Rhetorical Studies* [520].

217   Schilb, John. *Between the Lines: Relating Composition Theory and Literary Theory*. Portsmouth, N.H.: Heinemann-Boynton/Cook, 1996.

Literary theory defines rhetoric as irony, while composition theory defines rhetoric as persuasion. Theoretical differences were clear at two seminal conferences. The 1963 CCCC, site of the birth of modern composition studies, was marked by great interest in classical rhetoric, with its stable, unitary subject who could make rational choices about language use. In contrast, the 1966 Johns Hopkins conference, "The Languages of Criticism and the Sciences of Man," introduced Jacques Derrida, Roland Barthes, and Jacques Lacan to American academics and featured a poststructuralist view of the subject as unstable, fragmented, and determined by texts. Composition studies remained firmly subordinate in English departments of the 1960s so as to protect the elite status of the cultural capital regulated by the literature faculty. Yet both composition studies and literary studies wrongly neglected to attempt to form politically active citizens. Postmodernism has debilitated both fields. Its epistemology can help students understand power relations but oversimplifies politics. Its artistic strategies are not adequate for civic action. Its global cultural trends may be studied usefully, but only if connected to students' everyday lives. Composition studies and literary studies have recently converged in their interest in personal writing, which helps students learn the way self-identities are constructed but which can degenerate into self-indulgence, as practiced, for example, by Jane Tompkins. The fields have also converged in their attention to collaboration, which literary studies should learn from composition studies to value. At the same time, composition studies needs to learn from literary studies to be suspicious of the ethical problems posed by collaboration. The fields have also converged in their questioning of the efficacy of theory, but as a critique of the work of Stanley Fish shows, theories that are tested by pedagogy, as those of composition studies are and those of literary studies should be, do not present the totalizing threats against which Fish inveighs.

218   Selzer, Jack, ed. *Understanding Scientific Prose*. Madison: Univ. of Wisconsin Press, 1993.

Thirteen essays analyze a single scientific essay, "The Spandrels of San Marco," by Stephen Jay Gould and R. C. Lewontin. Each analysis uses a different critical method in order to "domesticate new methods of practical criticism," to show their usefulness when applied to scientific discourse, and to reveal the complexities of scientific prose. Essays include Charles Bazerman, "Intertextual Self-Fashioning: Gould and Lewontin's Representations of the Literature"; Susan Wells, "'Spandrels,' Narration, and Modernity"; Carl G. Herndl, "Cultural Studies and Critical Science"; Mary Rosner and Georgia Rhoades, "Science, Gender, and 'The Spandrels of San Marco'"; Carolyn Miller and S. Michael Halloran, "Reading Darwin, Reading Nature; or, On the Ethos of Historical Science"; John Lyne, "Angels in the Architecture: A Burkean Inventional Perspective on 'Spandrels'"; Gay Gragson and Jack Selzer, "The Reader in the Text of 'The Spandrels of San Marco'"; Debra Journet, "Deconstructing 'The Spandrels of San Marco'"; Greg Myers, "Making Enemies: How Gould and Lewontin Criticize"; and Stephen Jay Gould, "Fulfilling the Spandrels of World and Mind." Includes the original article by Gould and Lewontin.

219   Selzer, Jack and Sharon Crowley, eds. *Rhetorical Bodies*. Madison: Univ. of Wisconsin Press, 1999.

A product of the Fifteenth Penn State Conference on Rhetoric and Composition in 1997, this book includes sixteen essays on material rhetoric or rhetoric's materiality. Chapters include Jack Selzer, "Habeas Corpus: An Introduction"; Carole Blair, "Contemporary U. S. Memorial Sites as Exemplars of Rhetoric's Materiality"; Karyn Hollis, "Material of Desire: Bodily Rhetoric in Working Women's Poetry at the Bryn Mawr Summer School, 1921–1938"; Peter Mortensen, "Figuring Illiteracy: Rustic Bodies and Unlettered Minds in Rural America"; Lester Faigley, "Material Literacy and Visual Design"; Christina Haas, "Materializing Public and Private: The Spatialization of Conceptual Categories in Discourses of Abortion"; J. Blake Scott, "Rhetoric and Technoscience: The Case of Confide"; Yameng Liu, "Dick Morris, Ideology, and Regulating the Flow of Rhetorical Resources"; Celeste Condit, "The Materiality of Coding: Rhetoric, Genetics, and the Matter of Life"; Sharon Crowley, "Afterword: The Material of Rhetoric."

220 Trimbur, John. "Composition and the Circulation of Writing." CCC 52.2 (December 2000): 188–219.

College students' writing does not often circulate beyond "trade papers with a partner," yet the circulation of writing, the complex delivery systems through which writing circulates, should figure more prominently in writing instruction. Composition's tendency to figure classroom life as a middle-class family drama foreshortens the delivery system by linking production directly to consumption within the intimate space of the classroom/home. In addition, cultural studies' approaches to teaching writing, by their focus on critique and interpretation, also neglect other moments in the circulation of cultural forms and products while encoding and decoding restrict analysis to production and consumption. Marx's the *Grundrisse* offers a conceptual model that challenges a linear model of circulation by insisting that the *use* value of cultural products should not be separated from their *exchange* value. When exchange value and use value are united dialectially, as they are in Marx's notion of the commodity, we avoid the fallacy that by changing the manner of writing (the style) one can solve the problem of circulation. Delivery is inseparable from the circulation of writing and the widening diffusion of socially useful knowledge. Thus, assignments should problematize expertise from within the process of production and circulation, not erase the materiality of writing or isolate an education in writing from the means of production and delivery.

221 Villanueva, Victor, Jr., ed. *Cross-Talk in Comp Theory: A Reader.* Urbana, Ill.: NCTE, 1997.

Forty-one previously published essays have been chosen to demonstrate generative debates over basic issues in the contemporary field of composition studies. Section One addresses the writing process and includes Janet Emig, "Writing as a Mode of Learning" [291]; Nancy Sommers, "Revision Strategies of Student Writers and Experienced Adult Writers" [320]; Walter Ong, "The Writer's Audience Is Always a Fiction" [312]; and Lisa Ede and Andrea Lunsford, "Audience Addressed/Audience Invoked: The Role of Audience in Composition Theory and Pedagogy" [308]. Section Two proposes definitions of discourse and advice on its teaching, including James Kinneavy, "The Basic Aims of Discourse" [see 194]; Patrick Hartwell, "Grammar, Grammars, and the Teaching of Grammar" [333]; and Stephen P. Witte and Lester Faigley, "Coherence, Cohesion, and Writing Quality" [301]. Section Three presents work on developmental schemes and writing instruction, including Linda Flower and John R. Hayes, "A Cognitive Process Theory of Writing" [232] and Patricia Bizzell, "Cognition, Convention, and Certainty: What We Need to Know about Writing" [157]. Writing in society is addressed in Section Four, including Kenneth A. Bruffee, "Collaborative Learning and the 'Conversation of Mankind'" [164] and John Trimbur, "Consensus and Difference in Collaborative Learning" [402]. Section Five looks at controversies over voice, including David Bartholomae, "Writing with Teachers: A Conversation with Peter Elbow" [145]; Peter Elbow, "Being a Writer vs. Being an Academic: A Conflict in Goals," [174]; Elizabeth A. Flynn, "Composing as a Woman" [491]; and Lisa D. Delpit, "The Silenced Dialogue: Power and Pedagogy in Educating Other People's Children" [448]. Section Six looks briefly at developing issues, including James A. Berlin, "Rhetoric and Ideology in the Writing Class" [149]; and Patricia Bizzell, "'Contact Zones' and English Studies" [156].

222   Vitanza, Victor, ed. *PRE/TEXT: The First Decade*. Pittsburgh: Univ. of Pittsburgh Press, 1993.

Ten essays from the journal: Paul Kameen, "Rewording the Rhetoric of Composition"; Louise Wetherbee Phelps, "The Dance of Discourse"; Patricia Bizzell, "Cognition, Convention, and Certainty" [157]; S. Michael Halloran, "Rhetoric in the American College Curriculum" [96]; C. Jan Swearingen, "The Rhetor as Eiron"; William Covino, "Thomas De Quincey in a Revisionist Rhetoric"; Charles Bazerman, "The Writing of Scientific Non-Fiction"; Sharon Crowley, "Neo-Romanticism and the History of Rhetoric"; John Schilb, "The History of Rhetoric and the Rhetoric of History"; and Susan Jarratt, "Toward a Holistic Historiography." Includes a history of the journal by Vitanza, a comment by James Berlin, and afterwords by David Bartholomae and Steven Mailloux.

223   Warnick, Barbara. "Rhetorical Criticism of Public Discourse on the Internet: Theoretical Implications." *Rhetoric Society Quarterly* 28 (Fall 1998): 73–84.

Humanists have avoided analyzing computer-mediated communication (CMC), perhaps because it disrupts traditional notions of author and audience, all of whom may be anonymous, and text, which is destabilized by hypertext links. Nevertheless, cyberspace communicators are still trying to persuade, and rhetoricians can analyze their practices. Especially important will be to discern how these practices connect with moral judgments. Rhetorical criticism of hypertext can look for patterns among a large number of texts, whose boundaries are usually blurred. Rhetorical criticism of audience can look at how different groups are characterized or characterize themselves, policing their own online ethos. Ethical questions include whether computer-simulated political activities affect participation in the real-world public sphere; whether CMC promotes hyperconformity and suppresses dissenting opinions, thus truncating deliberation; and whether access is improved the more technical expertise one claims to possess — often a form of sexist elitism.

224   Weaver, Richard M. "Language Is Sermonic." *Dimensions of Rhetorical Scholarship*. Ed. Robert E. Nebergall. Norman: Univ. of Oklahoma Dept. of Speech, 1963. 49–64. Rpt. in Bizzell and Herzberg [41].

Rhetoric should be restored to its once prominent place in the curriculum, for it is "the most humanistic of the humanities," concerned with the intimate details of human feelings, needs, and historical pressures in its attempt to find ways to persuade people to right action. Rhetoric is therefore incompatible with science — the search for universals. To study rhetoric is to evaluate the force of appeals to action — an "existential, not hypothetical" concern. Finally, all speech is rhetorical — intended to persuade, never neutral — and all language is value-laden, a system for making predications and propositions: "We are all of us preachers."

225   Wells, Susan. "Rogue Cops and Health Care: What Do We Want from Public Writing?" CCC (October 1996): 325–41.

The public sphere we want our students to enter is not unitary and must be constructed, as an analysis of Clinton's failed health-care initiative shows. A pre-established national forum where citizens make decisions face to face does not exist. Civic discursive spaces are local, ephemeral, and often crisis-driven. As Jürgen Habermas explains, public discourse comprises a shifting ensemble of practices into which individuals enter and try to make their private experiences intelligible. Access varies with individuals' different social locations. If we want to teach our students to write for this kind of public sphere, assignments that focus on a general topic, such as gun control, or a genre, such as a letter to the (imaginary) editor, are inadequate. Rather, the focus should be on the problem of constructing a public sphere. Students can be given practice negotiating the agreements that allow local public spheres to exist, concentrating on actions to be accomplished, not on the identities of the communicators. Wells suggests four strategies: focus classroom activities on cultural studies and thus make the classroom itself, at least potentially, a public sphere; analyze examples of public discourse, especially those that express resistance to the dominant culture; provide students with internships that require writing that enters a public sphere; and ask students to analyze and produce examples of academic writing that is intended for a public sphere rather than an expert audience.

Composing, Literacy,
and the Rhetorics of Writing

The Process Movement

226   Britton, James, et al. *The Development of Writing Abilities (11–18)*.
       London: Macmillan Education, 1975.

       A study of about two thousand papers written by British schoolchil-
       dren between the ages of eleven and eighteen suggests that their writ-
       ing falls into three categories: transactional (communicating infor-
       mation); poetic (creating beautiful verbal objects); and expressive
       (exploring ideas and relating them to feelings, intentions, and other
       knowledge). Most school writing is transactional, but this emphasis
       is wrong because children use expressive writing as a mode of learn-
       ing. Transactional writing, with its complex sense of audience, can
       develop only from expressive facility. Transactional writing puts the
       writer in a passive, spectator role, whereas expressive writing encour-
       ages an active, participant role.

227   Cooper, Marilyn M. "The Ecology of Writing." CE 48 (April 1986):
       364–75. Rpt. in Cooper and Holzman [446].

       Cognitive-process models of composing rely too heavily on the im-
       age of a solitary author. A better, ecological model would situate the
       writer and the writer's immediate context in larger social systems, of
       which there are several. The system of ideas integrates private expe-
       rience with public knowledge. The system of purposes links the ac-
       tions of many different writers. The system of interpersonal relations
       connects writers in terms of social and linguistic conventions. The
       system of cultural norms reflects the attitudes of social groups to which
       writers belong. The system of textual forms marks generic conven-
       tions and innovations. These systems make up the material circum-
       stances that constrain writers and are in turn subject to the writer's
       power to shape and change them through interpretation.

228   Emig, Janet. *The Composing Processes of Twelfth Graders*. Urbana, Ill.:
       NCTE, 1971.

       Eight twelfth graders were asked to "compose aloud" while writing
       three essays. Extensive interviews with one of the students form a
       case study showing that twelfth graders compose in two modes: re-
       flexive and extensive. Reflexive writing concerns the writer's feel-
       ings and personal experience. The style is informal, and several kinds
       of exploratory writing accompany drafts. The student usually initiates
       reflexive writing and is its primary audience. Extensive writing fo-
       cuses on information to be conveyed to a reader. The style is more
       formal, and much less time is spent on planning and drafting than in
       the reflexive mode. The directive to write usually comes from the

teacher, who is the primary audience. Twelfth graders write much more often, though less well, in the extensive than in the reflexive mode. They should have more opportunities to write reflexively in school. This study has been influential because of its conception of composing as a process, its suggestion that the composing process should be taught and studied, and its method of composing aloud.

229   Faigley, Lester. "Competing Theories of Process: A Critique and a Proposal." CE 48 (October 1986): 527–42. Rpt. in Graves [376] and in Perl [239].

Three theories of the composing process — expressive, cognitive, and social — characterize the discipline of composition. The expressive theory embodies a neoromantic view of process that invokes the ideas of integrity, spontaneity, and originality. Integrity — or sincerity — becomes an evaluative category; spontaneity suggests the organic unfolding of writing; and originality changes from genius to self-actualization. The cognitive theory uses notions of cognitive development to explain how writing is learned, while using a cybernetic model (feedback, memory, processing) of the individual composing process. Cognitive theory created a science consciousness in composition researchers. Several lines of research — poststructuralism, sociology of science, ethnography, and Marxism — combine to form the social theory, which explains writing as a function of the activities of the writer in a discourse community. These process methods are superior to previous methods; they validate student writing, examine writing behavior, and investigate the social systems that stand in relation to the act of writing.

230   Flower, Linda. *The Construction of Negotiated Meaning: A Social Cognitive Theory of Writing*. Carbondale: Southern Illinois Univ. Press, 1994.

Literacy is a constructive process, an attempt to create meaning as part of social action. Literacy is shaped by literate, social, and cultural practices of a community, but, at the same time, it is a personal attempt to communicate. The issues of positioning within a community, communicative intent, and mediating social practices overshadow the mechanical concerns usually associated with literacy. A social-cognitive view of literacy, which situates the individual within a social context, explains more of the diversity and complexity of literate action. Such action occurs between the poles of thought (interpreting, problem-solving, reflecting) and culture (the texts, voices, and knowledge out of which interpretations are built). To examine an individual's thinking within the context of literate action can reveal the underlying logic of literate performance. Other metaphors for meaning-making, such as reproduction and conversation, are too limited to account for the individual's engagement in the process. Negotiation better describes the individual's agency within social constraints. Writers can articulate their strategic knowledge (goals, strategies, and awareness) to reveal their processes of meaning-construction in social settings.

231   Flower, Linda S. "The Construction of Purpose in Writing and Reading." *CE* 50 (September 1988): 528–50.

Purpose emerges from the interactions of individual language users with social and cultural contexts. A cognitive view of a writer's purpose would see it not as a unitary, conscious intention but rather as a web of intertwined goals and plans, not all of which are fully conscious or rationally attributable to immediate context and text content. The writer deals with this web through a constructive planning process in which goals are prioritized to help guide the composing process even as the goal hierarchy may be revised during composing. Good planners are opportunistic. A reader constructs a similar web or scenario made up of goals and plans (again not necessarily fully conscious) for using or responding to the reading. The reader's web also includes estimates of the author's purposes, forecasts of what may be coming next in a difficult or lengthy text, and so on. Framing such scenarios helps a reader group information and responses drawn from a text and isolate trouble spots that need more interpretation. Expert writers and readers generate more complex webs than do novices.

232   Flower, Linda S., and John R. Hayes. "A Cognitive Process Theory of Writing." *CCC* 32 (December 1981): 365–87.

The structure of the composing process is revealed by "protocol analysis" — asking writers to think aloud while writing and then analyzing the writers' narratives. The three elements of the composing process are the task environment, which includes such external constraints as the rhetorical problem and text produced so far; the writer's long-term memory, which includes knowledge of the subject and knowledge of how to write; and the writing processes that go on inside the writer's head. This last category comprises a planning process, subdivided into generating, organizing, and goal setting; a translating process, in which thoughts are put into words; and a reviewing process, subdivided into evaluating and revising. The whole process is regulated by a monitor that switches from one stage to another. The process is hierarchical and recursive. All writers exhibit this process, but poor writers carry it out ineffectively.

233   Flower, Linda, David L. Wallace, Linda Norris, and Rebecca E. Burnett, eds. *Making Thinking Visible: Writing, Collaborative Planning, and Classroom Inquiry.* Urbana, Ill.: NCTE, 1994.

A report on Carnegie Mellon's Making Thinking Visible project, a four-year collaboration among thirty-three high-school and college teachers, in which students and teachers attempted to document the processes of thinking about writing and teaching writing. Some of the twenty-seven chapters are brief accounts of classroom and teaching discoveries. Others are full essays, including Linda Flower, "Teachers as Theory Builders"; Linda Flower, "Writers Planning: Snapshots from Research"; David Wallace, "Teaching Collaborative Planning: Creating a Social Context for Writing"; Leslie Byrd Evans, "Transcripts as a Compass to Discovery"; James Brozick, "Using the Writing Attitude Survey"; David Wallace, "Supporting Students' Intentions for Writing"; and Wayne Peck, "The Community Literacy Center: Bridging Community- and School-Based Literate Practices."

234   Fox, Tom. *The Social Uses of Writing: Politics and Pedagogy*. Norwood, N.J.: Ablex, 1990.

Case studies show how freshmen use writing to negotiate conflicts between academic values and values they hold as a consequence of race, gender, and class. Teachers' responses to the students' writing are affected, in turn, by their own culturally constructed values. These tensions between culture-based values can be the topic of study in an interactive pedagogy that helps students see how such socially constructed values as beauty, objectivity, and upward mobility affect their writing. Interactive pedagogy, moreover, seeks to replace evaluation with interpretation and to bring student and academic discourse together instead of seeking to move students to a univocal academic discourse.

235   Greene, Stuart. "Making Sense of My Own Ideas: The Problems of Authorship in a Beginning Writing Classroom." *Written Communication* 12 (April 1995): 186–218.

A detailed study of two students composing research papers shows that Vuong relied heavily on what he thought was the teacher's definition of the task, namely, to summarize the ideas in the source texts. He structured his paper as a comparison of different authors. Writing about cultural literacy, Vuong, a Hmong immigrant, had strong opinions about the topic based in his own experience, but he did not want to bring these opinions into his paper. He avoided acting as arbiter among the texts he summarized. On the other hand, Jesus initially defined his task as permitting the use of his own experience as well as source texts. He structured his paper as a set of topics addressing aspects of a problem he identified in a central source text. Unlike Vuong's paper, Jesus's paper expressed a strong point of view throughout, clearly distinguished from the ideas of the authors he discussed. Greene urges writing teachers to realize that different cultural and educational backgrounds may prompt students to choose different composing strategies. Explicit classroom discussion of the authorial roles students might adopt in their writing would be helpful.

See: John Hagge, "The Process Religion and Business Communication" [587].

236   McComiskey, Bruce. *Teaching Composition as a Social Process*. Logan: Utah State Univ. Press, 2000.

"Social-content" composition courses treat cultural theory as content to be mastered while "social-process" writing instruction situates composing within particular sociopolitical contexts. A balanced approach to the three levels of composing — textual, rhetorical, and discursive — leads students to the fullest understanding of their writing processes. The post-process movement in composition studies, characterized here as social-process rhetorical inquiry, extends rather than rejects the writing process movement. Informed by cultural studies methodologies, social-process rhetorical inquiry is a set of heuristic questions, intended to guide student inquiry and instructional practice, based on the cycle of production, distribution, and consumption. Rather than focusing on a single moment or text to analyze, social-process rhetorical inquiry focuses on both the processes and products of discourse. Students are asked to produce both critical essays and practical documents that reconcile competing discourses. Through assignments in critical discourse analysis, students are prepared for participation in postmodern communal democracies.

237   Nelson, Jennie. "Reading Classrooms as Text: Exploring Student Writers' Interpretive Practices." CCC 46 (October 1995): 411–29.

Students enter college classrooms with many strategies for responding to writing assignments that have been successful for them in past schooling. These strategies typically include "reading" the entire classroom experience for clues to the teacher's expectations. Interviews with several student writers reveal, for example, that professors' grades and written comments on papers influence how students define and pursue writing tasks much more than professors' statements about such tasks. Also, while overly vague assignments can confuse students, overly explicit ones can also do damage when they are interpreted as a "blueprint for the final product," thus short-circuiting students' creative thinking. Students write better when assignments and the entire classroom atmosphere encourage them to participate in defining their intellectual tasks.

238   Penrose, Ann M., and Barbara M. Sitko, eds. *Hearing Ourselves Think: Cognitive Research in the College Writing Classroom*. New York: Oxford Univ. Press, 1993.

Cognitive research, investigating the relationship between how writers think about the writing process and the way they engage in the process, reveals much about the factors that determine how easy and successful writing will be. Process research in the classroom — methods for critical reflection on ways of learning and writing — can lead to an understanding by students and teachers of the ways that writers choose and can improve their writing strategies. Ten essays explain cognitive classroom research and its application to teaching: Ann Penrose and Barbara Sitko, "Introduction: Studying Cognitive Processes in the Classroom"; Christina Haas, "Beyond 'Just the Facts': Reading as Rhetorical Action"; Stuart Greene, "Exploring the Relationship between Authorship and Reading"; Ann Penrose, "Writing and Learning: Exploring the Consequences of Task Interpretation"; Lorraine Higgins, "Reading to Argue: Helping Students Transform Source Texts"; Jennie Nelson, "The Library Revisited: Exploring Students' Research Processes"; Rebecca Burnet, "Decision-Making during the Collaborative Planning of Coauthors"; Karen Schriver, "Revising for Readers: Audience Awareness in the Writing Classroom"; Barbara Sitko, "Exploring Feedback: Writers Meet Readers"; and Betsy Bowen, "Using Conferences to Support the Writing Process."

239   Perl, Sondra, ed. *Landmark Essays on Writing Process*. Davis, Calif.: Hermagoras Press, 1994.

Eighteen essays, arranged chronologically, beginning with Janet Emig's "The Composing Process: Review of the Literature" (1971). Essays include Sondra Perl, "The Composing Processes of Unskilled College Writers"; Linda Flower and John Hayes, "The Cognition of Discovery: Defining a Rhetorical Problem"; Nancy Sommers, "Revision Strategies of Student Writers and Experienced Adult Writers" [320]; Mike Rose, "Rigid Rules, Inflexible Plans, and the Stifling of Language: A Cognitivist Analysis of Writer's Block"; Sondra Perl, "Understanding Composing"; Ann Berthoff, "The Intelligent Eye and the Thinking Hand"; James Reither, "Writing and Knowing: Toward Redefining the Writing Process"; Lester Faigley, "Competing Theories of Process: A Critique and a Proposal" [229]; Min-Zhan Lu, "From Silence to Words: Writing as Struggle" [462]; Elizabeth Flynn, "Composing as a Woman" [491]; and Nancy Sommers, "Between the Drafts."

240   Rose, Mike, ed. *When a Writer Can't Write: Studies in Writer's Block and Other Composing Process Problems*. New York and London: Guilford Press, 1985.

Eleven essays address the social and psychological constraints that contribute to serious hesitations and false starts in writing. They include Donald H. Graves, "Blocking and the Young Writer"; Stan Jones, "Problems with Monitor Use in Second Language Composing"; David Bartholomae, "Inventing the University" [144]; and Mike Rose, "Complexity, Rigor, Evolving Method, and the Puzzle of Writer's Block: Thoughts on Composing Process Research."

241   Rose, Mike. *Writer's Block: The Cognitive Dimension*. Carbondale and Edwardsville: Southern Illinois Univ. Press, 1984.

A number of case studies of students who frequently experienced writer's block and some who seldom blocked show that writers who block frequently may rely on context-independent rules for good writing, edit individual sentences as they are being written, plan only after beginning to write, or interpret writing assignments too narrowly in light of their limited knowledge of discourse modes. Writers who seldom block are "opportunists" who treat what they know about writing as strategies, not rules, which can be varied in different writing situations. The capacities to write well and to enjoy writing are not related to blocking. This study suggests that no composing method should be taught as if applicable to all writing situations.

242   Schreiner, Steven. "A Portrait of the Student as a Young Writer: Re-evaluating Emig and the Process Movement." CCC 48 (February 1997): 86–104.

In *The Composing Processes of Twelfth Graders*, Janet Emig compares her research subject Lynn unfavorably with established literary writers. Emig suggests that Lynn writes too easily because she relies on stale academic strategies and avoids personally painful topics. Hence Emig advocates a pedagogy that would encourage Lynn to work over her writing more and to delve into self-expressive topics — an early and influential version of writing-process pedagogy. But this pedagogy, following Emig, ignores how Lynn's (and other students') strengths as a writer emerge not just from natural talent but also from sophisticated schooling and conditions of race and class privilege that equip her (but perhaps not other students) to be considered as a potential literary writer. Thus, process pedagogy risks neglecting important educational and cultural differences among students.

243   Tobin, Lad, and Thomas Newkirk, eds. *Taking Stock: The Writing Process Movement in the 90s*. Portsmouth, N.H.: Heinemann-Boynton/Cook, 1994.

Sixteen essays examine the history, theory, successes, problems, and prospects of writing-process pedagogy. Essays include: James Moffett, "Coming Out Right"; Lisa Ede, "Reading the Writing Process"; Donald Murray, "Knowing Not Knowing"; Ken Macrorie, "Process, Product, and Quality"; Mary Minock, "The Bad Marriage: A Revisionist View of James Britton's Expressive Writing Hypothesis in American Practice"; Peter Elbow, "The Uses of Binary Thinking: Exploring Seven Productive Oppositions"; Thomas Recchio, "On the Critical Necessity of 'Essaying'"; and James Britton, "There Is One Story Worth Telling."

Literacy

244   Barton, David. *Literacy: An Introduction to the Ecology of Written Language*. Malden, Mass.: Blackwell Publishers, 1994.

An ecological metaphor for literacy ("a set of social practices associated with particular symbol systems and their related technologies") allows social, psychological, and historical approaches to literacy studies to be brought together. In an ecological model, literacy is practices and events, rather than formal learning, and develops from a constructivist theory of language. Readers are introduced to key terms and definitions, to important research (Scribner and Cole; Heath; Street), to the relation of spoken and written language, and to writ-

ing systems and other notations. Other chapters cover the development of printing, emergent literacy, the literary view of literacy, school
practices, issues in adult literacy, and global literacy.

245   Barton, David and Mary Hamilton. *Local Literacies: Reading and Writing in One Community*. New York: Routledge, 1998.

A description and investigation of literacy in one local community
of Lancaster, England, presented as a microcosm of change and con-
tinuity in literacy practices. Sixty-five people in the neighborhood
of Springside were interviewed, with twelve selected for the case studies; data collection included a collaborative ethnography stage. Four
people are profiled in-depth in terms of their literacy life and history
with such topics as education, getting things done in the community,
living a local life, and leisure and pleasure. As a set of social practices
inferred from events that are mediated by written texts, literacy may
serve multiple functions in any given activity; for example, literacy
acts as evidence, display, threat, and/or ritual, and people can be incorporated into the literacy practices of others without reading or
writing a single word. Despite wide diversity of literacies in the home,
there was also coherence in the diversity; broad patternings included
the gendering of home practices; the intertwining of literacy and
numeracy practices; and the significance of multilingual experience
of literacy. Literacies are used for collective goals but also to make
sense of events in individuals' lives. Over 50 "asides" illustrate cooking literacy, learning at work, family traditions of reading, dealing
with dyslexia, doing the accounts, helping with the homework, computers in the home, and others.

246   Bernstein, Basil. *Class, Codes, and Control*. New York: Schocken,
1975.

School writing and speaking tasks call for the use of the elaborated
code — a formal way of using language that explicitly identifies context and carefully fills in transitions and details for an anonymous
reader. Most everyday speech, however, calls only for the restricted
code, which is highly context dependent. Socioeconomic class tends
to determine whether children learn how to use the elaborated code
at home, hence whether they can readily perform the kind of linguistic tasks assigned and expected at school. Working-class children
experience social relations in which elaborated code use is rare, unlike middle-class children, who can distinguish the codes and when
to use them. Thus, working-class children are often judged to be stu-
pid when they only lack access to school-like linguistic forms.

247   Bleich, David. *The Double Perspective: Language, Literacy and Social
Relations*. New York: Oxford Univ. Press, 1988.

We learn how to communicate by internalizing the double perspective of speaker and interlocutor first experienced as small children in
dialogue with our parents. Effective adult communication is never
an assertion of will but part of an oscillation between socially con-

structed pairs of opposing concepts. In teaching, a productive oscillation is needed between the classroom, in which subjective expression and collaboration are encouraged, and the academy, which valorizes "objective" scholarship produced by "independent" thought. In this as in other pairs of perspectives, one term must not be privileged: A double perspective is to be maintained. Bleich gives many examples of assignments and student work to illustrate his pedagogy.

248   Bloome, David, ed. *Classrooms and Literacy*. Norwood, N.J.: Ablex, 1989.

Eleven essays explore the idea that literacy education is a function of the curriculum as a whole and the school as a social institution. Includes David Bloome, "Beyond Access: An Ethnographic Study of Reading and Writing in a Seventh Grade Classroom"; Catherine Snow et al., "Giving Formal Definitions: An Oral Language Correlate of School Literacy"; Thomas Eisemon and Theresa Rogers, "The Acquisition of Literacy in Religious and Secular Schools"; Jay Lemke, "Social Semiotics: A New Model for Literacy Education"; and Patricia Stock and Jay Robinson, "Literacy as Conversation: Classroom Talk as Text Building."

249   Brandt, Deborah. "Accumulating Literacy: Writing and Learning to Write in the Twentieth Century." *College English* 57.6 (October 1995): 649–68.

Literacy practices in the twentieth century expanded both vertically and horizontally — as a result of rising levels of formal schooling, and "residual" materials and practices that get passed on, transformed, or assimilated. Interview participants from across four generations relate their early childhood experiences with literacy, schooling or training, and their uses and inheritances of language as adult writers. Two extended examples illustrate how individuals transform or adapt "residual literacy" — that is, practices and materials from earlier times "that linger at the scenes of contemporary literacy learning." As technologies and documentary practices evolve, old forms don't disappear but are transformed: a son gives his mother his used computer, and she passes on her manual typewriter to her grandchildren to play with; or a son draws upon his father's sermons in a C.M.E. church to write his own administrative and professional texts. Literacy needs to be defined in light of the "piling up" of artifacts and the ubiquity of print.

250   Brandt, Deborah. *Literacy as Involvement: The Acts of Writers, Readers, and Texts*. Carbondale: Southern Illinois Univ. Press, 1990.

The oral-literate dichotomy and the accompanying assumption that text literacy requires the ability to manage decontextualized language are in error. Rather, all forms of literacy are deeply context-bound, and reading and writing are forms of social interaction and intersubjectivity.

251   Chiseri-Strater, Elizabeth. *Academic Literacies: The Public and Private Discourse of University Students*. Portsmouth, N.H.: Heinemann-Boynton/Cook, 1991.

Detailed case studies of two college writers reveal linguistic resources that are not always recognized by the university. The academy favors lecture-recitation and combative debate formats that suited one of the students, while the other found less agonistic ways of communicating and learning. Both students used nonverbal expression, like visual images and dance, as aids to learning, even though these media were rarely valued in coursework. The development of multiple literacies can be fostered by adopting collaborative learning strategies and writing assignments that breach the traditional separation between public knowledge and private life.

252   Cook-Gumperz, Jenny. *The Social Construction of Literacy*. Cambridge: Cambridge Univ. Press, 1986.

Ten essays investigate the settings in which and means by which literacy is acquired. Includes Jenny Cook-Gumperz, "Literacy and Schooling: An Unchanging Equation?"; John Gumperz, "Interactional Sociolinguistics in the Study of Schooling"; Gordon Wells, "The Language Experience of Five-Year-Old Children at Home and at School"; James Collins, "Differential Instruction in Reading Groups"; and Herbert Simons and Sandra Murphy, "Spoken Language Strategies and Reading Acquisition."

253   Cushman, Ellen. *The Struggle and the Tools: Oral and Literate Strategies in an Inner City Community*. Albany: State Univ. of New York Press, 1998.

In daily struggles with public service agencies, inner-city residents demonstrate sophisticated linguistic strategizing and draw upon a wide variety of literacy tools. Faced with eviction, for example, residents collaborated on ways to find housing, including rehearsing conversations and sharing years of experiences with racism and bureaucracy. Through a cyclic process of learning, deploying, and assessing their oral and literate strategies for interactions with gatekeepers, the subjects of this study practiced language transfer, code-switching, and metadiscourse. Based on over three years of fieldwork, these findings challenge the notion of "illiteracy" as well as the concept of false consciousness. Cushman advocates an activist methodology and more studies of extracurricular literacies.

254   Daniell, Beth. "Against the Great Leap Theory of Literacy." *PRE/TEXT* 7 (Fall–Winter 1986): 181–93.

Literacy scholarship is divided into two camps, those who embrace and those who oppose the Great Leap theory. This theory holds that literacy shifts a culture's perception from holistic to analytic. It is advanced by Eric Havelock [263], Walter Ong, S.J. [274, 275], and Thomas Farrell [257]. But the conflation of thought itself with the qualities of formal discourse prejudices the characterization of oral communities, equating Western forms of academic thinking with human intelligence. The theory also permits broad generalization about language competence and cognitive ability from small language samples. Many researchers oppose this theory, having found that a continuum from oral to literate or a complex intermixing of these forms of discourse more accurately describes the language use of particular societies.

255   Daniell, Beth. "Narratives of Literacy: Connecting Composition to Culture." CCC 50.3 (February 1999): 393–410.

Lyotard's theory of grand narratives and little narratives helps to illustrate a number of issues in the relationship of literacy and composition. The "Literacy for Liberation Narrative," for example, largely informed by Freire, attempts to refute the "Great Leap Narrative," but in our tendency to buy into the narrative of literacy heroism, composition scholars have largely misunderstood Freire's Catholic and spiritual vision of education. Recent studies tend to be little narratives of literacy, most of which argue that literacy cannot be neatly linked to either freedom or oppression. The little narratives connect composition to culture by studying writing in everyday life and by representing the ideological contradictions of literacy.

256   DeStigter, Todd. "The *Tesoros* Literacy Project: An Experiment in Democratic Communities." *Research in the Teaching of English* 32 (February 1998): 10–42.

A ten-week collaboration between ESL (Latino) students and at-risk Anglo students put into practice John Dewey's ideas about the importance of relationships to democratic communities. This project attempts to resolve, not just to critique, the inequities in the educational environment of Addison High, where students collaborated weekly on reading and writing projects and, in the process, established affective relationships and illustrated the importance of valuing difference.

See: Janet Carey Eldred and Peter Mortensen, "Reading Literacy Narratives" [421].

257   Farrell, Thomas J. "I.Q. and Standard English." CCC 34 (December 1983): 470–84.

There is no genetic cause for black children's persistently lower scores on I.Q. tests. Black English communities, however, exhibit many patterns of oral, rather than literate, language use. If I.Q. tests measure cognitive abilities valued by society, and if the acquisition of literacy confers these abilities, the low I.Q. scores of black children can be attributed to their orality — their ignorance of Standard English, which is shaped by literacy. Thus, their cognitive abilities may be enhanced by teaching them to speak and write Standard English. See also "Responses to Thomas J. Farrell, 'I.Q. and Standard English,'" CCC 35 (December 1984): 455–77.

258   Freire, Paulo. *Pedagogy of the Oppressed.* Trans. Myra Bergman Ramos. New York: Seabury, 1968.

Pedagogy can be liberating if it truly enables the oppressed to name the world for themselves rather than merely imposing the knowledge of the dominant group. The banking approach to education, in which the teacher knows, thinks, speaks, and disciplines, treats people as adaptable and manipulable rather than as agents in the world with the power to create and transform. Liberating education consists of acts of cognition, not transfers of information. Teaching from generative themes drawn from the lives of the students can lead to critical consciousness as the students come to understand the situation in which they live, gain the power to name it, and see the possibility of changing it themselves.

259   Freire, Paulo, and Donaldo Macedo. *Literacy: Reading the Word and the World.* South Hadley, Mass.: Bergin and Garvey, 1987.

Literacy is a form of cultural politics, in the United States as elsewhere. It may reproduce the existing social formation or promote emancipatory change. Critical literacy encourages cultural production rather than reproduction, enabling people to tell their own stories about their individual and collective experience.

260   Gere, Anne Ruggles. "Kitchen Table and Rented Rooms: The Extracurriculum of Composition." CCC 45.1 (February 1994): 75–92.

In urban centers and small farming communities, countless writers gather regularly in self-sponsored workshops to share their writing. Participants gain confidence, hone their craft, contribute positive criticism, and create opportunities for performance and publication. These writing groups and the writing development they encourage are not accounted for in histories of composition studies, characteristically neglectful of extracurricular literary clubs and other literacy practices outside of formal education. Gere identifies self-help guides for writers, many used by groups that developed across gender, class, and racial lines: there were clubs for white women, African American women, and working-class women — all of which contributed to and sustained composition's extracurriculum. Motivated by desire, writers who participate in these groups remind composition teachers that "an unswerving concentration on professionalism" blinds us to the cultural work that writing accomplishes. Writers often write for the love of it, to enact power, and to perform.

261   Graff, Harvey. *The Labyrinths of Literacy: Reflections on Literacy Past and Present.* Pittsburgh: Univ. of Pittsburgh Press, 1995.

Sixteen previously published essays by Graff exploring the history of literacy and the implications of that history. Present-day conceptions of literacy are historically grounded, reflecting the oversimple view of literacy as the key to civilization (dominant until quite recently) yet serving as the basis of a more complex understanding of literacy at present. The connection between literacy and social development was based on untested assumptions and ideological predispositions: Literacy was mistaken for a neutral technology; alphabetic literacy was extolled, to the exclusion of other significant literacies; a false dichotomy was discerned between literacy and orality; and a hierarchy that irrevocably harmed individuals and societies perceived as illiterate was erected. Critical theory and social history have worked to test and correct these conceptions, revealing a far more complex understanding of the nature and types of literacy, the ways that literacies are learned and used, the functions of literacy in communities, and the policies that have been employed to foster — or impede — literacy.

262   Graff, Harvey J. *The Legacies of Literacy: Continuities and Contradictions in Western Culture and Society.* Bloomington: Indiana Univ. Press, 1987.

Graff reviews classical and medieval education but concentrates on the advent of print literacy in the Renaissance, exploring its consequences for popular schooling in eighteenth and nineteenth century Europe and America. He examines literacy in the social context to determine who achieves literacy, what kind of literacy is achieved, and what purposes literacy serves.

263   Havelock, Eric. *Preface to Plato.* Cambridge: Belknap Press of Harvard Univ. Press, 1963.

Plato's attack on poetry was in fact an attack on the use of oral poetry as the archive of Greek culture and the means of cultural instruction. Poetry distorts truth, Plato charges, making it entirely inappropriate for this task. Behind this attack is a rejection of oral forms of cultural preservation and transmission. In nonliterate societies, oral literature is the only means of preserving and handing on collective knowledge. Oral literature is didactic, teaching accepted beliefs and practices. Poetic form is an aid to memorization. Writing, which developed between the time of Homer and Plato, changes all of this by allowing cultural information to be stored more permanently and transmitted more reliably. Poetic form is no longer necessary, as a result of which, propositional forms, including logic, developed. The effect was a cognitive revolution based on alphabetic literacy, changing fundamentally the way that people thought.

264   Heath, Shirley Brice. *Ways with Words: Language, Life, and Work in Communities and Classrooms.* New York: Cambridge Univ. Press, 1983.

Research in three Carolina communities reveals socially conditioned patterns of oral and written language use, but no clear distinctions between literate and oral or preliterate groups.

265   Hirsch, E. D. *Cultural Literacy: What Every American Needs to Know.* Expanded ed. New York: Vintage, 1988.

Effective communication requires not only encoding and decoding skills — technical literacy — but also background knowledge shared among interlocutors — cultural literacy. Effective communication in a democracy requires a shared national culture. The contents of this culture, in the United States, have been largely determined by history: knowledge that has traditionally been important continues to be so for that very reason. Thus the cultural knowledge of dominant groups tends to predominate. Nevertheless, this cultural knowledge need not be elitist if it is taught to everyone in school and becomes the property of all. Curriculum planning should attend to conveying this cultural literacy. Includes an appendix listing several hundred names, dates, and ideas put forward as the basis of American cultural literacy.

266   Horsman, Jennifer. *Something in My Mind besides the Everyday: Women and Literacy*. Toronto: Women's Press, 1990.

Literacy programs often assume that their clients are completely illiterate and even unintelligent, that traditional school literacy is what they need, and that any failure to complete the program is owing to the individual's lack of motivation. Interviews with twenty-three women enrolled in literacy programs and ten workers in the programs suggest, to the contrary, that learners have varied abilities and a variety of personal and career goals related to literacy. They want to end their dependence on social-service agencies. They are often hampered in their efforts by the complex demands of life in disadvantaged socioeconomic settings and by the debilitating links between many literacy programs and the very social agencies the students wish to escape. Literacy programs need to listen more to learners' self-definitions of their needs and to encourage the use of literacy for social criticism.

267   Kintgen, Eugene R., Barry M. Kroll, and Mike Rose, eds. *Perspectives on Literacy*. Carbondale: Southern Illinois Univ. Press, 1988.

Twenty-eight major essays on the theory, history, and pedagogical and social implications of literacy. Essays include Jack Goody and Ian Watt, "The Consequences of Literacy"; Walter J. Ong, S.J., "Some Psychodynamics of Orality"; Sylvia Scribner and Michael Cole, "Unpackaging Literacy"; Harvey J. Graff, "The Legacies of Literacy"; Eric A. Havelock, "The Coming of Literate Communication to Western Culture"; David R. Olson, "From Utterance to Text"; John U. Ogbu, "Literacy and Schooling in Subordinate Cultures"; Yetta Goodman, "The Development of Initial Literacy"; Shirley Brice Heath, "Protean Shapes in Literacy Events"; Paulo Freire, "The Adult Literacy Process as Cultural Action for Freedom"; Carl Kaestle, "The History of Literacy and the History of Readers"; Jay Robinson, "The Social Context of Literacy"; David Bartholomae, "Inventing the University" [144]; Kyle Fiore and Nan Elsasser, "'Strangers No More': A Liberatory Literacy Curriculum" [450]; and William Diehl and Larry Mikulecky, "The Nature of Reading at Work."

268   Knoblauch, C. H., and Lil Brannon. *Critical Teaching and the Idea of Literacy*. Portsmouth, N.H.: Heinemann-Boynton/Cook, 1993.

Critical teaching aims to prepare students to live comfortably with cultural diversity and to work actively for social and economic justice. These goals have been hampered by the scare tactics of those who, like Dinesh D'Souza, deride political correctness but have much more power than those they warn against. Critical teaching is also thwarted by limiting models of literacy: the functionalist model, emphasizing supposedly practical skills; the cultural-literacy model, inculcating Western culture; and the expressivist model, celebrating personal growth while disguising political realities. A preferable model is critical literacy, which, as Paulo Freire argues, empowers students to name the inequities in their world and work to change them.

269   Lee, Carol D. and Peter Smagorinsky, eds. *Vygotskian Perspectives on Literacy Research: Constructing Meaning through Collaborative Inquiry*. New York: Cambridge Univ. Press, 2000.

Central tenets of Vygotsky's theory have influenced current debates in literacy research and in activity theory; the centrality of language and the inherently social nature of literacy learning and practice have provided the basis for modern analysis, and Vygotsky's ideas have also been modified through the studies that draw on them. Eleven chapters, following an introduction by the editors, include the following: James V. Wertsch, "Vygotsky's Two Minds on the Nature of Meaning"; LeeAnn G. Putney, et al., "Consequential Progressions: Exploring Collective-Individual Development in a Bilingual Classroom"; Kris D. Gutierrez and Lynda D. Stone, "Synchronic and Diachronic Dimensions of Social Practice: An Emerging Methodology for Cultural-Historical Perspectives on Literacy Learning"; Carol D. Lee, "Signifying in the Zone of Proximal Development"; Arnetha F. Ball, "Teacher's Developing Philosophies on Literacy and their Use in Urban Schools: A Vygotskian Perspective on Internal Activity and Teacher Change"; Luis C. Moll, "Inspired by Vygotsky: Ethnographic Experiments in Education."

270   Lunsford, Andrea A., Helene Moglen, and James Slevin, eds. *The Right to Literacy*. New York: MLA, 1990.

Twenty-nine compact essays address the public and professional issue of literacy, the literacy problems of particular social groups, and political and pedagogical concerns. Essays include Theodore Sizer, "Public Literacy: Puzzlements of a High School Watcher"; Jacqueline Jones Royster, "Perspectives on the Intellectual Tradition of Black Women Writers"; James Moffett, "Censorship and Spiritual Education"; Deborah Brandt, "Literacy and Knowledge"; Glynda Hull and Mike Rose, "Toward a Social-Cognitive Understanding of Problematic Reading and Writing"; and Shirley Brice Heath, "The Fourth Vision: Literate Language at Work."

271   Macedo, Donaldo. *Literacies of Power: What Americans Are Not Allowed to Know.* Boulder: Westview Press, 1994.

Drills in discrete skills give people sufficient literacy to decode but not to demystify government propaganda. Adding a cultural-literacy component to education perpetuates cultural genocide on those who do not belong to the majority culture, if the model favors Western culture, as does E. D. Hirsch's. Following Paulo Freire, we should encourage multilingual, multicultural literacy education in order to effect change toward social justice. Macedo testifies to the value of such education from personal experience.

272   Moss, Beverly J. *Literacy across Communities.* Cresskill, N.J.: Hampton, 1994.

Five of the six essays in this collection study nonacademic literacy practices in mainstream communities: Marcia Farr, "En Los Dos Idiomas: Literacy Practices among Chicano Mexicanos"; Gail Weinstein-Shr, "From Mountaintops to City Streets: Literacy in Philadelphia's Hmong Community"; Daniel McLaughlin, "Toward a Dialogical Understanding of Literacy: The Case of Navajo Print"; Jabari Mahiri, "Reading Rites and Sports: Motivation for Adaptive Literacy of Young African-American Males"; and Beverly Moss, "Creating a Community: Literacy Events in African-American Churches." In the final essay, "World Travelling: Enlarging Our Understanding of Nonmainstream Literacies," Elizabeth Chiseri-Strater comments on the preceding studies and recommends, following them, that teachers should function as coaches, not authority figures; that classrooms should be collaborative learning communities; and that school-home communication should become bidirectional.

273   Murray, Denise E., ed. *Diversity as Resource: Redefining Cultural Literacy.* Alexandria, Va.: TESOL, 1992.

Twelve essays illustrate and develop an approach to multicultural literacy that explicitly answers E. D. Hirsch's program for a primarily Western common culture in the United States. Essays include Keith Walters, "Whose Culture? Whose Literacy?"; Anna Soter, "Whose Shared Assumptions? Making the Implicit Explicit"; Denise Murray, Patricia Nichols, and Allison Hecht, "Identifying the Languages and Cultures of Our Students"; Evelyn Baker Dandy, "Sensitizing Teachers to Cultural Differences: An African American Perspective"; Olga Vasquez, "A Mexicano Perspective: Reading the World in a Multicultural Setting"; Ann Johns, "Toward Developing a Cultural Repertoire: A Case Study of a Lao College Freshman"; Daniel McLaughlin, "Power and the Politics of Knowledge: Transformative Schooling for Minority Language Learners"; and Patricia Nichols, "Language in the Attic: Claiming Our Linguistic Heritage."

274   Ong, Walter J., S.J. "Literacy and Orality in Our Times." *ADE Bulletin* 58 (September 1978): 1–7. Rpt. in Enos [449] and in Young and Liu [295].

Writing is essential for analytic, linear, and sequential thought, in contrast to speech, which is "rhapsodic" — loosely constructed of clichés, proverbs, and other "loci" (topoi). Students, particularly those from highly oral cultural communities, must move from the oral to the written form of thought; their writing often has the loose structure of conversation. It can be helpful to teach students about the contrast between oral and written thought, but it is essential for writing teachers to know about the differences. See also Ong [275].

275   Ong, Walter J., S.J. *Orality and Literacy: The Technologizing of the Word.* New York: Methuen, 1982.

Ong applies Eric Havelock's theory of cognitive differences between oral and literate cultures to modern society. See Ong [274]; Daniell [254].

276   Pattison, Robert. *On Literacy: The Politics of the Word from Homer to the Age of Rock.* New York: Oxford Univ. Press, 1982.

Historical and cross-cultural study focusing on ideological implications of different definitions and forms of literacy. Literacy, finally, cannot be defined as a mechanical skill, a touchstone of civility, or a prerequisite for economic advancement but as consciousness of the problems raised by language.

277   Roberts, Peter. *Education, Literacy, and Humanization: Exploring the Work of Paulo Freire.* Westport, Conn.: Bergin & Garvey, 2000.

If educators from the First World are to avoid the danger of domestication, Freire's writings and pedagogical practice must be properly contextualized and studied in a holistic and critical manner. Reading Freire's entire pedagogical history as a narrative of hope, and the process of reinventing Freire's ideas, begins with acknowledging the particular social circumstances under which his pedagogy was forged. When we engage in critical, dialogical praxis, we pursue the idea of humanization, which is a continuous, unfinished process and makes problematic the tendency among Western educators to reduce Freirean theory to a set of methods. Freire's works contain a number of binary oppositions, but his later writings suggest that there is no single antithesis to liberating education. In Freirean programs of adult literacy education, dialogue is pivotal, and to become literate in the sense Freire intends requires not merely a mastery of signs and symbols, but also a willingness to participate in the process of building and rebuilding one's society. Despite accepting a number of insights from postmodernists, Freire remained essentially a modernist, resulting in strong criticism such as charges of antidialogue and criticisms of universalist thought. The "stages" model of conscientization and an individualist view of critical consciousness should be rejected in order to concentrate on the link between conscientization and praxis; Freire's ideal can be reassessed in light of postmodernist notions of multiple subjectivities.

See: Jacqueline Jones Royster, *Traces of a Stream: Literacy and Social Change Among African American Women* [130].

278   Scribner, Sylvia, and Michael Cole. *The Psychology of Literacy.* Cambridge: Harvard Univ. Press, 1981.

Research among the African Vai, a people with widely varying degrees of literacy, reveals no pattern of cognitive gains associated with literacy.

279   Sheridan, Dorothy, Brian Street, and David Bloome. *Writing Ourselves: Mass-Observation and Literacy Practices.* Cresskill, N.J.: Hampton Press, 2000.

Because the everyday literacy practices of ordinary people are made nearly invisible, the Mass-Observation Project at the University of Sussex offers a unique institutional context for writing and the means of understanding the nature of writing in Britain in the late twentieth century, illustrating the intimate relationships between literacy practices and social life. Begun in 1937 as an effort to establish an "anthropology of our own people," Mass-Observation asked "ordinary people" to record their lives and submit their writings to the Archive. Re-launched in 1981, the Project today sends volunteer observers or correspondents directives three times a year (e.g., "keep a diary for the day of the 1981 Royal Wedding"). The Archive places recently received material directly in the public domain. Mass-Observation is closely linked with the intellectual history of the discipline of social anthropology in the U.K.; more importantly, Mass-Observation material provides a way of exploring cross-cultural literacy practices, the social uses and meanings of reading and/or writing. Mass-Observers' commentaries on their own writing practices, in particular, adopt an ethnographic perspective on literacy. The dialogues of nine Mass-Observation correspondents are constructed to illustrate how writing is implicated in the exercise of power, definitions of personhood, and the creation and transformation of social space.

280   Street, Brian, ed. *Cross-Cultural Approaches to Literacy.* New York: Cambridge Univ. Press, 1993.

Opposing a psycholinguistic focus on discrete reading and writing skills, this collection illustrates approaches to literacy informed by anthropology and focused on social contexts and practices. Twelve essays study literacies around the world, many in nonacademic settings. Includes Kathleen Rockhill, "Gender, Language, and the Politics of Literacy"; Miriam Camitta, "Vernacular Writing: Varieties of Literacy among Philadelphia High School Students"; Amy Shuman, "Collaborative Writing: Appropriating Power or Reproducing Authority?"; Gail Weinstein-Shr, "Literacy and Social Process: A Community in Transition"; and an introduction by Street.

281   Street, Brian V., ed. *Literacy and Development: Ethnographic Perspectives.* New York: Routledge, 2001.

The contributors to this volume are ethnographers of literacy projects who have spent many years conducting in-depth qualitative studies of everyday literacies in different parts of the world. Essays address educational interventions, the broader contexts of development interventions, and the specific aspects of development agendas. Included is an introduction by the editor, an afterword, and ten chapters, including Caroline Dyer and Archana Choksi, "Literacy, Schooling and Development: Views of Rabari Nomads, India"; Martha Wagar Wright, "More Than Just Chanting: Multilingual Literacies, Ideology and Teaching Methodologies in Rural Eritrea"; Priti Chopra, "Betrayal and Solidarity in Ethnography on Literacy: Revisiting Research Homework in a North Indian Village"; Pat Herbert and Clinton Robinson, "Another Language, Another Literacy? Practices in Northern Ghana"; Anna Robinson-Pant, "Women's Literacy and Health: Can an Ethnographic Researcher Find the Links?"; Shirin Zubair, "Literacies, Gender and Power in Rural Pakistan."

282   Stubbs, Michael. *Language and Literacy: The Sociolinguistics of Reading and Writing.* London: Routledge and Kegan Paul, 1980.

A functional or sociolinguistic theory of literacy accounts for the relationship between spoken and written language and delineates the "communicative functions served by different types of language in different social settings." Although spoken language is usually learned before written language, speech is much more variable than writing, the orthography of which often does not reflect pronunciation. Written language is thus semiautonomous from and often higher in prestige than spoken language. These differences make writing difficult to learn for children whose spoken language varies widely from the written form dominant in school. Psychological theories of verbal deprivation that purport to explain these difficulties are reductive. All languages are equally effective media of communication. Language-learning difficulties must be understood in terms both of children's varied social experiences with language and of their teachers' attitudes toward their preferred language forms.

283   Taylor, Denny, and Catherine Dorsey-Gaines. *Growing Up Literate: Learning from Inner-City Families.* Portsmouth, N.H.: Heinemann, 1988.

Detailed ethnographic study of poor urban black families, depicting them as creating productive environments for literacy learning.

284   Tuman, Myron C. *A Preface to Literacy: An Inquiry into Pedagogy, Practice, and Progress.* Tuscaloosa: Univ. of Alabama Press, 1987.

Discussions of literacy present conflicting definitions of the term, from transcription of speech and minimal reading ability (the unproblematic model) to sophisticated interpretive skills that require inferring a context to find meaning in a message (the problematic model). These definitions have supported particular ideological agendas that affect our understanding of litera·y education.

285   Villaneuva, Victor, Jr. *Bootstraps: From an American Academic of Color.* Urbana, Ill.: NCTE, 1993.

Linguistic deficit theories are grossly inadequate to explain the school difficulties of students from minority social groups, who are stigmatized by color and social class, unlike immigrant students, even if their native language is English. Particularly disadvantaged are students of castelike minorities that have been economically and culturally colonized by dominant U.S. culture. The dominant culture requires racelessness and abandonment of the home culture as conditions of acceptance, making biculturalism a difficult option. These students need to develop a critical consciousness of the historically generated social conditions that block their freedom and to become conscious intellectuals who can lead progressive social change. Educators should hold minority students to high standards while teaching forms of literacy that foster cultural and linguistic diversity, and political analyses that address the economic decline and individualistic fragmentation of postmodern life.

286   Yagelski, Robert P. *Literacy Matters: Writing and Reading the Social Self.* New York: Teachers College Press, 2000.

Exploring the nature of literacy and its ambiguous role in our lives begins by defining literacy as a local act of self-construction within discourse. Outmoded beliefs about literacy that continue to drive conventional English curricula in American schools do not help us to understand the specific acts of reading and writing that students engage in or the complexities and contradictions involved in literate acts. Children receive mixed messages about literacy, in part because school-based literacy instruction is centered mostly on individual abilities and achievements and ignores the fact that official literacies can marginalize as well as empower. The task of the literacy educator is to enable learners to understand how literacy functions as a means of participation in ever-shifting discourses that shape our lives. Exploring how individual texts come to be and what they mean to individual writers and readers working within complex, inherently social contexts and discourses can illuminate the local nature of literacy in the context of its basic social functions. An adequate understanding of literacy requires accounting for tension between individual writer and social context and should understand the ways in which new literacy technologies might be redefining the value of literacy in an increasingly technological and multicultural world.

Invention and Pre-Writing

287   Berthoff, Ann E. *Forming/Thinking/Writing: The Composing Imagination.* Rochelle Park, N.J.: Hayden, 1978.

Writing is a process of making meaning, of discovering how we think and feel about the world as we try to shape our thoughts in language. This textbook offers a series of "assisted invitations" to explore the composing process, from simple observation to forming concepts and writing critically about one's own knowledge.

288   Brent, Doug. *Reading as Rhetorical Invention: Knowledge, Persuasion, and the Teaching of Research-Based Writing.* Urbana, Ill.: NCTE, 1992.

A rhetoric of discourse consumption explains how people come to be persuaded by the texts they read and how they decide among texts' competing claims. Assuming that texts can convey shareable good reasons for belief, readers adjudicate among them, granting or withholding assent on the basis of the text's match with what the reader already knows and believes. The richer the reader's repertoire of knowledge and examined belief, the more readily she can learn from reading. This ability to learn from texts is the fundamental academic research skill. It can be taught, even to beginners, by emphasizing that the purpose of research is not to retrieve data but to converse about it, that all texts are biased, that gut feelings of commitment to one text over another can be trusted, and that research is recursive.

289   Coe, Richard M. "If Not to Narrow, Then How to Focus: Two Techniques for Focusing." CCC 32 (October 1981): 272–77.

The typical advice of textbooks to narrow a topic to one of its parts or to focus on one aspect of a topic may limit students to trivial topics or choke off development of ideas. Instead, students should shape a topic by looking for a contradiction in it and resolving the contradiction as the thesis of the essay.

290   Comprone, Joseph. "Kenneth Burke and the Teaching of Writing." CCC 29 (December 1978): 336–40.

Burke's theory of language as symbolic action is applicable to writing as an active process. The pentad can be used as a heuristic in the invention stage by focusing on agent and scene as a way to interpret experience and, later, in the drafting stage by focusing on agency and purpose as a way to move the audience. Burke's concept of "terministic screens" can help writers understand the need to translate their worldviews for an audience, and the concept of "identification" can point to persuasive techniques. Comprone restates the pentad as a set of questions for the writer. Cf. Burke [166, 167].

See: Sharon Crowley, *The Methodical Memory* [91].

291   Emig, Janet. "Writing as a Mode of Learning." CCC 28 (May 1977): 122–28. Rpt. in Young and Liu [295].

Writing is a uniquely valuable mode of learning. It simultaneously engages the hand, the eye, and both hemispheres of the brain. Writing requires an emotional commitment and is self-paced. The written product provides immediate feedback on learning and a record that can be reconsidered and revised at leisure. The stages of the writing process, embodied in notes, outlines, and drafts, also provide a record of the growth of learning.

292   LeFevre, Karen Burke. *Invention as a Social Act*. Carbondale: Southern Illinois Univ. Press, 1987.

American composition pedagogy has long been based on the Platonic view that invention is the act of the individual writer who searches for truth by self-examination. This view is supported by ubiquitous myths of individualism in America. Although there is real value in this perspective, a more complete account must recognize that invention is social and collaborative: the individual author has been influenced by society; all human acts are dialectical responses to context; writing refers to an audience, internal or external; and the classical context of rhetoric is explicitly social. Thus, there are four perspectives on invention. In the Platonic view, invention is private. The internal-dialogic view projects a Freudian self made up of contesting inner voices, strongly influenced by internalized social values. The collaborative view follows George Herbert Mead in locating meaning in the symbolic interactions of a group of people. And the collective view follows Emile Durkheim's theory that social institutions and cultural traditions affect individual choices. The social view of invention suggests ways that composition research and pedagogies can go beyond personal assumptions about authorship.

293   Murray, Donald M. "Write before Writing." CCC 29 (December 1978): 375–82.

Professionals go through an elaborate pre-writing process, for which teachers would do well to allow time. The first stage is delay, when the writer collects information, develops a concern for the subject and a sense of the audience, and feels the deadline approaching. Next comes rehearsal, talking about what will be written and making notes, outlines, and finally a tentative draft. Eight signals — such as genre, the sense that one's writing is fitting into a known form, or point of view, the development of a strong position on the subject — help the writer to the final draft.

294   Young, Richard E., Alton L. Becker, and Kenneth L. Pike. *Rhetoric: Discovery and Change*. New York: Harcourt, Brace and World, 1970.

Rhetoric is the study of methods for discovering ideas and changing the attitudes of one's audience about those ideas. Humans render the chaos of external reality intelligible through three cognitive activities: sorting perceptions by simple comparison and contrast with other perceptions, looking at the range of variation among the set of similar perceptions, and looking at the distribution of these perceptions across a range of experience. The subject can be considered in three ways in each activity: as an isolated "particle," in itself; as a dynamic "wave" and as a "field," in relation to other subjects. Out of this nine-part heuristic comes an understanding of the subject as a problem to be solved in writing. To persuade the audience, it is better to avoid an adversary posture and to adopt a three-step method devised by psychotherapist Carl Rogers: (1) convince your reader that you truly understand his position; (2) compare the worldviews that support your position and your reader's, to exploit the similarities between those views; and (3) move your reader toward your position. This textbook, seldom used in undergraduate courses, was a very influential work on invention and persuasion methods derived from psychology and linguistics.

295   Young, Richard, and Yameng Liu, eds. *Landmark Essays on Rhetorical Invention in Writing*. Davis, Calif.: Hermagoras Press, 1994.

Nineteen essays arranged chronologically, beginning with Kenneth Burke, "The Five Master Terms" (1943). Essays include Wayne Booth, "The Rhetorical Stance" [161]; Kenneth Pike, "Beyond the Sentence"; D. Gordon Rohman, "Pre-Writing: The Stage of Discovery in the Writing Process"; Chaïm Perelman, "Rhetoric and Philosophy"; S. Michael Halloran, "On the End of Rhetoric, Classical and Modern"; Janet Emig, "Writing as a Mode of Learning" [291]; Walter Ong, "Literacy and Orality in Our Times" [274]; James Britton, "Shaping at the Point of Utterance"; Douglas Park, "The Meanings of 'Audience'"; and James Kinneavy, "Kairos: A Neglected Concept in Classical Rhetoric."

Arrangement

296   Braddock, Richard. "The Frequency and Placement of Topic Sentences in Expository Prose." Research in the Teaching of English 8 (Winter 1974): 287–302.

Do good expository paragraphs begin with explicit topic sentences? In twenty-five essays by professional writers, fewer than half of the paragraphs have topic sentences at all, and fewer than half of those topic sentences are simple and direct. Other kinds of topic sentences are delayed-completion, assembled (in which the topic-sentence ideas are scattered through the paragraph), and inferred. First Braddock Award winner.

297   Christensen, Francis. "A Generative Rhetoric of the Paragraph." CCC 16 (October 1965): 144–56. Rpt. in *The Sentence and the Paragraph* [299]; in Francis Christensen, *Notes Toward a New Rhetoric: Six Essays for Teachers* (New York: Harper and Row, 1967); and in Francis Christensen and Bonniejean Christensen, eds., *Notes Toward a New Rhetoric: Nine Essays for Teachers* (New York: Harper and Row, 1978).

Paragraph structure resembles sentence structure (cf. [324]). The topic sentence, usually the first sentence, is analogous to the main clause, and supporting sentences, working at lower levels of generality, are analogous to modifying phrases. Relations between sentences in a paragraph are coordinate or subordinate. Most paragraphs exhibit both kinds of relation, even when there is no topic sentence or when the paragraph includes unrelated sentences. Students should practice diagramming paragraphs by level of generality to see where coordinate and subordinate additions are needed. Cf. Braddock [296].

298   Eden, Rich, and Ruth Mitchell. "Paragraphing for the Reader." CCC 37 (December 1986): 416–30, 441.

While research shows that paragraphs in admired professional writing don't necessarily contain topic sentences or follow prescribed patterns, textbooks continue to offer these "rules." Writers should be taught, instead, reader-oriented paragraphing. Readers expect to see paragraphs and project several qualities upon them. Most important, readers will always treat the first sentence of a paragraph as the orienting statement, so writers should ask only if their first sentence orients the reader as they wish. Moreover, this consideration should arise only during the editing process and not — as generative theories of paragraphing suggest — during composing itself. Paragraphing shapes the reader's interpretation of the text. Ineffective paragraphing usually comes from thinking of paragraphs as formal structures related only to the material.

299   *The Sentence and the Paragraph.* Urbana, Ill.: NCTE, 1963.

This important collection comprises essays by Francis Christensen on the generative rhetoric of the sentence and the paragraph [297, 324] as well as his "Notes Toward a New Rhetoric: Sentence Openers; A Lesson from Hemingway." It also includes Alton L. Becker, "A Tagmemic Approach to Paragraph Analysis," and a symposium on the paragraph by Francis Christensen, Alton L. Becker, Paul C. Rodgers, Jr., Josephine Miles, and David H. Karrfalt.

300   Winterowd, W. Ross. "The Grammar of Coherence." CE 31 (May 1970): 328–35. Rpt. in Corbett, Meyers, and Tate [171].

Transformational grammar shows how case and syntax hold sentences together, but these features do not fully explain the coherence either of sentences or of larger units of discourse. Seven transitional relations account for coherence: coordinate (expressed, for example, by *and*); obversative (*but*); causative (*for*); conclusive (*so*); alternative (*or*); inclusive (the colon); and sequential (*first . . . second*).

301   Witte, Stephen P., and Lester Faigley. "Coherence, Cohesion, and Writing Quality." CCC 32 (May 1981): 189–204.

According to M. A. K. Halliday and Ruqaiya Hasan, cohesive ties, the semantic relations that hold a text together, fall into five classes: substitution and ellipsis, more common in speech than in writing; reference (the use of pronouns and definite articles); conjunction; lexical reiteration (repeating words or synonyms); and collocation (common word groups). Better writers use more ties. Coherence, however, depends on more than cohesive ties. It also requires setting discourse in the appropriate context for the audience. Collocation may be the best indicator of coherence.

Argument

302   Emmel, Barbara, Paula Resch, and Deborah Tenney, eds. *Argument Revisited, Argument Redefined: Negotiating Meaning in the Composition Classroom.* Thousand Oaks, Calif.: Sage Publications, 1996.

The nine essays in this volume survey current methods for teaching argument and, in general, evaluate them from the perspective that successful argument, both as genre and as process, negotiates across cultural boundaries rather than supposedly subduing all possible readers or hearers with logic. Contributors are John T. Gage, "The Reasoned Thesis: The E-word and Argumentative Writing as a Process of Inquiry"; Barbara Emmel, "Evidence as a Creative Act: An Epistemology of Argumentative Inquiry"; Richard Fulkerson, "The Toulmin Model of Argument and the Teaching of Composition"; Doug Brent, "Rogerian Rhetoric: Ethical Growth through Alternative Forms of Argumentation"; Jeanne Fahnestock and Marie Secor, "Classical Rhetoric: The Art of Argumentation"; Pamela J. Annas and Deborah Tenney, "Positioning Oneself: A Feminist Approach to Argument"; Judith Summerfield, "Principles for Propagation: On Narrative and Argument"; Mariolina Salvatori, "The 'Argument of Reading' in the Teaching of Composition"; and David Bartholomae, "The Argument of Reading."

303   Fahnestock, Jeanne, and Marie Secor. "Teaching Argument: A Theory of Types." CCC 34 (February 1983): 20–30. Rpt. in Corbett, Myers, and Tate [171].

Argument can be taught by the logical/analytic, content/problem-solving, or rhetorical/generative approaches. The first does not work because formal logic is not the logic of discourse, as shown by Perelman [209]. The second approach works better because students infer argumentative techniques by taking stands on controversial issues, but the issues tend to take over the course. The rhetorical/generative approach is best because it teaches forms of argument that are transferable to a wide variety of situations. Most arguments take one of four forms: categorical propositions, causal statements, evaluations, and proposals. Students should learn to write an argument of each kind, in this sequence, on their own topics.

304   Gage, John T. "Teaching the Enthymeme: Invention and Arrangement." *Rhetoric Review* 2 (September 1983): 38–50.

Structural formulae for constructing essays do not acknowledge the extent to which audience affects invention and arrangement. The enthymeme, however, properly understood as a large-scale heuristic and not a sentence-level device, can help the writer consider the questions that concern a particular audience, the probable answers to those questions, potential strategies for presenting those answers, and the shared premises that make reasons persuasive. It can thus provide the basic structure of a whole argument. Teaching the enthymeme helps writers see their rhetorical situation and understand logic as a function of audience assumptions.

305   Kneupper, Charles W. "Teaching Argument: An Introduction to the Toulmin Model." CCC 29 (October 1978): 237–41.

Stephen Toulmin's model of argumentation has three parts: the claim or issue, which concludes the argument; the data, or evidence for the claim; and the warrant, which is the general principle that links data and claim. In simple arguments, the warrant may be assumed. If the warrant is specified, then three more elements enter the model: the qualifier, an acknowledgment that the claim is probably but not certainly true; the reservation, which spells out constraints on the warrant; and the backing, which supports the warrant. Teaching students to analyze essays according to this model will improve their ability to write coherently and argue reasonably.

See: Catherine E. Lamb, "Beyond Argument in Feminist Composition" [503].

306   Schroeder, Christopher. "Knowledge and Power, Logic and Rhetoric, and Other Reflections in the Toulmin Mirror: A Critical Consideration of Stephen Toulmin's Contributions to Composition." *Journal of Advanced Composition* 17 (1997): 95–107.

Philosopher Stephen Toulmin's model of practical reasoning has proved tremendously useful in composition classes. However, writing teachers should be aware of a number of problems with it. Toulmin's model does not distinguish between logically valid and merely probable arguments. It does not require consideration of all available data; on the contrary, it encourages selecting data, perhaps misleadingly, to fit the claim and warrant. The model tends toward relativism in that warrants are presumed not to be universally applicable but to require backing, which depends for acceptance on audience belief. It ignores ethos and pathos as argumentative strategies. It can be used to structure not an entire essay but only individual arguments within the larger text. The most serious problem with the Toulmin model, however, is that it depoliticizes argument, drawing attention away from the social and political power issues that generate claims and legitimate warrants. The function of ideology is obscured. For example, the model itself, fundamentally hierarchical, could be analyzed as an example of masculine thinking, but nothing in the Toulmin approach suggests subjecting it to such analysis.

307   Sosnoski, James J. "Explaining, Justifying, Configuring." *Modern Skeletons in Postmodern Closets: A Cultural Studies Alternative.* Charlottesville: Univ. Press of Virginia, 1995. 70–79.

There are three kinds of academic arguments. "Explanations" work from premises that are established laws, to explain events and give evidence as to how and why they occurred. Such arguments are typical of the natural sciences. "Justifications" work from premises that are not laws but that have to be justified to the audience; they work only for audiences that accept the premises. Such arguments are typical of the social sciences and of literary criticism — for example, of a particular critical school. "Configurations" appeal to the audience's experiences, and they work to the extent that the experience they present or refer to matches the audience's. Literary arguments may also be configurations, when they ask the audience to share the critic's reading experience. Sosnoski analyzes problems with literary criticism that treats its own interpretive premises as established laws. He prefers that literary arguments be configurations, because these work best in accounting for cultural differences among diverse audience members. For the same reason, configurations are the best arguments to use in conveying academic knowledge to the general public.

Audience

308   Ede, Lisa, and Andrea Lunsford. "Audience Addressed/Audience Invoked: The Role of Audience in Composition Theory and Pedagogy." CCC 35 (May 1984): 155–71. Rpt. in Corbett, Myers, and Tate [171].

Two divergent views of audience face the writing teacher, one claiming that it is crucial to writing instruction to identify a real audience (the audience addressed), the other claiming that the audience is fictional and a function of signals given in texts (the audience invoked). Both views miss the dynamic quality of rhetorical situations and the interdependence of reading and writing. To emphasize the audience as addressed tends to undervalue both invention and ethics of language use in the effort to adapt to the "real" audience. On the other side, Ong's view of the audience as a fiction (see [312]), which contrasts the speaker's real, present audience with the writer's distant one, tends to overstate the reality of the speaker's audience as compared with the writer's. Rather, both senses of audience must be understood within the larger rhetorical situation and the many possible roles that may be taken by real readers and imagined by the writer. Braddock Award winner.

309   Elbow, Peter. "Closing My Eyes as I Speak: An Argument for Ignoring Audience." CE 49 (January 1987): 50–69. Rpt. in Graves [376] and in Corbett, Myers, and Tate [171].

Writers should think about their audience, but not always. Some audiences help writers think better, others inhibit or intimidate. Faced with the latter, it is better to ignore the audience or pretend the audience is friendly during the early stages of writing. Not only can this overcome a block, it may lead to new thinking and knowledge. Indeed, this writer-based prose can be better than reader-based prose, in the same way that journal writing can be stronger than formal audience-directed writing. Writing to an audience has been characterized as the higher level cognitively, yet the ability to turn off the audience, to experiment with a more poetic form of language, should be seen as a higher level still.

310   Kirsch, Gesa, and Duane H. Roen. *A Sense of Audience in Written Communication*. Newbury Park, Calif.: Sage Publications, 1990.

Ten essays on the history and theory of audience as a rhetorical concern and six essays reporting on empirical studies of writers' conceptions and use of audience include R. J. Willey, "Pre-Classical Roots of the Addressed/Invoked Dichotomy of Audience"; Stuart Brown and Thomas Willard, "George Campbell's Audience"; Barbara Tomlinson, "Ong May Be Wrong: Negotiating with Nonfictional Readers"; Bennett Rafoth, "The Concept of Discourse Community: Descriptive and Explanatory Adequacy"; Louise Wetherbee Phelps, "Audience and Authorship: The Disappearing Boundary"; Gesa Kirsch, "Experienced Writers' Sense of Audience and Authority: Three Case Studies."

311   Kroll, Barry M. "Writing for Readers: Three Perspectives on Audience." *CCC* 35 (May 1984): 172–85.

Three conceptions of audience are influential in composition teaching: rhetorical, informational, and social. The rhetorical perspective draws from classical theory and recommends adapting speech or writing to the characteristics of the audience. This advice is generally good, but the perspective is flawed: it casts audiences as adversarial, it ignores the impossibility of characterizing most audiences, and it takes an unsophisticated view of reader psychology. The second approach is that writing must convey information to the reader effectively, by attending to the difficulties readers have extracting meaning from texts. But this model, criticized thoroughly by Dillon [173], tends to give a mechanistic and reductive account of text-processing. The third approach is that writing is a social activity like all communication, requiring a decentering from the self that allows the speaker or writer to take another's perspective. Collaborative writing and reader feedback support this approach pedagogically. The "sense of audience" promoted here, though, is vague, and it can be objected that writing is not social but rhetorical, more connected to genre and convention than to social knowledge.

312   Ong, Walter J., S.J. "The Writer's Audience Is Always a Fiction." *PMLA* 90 (January 1975): 9–21.

Writers project audiences for their work by imagining the presumptive audiences of other pieces of writing. Readers seem willing to be fictionalized in this way — to be the audience projected by the writer — as long as the reader's role is familiar or the writer creates a new role persuasively. Thus, the writer's style or voice is a way of addressing an imagined audience that will respond in the desired way.

313   Park, Douglas. "The Meanings of 'Audience.'" *CE* 44 (March 1982): 246–57. Rpt. in Corbett, Myers, and Tate [171] and in Young and Liu [295].

Audience, a crucial part of teaching writing, is difficult to define and to apply. The meanings tend to diverge, on the one hand, toward real people with a set of beliefs and expectations to which the discourse must be adjusted, and, on the other, toward a fictional audience implied by the text itself. In both cases, audience refers to aspects of knowledge and motivation that form the contexts for discourse. Even when identified, its characteristics remain complex; the general audience is that much more elusive. Instead of asking about audience, we might more usefully ask about the conventions that make a piece of writing meaningful to a range of readers, beginning with generally accepted conventions of form and moving toward more particular conventions associated with the subject or genre. Using the class as audience does not solve the problem of defining the appropriate rhetorical contexts. We ask our students to act in sophisticated ways when we call for sensitivity to audience, but we lack a clear understanding of the kinds of writing we ought to teach and fall instead into teaching vaguely defined general writing skills.

314   Petraglia, Joseph. "Spinning Like a Kite: A Closer Look at the Pseudotransactional Function of Writing." *Journal of Advanced Composition* 15 (1995): 19–33.

Transactional writing aims to get things done in the world, such as informing, persuading, or instructing. Most writing in composition classes, however, is pseudotransactional: while students are asked to consider audience, purpose, and appropriate persona, which seem to be rhetorical concerns, assignments often pose hypothetical cases while serving primarily as occasions for grading. Thus, students do not develop a truly rhetorical, self-reflective grasp of discursive practices. Composition teachers have failed to deal with the problem of pseudotransactionality. They either deny it through expressivist pedagogies claiming that students will provide "their own" purposes for writing, or escape it through assigning collaborative work, writing that tests knowledge of reading, or writing-across-the-curriculum. Composition scholars must not let their postmodern skepticism about the possibility of determining assignments' "authenticity" or "reality" prevent them from addressing this problem.

315   Porter, James E. *Audience and Rhetoric: An Archeological Composition of the Discourse Community.* Englewood Cliffs, N.J.: Prentice-Hall, 1992.

From the Western rhetorical tradition, we have inherited a conception of "audience" as a group of real people passively listening to an oral discourse, mere receivers of the communicator's message. Contemporary theory has disrupted this conception, however, with claims that "audience" is actually imagined by the author or called up by the text itself, or even that the notion of discrete individuals who could send or receive messages is problematic. With a survey of conceptions of audience from Aristotle to George Campbell to the New Rhetoric, reader-response criticism, and social constructionism, Porter shows that other disciplinary concerns, as well as cultural and political trends, tend to influence what concept of audience prevails. Porter advocates adherence to a social constructionist view in which the audience collaborates with the writer or speaker in various ways from the beginning of the composing process.

Revision

316   Beach, Richard. "Self-Evaluation Strategies of Extensive Revisers and Non-Revisers." CCC 27 (May 1976): 160–64.

In a limited study of revising, the students who typically revised drafts very little tended to evaluate their drafts in terms of form: "choppy," "awkward," "wordy," and the like. They did not consider content important when revising. The more extensive revisers tended to locate the "centers of gravity" in early drafts and to evaluate drafts in terms of the development of ideas. The extensive revisers found that their evaluations of each draft were helpful guides to further revision and occasions for predicting solutions to problems in a draft.

317   Faigley, Lester, and Stephen P. Witte. "Analyzing Revision." CCC 32 (December 1981): 400–414.

Revisions can be classified as either surface changes or text-based changes. Surface changes do not affect the information content of the text. They can be subdivided into formal changes, such as spelling, and meaning-preserving changes, such as substitutions. Text-based changes do affect the content. They can be subdivided into microstructure changes, which affect local content only, and macrostructure changes, which affect the gist of the whole text. This taxonomy complements studies of revision such as Sommers's [320] by providing a way of indicating the significance of revision changes. "The major implication of this study . . . is that revision cannot be separated from other aspects of composing." Revision studies have not determined what causes writers to revise.

318   Flower, Linda S., John R. Hayes, Linda Carey, Karen Schriver, and James Stratman. "Detection, Diagnosis, and the Strategies of Revision." CCC 37 (February 1986): 16–55.

Successful writers revise in order to adapt the text to their goals. Revision requires knowledge about texts, knowledge about strategies for revising, and a clear intention to use this knowledge to achieve a goal. Beginning writers must clear three hurdles in learning revision: detecting problems in the text, diagnosing the problems, and selecting a strategy. Detecting problems calls for a review of the text, testing it against an imagined ideal text that fulfills the writer's intentions. Many beginning writers see not the actual text but the intended text when they read their own drafts, and many do not form a clear sense of the gist of their own writing. These problems are often compounded by too narrow an intention or the lack of a clear sense of intention. Intention reflects knowledge, so beginning writers may focus on proofreading, which they know to be a feature of finished writing. A stronger sense of purpose and audience brings other features into focus. Diagnosis places problems, once detected, into conceptual categories related, for example, to style or audience. Writers may detect problems and simply do local rewriting. But diagnosis suggests more elaborate revising strategies in response to well-defined problems of knowledge and intention. Braddock Award winner.

319   Mlynarczyk, Rebecca Williams. "Finding Grandma's Words: A Case Study in the Art of Revising." *Journal of Basic Writing* 15 (Summer 1996): 3–22.

A detailed case study of one basic writer reveals that her tendency to revise for surface features only, typical of many student writers, was encouraged by her teacher's being very focused and directive in written and oral comments on a draft. When the teacher abandoned this evaluative role and stopped trying to "fix" the paper according to her own conception of what it should be, but rather discussed the essay content empathetically with the student, the student revised substantively. Mlynarczyk concludes that more open-ended comments addressed to essay content will best encourage substantive revision.

320   Sommers, Nancy. "Revision Strategies of Student Writers and Experienced Adult Writers." CCC 31 (December 1980): 378–88. Rpt. in Enos [449] and in Perl [239].

Revision is a recursive process essential to developing ideas, not merely the last stop in a train of writing tasks. Students usually describe revision as choosing better words and eliminating repetition. They revise to develop ideas only when redrafting the opening paragraph. Adults, on the other hand, usually describe revision as the process of finding the form of an argument and accommodating the audience. Adult writers are more likely to add or delete material and to rearrange sentences and paragraphs as they revise.

321   Yagelski, Robert P. "The Role of Classroom Context in the Revision Strategies of Student Writers." *Research in the Teaching of English* 29 (May 1995): 216–38.

Students in a twelfth-grade advanced composition class focused 81.7 percent of revisions on surface and stylistic changes and only 18.3 percent on more substantive structural and content changes. This occurred even though the class emphasized the writing process, requiring two drafts of each of ten papers, reviewed by peers and by the teacher, and providing class time for rewriting. Evidently, the students' revision choices were strongly influenced by the teacher's retaining all authority for determining what constitutes "good" writing and by her emphasizing correctness as its most important criterion.

Style, Grammar, and Usage

322   Baron, Dennis. *Guide to Home Language Repair*. Urbana, Ill.: NCTE, 1994.

Based on Baron's radio call-in show on grammar and the vagaries of English. Baron answers questions (as "Dr. Grammar") and offers advice on dealing with the Language Police (William Safire and his ilk), the demands of politically correct language, the peculiarities of English spelling, jargon, plagiarism, and sundry other topics.

323   Baron, Dennis E. *Grammar and Good Taste: Reforming the American Language*. New Haven: Yale Univ. Press, 1982.

After the Revolution, English supplanted Latin and Greek as the dominant language of instruction in American schools. Patriots sought to differentiate American from British English by establishing native standards of spelling, grammar, and pronunciation. Some advocated the formation of an American Academy, like the French Academy, to set these standards. The authors of popular grammar textbooks also attempted to set standards. Although no uniform "Federal grammar" emerged, the link between correct grammar and patriotism led to the association of correctness with good morals in general, and hence with social prestige. The link between grammar and morality also fostered intense anxiety about correctness that continues to this day.

See: Francis Christensen, "A Generative Rhetoric of the Paragraph" [297].

324   Christensen, Francis. "A Generative Rhetoric of the Sentence." CCC 14 (October 1963): 155–61. Rpt. in *The Sentence and the Paragraph* [299]; in Francis Christensen, *Notes Toward a New Rhetoric: Six Essays for Teachers* (New York: Harper and Row, 1967); and in Francis Christensen and Bonniejean Christensen, eds., *Notes Toward a New Rhetoric: Nine Essays for Teachers* (New York: Harper and Row, 1978).

Professional writers write "cumulative" sentences, in which modifying words and phrases are added before, within, or after the base clause. The modifiers work at different levels of abstraction and add to the sentence's texture. Students should practice writing cumulative descriptions of objects and events in single sentences, which will make style and content more complex simultaneously. See also Christensen [297].

See: Connors, Robert J. "The Erasure of the Sentence" [85].

325   Corbett, Edward P. J. "Approaches to the Study of Style." In *Teaching Composition: Twelve Bibliographic Essays*. Ed. Gary Tate [40].

This bibliographic essay discusses works on literary style and stylistics, the history of English prose style, theories of style, teaching the analysis of prose style, and teaching students how to improve their writing style.

326   Crew, Louie. "Rhetorical Beginnings: Professional and Amateur." CCC 38 (October 1987): 346–50.

Most amateurs begin an essay by stating their purpose, giving background, or telling results. Professionals hold those moves in reserve. Sixty percent of professionals, compared with 10 percent of student amateurs (in the given sample), begin with narratives. Such openings dramatize the subject and are brief. Professionals use indirection, drop hints, or cite experts in order to contradict them, and use oblique quotations, whereas amateurs attempt to be direct. Amateurs use rhetorical questions and truisms, while professionals rarely do. But when these professional strategies are pointed out, student amateurs learn them quickly.

327   D'Eloia, Sarah. "The Uses — and Limits — of Grammar." *Journal of Basic Writing* 1 (Spring–Summer 1977): 1–20. Rpt. in Corbett, Myers, and Tate [171] and in Enos [449].

Students should learn grammar as part of the writing process. Mina Shaughnessy's work [472] helps us distinguish between true grammar errors and merely accidental errors in student writing. Teachers can address the grammar-based errors through such techniques as dictation, narrowly focused editing, paraphrasing, and imitation. D'Eloia gives much useful advice for teaching grammar.

328   Elbow, Peter. "Reflections on Academic Discourse: How It Relates to Freshmen and Colleagues." *College English* 53 (February 1991): 135–55.

Academic writing teaches valuable habits of mind. But a composition course should not be devoted entirely to teaching academic discourse, because then it will not encourage students to write by choice. Also, the course will not give them practice in two important kinds of nonacademic writing, that which renders rather than explains experience and that which describes disciplinary concepts in the students' own language. Furthermore, academic discourse is difficult to teach because so many varieties of it exist. Nevertheless, some generic features of academic style can be described: academic writing concentrates on giving reasons and evidence for the views expressed; it acknowledges the writer's interests without letting them dominate; it contains frequent signposts to its internal structure; it tends to be explicit about views expressed but indirect about the writer's personal reasons for holding these views; it uses specialized language or jargon; its sentences tend to be long and complex; it projects a tone of authority, often augmented by citations, and exclusion of nonexperts. Elbow recommends teaching only the more intellectual aspects of academic style, such as reliance on reasoning and evidence, and he gives suggestions for how to do so. Students will be inhibited in their writing and thinking if they have to try to adopt all characteristics of academic style at once, he argues. Moreover, even this list of generic features must be tentative in light of how quickly academic discourse is currently changing and diversifying.

See: Erasmus, *Copia* [56].

329   Faigley, Lester. "Names in Search of a Concept: Maturity, Fluency, Complexity, and Growth in Written Syntax." CCC 31 (October 1980): 291–300.

Recent research on syntactic maturity in student writing has relied too uncritically on the measures of complexity devised by Kellogg Hunt. Such research, aimed at testing the efficacy of sentence combining, finds increased T-unit and clause lengths in student writing, but no connection has been established between such complexity and the overall quality of the writing. Moreover, designating writing as more or less mature on the basis of such measures is problematic because T-unit and clause length in adult writing vary with discourse aims. Similarly, fluency depends on intersentence, not intrasentence, relations. We have no adequate description of syntactic complexity because we have no reliable generative grammar. Nonetheless, writing pedagogy emphasizes syntax to the detriment of coherence in the essay as a whole.

330   Finegan, Edward. *Attitudes toward English Usage*. New York: Teachers College Press, 1980.

The war between prescriptive grammar and descriptive linguistics has a long history — from Swift and Johnson to the battle of *Webster's Third*. In the attempt to halt the "degradation" of English, prescriptivists developed the doctrine of correctness, the idea that there are right and wrong grammatical forms. This doctrine dominated language study through the 1800s and continues to dominate teaching and public attitudes toward language. Descriptive linguistics holds that usage determines the language, that different forms have different functions, that spoken language is the language, and that change is inevitable. Although this position has led to modern forms of linguistics, it has not, apparently, changed the general attitude that links "correct" grammar to propriety and even morality. Finegan wittily summarizes the work of teachers and writers on both sides of the war, popular and scholarly, including excellent discussions of the NCTE, Noam Chomsky, Labov [460], and others.

331   Flannery, Kathryn T. *The Emperor's New Clothes: Literature, Literacy, and the Ideology of Style*. Pittsburgh: Univ. of Pittsburgh Press, 1995.

There is no inherently good style. Rather, the style preferred by socially powerful groups becomes established as good. This style is part of the group's cultural capital, helping them maintain their power. Since the late Renaissance, the clear, simple, objective style praised by the Royal Society has been promoted by Western educational institutions. Behind "style talk" that treats style as politically neutral is a conservative agenda of maintaining the cultural status quo, as can be seen in T. S. Eliot's elevation of Francis Bacon's work as model prose. E. D. Hirsch follows the same agenda with his doctrine of "communicative efficiency" in *The Philosophy of Composition*. Literacy education has the institutional role of teaching the plain style to the masses, while literature, with its premium on artifice, remains privileged discourse. Resisting this agenda requires a rhetorical conception of style that valorizes artifice and a range of styles for everyone.

332   Harris, Muriel, and Katherine E. Rowan. "Explaining Grammatical Concepts." *Journal of Basic Writing* 6 (Fall 1989): 21–41.

Editing is a process of detection, diagnosis, and rewriting, not a single final step in the composing process. But prescriptive grammar often does not help unpracticed writers. As Patrick Hartwell [333] argues, most grammar rules are COIK — clear only if known. Learning grammatical terminology, however, is not the same as learning the grammatical concepts necessary for editing. To help students learn the concepts, four techniques are useful: provide background information (i.e., prerequisite concepts) when needed; define critical attributes of the concept; use a variety of examples; and in practice sessions, lead students to formulate questions they can ask themselves.

333   Hartwell, Patrick. "Grammar, Grammars, and the Teaching of Grammar." *CE* 47 (February 1985): 105–27. Rpt. in Enos [449].

The debate about whether grammar instruction improves writing will not be resolved by empirical studies. These studies suggest that grammar instruction has no effect on writing, and they have been attacked by proponents of such instruction. Grammar may be defined in five ways: (1) The internalized rules shared by speakers of a language. These rules are difficult to articulate and are learned by exposure to the language. (2) The scientific study of the internalized rules. Different theories of language generate different systems of rules. These rules do not dictate the actual use of grammar in the first sense. Researchers find no correlation between learning rules and using them, or between using rules and articulating them. (3) The rules promulgated in schools. These are simplifications of scientific grammars and are therefore even further from grammar as used by speakers of the language. They reflect the questionable belief that poor grammar is a cognitive deficiency. Metalinguistic awareness, including some knowledge of grammar, seems to be central to print literacy, but the awareness appears to follow, not generate, print literacy. (4) Grammar as usage: a set of exceptions to grammar rules. (5) Grammar as style: the use of grammatical terms in manipulating style. Much research suggests that active use of language improves writing more than instruction in any grammar.

See: Richard Haswell, "Minimal Marking" [357].

334   Haussamen, Brock. *Revising the Rules: Traditional Grammar and Modern Linguistics*. Dubuque: Kendall Hunt, 1993.

The prescriptive rules of grammar were divorced from descriptive linguistics in the nineteenth century, and trying to remarry them is difficult. The tradition of grammar handbooks is long and deeply ingrained, while linguistics has focused on oral language and theory. Descriptive grammar does, however, have much to offer about grammar conventions that can enliven and improve the grammar we teach to students. Haussamen, a community college teacher, offers new descriptions of old conventions including verb tense, agreement, passive voice, pronoun agreement, and punctuation, all in aid of a more rhetorical approach to grammar.

335   Horner, Bruce. "Rethinking the 'Sociality' of Error: Teaching Editing as Negotiation." *Rhetoric Review* 11 (1992): 172–99; Rpt. in Bruce Horner and Min-Zhan Lu [458].

Writing teachers now generally agree that what counts as "error" in writing is socially determined, yet we continue to treat discrete errors in student papers as failures in the writer's knowledge of correct forms. Rather, we should see errors as instances of the writer's and reader's failure to negotiate an agreement on how their relationship is to be actualized in the text, that is, agreement on the features the text that permits a satisfying relationship will need to have. Such negotiation could help determine, for example, whether a sentence fragment is to be regarded as an error or as a stylistic device. "Basic writers," then, are those who are inept at such negotiation. They need to be taught what it is and how to do it, including how to make decisions about when or whether to use variant dialects of English. Horner concludes with some pedagogical suggestions for how to help basic writers learn to enter into such negotiations while revising their work.

336   Hunter, Susan, and Ray Wallace, eds. *The Place of Grammar in Writing Instruction: Past, Present, Future*. Portsmouth, N.H.: Heinemann-Boynton/Cook, 1995.

Grammar was long regarded as an essential element in the teaching of writing, an attitude criticized and discarded in more recent times. However, the usefulness and methods of grammar instruction are still debated, with some good arguments appearing for at least limited grammar instruction keyed to students' writing. Sixteen essays explore grammar instruction past, present, and future, including Cheryl Glenn, "When Grammar Was a Language Art"; Gina Claywell, "Reasserting Grammar's Position in the Trivium in American Composition"; John Edlund, "The Rainbow and the Stream: Grammar as System versus Language in Use"; R. Baird Shuman, "Grammar for Writers: How Much Is Enough?"; Stuart Brown, Robert Boswell, and Kevin McIlvoy, "Grammar and Voice in the Teaching of Creative

Writing"; and David Blakesly, "Reconceptualizing Grammar as an Aspect of Rhetorical Invention."

337   Kline, Charles R., Jr., and W. Dean Memering. "Formal Fragments: The English Minor Sentence." *Research in the Teaching of English* 11 (Fall 1977): 97–110.

Grammar handbooks, if they do not simply forbid using sentence fragments, give few guidelines for using them effectively. A survey of samples of formal prose shows that accomplished writers use fragments often and in predictable ways. Kline and Memering list and explain the conditions in which fragments are effectively used and argue that such effective fragments should be called "minor sentences" (following Richard Weaver's suggestion) and taught as a stylistic option.

338   Lanham, Richard A. *Analyzing Prose*. New York: Charles Scribner's Sons, 1983.

The dominant theory of prose style prizes clarity, brevity, and sincerity. This theory tries to make prose transparent; it reduces rhetoric to mere ornament; it runs counter to common sense, to what we value in literature, and to the fact that context defines its three main terms. Classical rhetorical terms provide an alternative way to describe prose style. Noun style relies on "be" verbs, prepositional phrases, and nominalized verbs. Verb style uses active verbs. Parataxis is the absence of connecting words between phrases and clauses, and paratactic style uses simple sentences and prepositional phrase strings. Hypotaxis is the use of connecting words, hence a highly subordinated style. Either style may use asyndeton (few connectors) or polysyndeton (many connectors). The "running" style uses parataxis: it is characterized by a serial record of ideas with many parenthetical additions. "Periodic" style is hypotactic: highly organized, reasoned, and ranked. Other stylistic devices (isocolon, chiasmus) affect these styles differently. Descriptive analysis should also account for visual and vocal form, the use of several common and effective tropes and schemes, and high and low diction. The reader's self-consciousness about style tends to direct judgments of style as clear or opaque, but determining the appropriateness of style to a range of purposes through descriptive analysis is a better way to judge prose.

339   O'Hare, Frank. *Sentence-Combining: Improving Student Writing without Formal Grammar Instruction*. Urbana, Ill.: NCTE, 1973.

Although teaching transformational grammar is no more helpful in improving student writing than instructing in traditional grammar, practice in sentence-combining (originally used as a way of teaching grammar) leads to increased syntactic maturity, even in the absence of formal grammar training of any kind. See Donald Daiker, Andrew Kerek, and Max Morenberg, "Sentence-Combining and Syntactic Maturity in Freshman English," CCC 29 (February 1978): 36–41. Cf. Faigley [329].

340   Ohmann, Richard. "Use Definite, Specific, Concrete Language." *CE* 41 (December 1979): 390–97. Rpt. in Corbett, Myers, and Tate [171].

One of the most common revision maxims given in rhetoric textbooks is to substitute concrete for abstract language. This advice springs from an ideology of style that values ahistoricism (focus on the present moment), empiricism (focus on sensory data), fragmentation (objects seen outside the context of social relations), solipsism (focus on individual's perceptions), and denial of conflict (reported facts have the same meaning for everyone). Following this advice may trap students in personal experience and inhibit their ability to think critically about the world. Students need to practice the relational thinking made possible by abstractions and generalizations.

See: National Council of Teachers of English, *The Sentence and the Paragraph* [299].

341   Weathers, Winston. "Teaching Style: A Possible Anatomy." CCC 21 (May 1970): 144–49. Rpt. in Corbett, Myers, and Tate [171].

To teach style, we must convince students that they must master style to express themselves with individuality and to communicate vividly. We must give students a way to recognize and imitate different styles, to incorporate them into extended discourse, and to suit style to the rhetorical situation. Finally, we must demonstrate our own ability to vary style in writing done in front of the class.

Response and Evaluation

342   Anson, Chris M. *Writing and Response: Theory, Practice, and Research.* Urbana, Ill.: NCTE, 1989.

Seventeen essays include Anson, "Response to Writing and the Paradox of Uncertainty"; David Bleich, "Reconceiving Literacy: Language Use and Social Relations"; Louise Phelps, "Images of Student Writing: The Deep Structure of Teacher Response"; Martin Nystrand and Deborah Brandt, "Response to Writing as a Context for Learning to Write"; Susan Wall and Glynda Hull, "The Semantics of Error: What Do Teachers Know?"; Thomas Newkirk, "The First Five Minutes: Setting the Agenda in a Writing Conference"; Richard Beach, "Demonstrating Techniques for Assessing Writing in the Writing Conference" [392].

See: Richard Beach, "Demonstrating Techniques for Assessing Writing in the Writing Conference" [392].

See: John D. Beard, Jone Rymer, and David L. Williams, "An Assessment System for Collaborative Writing Groups: Theory and Empirical Evaluation" [581].

343   Belanoff, Pat. "The Myth of Assessment." *Journal of Basic Writing* 10 (Spring 1991): 54–66.

There are four myths of assessment. The first is that we know what we're testing for. Tests assume, falsely, that we can judge when writing is good enough for some purpose, to satisfy a requirement or to graduate, and they assume that we know what constitutes improvement. The second myth is that we know what we are testing. We cannot test ability, though: we simply judge the quality of a hastily written product, the result of a meaningless task, without reference to the writer at all. The third is that we agree both on criteria and on whether individual papers meet the criteria. But because texts do not contain meaning, readers inevitably differ about whether abstract criteria have been met. The final myth is that there is a standard of good writing that can be applied uniformly, an obvious misapprehension. Even communal portfolio assessment does not eliminate differences in judgment, but, by promoting discussion of teaching and criteria, it improves teaching, and, moreover, appears to be the best way to approach consensus.

344   Belanoff, Pat, and Marcia Dickson. *Portfolios: Process and Product.* Portsmouth, N.H.: Heinemann-Boynton/Cook, 1991.

Twenty-three essays on both practical and theoretical dimensions of portfolio assessment. Units cover proficiency testing, program assessment, using portfolios in courses, and political issues. Essays include Peter Elbow and Pat Belanoff, "State University of New York at Stony Brook Portfolio-based Evaluation Program"; David Smit, Patricia Kolonosky, and Kathryn Seltzer, "Implementing a Portfolio System"; Roberta Rosenberg, "Using the Portfolio to Meet State-Mandated Assessment"; Anne Sheehan and Francine Dempsey, "Bridges to Academic Goals: A Look at Returning Adult Portfolios"; Richard Larson, "Using Portfolios in the Assessment of Writing in the Academic Disciplines"; Jeffery Sommers, "Bringing Practice in Line with Theory: Using Portfolio Grading in the Composition Classroom"; Pamela Gay, "A Portfolio Approach to Teaching a Biology-Linked Basic Writing Course"; and Marcia Dickson, "The WPA, the Portfolio System, and Academic Freedom." Includes a cumulative bibliography of works cited.

345   Belanoff, Pat, and Peter Elbow. "Using Portfolios to Increase Collaboration and Community in a Writing Program." *WPA* 9 (Spring 1986): 27–40.

Students prepare portfolios of three composition-course papers — one narrative or expressive, one formal essay conceptually organized, and one text analysis — plus cover sheets describing their writing processes and an unrevised piece of in-class writing. Students submit one or two pieces at midsemester to be evaluated without prejudice. Grades are pass-fail only, assigned by a group of teachers. The student's own teacher can ask for a second reading. This testing process, unlike the proficiency exam, rewards the student for collaboration and revision. It also builds community among the teachers, who have two chances each semester to discuss writing and grading standards and slowly work toward consensus on some issues. The portfolio system encourages collaboration between teachers and students and gives the teacher's coaching role more credibility. Finally, the system increases collaboration between teachers and program directors by bringing the course content into the open.

346   Black, Laurel, Donald A. Daiker, Jeffrey Sommers, and Gail Stygall, eds. *New Directions in Portfolio Assessment: Reflective Practice, Critical Theory, and Large-Scale Scoring.* Portsmouth, N.H.: Heinemann-Boynton/Cook, 1994.

Twenty-six essays representing a variety of research approaches to the questions of the validity and perceived benefits of portfolio assessment. Essays include Pat Belanoff, "Portfolios and Literacy: Why?"; Edward White, "Portfolios as an Assessment Concept"; Peter Elbow, "Will the Virtues of Portfolios Blind Us to Their Potential Dangers?"; James Berlin, "The Subversions of the Portfolio"; Glenda Conway, "Portfolio Cover Letters, Students' Self-Presentation, and Teachers' Ethics"; John Beall, "Portfolios, Research, and Writing about Science"; James Reither and Russell Hunt, "Beyond Portfolios: Scenes for Dialogic Reading and Writing"; Nedra Reynolds, "Graduate Writers and Portfolios: Issues of Professionalism, Authority, and Resistance"; Irwin Weiser, "Portfolios and the New Teacher of Writing"; Gail Stygall, et al., "Gendered Textuality: Assigning Gender to Portfolios"; Robert Broad, "'Portfolio Scoring': A Contradiction in Terms"; David Smit, "A WPA's Nightmare: Reflections on Using Portfolios as a Course Exit Exam"; and Carl Lovitt and Art Young, "Portfolios in the Disciplines: Sharing Knowledge in the Contact Zone."

347   Charney, Davida. "The Validity of Using Holistic Scoring to Evaluate Writing: A Critical Overview." *Research in the Teaching of English* 18 (February 1984): 65–81.

A good test of writing ability must be both reliable (it must provide reproducible results) and valid (it must actually test what it claims to test). Many writing teachers have rejected quantitative tests as invalid, feeling that they do not actually measure writing ability. But qualitative tests are often unreliable, as raters disagree over what constitutes good writing. The use of holistically scored writing samples is now widely regarded as a reliable and valid testing method. But holistic scorers are often influenced by legibility, length, and unusual diction, casting doubt on the validity of this method.

348   Cooper, Charles R., and Lee Odell, eds. *Evaluating Writing: Describing, Measuring, Judging.* Urbana, Ill.: NCTE, 1977.

Six essays explain current techniques for assessing students' writing, including measures of syntactic complexity, intellectual maturity, and self-evaluating ability. Two important testing methods are described in Cooper and Odell, "Holistic Evaluation of Writing," and Richard Lloyd-Jones, "Primary Trait Scoring."

349   Cooper, Charles R., and Lee Odell, eds. *Evaluating Writing: The Role of Teachers' Knowledge about Text, Learning, and Culture*. Urbana, Ill.: NCTE, 1999.

A collection of seventeen essays covers a number of issues related to response, evaluation, and assessment, including describing students' writing, connecting teaching and evaluation, and examining assumptions and practices. Sections include assessment in four disciplines and the writing of dual-language students. Essays include Charles R. Cooper, "What We Know about Genres, and How It Can Help Us Assign and Evaluate Writing"; Richard W. Beach, "Evaluating Students' Response Strategies in Writing about Literature"; Arnetha F. Ball, "Evaluating the Writing of Culturally and Linguistically Diverse Students: The Case of the African American Vernacular English Speaker"; Chris M. Anson, "Reflective Reading: Developing Thoughtful Ways to Respond to Students' Writing"; Sandra Murphy and Mary Ann Smith, "Creating a Climate for Portfolios"; and Roxanne Mountford, "Let Them Experiment: Accommodating Diverse Discourse Practices in Large-Scale Writing Assessment."

350   Diederich, Paul. *Measuring Growth in English*. Urbana, Ill.: NCTE, 1974.

Diederich discusses factor analysis of readers' responses to essay tests; avoidance of reader bias; reliability of statistical results; standard deviation; comparative reliability of objective and essay tests; and design of tests. Appendices describe criteria for evaluating essay tests, sample essay topics, and sample objective questions. See Cooper and Odell [348] for newer testing methods, but Diederich's work is essential for explaining statistical problems.

351   Faigley, Lester, Roger D. Cherry, David A. Jolliffe, and Anna M. Skinner. *Assessing Writers' Knowledge and Processes of Composing*. Norwood, N.J.: Ablex, 1985.

Current methods of evaluating writing do not adequately reflect the research on composing that has prompted many writing programs to teach the composing process. Better evaluation would consider the literary, cognitive, and social dimensions of composing, and measure what writers know as well as what they do. Two methods developed for this study attempt to assess knowledge and process. In the first method, writers describe the knowledge they will apply to a given writing task (about situation, form, content, and so on). The second method is a "process log" of the actual writing experience. This book presents an extensive overview of research; the results of a study of writers' planning, writing, and revising and their task-related knowledge; and a thorough discussion of the relationship between theories of composing and theories of assessment.

352   Garrison, Roger. "One-to-One: Tutorial Instruction in Freshman Composition." *New Directions for Community Colleges* 2 (Spring 1974): 55–84.

Professional writers learn their craft by writing with the help of an editor. Freshman writers can learn the same way if the classroom is set up as a workshop in which students work independently, at their own pace, and consult the instructor for editorial guidance in brief conferences. The instructor should suggest writing projects tailored to each student's personal or career interests. Garrison provides detailed advice on commenting effectively in a short conference.

353   Greenberg, Karen. "Validity and Reliability Issues in the Direct Assessment of Writing." *WPA: Writing Program Administration* 16 (Fall–Winter 1992): 7–22.

Writing teachers prefer direct assessment — that is, holistically scored essay tests — to indirect, multiple-choice tests. Yet direct assessment is still criticized by the College Board on grounds of inter-rater unreliability, based on studies through the years that show greater reliability for indirect measures. But multiple-choice tests, scored mechanically, will always produce high reliability. Such tests, moreover, focus on the less important components of writing and reflect cultural bias. Differences in judgment on essays reflect the complexity of reading and writing, and good scoring procedures increase reliability. The validity of indirect assessment has long been challenged, yet the College Board — despite the evidence of their own study showing that a writing sample calling for two or more rhetorical tasks has greatest construct validity — champions a cost-effective test that includes multiple choice. Portfolio assessment is clearly more relevant to theory and classroom practice, but it does not yet include a model of good writing that will boost construct validity. Though research is needed in this area, there is sufficient reason to be comfortable with a commitment to direct assessment.

354   Greenberg, Karen, Harvey S. Wiener, and Richard A. Donovan, eds. *Writing Assessment: Issues and Strategies*. New York and London: Longman, 1986.

Twelve essays and an annotated bibliography (fifty-three entries) collected by the National Testing Network in Writing, which is based at the City University of New York. Included are Stephen P. Witte, Mary Trachsel, and Keith Walters, "Literacy and the Direct Assessment of Writing: A Diachronic Perspective"; Edward M. White, "Pitfalls in the Testing of Writing"; Gertrude Conlon, "'Objective' Measures of Writing Ability"; Roscoe C. Brown, Jr., "Testing Black Student Writers"; Gordon Brossell, "Current Research and Unanswered Questions in Writing Assessment."

355   Harris, Muriel. *Teaching One-to-One: The Writing Conference*. Urbana, Ill.: NCTE, 1986.

Conferences should be an integral part of teaching writing. Many teachers find conferences their most helpful pedagogical strategy, useful at every stage of the writing process, and capable of improving the writer's sense of audience and purpose. To have successful conferences, teachers should consider their goals, their role in the conference, meeting formats, and scheduling. Conversation should be purposefully directive or nondirective in keeping with the immediate goals. To diagnose student difficulties and provide help in solving problems, teachers should begin by diagnosing their own criteria, their teaching methods, and the composing styles of the students. Diagnosis leads to strategies for overcoming writer's block, for recognizing cultural differences, and for dealing with learning disabilities. Finally, the conference is a good setting for teaching grammar.

356 Haswell, Richard H., ed. *Beyond Outcomes: Assessment and Instruction Within a University Writing Program.* Ablex, 2001.

357 Haswell, Richard H. "Minimal Marking." *CE* 45 (October 1983): 600–604.

Marking compositions is unpleasant and largely unproductive as well: correcting surface errors has virtually no effect on students' writing. A way to address this level of writing, though, is not to correct errors but to indicate their presence in a line of writing by a check in the margin. This method challenges the student to find and correct the errors, most of which turn out to be careless. Conceptual errors are now easier to address; the teacher's commenting time can be spent on substance; and students move more effectively to mastery.

358 Horvath, Brooke K. "The Components of Written Response: A Practical Synthesis of Current Views." *Rhetoric Review* 2 (January 1985): 136–56. Rpt. in Corbett, Myers, and Tate [358].

The consensus of advice on formative evaluation (feedback on drafts as opposed to summative evaluation of final products) suggests that teachers should avoid correcting and rewriting students' papers and should instead ask questions, suggest changes, and assign new tasks. The goal of formative evaluation is to promote learning and help students approximate skilled writers' behavior. Teachers should remember to put responses in appropriate order (large-scale concerns before mechanics), leave the authorship with the student, and avoid unhelpful comments. Bibliography contains eighty-one annotated items.

359 Huot, Brian. "Toward a New Theory of Writing Assessment." *CCC* 47.4 (December 1996): 549–66.

Traditional writing assessment practices, rooted in positivism, are beginning to be redefined through revised views of validity that account for context, site specificity, and institutional needs. Placement or exit procedures at three universities illustrate "emergent assessment methods" focused on context while bypassing inter-rater reliability. Concerns about reliability are heightened in "contextually stripped environments" but can be just one way to judge a worthwhile assessment. Specific communicative tasks, created within a meaningful rhetorical situation, can eliminate testing technologies and will require different procedures through which to validate these procedures. An assessment scheme rich in context will emphasize local control and will make inter-rater reliability irrelevant.

360   Anson, Chris M. "Response and the Social Construction of Error." *Assessing Writing* 7(2000); 5–21.

Writing instructors remain unsettled about the role of error in response and evaluation, perhaps because there has been very little research on teacher *response to error*. Existing scholarship — numerous attempts to quantify errors — might be extended to explore the social dimensions of error in response to student writing; that is, to tell us what teachers are thinking when they encounter errors in student writing. What sources of knowledge *do* teachers act on in responding to students' errors? Many of the socially constructed decisions about hyphen usage, for example, that take place among editors and publishers, are slow to reach writing teachers, who do not always approach "correctness" as a shifting, constantly modified code of language conventions. The relationship between error and response may be explored through reflective practice and the use of instructional "filters," consciously applied to determine when instruction about error will benefit students. Reflection in action brings into the classroom various histories of conventions and more attention to the relationship between rule-breaking and style, persona, or context. Knowing more about the effects of error on our reading processes unites response practices with realistic, context-based instruction.

See: Priscilla S. Rogers, "Analytic Measures for Evaluating Managerial Writing" [594].

361   Rubin, Donnalee. *Gender Influences: Reading Student Texts*. Carbondale: Southern Illinois Univ. Press, 1993.

Reader-response theories argue that men and women respond differently to literary texts. Nevertheless, research in which a group of male and female teachers were asked to evaluate unidentified essays reveals little gender bias. Longitudinal study of two teachers, one male and one female, also reveals little bias. The better a teacher knows his or her students — through, for example, a pedagogy that uses frequent conferencing — the less gender bias the teacher exhibits. Blind evaluation increases the chance of distortion by essay topics or styles uncongenial to the evaluator's gender identity. A maternal model of teaching, which gives a responsive reading to all students, attends to the contexts of writing, and encourages independence, most tends to obviate gender bias.

362   Smith, Jane Bowman and Kathleen Blake Yancey, eds. *Self-Assessment and Development in Writing: A Collaborative Inquiry*. Cresskill, N.J.: Hampton Press, 2000.

Self-assessment is a phenomenon that can be approached in several ways: historical, theoretical, practical, ethical, and conceptual. Eleven chapters include Thomas L. Hilgers, Edna L. Hussey, and Monica Stitt-Bergh, "The Case for Prompted Self-Assessment in the Writing Classroom"; Susan Latta and Janice Lauer, "Student Self-Assessment: Some Issues and Concerns from Postmodern and Feminist Perspectives"; Rebecca Moore Howard, "Applications and Assumptions of Student Self-Assessment"; Chris M. Anson, "Talking about Writing: A Classroom-Based Study of Students' Reflections on Their Drafts"; Vicki Tolar Collins, "Freewriting in the Middle: Self-Help for College Writers Across the Curriculum"; Irwin Weiser, "Self-Assessment, Reflection, and the New Teacher of Writing."

363   Smith, Summer. "The Genre of the End Comment: Conventions in Teacher Responses to Student Writing." CCC 48.2 (May 1997): 249–68.

End comments on student papers can be understood as secondary speech genres, with "relatively stable content, style, and structure." Not interested in finding contradictions or measuring specificity in teachers' end comments, this study of 313 representative end comments seeks to determine the features of end comments and the range of options available to commenters. Sixteen primary genres were identified, grouped into three categories: judging, reader response, and coaching. The most frequently identified genres included "evaluation of development" and "suggestion for revision of current paper," and 88 percent of end comments begin with a positive evaluation. When patterns of selecting from the repertoire of commenting conventions do not vary, students may dismiss the commentary as generic and formulaic.

364   Sommers, Nancy. "Responding to Student Writing." CCC 32 (May 1982): 148–56. Rpt. in *Teaching Writing: Theories and Practices*. Ed. J. Travers. Glenview, Ill.: Scott, Foresman, 1988.

"Teachers' comments can take students' attention away from their own purposes in writing a particular text and focus that attention on the teachers' purpose in commenting." In this study, comments by teachers directed students to edit sentences and to rethink and expand the topic at the same time. This is contradictory advice, urging students to treat the text as finished while treating the subject as unfinished. Instead of using comments to justify grades, teachers should respond to the meaning and purpose of early drafts and leave editing corrections for later, thus encouraging students to revise more extensively rather than to patch up the text. Braddock Award winner.

365   Straub, Richard. "The Concept of Control in Teacher Response: Defining the Varieties of 'Directive' and 'Facilitative' Commentary." CCC 47.2 (May 1996): 223–51.

With remarkable consistency in the literature, teachers are urged to be facilitative and not directive in their responses to student writing. However, between these two extremes, teacher commentary can take a number of forms that resist a neat binary. Analyzing teacher commentary by *focuses* and *modes* illustrates the varying degrees of control that teachers exercise. Five teachers who wrote comments on the same student draft used different strategies for giving the student help and direction without usurping the student's choices. This study suggests that we "should not reject all directive styles of response any more than we should all adopt some standard facilitative style."

366   Walvoord, Barbara E. Fassler. *Helping Students Write Well: A Guide for Teachers in All Disciplines*. 2nd ed. New York: MLA, 1990.

To help students write well, teachers should communicate expectations clearly, respond to writing without rewriting students' papers for them, and use grades to coach as well as evaluate writing. Walvoord provides a wealth of practical advice, primarily for the novice writing teacher, with sample assignments, student papers, and comments.

367   White, Edward M. *Teaching and Assessing Writing*. 2nd ed. San Francisco and London: Jossey-Bass, 1994.

Assessment can have a damaging influence on writing instruction, but, used properly, may improve teaching and demonstrate the value of what we do. Formative assessment should be used to help students progress and to understand that product assessment is the inevitable end of writing in college. Writing teachers should, for example, help students learn how to take essay tests, which students will encounter frequently. External or summative assessment is similarly inevitable, and writing program administrators are well advised to understand the language of testing from a variety of perspectives, in an effort to produce fair and satisfactory tests. White offers much commonsense advice on testing, organizing holistic tests, program evaluation, and using testing and evaluation in teaching.

368   Yancey, Kathleen Blake. "Looking Back as We Look Forward: Historicizing Writing Assessment as a Rhetorical Act." CCC 50.3 (February 1999): 483–503.

The history of writing assessment can be traced in various ways. The one located in method sees three waves: the first in the form of objective tests, the second as holistically scored essays, and the third or most current as portfolio and programmatic assessment. In the first wave, reliability and testing specialists dominated the field; in the second wave, validity became a major concern, and the disciplinary machinery was developed to support and disseminate expertise in both writing and assessment. The third wave features a model of assessment that emphasizes validity and re-contextualizes reliability through multiple texts, different genres, and/or portfolios; more importantly, the third wave is creating knowledge both about assessment and our own practices. Only recently has assessment been seen as a knowledge-making endeavor. Understanding writing assessment as a rhetorical act that is both humane and ethical marks the most significant change of the last 50 years.

369   Yancey, Kathleen Blake, and Irwin Weiser, eds. *Situating Portfolios: Four Perspectives.* Logan: Utah State Univ. Press, 1997.

Twenty-four essays in four sections — Theory and Power; Pedagogy; Teaching and Professional Development; and Technology — address themes of collaboration, models, and reflection in classroom portfolios, teacher portfolios, and large-scale portfolio assessment. Essays include Peter Elbow and Pat Belanoff, "Reflections on an Explosion: Portfolios in the '90s and Beyond"; Brian Huot and Michael M. Williamson, "Rethinking Portfolios for Evaluating Writing: Issues of Assessment and Power"; Sandra Murphy, "Teachers and Students: Reclaiming Assessment via Portfolios"; Mary Ann Smith, "Behind the Scenes: Portfolios in a Classroom Learning Community"; William Condon, "Building Bridges, Closing Gaps: Using Portfolios to Reconstruct the Academic Community"; Robert P. Yagelski, "Portfolios as a Way to Encourage Reflective Practice among Preservice English Teachers"; Irwin Weiser, "Revising Our Practices: How Portfolios Help Teachers Learn"; Gail E. Hawisher and Cynthia L. Selfe, "Wedding the Technologies of Writing Portfolios and Computers: The Challenges of Electronic Classrooms"; and Kristine L. Blair and Pamela Takayoshi, "Reflections on Reading and Evaluating Electronic Portfolios."

370   Zak, Frances, and Christopher C. Weaver, eds. *The Theory and Practice of Grading Writing.* Albany: State Univ. of New York Press, 1998.

Fifteen essays address "our myopia on the subject of grading" and put grading into dialogue with current theory. Essays include Bruce W. Speck and Tammy R. Jones, "Direction in the Grading of Writing? What the Literature on the Grading of Writing Does and Doesn't Tell Us"; Kathleen Blake Yancey and Brian Huot, "Construction, Deconstruction, and (Over)Determination: A Foucaultian Analysis of Grades"; Michael Bernard-Donals, "Peter Elbow and the Cynical Subject"; Nick Carbone and Margaret Daisley, "Grading as a Rhetorical Construct"; Maureen Neal, "The Politics and Perils of Portfolio Grading"; Cherryl Smith and Angus Dunstan, "Grade the Learning, Not the Writing"; and Peter Elbow, "Changing Grading While Working with Grades."

Curriculum Development

Course Development

371   Bartholomae, David, and Anthony R. Petrosky. *Facts, Artifacts and Counterfacts.* Upper Montclair, N.J.: Boynton/Cook, 1986.

Basic writers can learn to use academic discourse in a course that asks them to read difficult nonfiction books and write about their reading processes. The students find that all reading requires interpretation and that interpretive methods are inevitably culture-bound. They thus come to see that their "problem" as basic writers consists in their use of nonacademic or imperfectly assimilated academic interpretive methods. As they become more familiar with the language and methods of the university, they can create authoritative, academically successful personae in their writing. This book explains the theory behind the authors' University of Pittsburgh course and reproduces course materials, including twenty-four sequenced writing assignments. It also includes chapters by their colleagues on revising, correcting errors, and using personal writing to develop a dialogue between student and text.

372   Dickson, Marcia. *It's Not Like That Here: Teaching Academic Writing and Reading to Novice Writers.* Portsmouth, N.H.: Heinemann-Boynton/Cook, 1995.

A major problem for novices entering the academic discourse community is that they do not understand how they can use their non-academic literacies and personal knowledge there. The Distanced/Personal writing course project attacks this problem by having students research and write about a topic like high-school education, about which they have some personal experience, a topic that can be explored both in the library and by ethnographic research in their home communities. Final papers synthesize these disparate sources. Several chapters give advice on how to help students read difficult academic material and interview others effectively.

373   Dixon, John. *Growth through English.* 3rd ed. 1967. London: Oxford Univ. Press for the National Association for the Teaching of English, NCTE, and MLA, 1975.

"Language is learnt in operation, not by dummy runs." Children need to do more writing in school for their own purposes of self-exploration or communicating personal experience. The development of writing ability thus becomes a social and cognitive process. English education should be based on a "growth model" rather than a "skills" or "cultural heritage" model. Reporting on his conclusions following the 1966 Dartmouth Conference, Dixon gives examples of student writing and suggestions for classroom practice at the elementary and middle-school levels, but his curriculum theory has also influenced college teachers. In this edition, Dixon recommends paying more attention to the students' social world and encouraging students to write in a wider variety of modes.

374   Elbow, Peter. *Writing with Power*. New York: Oxford Univ. Press, 1981.

Learning to master our writing makes us feel that we can express our ideas powerfully and move our audience. Writing well thus becomes an important way of relating to the world. This book works from the same premises as *Writing without Teachers* [397] with many more teaching suggestions, particularly on making writing responsive to audience.

375   Foster, David. *A Primer for Writing Teachers: Theories, Theorists, Issues, Problems*. 2nd ed. Portsmouth, N.H.: Boynton/Cook, 1993.

The teaching of writing has been influenced by a number of theories and traditions. The handbook tradition of error correcting still wields power in the field, although most writing teachers are now convinced that handbook exercises do not improve writing. The rhetorical tradition, revived in the last two decades, emphasizes the communication situation and connects with poststructuralist focus on context. The work of Piaget, Vygotsky, and Bruner in cognitive psychology has led to the development of a variety of cognitive-process models of writing that have been vastly influential in teaching and research. Constructivist views, drawing on the work of Rorty, Bakhtin, and Freire [258, 259], oppose the cognitivist view of language as expression of thought. Cognitive construction implies that mental constructs shape knowledge and understanding; social construction proposes that meaning is a function of social discourse. This perspective emphasizes the negotiation of communal discourse conventions in learning to write. Several discourse systems offer additional theoretical bases for teachers of writing. Relational systems (Burke [166, 167], Moffett [381], Britton [226]) emphasize the interaction between writer and audience; categorical systems (Kinneavy [194], classify topics, strategies, forms, and styles; "micro-rhetorics" (Christensen [297], Alton Becker) focus on the shaping of sentences and paragraphs. Writing teachers must also be aware of the relationship between literacy and dialect, the problems of measuring writing skills, and research in basic writing. Foster concludes with a chapter each on course planning and teaching methods.

See: Paulo Freire and Donaldo Macedo, *Literacy: Reading the Word and the World* [259].

376   Graves, Richard L., ed. *Rhetoric and Composition: A Sourcebook for Teachers and Writers*. 3rd ed. Portsmouth, N.H.: Boynton/Cook, 1990.

Thirty-one previously published essays collected as a resource for practicing writing teachers. Few of the essays from the previous edition appear in this one. There are sections on theory, motivating student writing, and style, as well as stories from the writing classroom. Essays include Maxine Hairston, "The Winds of Change"; Lester Faigley, "Competing Theories of Process" [229]; Robert Brooke, "Underlife and Writing Instruction"; Gabriele Lusser Rico, "Tapping Creative Potential for Writing"; Donald Murray, "Writing and Teaching for Surprise"; Valerie Krishna, "The Syntax of Error"; Francis Christensen, "A Generative Rhetoric of the Sentence" [324]; Winston Weathers, "Grammars of Style: New Options in Composition"; Stephen North, "The Idea of a Writing Center" [643]; Peter Elbow, "Closing My Eyes as I Speak: An Argument for Ignoring Audience" [309]; Linda Brodkey, "On the Subjects of Class and Gender in 'The Literacy Letters'" [444]; and Ann Berthoff, "Paulo Freire's Liberation Pedagogy."

See: Bruce Herzberg. "Community Service and Critical Teaching" [699].

377   Kail, Harvey. "Narratives of Knowledge: Story and Pedagogy in Four Composition Texts." *Rhetoric Review* 6 (Spring 1988): 179–89.

A course or a textbook is like a story about acquiring knowledge, a heroic quest; in the texts considered here, it is a myth of separation, initiation, and return. In Young, Becker, and Pike's *Rhetoric: Discovery and Change* [294], the hero's quest is to reunite the post-Babel world of epistemic alienation by overcoming barriers to communication through the exercise of tortuous heuristics and the disarming of opponents by Rogerian rhetoric, at once winning the trust of the audience and a glimpse of unclouded reality. In Berthoff's *Forming/Thinking/Writing* [287], the hero assails the Castle of Positivism to reclaim the imagination, sailing off on assisted invitations to examine magical objects that lead first to chaos and then to self-recognition. In Coles's *Teaching Composing*, the hero awakens from enchantment by the school, abandons its familiar language, enters the gap of silence between languages, and, with the help of classmate-comrades, gains the freedom of true individual identity. These and other such narratives are founded on social traditions — the Christian search for salvation or the romantic quest for a natural form of individual identity.

378   Kiniry, Malcolm, and Ellen Strenski. "Sequencing Expository Writing: A Recursive Approach." *CCC* 36 (May 1985): 191–202.

The basic-writing program at the University of California at Los Angeles uses a sequence of expository assignments, in order of increasing cognitive complexity, to introduce students to academic writing: listing, definition, seriation (e.g., chronology), classification, summary, comparison/contrast, analysis, and academic argument. These schema, abstracted from a survey of writing assignments in all departments, allow for development, recursivity (repetition of earlier tasks in later assignments), the use of model academic writing, and an introduction to the methods of reasoning in different academic disciplines.

379   Lindemann, Erika. *A Rhetoric for Writing Teachers*. 3rd ed. New York: Oxford Univ. Press, 1995.

Writing is a means of communication (sending a message to a reader in a particular context) as well as a process involving pre-writing, writing, and rewriting. Psychology and linguistics inform modern methods of teaching students to find ideas; choose words; shape effective sentences, paragraphs, and forms of discourse; and revise what they have written. Lindemann provides chapters on each step in the writing process, on premodern rhetoric, on modern grammar, on the evaluation of writing, and on the design of courses. The third edition provides an expanded bibliography and an outline of the history of composition and rhetoric.

380   Miller, Richard E. *As If Learning Mattered: Reforming Higher Education*. Ithaca: Cornell Univ. Press, 1998.

Theories that aim to reform education often have very little impact on what actually happens in classrooms, because academics tend to despise the bureaucratic labor that would make change possible. The few successful reforms have adapted to local conditions, not attempting to radically restructure the school day or the curriculum or to retrain teachers, but negotiating minor adjustments while taking these circumstances into account. The reformer who effects such changes must have the administrative ability of the bureaucrat as well as the creative insight of the intellectual. Miller illustrates how the bureaucrat-intellectual could function through case studies: Matthew Arnold in his role as inspector of schools; the Great Books approach; British cultural studies for open-admissions students; and ethnography as a means for student self-study.

381   Moffett, James. *Teaching the Universe of Discourse*. Boston: Houghton Mifflin, 1968.

English classes in grades K through 12 should focus on language as a symbol system that enables increasingly abstract thought. This view of language is realized in a curriculum that moves students through a "spectrum" of kinds of discourse — interior dialogue, conversation, correspondence, public narrative, and public generalization and inference — that are classified according to the distance between speaker/writer, hearer/reader, and subject. Moving through the spectrum requires increasing efforts to imagine one's audience and what they need to be told about the subject. Lessons can begin with drama performed in class, followed by narrative, moving from diaries and letters to memoirs and biographies. As narration becomes more anonymous, older students move to abstract reasoning. This curriculum is student-centered because it reflects children's cognitive development and because student writing is the principal content. An influential curriculum model, based on the principles developed at the 1966 Dartmouth Conference.

382   Muller, Herbert J. *The Uses of English*. New York: Holt, Rinehart and Winston, 1967.

Summarizing the conclusions agreed upon at the 1966 Dartmouth Conference, Muller makes several recommendations. Children in a democratic school system should not be grouped according to ability; the classroom should also be ethnically and socially diverse. The English curriculum should center on the child's cognitive development, and "good English" should not be taught prescriptively. Literature, not literary criticism, should be taught, with respect for personal responses. English teachers should connect writing with speaking to break down students' tendency to use academic jargon; bring drama into the classroom to foster social maturity and creativity; and use audiovisual media in the classroom and make the study of film, television, and other mass media part of English study. Alternatives to formal examinations should also be sought.

383   Murray, Donald M. *A Writer Teaches Writing*. 2nd ed. Boston: Houghton Mifflin, 1985.

Murray advocates teaching writing through a workshop approach, in which students and teachers seek the surprise of hearing the written voices that engage readers. Drawing on his experience as a Pulitzer Prize–winning journalist, Murray gives detailed advice on teaching the whole writing process, from syllabus design ("inviting writing") to evaluation (helping students learn to evaluate their own drafts).

See: Wayne Campbell Peck, Linda Flower, and Lorraine Higgins. "Community Literacy" [702].

384   Petrosky, Anthony R., and David Bartholomae, eds. *The Teaching of Writing: Eighty-Fifth Yearbook of the National Society for the Study of Education, Part II*. Chicago: Univ. of Chicago Press, 1986.

Eleven comprehensive essays directed to an audience of educators who are not composition specialists. Included are David Bartholomae, "Words from Afar"; John Gage, "Why Write?"; Patricia Bizzell, "Composing Processes: An Overview"; Arthur N. Applebee, "Problems in Process Approaches: Toward a Reconceptualization of Process Instruction"; Rexford Brown, "Evaluation and Learning"; and Paul Kameen, "Coming of Age in College Composition."

385   Reynolds, Mark, ed. *Two-Year College English: Essays for a New Century*. Urbana, Ill.: NCTE, 1994.

Nineteen essays on a variety of issues facing teachers of English in two-year colleges, including Janice Albert, "I Am Not the Look in Your Eyes"; Mary L. Needham, "This New Breed of College Students"; Mary Kay Morrison, " 'The Old Lady in the Student Lounge': Integrating the Adult Female Student into the College Classroom"; Smokey Wilson, "What Happened to Darlene? Reconstructing the Life and Schooling of an Underprepared Learner"; Kate Mangelsdorf, "Latina/o College Writing Students: Linguistic, Cultural, and Gender Issues"; Raelyn Agustin Joyce, "Aliteracy among Community College Students"; Claudia Barrett and Judith Wootten, "Today for Tomorrow: Program and Pedagogy for 21st-Century College Students"; Myrna Goldenberg and Barbara Stout, "Writing Everybody In"; Judith Rae Davis and Sandra Silverberg, "The Integration Project: A Model for Curriculum Transformation"; Ellen Andrews Knodt, "If at First You Don't Succeed: Effective Strategies for Teaching Composition in the Two-Year College"; Nell Ann Pickett, "A Quarter Century and Beyond: My Story of Teaching Technical Writing"; Jean Bolen Bridges, "Honors English in the Two-Year Colleges"; Mark Harris and Jeff Hooks, "Writing in Cyberspace: Communication, Community, and the Electronic Network"; Al Starr, "Community College Teaching: Endless Possibilities"; Bertie E. Fearing, "Renewed Vitality in the 21st Century: The Partnership between Two-Year College and University English Departments"; and Keith Kroll, "(Re)Viewing Faculty Preservice Training and Development."

386   Shor, Ira. *Critical Teaching and Everyday Life*. Boston: South End Press, 1980.

Open-admissions policies have brought increasing numbers of working-class students into American colleges. They need to learn how to distance themselves from their everyday experience in order to analyze it critically, a first step toward understanding and acting on their political situation. Shor shows howitical situation. Shor shows how encourages such analysis while reducing the teacher's authority. The most complete application of the ideas of Paulo Freire [258] to American education. Cf. Berthoff [153] and Fiore and Elsasser [450].

387   Shor, Ira, and Caroline Pari. *Critical Literacy in Action*. Portsmouth, N.H.: Heinemann-Boynton/Cook, 1999.

Seventeen previously published essays elaborating Freirean critical pedagogy, with a new introductory essay by Shor, "What Is Critical Literacy?" Other essays include Elsa Auerbach's essay on adult ESL teaching, "Teacher, Tell Me What to Do"; Beverly Tatum, "Teaching White Students about Racism: The Search for White Allies and the Restoration of Hope," which proposes alternatives to the oppressor/victim roles of whites and blacks; Tom Fox's critique of extant models of racial and linguistic differences, "Basic Writing as Cultural Conflict"; Terry Dean, "Multicultural Classrooms, Monocultural Teachers" [447]; Houston Baker's 1992 Presidential Address to the MLA, "Local Pedagogy; or, How I Redeemed My Spring Semester"; Jane Nagle, "Social Class and School Literacy," which challenges middle-class assumptions about the goals of working-class students; Dale Bauer, "The Other 'F' Word" [483]; Bruce Herzberg, "Community Service and Critical Teaching" [699]; and James Berlin, "Students (Re)Writing Culture," from *Rhetorics, Poetics, and Cultures* [515].

388   Small, Robert C., Jr., and Joseph E. Strzepek. *A Casebook for English Teachers: Dilemmas and Decisions*. Belmont, Calif.: Wadsworth, 1988.

Thirty-three cases dramatically present problems that call for ethical and pedagogical solutions, for example, dialect prejudice, sexual stereotyping, hostile reactions to group work, students unprepared for class, plagiarism, grade complaints, failed lessons, boring papers, unwillingness to participate in class discussion, and mechanical errors in papers. Each case is followed by analytic questions, suggestions for approaching the problem from different angles, possible pedagogical solutions or follow-up activities, and reading suggestions. Though designed for secondary-school teachers, most cases apply as well to college classes.

389   Summerfield, Judith, and Geoffrey Summerfield. *Texts and Contexts: A Contribution to the Theory and Practice of Teaching Composition*. New York: Random House, 1986.

Human discourse is produced in reaction to social contexts. People adopt a variety of roles constructed in discourse, roles that can be understood as occupying a position on a spectrum from participant in the social context to spectator of it. Participant texts tend to offer many sensory impressions of the context but little explanation of it. They also tend to be structured paratactically. Spectator texts tend to evaluate the social context from a critical distance, to seek connections among contexts, and to be structured hypotactically. Students can be stimulated to write in a variety of participant and spectator roles as they react to texts by others. They can thus test the purposes and effects of taking different roles, develop commitment in writing, and become more critical as readers.

See: Barbara E. Fassler Walvoord, *Helping Students Write Well: A Guide for Teachers in All Disciplines* [366].

390   Tate, Gary, Amy Rupiper, and Kurt Schick, eds. *A Guide to Composition Pedagogies*. NY: Oxford Univ. Press, 2001.

This collection of twelve original essays serves as an introduction to composition studies and its wide range of current pedagogies and also offers an overview of the pedagogical approaches important in the discipline. Process, expressive, rhetorical, collaborative, cultural studies, critical, feminist, community service, writing center, and basic writing pedagogies, as well as writing across the curriculum and technology and the teaching of writing, are each explained in a separate essay which includes bibliographic guides. Contributors include Lad Tobin, Christopher Burnham, William A. Covino, Rebecca Moore Howard, Diana George, John Trimbur, Ann George, Susan C. Jarratt, Laura Julier, Susan McLeod, Eric H. Robinson, Deborah Mutnick, and Charles Moran.

391   Williams, James D. *Preparing to Teach Writing: Research, Theory, and Practice*. 2nd ed. Mahwah, N.J.: Lawrence Erlbaum Associates, 1998.

Teachers of writing in college face an extensive field of theory and practice related to writing, rhetoric, classroom management, assignments, and assessment. In ten chapters, Williams presents exceptionally clear summaries of these concerns, offering theoretical background as well as practical options. Chapters include an overview of the history of rhetoric and its relation to writing instruction; explanations of the main current theories of composition; the workshop classroom; how to teach reading, grammar, and style; ESL, Ebonics, and non-standard English; and commenting on and assessing writing.

Collaborative Learning

392   Beach, Richard. "Demonstrating Techniques for Assessing Writing in the Writing Conference." CCC 37 (February 1986): 56–65.

Some students need instruction in assessing writing beyond either reader-based feedback or the teacher's identification of problems in the text. Such instruction can be offered in a conference in which the teacher first demonstrates describing, judging, and selecting appropriate revisions, then describes the rhetorical context of purpose and audience used as criteria for assessment, and finally asks the student to practice this technique. When writers describe their goals in rhetorical terms, they articulate the bases for making judgments, which leads to revision strategies. Students can be given an assessment form before the conference, asking them to describe goals and audience, identify problems, and suggest changes. In conference, the teacher can then focus on the students' difficulties with these categories, helping them see the nature of rhetorical goals, sensing dissonance between goals and the text, and so on.

See: John D. Beard, Jone Rymer, and David L. Williams, "An Assessment System for Collaborative Writing Groups: Theory and Empirical Evaluation" [587].

393   Brooke, Robert. *Writing and Sense of Self: Identity Negotiation in Writing Workshops.* Urbana, Ill.: NCTE, 1991.

Learning to write requires seeing oneself as a person who uses writing to solve problems and accomplish purposes in many areas of one's life, not only in school. To foster this vision, the writing class should encourage students to try on various social roles in their writing and to negotiate a writer's identity for themselves. The teacher should coach apprentices and offer instruction about writing (writing processes, formal rules, etc.) only as needed to help students write what they want. This approach also encourages students to use writing to address public problems beyond the classroom.

394   Brooke, Robert, Ruth Mirtz, and Rick Evans. *Small Groups in Writing Workshops.* Urbana, Ill.: NCTE, 1994.

Writing groups facilitate four elements that are essential to a writer's life: time for writing, ownership of the uses of writing, a community of responders, and exposure to other people's writing. Groups are complex communities, with social and emotional challenges for students. Such challenges are opportunities for learning to deal with differences of many kinds. Teachers are challenged, too, to see themselves as writers in communities and to formulate successful pedagogies. Teachers must, for example, facilitate student role experimentation in groups, design writing activities, provide rules for response, adjust rules as needed, monitor group dynamics, and evaluate group work. The authors give specific, detailed advice about teaching courses with small group workshops.

395   Bruffee, Kenneth A. "The Brooklyn Plan: Attaining Intellectual Growth through Peer-Group Tutoring." *Liberal Education* 64 (December 1978): 447–69.

Student tutors are sometimes more effective than teachers in helping other students gain confidence and ability in writing because the students are engaged socially and intellectually at once. In the Brooklyn Plan, tutors who have been trained in an advanced composition course help other students in expository composition. The tutors gain, too, by becoming more committed to quality in their own writing. Bruffee describes the tutor-training program.

See: Kenneth Bruffee, "Collaborative Learning and the 'Conversation of Mankind' " [164].

396   Bruffee, Kenneth A. *Collaborative Learning: Higher Education, Interdependence, and the Authority of Knowledge*. Baltimore: Johns Hopkins Univ. Press, 1993.

Collaborative learning embodies a nonfoundational conception of knowledge as communal consensus achieved by conversation. A foundational or cognitive conception that knowledge is a transferable entity now dominates university teaching. This view maintains the authority of knowledge and the authority of the teacher, challenged by collaboration and its assumption that knowledge is socially constructed. In college, students must enter new communities and cultures. Collaborative learning is the most effective way to gain such acculturation because it works as cultures really do, through social interaction. Conversation allows people to cross boundaries, to become more like others and learn a new discourse. Not only is collaboration more effective than top-down learning, it creates more critical acuity as well. Collaborative teachers use different teaching procedures: setting group tasks, managing the groups, and keeping time. The process teaches interdependence, vital in our interdependent world, while helping students understand the nature of knowledge and its creation.

See: Gregory Clark, *Dialogue, Dialectic, and Conversation* [169].

397   Elbow, Peter. *Writing without Teachers*. New York: Oxford Univ. Press, 1973.

Many writers have been trained to think that good writing proceeds from an organized outline through a near-perfect rough draft to an error-free final draft. This view is wrong for many writers, for it assumes that writers know exactly what they want to say before they begin writing. For those who don't (most of us), a better way to begin is "freewriting," deliberately unfocused but sustained written brainstorming from which a "center of gravity" for an organized essay can emerge. Working on drafts is then a process of "growing," or allowing the organization to remain flexible at first while you generate as many ideas as possible on your subject, and "cooking," or submitting your draft to constructive critical interaction with the demands of fellow writers, literary genres, or your own expectations. A group of people committed to working on their writing in this way can form a teacherless class. They can work on academic writing, too, if they understand that academic work is carried on by the interplay of the "doubting game" — radical skepticism about another's work — and the "believing game" — fully entering another's worldview.

See: Stephen M. Fishman and Lucille McCarthy, *John Dewey and the Challenge of Classroom Practice* [181].

398   Forman, Janis, ed. *New Visions of Collaborative Writing.* Portsmouth, N.H.: Boynton/Cook, 1992.

Nine essays extend the theory and practice of collaborative writing, including Anne Ruggles Gere and Laura Jane Roop, "For Profit and Pleasure: Collaboration in Nineteenth Century Women's Literary Clubs"; John Trimbur and Lundy Braun, "Laboratory Life and the Determination of Authorship"; Mary Lay, "The Androgynous Collaborator: The Impact of Gender Studies on Collaboration"; John Schilb, "The Sociological Imagination and the Ethics of Collaboration"; and Cynthia Selfe, "Computer-Based Conversations and the Changing Nature of Collaboration."

399   Gere, Anne Ruggles. *Writing Groups: History, Theory, and Implications.* Carbondale: Southern Illinois Univ. Press, 1987.

Since the eighteenth century, American college students have formed literary clubs — essentially writing groups — to coach one another on writing and speaking. Literary clubs that featured formal presentation and critique of papers were also popular among adults, at least until the twentieth century, and offered intellectual opportunities that were especially important to women. Writing groups work against alienation and the solo-performer view of the author. Vygotsky's theory that language development is socially conditioned, along with recent revisionist work on literacy as a communal phenomenon, partly explains why group work helps students write better. Groups work best when all members have agreed on clearly defined tasks and on ways to evaluate their performance on these tasks. Includes an extensive annotated bibliography.

See: Karen Burke LeFevre, *Invention as a Social Act* [292].

400   Lunsford, Andrea, and Lisa Ede. *Singular Texts/Plural Authors: Perspectives on Collaborative Writing.* Carbondale: Southern Illinois Univ. Press, 1990.

Despite the dominant trope of writing as a solitary act, the results of two surveys and follow-up interviews demonstrate that collaborative writing is a fact of life for many professionals, as it is for the authors. Descriptions of several writers and scenes of writing act as snapshots of "everyday, commonsense collaboration" and provide insights into the social process and contexts for collaborative writing for members of several academic disciplines. A history of the concept of authorship illustrates the complex role of the author in our culture; for example, destabilized by contemporary theories, concepts of individual authorship have nevertheless persisted in composition studies, alongside a developing pedagogy of collaboration. Because hierarchical modes of collaboration are dominant, dialogical modes often serve a subversive purpose by including a plurality of voices. Further studies of authorship and collaboration need to acknowledge material changes in technology and copyright laws in order to interrogate both theory and practice for social writing processes. Appendices include copies of the questionnaires, summaries of responses, and collaborative writing assignments.

See: Joan Mullin and Ray Wallace, *Intersections* [639].

401   Spear, Karen. *Sharing Writing: Peer Response Groups in English Classes.* Portsmouth, N.H.: Heinemann-Boynton/Cook, 1988.

Peer-response groups must first learn how groups work. Peer interaction needs to be seen as part of the composing process, and students need instruction in how to read each other's drafts to overcome confusion about sharing writing. Students' tendency to stand in for the teacher should be replaced by real collaborative behavior. The teacher's role is to recognize successful group work and foster it. Spear offers detailed advice on running a class with groups, focusing on interpersonal relationships.

402   Trimbur, John. "Consensus and Difference in Collaborative Learning." *CE* 51 (October 1989): 602–16.

The purpose of collaborative learning as described by Bruffee [395] and Wiener [403] is to help students experience the process of negotiating and reaching consensus. This goal has been attacked on the ground that it subjects individual students to leveling peer pressure. But since individuals must face peer pressure as part of living in society, collaborative learning can help them learn how to deal with it. Moreover, the collaborative approach can teach students how to deflect control by authorities to which they might be subject as isolated individuals. Some critics of collaborative learning caution that consensus may actually be acquiescence to prevailing social attitudes;

consensus would thus reproduce the oppressions of a nonegalitarian social structure. Richard Rorty, whose views are called upon to support collaborative learning, seems to exacerbate that danger by presenting consensus as a seamless conversational web that can be ruptured only occasionally by individuals. But, contrary to Rorty's thinking, most people participate in a variety of overlapping discourses that often come into conflict. Thus, a collaborative classroom would treat "dissensus," however muted, as the normal state of affairs in most discourse communities and would teach students to think of genuine consensus, following Habermas, not as something achievable but as a commitment to engage in polyvocal conversations as free from relations of domination as possible.

403   Wiener, Harvey S. "Collaborative Learning in the Classroom: A Guide to Evaluation." *CE* 48 (January 1986): 52–61. Rpt. in Corbett, Myers, and Tate [171].

In a collaborative classroom, students work in small groups on a task designed by the teacher. Each group reports its results to the whole class while the teacher mediates differences and highlights important features of the task. The teacher can bs of the task. The teacher can b a task-setter who must design problems that involve students in complex negotiations and provide guidelines for reaching consensus; as a classroom manager who must organize groups efficiently; as a facilitator who must help all students to participate while intervening minimally; and as a synthesizer who must help the class compare the groups' results and lead them to appreciate the intellectual purposes of the task rather than simply to seek the right answers.

Essay and Personal Writing

404   Anderson, Chris, ed. *Literary Nonfiction: Theory, Criticisms, Pedagogy.* Carbondale: Southern Illinois Univ. Press, 1989.

New Journalism and personal essays by contemporary men and women of letters are often studied in composition classes. This intersection of literature and rhetoric is explored in the seventeen essays in this volume, presenting readings of individual authors, theoretical commentary on the essay form, and pedagogical strategies. Essays include Charles Schuster, "The Nonfictional Prose of Richard Selzer"; Suzanne Clark, "Annie Dillard"; Carl H. Klaus, "Essayists on the Essay"; George L. Dillon, "Fiction in Persuasion: Personal Experience as Evidence and Art"; Peter Elbow, "Gretel Ehrlich and Richard Selzer"; John Clifford, "Responding to Loren Eiseley's 'The Running Man'"; and Pat Hoy II, "Students and Teachers under the Influence: Image and Idea in the Essay."

See: Akua Duku Anokye, "Oral Connections to Literacy" [440].

405   Bloom, Lynn Z. "The Essay Canon." *College English* 61 (March 1999): 401–30.

The essay is now read primarily in composition anthologies, whose contents thus reveal the essay canon of the time. In anthologies, an "essay" may be virtually any nonfiction prose piece, such as the Gettysburg Address. Short or abridged pieces are favored. They must also be teachable (not too difficult for first-year students, for example), provocative (according to writing teachers' proclivities), and suitable as models of form and style for undergraduate writing. Permissions costs must also be affordable. Bloom surveyed fifty-eight best-selling anthologies in multiple editions from World War II to the present, to compile the list printed here of most-anthologized authors and essays (in first place is George Orwell's "Politics and the English Language"). Bloom deplores the dull study questions that usually accompany essays in anthologies and the neglect of the genre by MLA and CCCC. More serious pedagogical and scholarly attention to the genre might result in a less conservative canon.

406   Coles, William E., Jr. *The Plural I: The Teaching of Writing.* New York: Holt, Rinehart and Winston, 1978. Upper Montclair, N.J.: Boynton/Cook, 1988.

Students produce "themewriting" — correct but meaningless prose — when teachers correct only for mechanics and style and never comment on content. Coles sets forth a thirty-lesson writing course that focuses on content by identifying an intellectual problem that the class will work on together throughout the semester. Assignments pose increasingly difficult questions about the common problem. Class discussion of students' essays creates a productive self-consciousness about using language.

407   Connors, Robert J. "Personal Writing Assignments." CCC 38 (May 1987): 166–83.

Through most of its history, instruction in rhetoric aimed to equip students to write or speak on any *objective* topic. The rhetor was to be knowledgeable and impersonal in treating subjects. In the seventeenth and, especially, the eighteenth centuries, personal tastes and feelings became more acceptable, particularly in essays and narratives. Nineteenth-century romanticism brought a dramatic shift in the direction of personal writing, and rhetoric instruction, following suit, came to emphasize everyday language (as opposed to Ciceronian high style), assignments that called upon personal experience (rather than abstract ideas), and invention methods for probing personal experience (rather than for searching academic knowledge). By the early twentieth century, novelty — one's own new experience — became a criterion for good writing. Several objective modes remained — impersonal or public topics were still assigned for exposition and argument exercises — but personal assignments remained an important, if contested, element of the composition curriculum.

See: Peter Elbow, *Writing without Teachers* [397].

408   Elbow, Peter, ed. *Landmark Essays on Voice and Writing*. Davis, Calif.: Hermagoras Press, 1994.

Seventeen essays, beginning with an analytical introduction by Elbow and including Mikhail Bakhtin, "Discourse in Life and Discourse in Art"; Walker Gibson, "The 'Speaking Voice' and the Teaching of Composition"; Barbara Johnson, "Translator's Introduction to Dissemination"; bell hooks, "When I Was a Young Soldier for the Revolution: Coming to Voice"; June Jordan, "Nobody Mean to Me Than You: And the Future Life of Willie Jordan"; I. Hashimoto, "Voice as Juice: Some Reservations about Evangelic Composition"; Lester Faigley, "Judging Writing, Judging Selves"; Toby Fulwiler, "Looking and Listening for My Voice"; and Randall Freisinger, "Voicing the Self: Toward a Pedagogy of Resistance in a Postmodern Age."

409   Harris, Jeanette. *Expressive Discourse*. Dallas: Southern Methodist Univ. Press, 1990.

All discourse can be described as expressive of the writer's ideas and feelings, and virtually no discourse is entirely expressive — that is, devoid of a desire to communicate. Thus, although the category "expressive discourse" is in a sense false, the concept has aided the development of composition pedagogy. Four types of expressive discourse have been promoted. (1) The interior text is the unwritten text in a writer's mind. It serves as the model of the text to be created and may drive the desire to see the text realized. (2) Generative texts include reading journals, summaries, position papers, personal reaction papers, and so on, which help prepare students for more formal writing. (3) Aesthetic discourse forms — poems, stories, and plays — are often taught on the questionable assumption that practicing these forms improves writing generally. (4) Experience-based discourse, or the essay on personal experience, is the type most often assigned in composition classes. There is no evidence that it helps students improve their writing. Moreover, such assignments tend to dichotomize personal writing and information-based writing when a preferable approach is to help students integrate the two.

410   Hollis, Karyn. "Liberating Voices: Autobiographical Writing at the Bryn Mawr Summer School for Women Workers, 1921–1938." CCC 45 (February 1994): 31–60.

The Bryn Mawr Summer School boasted a distinguished faculty, an innovative interdisciplinary curriculum, and an equally innovative pedagogy that included peer collaboration, guided revision, student publication, and links between personal experience and academic disciplines. Writing an autobiography was a key assignment. Today, some critics charge that the autobiographical sensibility is compromised by the masculine belief in a unified self. The Summer School assignments, however, show awareness of the need to be critical of the status quo and not present the themes of bourgeois life as norms. The most popular topic in the autobiographies is work. Most of the autobiographies show a shift from a narrative "I," typical of the unitary bourgeois consciousness, to "we," along with a shift from past to present tense, the "I" being critical and the "we" offering responses to exploitation. This identification with other workers, or with women, or with the family, is the voice of public resistance and empowerment, counteracting the powerless social atom represented by the "I" narrator. Follow-up studies show that many of the students went back to their communities to become civic, church, and union leaders. The "we" of collective subjectivity is rarely seen in student autobiography, but the sense of collective endeavor that supports it might well be encouraged as a way to change consciousness.

411   Macrorie, Ken. *Telling Writing*. Rochelle Park, N.J.: Hayden, 1970.

College students are urged to write dull, impersonal prose: "Engfish." They will write better and learn more if they see writing as a way of telling the truth about their experiences. This textbook contains lessons on telling facts, working through facts to large meanings, using a journal, sharpening word choice, and writing critically. See also *Uptaught* (Rochelle Park: Hayden, 1970), in which Macrorie describes how his dissatisfaction with his own teaching and school standards led him to develop the "telling writing" pedagogy.

See: Richard E. Miller, "Fault Lines in the Contact Zone" [198].

See: James Moffett, *Teaching the Universe of Discourse* [381].

412   Morgan, Dan. "Ethical Issues Raised by Students' Personal Writing." *College English* 60 (March 1998): 318–25.

Teachers who assign personal writing are often distressed by students' apparent disclosure of criminal behavior or severe emotional problems. Administrators should provide clear guidelines for when and how such self-disclosure should be reported; but teachers should realize that counseling services at many schools are inadequate. Sometimes, teachers just need to listen sympathetically while maintaining appropriate professional distance. Morgan also suggests that teachers emphasize audience and purpose in writing assignments, using sample papers from earlier classes to show what kinds of problems arise when explosively self-disclosing pieces are offered for class discussion. Teachers may also rule some topics out of bounds — illegal activities, for example — and may deal with self-disclosing drafts in conference. Teachers should seek readings (not commonly found in composition anthologies) that deal with the kinds of personal topics students usually choose, such as divorce or alcoholism, in appropriate ways. Morgan sensibly acknowledges the limitations of all these suggestions, but deplores the solution that abandons all personal writing assignments.

413   Schroeder, Christopher, Helen Fox, and Patricia Bizzell, eds. *ALT Dis: Alternative Discourses and the Academy*. Portsmouth, N.H.: Boynton/Cook, 2002.

Debate continues over the fundamental assumption that all students need to learn traditional academic discourse while many academics and students develop "hybrid," "mixed," "alternative," or "constructed" forms of academic discourse. Fifteen essays include the following: Patricia Bizzell, "The Intellectual Work of 'Mixed' Forms of Academic Discourses"; Malea Powell, "Listening to ghosts: An alternative (non)argument"; Jacqueline Jones Royster, "Academic Discourses or Small Boats on a Big Sea"; Sidney I. Dobrin, "A Problem with Writing (about) 'Alternative' Discourse"; Haixia Lan, "Contrastive Rhetoric: A Must in Cross-Cultural Inquiries"; Christopher Thaiss and Terry Myers Zawacki, "Questioning Alternative Discourses: Reports from Across the Disciplines"; LuMing Mao, "Re-Clustering Traditional Academic Discourse: Alternating with Confucian Discourse"; Laura Lai Long, "Full (dis)Course Meal: Some Words on Hybrid/Alternative Discourses"; Michael Spooner, "An Essay We're Learning to Read: Responding to Alt.Style."

414   Spellmeyer, Kurt. "A Common Ground: The Essay in the Academy." CE 51 (March 1989): 262–76.

Proponents of teaching academic discourse depict learning to write as constructing one's knowledge and one's very self through a discourse given by tradition. This approach ignores something universal in all uses of discourse, namely the individual writer's attempts to work out interpretations of experience that make sense to him or her, that allow him or her to retain or reconstruct a feeling of personal coherence. Unity within the writer and within the discourse is best achieved through a form that owes as little as possible to tradition, that contravenes convention for the sake of reproducing the personal viewpoint, yet recognizes stylistic constraints imposed by the attempt to make the personal viewpoint public. The essay best meets this need. Students should be encouraged to write essays in order to learn to put their own stamps on any discourse they employ.

415   Tobin, Lad. "Car Wrecks, Baseball Caps, and Man-to-Man Defense: The Personal Narratives of Adolescent Males." *College English* 58 (February 1996): 158–75.

Many male students write personal essays that celebrate acts of machismo in clichéd language. Both male and female teachers tend to overreact negatively to such essays. To better understand both these students' writing and their personal development, teachers should study how masculine identities are constructed in American culture — considering, for example, the significance of the automobile. They should be especially careful not to impose their own cultural agendas when coaching revision. They should force themselves to respond empathetically even to the most openly defiant or disengaged students. Tobin illustrates the success of these approaches through a semester's experience with one male student's writing.

416   Trimmer, Joseph F., ed. *Narration as Knowledge: Tales of the Teaching Life*. Portsmouth, N.H.: Heinemann-Boynton/Cook, 1997.

Deliberately avoiding academic methods of empirical or ethnographic reporting, the nineteen teachers included here tell stories about their teaching experiences in ways that attempt to make full use of the literary resources of the essay genre. Among the essays, which both exemplify and discuss personal writing, are Victor Villanueva, Jr., "Shoot-Out at the I'm OK, You're OK Corral"; Lad Tobin, "Reading and Writing about Death, Disease, and Dysfunction; or, How I've Spent My Summer Vacations"; Lynn Z. Bloom, "Subverting the Academic Master Plot"; Cecelia Tichi, "The Teflon Lesson and Why It Didn't Stick"; Sondra Perl, "Facing the Other: The Emergence of Ethics and Selfhood in a Cross-Cultural Writing Classroom"; and Wendy Bishop, "What We Don't Like, Don't Admit, Don't Understand Can't Hurt Us, Or Can It? On Writing, Teaching, Living."

417   Yancey, Kathleen Blake, ed. *Voices on Voice*. Urbana, Ill.: NCTE, 1994.

Voice as a metaphor for style signals a focus on the writer as an individual, on the drive to express oneself, and on the search for personal authenticity, for a distinctive or a natural sound, and for control of various personae that may inhabit a text or speak to a particular discourse community or speak within a particular culture. Eighteen essays explore the range of meanings and pedagogical uses of the idea of voice, including Peter Elbow, "What Do We Mean When We Talk about Voice in Texts?"; Doug Minnerly, "Affect and Effect in Voice"; Nancy Allen and Deborah Bosley, "Technical Texts/Personal Voice: Intersections and Crossed Purposes"; Carl Klaus, "The Chameleon 'I': On Voice and Personality"; Margaret Woodworth, "Teaching Voice"; John Albertini, Bonnie Meath-Lang, and David Harris, "Voice as Muse, Message, and Medium: The Views of Deaf College Students"; Tom Carr, "Varieties of the 'Other': Voice and Native American Culture"; John Powers and Gwendolyn Gong, "East Asian Voice and the Expression of Cultural Ethos"; Susan Brown Carlton, "Voice and the Naming of Woman"; Randall Freisinger, "Voicing the Self: Toward a Pedagogy of Resistance in a Postmodern Age"; and Peter Elbow and Kathleen Blake Yancey, "An Annotated and Collective Bibliography of Voice."

Literature and Composition

418   Berthoff, Ann E. "Is Reading Still Possible?" *The Sense of Learning* [151].

To read is necessarily to interpret. As we construe the letters, words, and sentences, we construct meaning in light of both what we imagine, from other reading experiences, will be coming next, and what meanings we have just made in working with the particular text. Constructing a plausible reading of a text is like translating it from one language to another. In the process of constructing meaning, the reader must tolerate ambiguity as different possible interpretations develop. There may be variant readings but also incorrect ones. These processes of simultaneously construing and constructing are also at work both when we listen effectively (a hint here to improve student note-taking) and when we write. Always we are using signs to actively make sense of the world.

See: Linda Brodkey, "Modernism and the Scene(s) of Writing" [162].

419   Crowley, Sharon. "Literature and Composition: Not Separate but Certainly Unequal." *Composition in the University: Historical and Polemical Essays* [172].

English as a university discipline at first studied not literature but philology and composition. Literature came to be the focus only in the late nineteenth century with the professionalization of academic work in English, providing both material to study and a justification for studying it, namely that literature was supposedly an ideal repository of human experience that cultivated moral sensibility. Good taste in literature, then, because it was based on moral qualities, seemed to justify the social privilege of those who possessed it. Concomitantly, composition was despised because to need such instruction was to show that one did not possess good taste. Yet composition was able to displace rhetoric in English departments because at least it focused on self-expression, as literature does, and not on public persuasive discourse, as rhetoric does. What has been taught in composition since 1900? Process has been suppressed because literary scholars did not want to sully the glamour of their artists' inspiration by imagining them revising. One prevailing approach has taught literature as an aid to elevating students' taste — and therefore their morals. The other most prevalent approach has aimed to teach universally applicable writing skills as a service to the university. A third approach, which taught literature as a source of stylistic models and community values, dwindled along with rhetoric generally. Crowley discusses the use of the first approach at Harvard, Yale, and Princeton. The second approach, usually found at less elite schools, encouraged a lot of writing on personal topics, which the teacher corrected — this developed into what is now known as "current-traditional rhetoric," with its focus on form and correctness. Crowley discusses a few challenges to approaches one and two but says that the skills approach, leavened with more or less literature, prevailed in most programs until around 1970.

420   Eberly, Rosa A. *Citizen Critics: Literary Public Spheres.* Urbana and Chicago: Univ. of Illinois Press, 2000.

Four case studies of nonexpert citizen critics writing in literary public spheres offer an account of discursive processes and forms of public criticism. Texts considered "literary" can be studied empirically: the interpretive practices of actual readers writing publicly about problematic literary texts (James Joyce's *Ulysses*, Henry Miller's *Tropic of Cancer*, Bret Easton Ellis's *American Psycho*, and Andrea Dworkin's *Mercy*) illustrate rhetorical approaches to the study and practice of interpretation. Interpretations are shaped not only by broad cultural assumptions but also by inventional strategies, *topoi* in particular, with cultural texts playing an important role in reinvigorating participatory democratic practice. Public criticism rather than literary criticism may offer a way to study how literature has affected society. Rhetorical theory offers possibilities for studying how fictional texts and the public debate around them influence social practices around such topics as obscenity, community standards, public interest, or social value vs. literary merit. This book ends with a discussion of classrooms as protopublic spaces.

421   Eldred, Janet Carey, and Peter Mortensen. "Reading Literacy Narratives." CE 54 (September 1992): 512–39.

Sociolinguistic scholarship on literacy provides critical insights into literary works that feature narratives of literacy acquisition. This scholarship has exploded the myth that increased literacy brings social progress and individual advancement, a myth that can be found in literature. Literacy scholarship also calls attention to the ways that literacy acquisition affects the formation of new identities, seen in narratives of socialization. In literature of the contact zone (see Pratt [212]), people struggle with literacy imposed by colonizers. A number of literary works, like Shaw's *Pygmalion*, focus on literacy narratives.

422   Horner, Winifred Bryan, ed. *Composition and Literature: Bridging the Gap*. Chicago: Univ. of Chicago Press, 1983.

This important collection of twelve essays on the theoretical and pedagogical relationships between composition and literature includes J. Hillis Miller, "Composition and Decomposition: Deconstruction and the Teaching of Writing"; Wayne C. Booth, "LITCOMP: Some Rhetoric Addressed to Cryptorhetoricians about a Rhetorical Solution to a Rhetorical Problem"; Nancy R. Comley and Robert Scholes, "Literature, Composition, and the Structure of English"; Elaine P. Maimon, "Maps and Genres: Exploring Connections in the Arts and Sciences" [662]; Walter J. Ong, S.J., "Literacy and Orality in Our Times" [274]; and E. D. Hirsch, Jr., "Reading, Writing, and Cultural Literacy."

423   Lanham, Richard A. *Literacy and the Survival of Humanism*. New Haven: Yale Univ. Press, 1983.

Nine essays on the place of the humanities in the university curriculum. Unless literature and composition are reconciled, not only will the study of literature perish but our nation will descend into illiteracy and political conflicts among our disparate languages and cultures. Humanities teachers must abandon the notion that language is a neutral medium for exchanging information or expressing oneself.

If language were employed only for such rational purposes, humanistic study would be superfluous. A more accurate notion of human motivation is now emerging from interdisciplinary work in the biological and social sciences. This "post-Darwinian synthesis" depicts human beings as motivated by the desire to play games as well as to satisfy appetites. Humanism can offer crucial insight into game-playing motives, particularly as expressed in styles of language use, and into the ways human beings collaboratively construct self and reality. In the final essay, Lanham outlines the UCLA composition program designed to inculcate "post-Darwinian humanism."

424   Lindemann, Erika, and Gary Tate. "Two Views on the Use of Literature in Composition." CE 55 (March 1993): 311–21.

Lindemann and Tate recap here a debate staged at the 1992 CCCC. In "Freshman Composition: No Place for Literature," Lindemann argues against including imaginative literature — poetry, fiction, and drama — in the first-year composition course. This course should focus on academic discourse, and students should read and write texts from a variety of disciplines. Including literature risks shifting the focus from students' active composing processes to their passive consuming of texts and the teacher's ideas about the texts or about current critical theory. In "A Place for Literature in Freshman Composition," Tate implies that literature has already been eliminated from first-year classes merely to satisfy a fad for rhetoric. But writing teachers usually are not competent to teach the discourses of disciplines other than their own, and deciding which ones to treat becomes problematic in a class of diverse majors. Moreover, teaching literature allows teachers and students to discuss and enjoy the most stylistically accomplished products of the human imagination that our culture has produced, a powerful inspiration to student writers. For further discussion of the issues raised here, see a symposium in the March 1995 CE with essays by Lindemann, Tate, Erwin R. Steinberg, Michael Gamer, and Jane Peterson.

See: Steven Mailloux, *Reception Histories: Rhetoric, Pragmatism, and American Cultural Politics* [197].

425   McQuade, Donald. "Composition and Literary Studies." *Redrawing the Boundaries: The Transformation of English and American Literary Studies*. Ed. Stephen Greenblatt and Giles Gunn. New York: MLA, 1992.

Composition studies continues to be an academic borderland, a contested territory, seen by outsiders as the site of political struggle over institutional resources and by insiders as a burgeoning area of scholarship and pedagogy dealing with critical issues of power, race, class, gender, and ethnicity at the beginning of every instructional hour. Despite efforts to cast it in a healing role, composition remains a fracture separating literary criticism and rhetoric. In the nineteenth century, as belletristic rhetoric spawned literary studies, composition was placed in a subservient role, a development that was exacerbated by New Criticism and by the general degradation of teaching. The class division persists today. Composition has, in the past two decades, developed and professionalized through vigorous scholarship, while scholars like Wayne Booth, Richard Lanham, and Robert Scholes have shown ways to draw the two fields together by extending our understanding of textuality — all without healing the rift. The work should not be abandoned; however, our students should be taught that there is a continuum from literature to composition on which they can locate their own work.

426   Petrosky, Anthony R. "From Story to Essay: Reading and Writing." CCC 33 (February 1982): 19–36.

Reading comprehension is not a simple matter of seeing the information in the text but of formulating it through schemata, or culturally determined cognitive frameworks of understanding. Bartholomae's work on basic writers [441] suggests that writing, like reading, is a process of forming through schemata. The literary pedagogy of Louise Rosenblatt, Norman Holland, and David Bleich provides a way to unite reading and writing instruction productively.

427   Ponsot, Marie, and Rosemary Deen. *Beat Not the Poor Desk*. Upper Montclair, N.J.: Boynton/Cook, 1982.

Writing teachers can facilitate student writing, even under the constraints of time and circumstance, by eliminating class activities that are not writing and by providing opportunities for error-free practice of the elemental skill of writing. Writing should be prolific and guided by the whole structure of the essay. Teachers trained in literature can provide images of the shape of essays: the fable offers a structure for a story with a conclusion, and the parable creates a need for a thesis and clear point of view. Such shapes can be developed inductively and can help make the transition to a sense of other shapes for exposition. The authors describe intermediate steps, many possible shapes for essays, class activities, sample essays, syllabi, ways of teaching grammar, writing about literature, and organizing collaboration. Mina P. Shaughnessy Prize winner.

See: John Schilb, *Between the Lines: Relating Composition Theory and Literary Theory* [217].

428   Steinberg, Erwin R., Michael Gamer, Erika Lindemann, Gary Tate, and Jane Peterson. "Symposium: Literature in the Composition Classroom." CE 57 (March 1995): 265–318.

Five scholars respond to an earlier debate between Lindemann and Tate [424] on whether imaginative literature — poetry, fiction, and drama — should be taught in the first-year composition course.

Advanced Composition

429   Adams, Katherine H. "Bringing Rhetorical Theory into the Advanced Writing Class." *Rhetoric Review* 3 (1985): 184–89.

Rhetorical theory and research in writing can enhance advanced writing courses. Advanced students are capable of appreciating empirical research. They identify, for example, with the problems attested to by writers in protocol analyses and learn from the research on the effects of revision. Testimony by professional writers can encourage students to see the connection between writing and their own disciplines and careers. Grounding in the history of rhetoric reinforces students' sense of the importance and value of speaking to real audiences. The theories of Plato and others can be effectively applied to current examples of attempted persuasion. Research on heuristics can be an antidote to the current-traditional model that most students learned in freshman composition. This material does not need to become the course, but can be incorporated in workshops and discussions.

430   Adams, Katherine H. *A History of Professional Writing Instruction in American Colleges*. Dallas: Southern Methodist Univ. Press, 1993.

Professional writing courses began around 1900 as attempts to meet the need for instruction beyond freshman composition and to respond to vocational and professional pressures on the university. At first, instructors were literature faculty, but soon professional writers were brought in. These professionals taught genres and formats particular to their fields — poetry, journalism, business, technology. This training expanded to study of actual rhetorical situations in the field. Soon, as such courses seemed increasingly anomalous in English departments, journalism became a separate program. Creative writing, linked to literature, remained in English. Technical and business writing never gained sufficient support from business and technical departments to become independent programs and so remained peripheral parts of English departments. After World War II, more advanced writing courses and programs appeared, typically following public events: scientific writing grew during the space race, journalism following Watergate. Professional writing courses have always been dogged by the question of whether they are necessary: could practical writing be learned better out in the field? Were theory-based courses worthwhile? Were they good uses of curricular time? Despite such questions, many schools now offer professional-writing minors and majors, a trend that appears likely to continue.

431   Adams, Katherine H. *Progressive Politics and the Training of America's Persuaders*. Mahwah, N.J.: Lawrence Erlbaum Associates, 1999.

Toward the end of the nineteenth century, as rhetoric shrank to freshman composition, a number of forces combined to create advanced composition courses. In traditional universities like Harvard, advanced writing courses were designed to improve sophistication and fluency. The Progressive movement, though focused educationally on lower schools, influenced the creation of journalism courses and programs at the turn of the twentieth century through its emphasis on citizenship. Advanced courses in journalism spawned imitators in engineering schools, which began to offer business and technical writing. At the same time, the creation of land grant colleges with their agricultural, commercial, and technical specialization led naturally to advanced courses in business and technical writing, business journalism, and advertising. During this period and since, instruction in persuasive writing — despite the importance of persuasion in American public and business life — remained absent from the general curriculum, even while advanced writing courses developed a wide range of persuasive skills.

432   Adams, Katherine H., and John L. Adams, eds. *Teaching Advanced Composition: Why and How?* Portsmouth, N.H.: Boynton/Cook, 1991.

Nineteen essays, seven on theory and the problem of distinguishing advanced from freshman courses, and twelve on approaches to teaching. Essays include Elizabeth Penfield, "Freshman English/Advanced Writing: How Do We Distinguish the Two?"; William Covino, "The Grammar of Advanced Writing"; Michael Carter, "What Is Advanced about Advanced Composition? A Theory of Expertise in Writing"; Michael Keene and Ray Wallace, "Advanced Writing Courses and Programs"; Mary Fuller, "Teaching Style in Advanced Writing Courses"; Sam Watson, "Letters on Writing — A Medium of Exchange with Students of Writing"; Jeanne Fahnestock, "Teaching Argumentation in the Junior-Level Course"; Timothy Donovan and Janet Carr, " 'Real World' Research: Writing Beyond the Curriculum"; and Lynn Bloom, "Creative Nonfiction, Is There Any Other Kind?" Includes "Afterword: Needed Scholarship in Advanced Composition" by Gary Olson, and an annotated bibliography of twenty-eight articles on advanced composition.

433   Covino, William A. "Defining Advanced Composition: Contributions from the History of Rhetoric." *Journal of Advanced Composition* 8 (1988): 113–22.

In their demand for rigor in managing broad and difficult topics and reducing their complexity, advanced composition courses reflect a post-Cartesian notion of advanced knowledge as schematized and well-ordered. Advanced writing students must demonstrate mastery of the conventions of closure, both in composition and, often, in an academic discipline as well. But the post-Cartesian model can be challenged by the older Classical definition of advanced rhetors as more tolerant of ambiguity. Poor rhetors must rely on formulae, whereas better ones probe and search freely. Plato and Cicero depict questioning dialogists as superior to those who seek simple answers or summaries. Montaigne, Vico, and De Quincey criticize Descartes and support the dialogic-dialectical approach to the lost art of rhetoric. As a model for advanced composition, the dialogic approach suggests that research and writing be used to defer judgment, to explore a variety of perspectives on an issue, and to set aside conviction in order to practice rhetoric.

434   Hairston, Maxine. "Working with Advanced Writers." CCC 35 (1984): 196–208.

Advanced writers — honors freshmen and other students taking an elective advanced expository writing course — are reluctant to change writing habits that are earning them good grades, despite felt dissatisfaction with their own writing. Their writing is correct, wordy (repetitive and inflated), heavily nominalized, impersonal, unrealistically ambitious, overly generalized, and without much sense of audience. Their personalities are hidden behind the mask of a bureaucrat or pedantic scholar. They see this style as officially sanctioned; it has earned them rewards, and it is also safe. To persuade them to try anything new, a safe classroom is necessary, where grades are downplayed, risk is rewarded, and a writing community is formed.

435   Olson, Gary A., and Julie Drew, eds. *Landmark Essays on Advanced Composition*. Mahwah, N.J.: Lawrence Erlbaum Associates, 1996.

Twenty-four previously published essays and an extensive bibliography on the history, curriculum, and theory of advanced composition. Included are several surveys of the field from 1980 and 1990; the 1967 CCCC guidelines for advanced composition; William Covino, "Defining Advanced Composition: Contributions from the History of Rhetoric" [433]; Carol Snyder, "Analyzing Classifications: Foucault for Advanced Writers" [438]; Susan Hilligoss, "Preoccupations: Private Writing and Advanced Composition"; Katherine Adams, "Bringing Rhetorical Theory into the Advanced Writing Class" [429]; and Kate Ronald, "The Politics of Teaching Professional Writing."

436   Ramage, John. "From Profession to Discipline: The Politics of Establishing a Writing Concentration." *Coming of Age: The Advanced Writing Curriculum*. Portsmouth, N.H.: Heinemann-Boynton/Cook, 2000.

The development of an advanced undergraduate writing program usually entails the following: resistance from literature colleagues worried about encroachment; the necessity of collectively defining and enacting a disciplinary identity; and the likelihood of having to debate "secession" (from the English department) and "abolition" (of first-year composition). The toughest issues often have less to do with resources and institutional support than with department-internal politics. Local circumstances will guide answers, but critical factors can be identified that need to be accounted for by any program undergoing the change of identity that is effected by instituting an advanced undergraduate writing curriculum.

437   Shamoon, Linda K., Rebecca Moore Howard, Sandra Jamieson, and
       Robert A. Schwegler. *Coming of Age: The Advanced Writing Curriculum*. Portsmouth, N.H.: Heinemann-Boynton/Cook, 2000.

       Advanced composition has come to take a wide range of shapes and
       forms, reflecting new developments in the teaching of writing. The
       thirty-four entries here reflect the emerging variety of advanced composition from traditional business and technical writing courses to
       visual communication, civic discourse, and cultural studies courses.
       Each short essay provides both theoretical discussion and practical
       information on assignments and syllabi. Included are Lynn Bloom,
       "Advancing Composition"; Deepika Bahri, "Postcolonial Writing";
       Rebecca Howard, "Style, Race, Culture, Context"; Richard Leo Enos,
       "The History of Rhetoric"; Sandra Jamieson, "Theories of Composing"; Dennis Baron, "Literacy and Technology"; John C. Bean, "Seeking the Good: A Course in Advanced Argument"; Patricia Bizzell,
       "Writing as a Means of Social Change"; Diana George, "Cultural
       Studies"; Bruce Herzberg, "Civic Literacy and Service Learning";
       Johndan Johnson-Eilola, "Computers and Communication"; Mary
       Lay, "Technical Communication"; Kitty O. Locker, "Writing for and
       about Business and Nonprofit Organizations"; and John Ramage,
       "From Profession to Discipline: The Politics of Establishing a Writing Concentration" [436].

438   Snyder, Carol. "Analyzing Classifications: Foucault for Advanced
       Writers." CCC 35 (1984): 209–16.

       Classifications structure discourse in the disciplines, and advanced
       students are often expected to explain them in their papers. But students typically misunderstand the provisional nature of classification
       schemes, treating them as permanent and not subject to analysis or
       change. They can learn much from Foucault, who compares earlier
       and later classification systems in a field to see changes in the ways
       that we conceive our subjects. Foucault also analyzes classification
       schemes as codes with the power to shape social and intellectual reality and to vest that power in certain people and institutions. Students readily add their own examples to Foucault's pictures of the
       division of people into categories and their distribution into social
       and physical spaces. Taught to identify the object of classification,
       the exclusions of the classifying scheme, the people who use the
       scheme, and the time and space frames of the scheme, students are
       able to analyze classification systems in their own disciplines, discovering much about the field's history and lines of power.

439   Trimbur, John. "The Problem of Freshman English (Only): Toward
       Programs of Study in Writing." *WPA: Writing Program Administration*
       22.3 (Spring 1999): 9–30.

       Despite the powerful sense of mission that accompanies the first-year
       course in writing, our attachment to a single course leads to an
       oversaturation of the curriculum while the single-minded focus on

the first-year course also makes it difficult to compare models and theorize program design. Programs of study in writing would position the first-year course as introductory to the intellectual study of writing, a move that would help to expand the forum for negotiating differences in the theories and agendas that currently divide the field. The assumption that writing instruction must take place in English-Only environments can be traced to its origins, where the formation of the first-year course severed writing in English from its association with classical languages. English achieved its dominance both as a department and as a modern language in part because of the required first-year course, and mastery of English Only has made Freshman English First Worldist at the level of both language and culture. Program design must intersect with multiple constituencies and serve multiple purposes without departmentalizing knowledge. One of the central challenges facing program design is to imagine writing instruction and curriculum from an internationalist perspective.

Basic Writing

440   Anokye, Akua Duku. "Oral Connections to Literacy: The Narrative." *Journal of Basic Writing* 13 (Fall 1994): 46–60.

Oral narratives can help students appreciate their classmates' cultural and racial diversity and generate a variety of themes for writing. Class discussion of the secrets of storytelling and the ways that tales are told in different cultures is a preliminary to an assignment to tell a familiar folk tale that represents some strongly held value. Folk tales reveal both common themes and cultural differences, oral presentation makes students aware of the need to adapt to the audience, and the stories lead to self-awareness as well as cross-cultural understanding. A second assignment is to tell a family story that goes as far back in history as possible, and a third is to tell a personal life narrative. These assignments generate exciting class discussion about cultures and about composition — anticipating questions and confusion, choosing language both for comprehension and effect, clarifying central ideas, and choosing rhetorical forms. Moving to journal and essay writing, students write the stories themselves, or reflect on cultural difference, stereotypes, customs, or history. Discussions also generate criteria for peer-group response. Such assignments help us fulfill our obligation to open windows on the world for our students.

441   Bartholomae, David. "The Study of Error." CCC 31 (October 1980): 253–69. Rpt. in Corbett, Myers, and Tate [171].

"Basic writing" is not a simplified course for the cognitively or linguistically deficient, but a kind of writing produced by an adult who is, in effect, learning a second language called formal written discourse. While learning the new language, the writer produces a personal version of it, an "interlanguage." More research is needed to discover how students produce their interlanguages. One research technique is to ask students to read their work aloud: students will often orally correct written errors without noticing the difference between written and spoken versions. The researcher can point this out and discuss the reasons for the error. Bartholomae uses error analysis and miscue analysis procedures developed by English as a Second Language (ESL) and reading instructors. Braddock Award winner.

442   Bartholomae, David. "The Tidy House: Basic Writing in the American Curriculum." *Journal of Basic Writing* 12 (Spring 1993): 4–21.

Basic writing cannot be a course in which students are taught skills preparatory to reading and writing: it must be a course that engages them in the difficult materials the academy regards as its best possessions and should treat their writing seriously as texts in the course. Even a basic writing course that strives for these laudable goals risks patronizing basic writers as recipients of liberal outreach — and worse, ensuring that the category "basic writer" will remain marked and filled — if the course asks students to shape their writing under a single controlling idea, to produce linear arguments, and to exclude the tangential. Such writing makes it impossible to acknowledge the very specifics of race, gender, and class that have contributed to their status as basic writers. Basic writing should adopt the arts of the contact zone (see Pratt [212]), in which unequal cultures struggle and, in so doing, produce texts of uncertain genre. At the same time, we must remember that students need to become more accomplished at controlling their writing to bring in their history and culture; we should not see all nonstandard features as deliberately unconventional. Basic writing, which once served the strategic purpose of making us change the way we talked about students and curriculum, has tended to become fixed. That status must be questioned.

443   Bizzell, Patricia. "What Happens When Basic Writers Come to College?" *CCC* 37 (October 1986): 294–301. Rpt. in Bizzell [156].

When basic writers begin to learn academic discourse, they are acquiring not only a new dialect (Standard English) and new genres but also a new worldview. Their difficulties may often stem more from conflicts between this new worldview and their home worldviews than from purely linguistic differences. Therefore, to understand and help them, writing teachers should learn more about both the worldviews basic writers bring to college and the academic worldview. The final position in William Perry's scheme of college-level intellectual development can be taken as a model of the academic worldview. We should be cautious about applying models from orality-literacy theory or European class-based analyses of educational differences to American basic writers; still, we might explore whether the relativism described by Perry is especially off-putting to basic writers from communities that cohere around traditional authorities. Even so, there are some grounds for hope that basic writers can become bicultural in their own and the academic worldviews.

444   Brodkey, Linda. "On the Subjects of Class and Gender in 'The Literacy Letters.'" *CE* 51 (February 1989): 125–41. Rpt. in Graves [376].

In the postmodern view, the self is constructed in discourse along ideological lines that determine who can create a privileged position and who will be denied such "authority." Basic writers' resistance to academic discourse may be construed as their rejection of the vulnerable subject position this discourse offers them. Academic discourse, therefore, was eschewed for the sake of encouraging fluency in the "Literacy Letters" — personal letters exchanged between six teachers taking a graduate course in teaching composition and six adult students in a basic writing class. The teachers did not correct the letters they received, and the students did not ask for corrections. Still, the teachers asserted their authority to control the discourse by refusing to respond to passages that suggested social-class or gender differences between teacher and student. The teachers maintained the image of classless and sexless academic writing. To authorize basic writers, class, race, and gender issues that affect them must be acknowledged as classroom realities, even if such acknowledgment threatens the teacher's privileged position.

445   Brooks, Charlotte K., ed. *Tapping Potential: English and Language Arts for the Black Learner*. Urbana, Ill.: NCTE, 1985.

Produced by the NCTE Black Caucus, this collection of forty-three essays on teaching reading, writing, and literature at levels K through 16 includes Clara Alexander, "Black English Dialect and the Classroom Teacher"; Darwin Turner, "Black Students, Language, and Classroom Teachers" and "Black Experience, Black Literature, Black Students, and the English Classroom"; Geneva Smitherman, "'What Go Round Come Round': *King* in Perspective" (see [473]); Miriam Chaplin, "Implications in Personal Construct Theory for Teaching Reading to Black Students"; Robert Fowler, "The Composing Processes of Black Student Writers"; Vivian Davis, "Teachers as Editors: The Student Conference"; William Cook, "The Afro-American Griot"; and Mildred Hill-Lubin, "Putting Africa into the Curriculum through African Literature."

446   Cooper, Marilyn M., and Michael Holzman. *Writing as Social Action*. Portsmouth, N.H.: Heinemann-Boynton/Cook, 1989.

Fifteen essays, eight previously published, by the authors separately and collaboratively, focusing on literacy education, include "The Ecology of Writing" [227], "Women's Ways of Writing," and "Why Are We Talking about Discourse Communities? or, Foundationalism Rears Its Ugly Head Once More" (all by Cooper); "A Post-Freirean Model for Adult Literacy Education" [457] and "The Social Context of Literacy Education" (both by Holzman); and "Talking about Protocols" (by Cooper and Holzman).

447   Dean, Terry. "Multicultural Classrooms, Monocultural Teachers." *CCC* 40 (February 1989): 23–37. Rpt. in Corbett, Myers, and Tate [171].

The greater the distance between a student's home culture and American academic culture, the greater the likelihood that the student will not succeed in school. This problem can be addressed by including the home culture in the curriculum, involving people from the home culture in the school, allowing students to shape some learning tasks according to their own interests and needs, and encouraging teachers to be advocates who will prevent culture-conflict "problems" from being blamed on the students. If the negotiation between home and school culture is studied sensitively in class, students can become comfortably bicultural. Students can write about cultural similarities and contrasts that they have observed, about their own cultural identities, and about their experiences in language learning. Monocultural teachers should avoid making assumptions about how students view their cultural identities and the transition to school culture.

See: Sarah D'Eloia, "The Uses — and Limits — of Grammar" [327].

448   Delpit, Lisa D. "The Silenced Dialogue: Power and Pedagogy in Educating Other People's Children." *Harvard Educational Review* 58 (August 1988): 280–98.

A set of practices or rules for getting, maintaining, and exercising power operates in the classroom as in society at large. Those without power (people of color) benefit from being told what the rules are, but those with power (white people) are often unaware of the existence of the rules or are at least very reluctant to acknowledge them. Indeed, one rule for exercising power is not to acknowledge that you have it. White middle-class teachers must listen to teachers of color who tell them to be more directive and explicit about the rules with students of color, even if doing so violates the whites' liberal sensibilities. Being more directive may mean being explicit, not only about general rules of conduct in the negotiation of power but also about specific rules for writing powerfully and correctly.

See: Anne DiPardo, *A Kind of Passport* [625].

449   Enos, Theresa, ed. *A Sourcebook for Basic Writing Teachers*. New York: Random House, 1987.

Forty-two essays and parts of books and three bibliographies, some previously published. Included are Walter J. Ong, S.J., "Literacy and Orality in Our Times" [274]; Mike Rose, "Remedial Writing Courses: A Critique and a Proposal" [469]; E. D. Hirsch, Jr., "Cultural Literacy"; Paulo Freire, "The Adult Literacy Process as Cultural Action for Freedom"; David Bartholomae and Anthony R. Petrosky, "Facts, Artifacts, and Counterfacts: A Basic Reading and Writing Course for the College Curriculum" [371]; Patrick Hartwell, "Grammar, Grammars, and the Teaching of Grammar" [333]; Sarah D'Eloia, "The Uses — and Limits — of Grammar" [327]; Ira Shor, "Reinventing Daily Life: Self-Study and the Theme of 'Work' "; Mina P. Shaughnessy, "Vocabulary" and "Beyond the Sentence" [472]; Nancy

Sommers, "Revision Strategies of Student Writers and Experienced Adult Writers" [320]; Ann E. Berthoff, "Recognition, Representation, and Revision"; and Kenneth A. Bruffee, "Writing and Reading as Collaborative or Social Acts." This collection is an excellent introduction to the field of composition studies as a whole.

450   Fiore, Kyle, and Nan Elsasser. " 'Strangers No More': A Liberatory Literacy Curriculum." CE 44 (February 1982): 115–28. Rpt. in Kintgen, Kroll, and Rose [267].

Paulo Freire's "generative themes" [258] help a college writing class of adult Bahamian women move from personal reflections on their families to social analysis of marriage in the Bahamas, thus developing their critical thinking and writing abilities at the same time.

451   Fox, Tom. Defending Access: A Critique of Standards in Higher Education. Portsmouth, N.H.: Boynton/Cook, 1999.

Lack of access remains the most crucial problem in higher education — not a crisis of standards — and we must, accordingly, abandon the notion that skills alone provide access. A brief account of literacy learning among African Americans provides a dramatic contrast to the institutional history of composition and illuminates the ideologies of access and exclusion. John Ogbu's theory of oppositional culture explains, in part, why initiation doesn't work as a curricular strategy. What is needed are constant critiques of the ideologies that reduce writing courses to service and skills. Efforts to transform the structures that work against access can begin by imagining writing program administration as a set of coordinated actions. Similarly, standards for teaching writing are part of coordinated political action, where standards are in a critical relationship with social and political change.

452   Giannasi, Jenefer M. "Language Varieties and Composition." In Teaching Composition: Twelve Bibliographic Essays. Ed. Gary Tate [40].

This bibliographic essay discusses works on dialectal varieties of American English, including Black English; differences between spoken and written dialects; social and cultural factors affecting dialect variation and choice (sociolinguistics); and usage.

453   Gilyard, Keith. Voices of the Self: A Study of Language Competence. Detroit: Wayne State Univ. Press, 1991.

Native Black English speakers in an urban public school environment can acquire Standard English language skills and "sociolinguistic competence" if they are encouraged to see their experience according to a transactional model that emphasizes their ability to negotiate and manipulate school language expectations in response to their own belief systems and personal traits. Gilyard surveys research on code-switching, bidialectalism, and the sociopolitical dimensions of schooling, interspersing these scholarly discussions with narratives of his own experience as one such urban Black English speaker making his way through school.

454   Gunner, Jeanne. "Iconic Discourse: The Troubling Legacy of Mina Shaughnessy." *JBW* 17.2 (Spring 1998): 25–42.

Examining the constraining discursive rules that are the legacy of Mina Shaughnessy (in the iconic sense) helps to understand the nature of the conflicts in the field of basic writing. Two primary discourses — iconic and critical — have shaped discussions in basic writing over the last twenty years and operate as systems of linguistic constraint. Iconic discourse reproduces the field according to certain laws while critical discourse is transgressive. Iconic discourse makes it impossible within the discourse to reconceptualize without seeming at once to betray and dehistoricize; it also constructs an idealized identity for the basic writing teacher, a heroic teacher-figure that remains as the central value in the academic enterprise. Iconic discourse contextualizes and thus constrains its subject(s), evident by the degree of resistance met by authors who engage in critical discourse, which constructs no heroes and is highly theoretical and political. Speaking outside of established discursive parameters, critical discourse is perceived as betrayal.

455   Harris, Joseph. "Negotiating the Contact Zone." *Journal of Basic Writing* 41.1 (1995): 27–42.

Metaphors of growth and initiation dominated discussions of teaching writing until the late 1980s, when the idea of struggle or conflict became popular, largely through Mary Louise Pratt's "contact zones." Pratt imports difference into her classroom (through her choices of texts) but does not engage with differences among *students* or offer strategies for students to communicate about and across differences. Pratt's conceptualization of the contact zone is problematic because of the superficiality of the engagement with otherness. When students retreat to "safe houses," for example, difference is valorized but the conflict remains. Working on *how* differences get negotiated promises a more expansive view of intellectual life.

See: Muriel Harris and Katherine E. Rowan, "Explaining Grammatical Concepts" [332].

456   Haswell, Richard. *Gaining Ground in College Writing: Tales of Development and Interpretation.* Dallas: Southern Methodist Univ. Press, 1991.

New information about development and new theory about human change invites a new study into how students' writing changes during college based on a model that sees writing development as three-dimensional — an educational lifework, including growth and maturation yet firmly embedded in culture. An assortment of interpretive frames causes clashes between developmental and nondevelopmental tales of interpretation, many of which compromise the engagement between teacher and student. Writing teachers should conceive of pedagogical tasks — evaluation, models, diagnosis, curriculum — as *narrative*. Evaluation and course content should be based not on the growth but on the *maturing* of students, when maturing is defined as generative change towards cultural standards. The transformative approach offers idiographic frames of action for individuals to try rather than nomothetic categories — general interpretations rather than explanatory laws. The paradoxical bind between writing instruction and writing style cannot be entirely overcome, but the transformative offers a guide for such issues as solecisms, rate of production, sentence sense, organization, and remediality. An instrumental perspective generates a distinct understanding of pedagogical sequencing; however, a lifework tale of sequence has teachers joining students in some work, not imitating educational disciplines. Similarly, lifework developmental perspectives should inform curriculum and (true) diagnosis. Parts of this book are informed by empirical data from a study analyzing first-week diagnostic essays, end-of-course essays, and similar essays written by college graduates employed in business, government, and industry.

457 Holzman, Michael. "A Post-Freirean Model for Adult Literacy Education." CE 50 (February 1988): 177–89. Rpt. in Cooper and Holzman [446].

In economically underdeveloped countries, many literacy educators use Paulo Freire's [259] methods with adult students. Here, an "animator" helps students develop literacy materials from their experience that foster insight into the politically oppressive conditions of their lives and the determination to change these conditions. In being so ideologically directive, though, Freirean pedagogy risks appropriating learners' responsibility for their own literacy goals. A post-Freirean model urges the teacher to wait for local initiative and to help student groups organize for whatever educational purposes — including literacy — they feel necessary.

See: Bruce Horner, "Rethinking the 'Sociality' of Error: Teaching Editing as Negotiation" [335].

458 Horner, Bruce, and Min-Zhan Lu. *Representing the "Other": Basic Writers and the Teaching of Basic Writing.* Urbana, Ill.: NCTE, 1999.

An analysis of the dominant discourse on basic writing begins by situating basic writing socially and historically and by examining representations of basic writers. Key terms and assumptions work to privilege some practices and marginalize others; these cultural materialist readings address a range of research and teaching practices. Essays include four by Horner — "The 'Birth' of Basic Writing"; "Mapping Errors and Expectations for Basic Writing: From the 'Frontier Field' to 'Border Country' "; "Rethinking the 'Sociality' of Error: Teaching Editing as Negotiation"; and "Some Afterwords: Intersections and Divergences" — and four by Lu — "Conflict and Struggle: The Enemies or Preconditions of Basic Writing?"; "Importing 'Science': Neutralizing Basic Writing"; "Redefining the Legacy of Mina Shaughnessy: A Critique of the Politics of Linguistic Innocence"; and "Professing Multiculturalism: The Politics of Style in the Contact Zone."

459   Kells, Michelle Hall, and Valerie Balester, eds. *Attending to the Margins: Writing, Researching, and Teaching on the Front Lines.* Portsmouth, N.H.: Heinemann-Boynton/Cook, 1999.

So-called nontraditional students, including those whose native language is not English, whose home culture is not derived from northern Europe, and/or whose social class is disadvantaged, now make up the majority of students in many classrooms. The so-called marginalized have come to the center of the educational enterprise in the schools where the ten contributors to this volume teach. These students need to learn traditional academic discourse, but in order to learn, they need to draw on the cultural resources they bring to the classroom. Specific suggestions on pedagogies to help these students do so can be found in Donna Dunbar-Odom, "Speaking Back with Authority: Students as Ethnographers in the Research Writing Class"; Caroline Pari, "Developing Critical Pedagogy for Basic Writing at a CUNY Community College"; Mike Palmquist, Donna LeCourt, and Kate Kiefer, "Talking across Differences: Building Student/Teacher Dialogue through Instruction in Computer-Supported Writing Classrooms"; Randall Popken, "Adult Writers, Interdiscursive Linking, and Academic Survival"; Maureen Neal, "Abdominal Conditions and Other Cretins of Habit: Hyperfluency and the Acquisition of Academic Discourse"; Barbara Gleason, "Something of Great Constancy: Storytelling, Story Writing, and Academic Literacy"; Margaret A. McLaughlin and Eleanor Agnew, "Teacher Attitudes Toward African American Language Patterns: A Close Look at Attrition Rates"; Michelle Hall Kells, "Leveling the Linguistic Playing Field in First-Year Composition"; Alan Hirvela, "Teaching Immigrant Students in the College Writing Classroom"; and Sharon Dean and Barbara Wenner, with Rosalyn Haugabrook, "Skin Deep: Toward an Equality of Disclosure." Sections of the book are introduced by Kells and Balester, Ira Shor, Victor Villanueva, and Akua Duku Anokye.

460   Labov, William. *The Study of Nonstandard English.* Urbana, Ill.: NCTE, 1970.

Nonstandard dialects of English, such as Black English, should not be seen as error-ridden deviations from the standard form — but neither should they be seen as separate languages. Comparative studies reveal that nonstandard forms express many of the same logical relations among elements in a sentence that the standard form does, in different yet regular ways. Almost all native speakers of English can use more than one dialect of the language, and almost all have at least some acquaintance with the standard form. Social class tends to determine which dialect a person feels most comfortable using. Nonstandard dialects tend to be socially stigmatized, even by those who feel most comfortable using them. Teachers must be aware of the grammatical structures and conventions governing social use of dialects to mediate between the dialects and Standard English. Some in-class speaking, reading, and writing in the students' dialects may help them to learn the standard form more quickly with less damage to their self-esteem.

461   Lu, Min-Zhan. "Conflict and Struggle: The Enemies or Preconditions of Basic Writing?" CE 54 (December 1992): 887–913.

When students from marginalized cultures enter the academy, they experience the pain of learning to live with multiple, conflicting points of view, but also the exhilarating creativity and insight that their borderland consciousness makes possible. Early work in basic-writing pedagogy sought to alleviate this pain, ignoring the accompanying benefits. Thomas Farrell and Kenneth Bruffee proposed acculturation as the cure, welcoming students into the intellectually superior academic community. This approach calmed colleagues who feared that basic writers would bring destructive change to the academy. Mina Shaughnessy, in contrast, offered accommodation, promising that students could accept the academic worldview without abandoning home allegiances. This approach also spared the academy from change. But the real task of the basic writer is neither to conform to nor abandon a monolithic discourse community, but to find innovative discursive strategies for negotiating the boundaries. Basic writers are complex selves, not to be essentialized as products of a single cultural group. The academy must adjust to these border-crossers' new discursive forms.

462   Lu, Min-Zhan. "From Silence to Words: Writing as Struggle." CE 49 (April 1987): 437–48. Rpt. in Perl [239].

Lu describes her experiences in negotiating among different worlds: her early schooling in Maoist China, her parents' Western education, her graduate work in Pittsburgh. Dealing with the often painful conflicts among these worlds, Lu attests, helped her grow as a thinker and writer. She concludes that writing teachers should avoid making only one kind of discourse acceptable in their classrooms. Students, however, should not be led to believe that they can move freely among the discourses they know and at the same time keep each discourse pure. Instead, the conflict of discourses — in the classroom and in one's head — should be a topic of reflection.

463   Lunsford, Andrea A. "The Content of Basic Writers' Essays." CCC 31 (October 1980): 278–90.

A sample of five hundred entrance exams suggests that basic writers focus on personal experience, using it as conclusive evidence or evaluating abstract questions solely in terms of personal effects; rely on clichéd maxims in place of generalizations; see themselves as passive victims of authority; and use stylistic features (such as personal pronouns) that reflect these content characteristics. All of this suggests that basic writers are arrested in what Piaget and Vygotsky call the "egocentric stage" of cognitive development. A similar study by Susan Miller suggests that they are also stuck in what Kohlberg calls the "conventional" stage of moral development. Basic writers might be helped, therefore, by a curriculum that asks them to solve increasingly abstract cognitive problems.

464   McNenny, Gerri and Sallyanne H. Fitzgerald, eds. *Mainstreaming Basic Writers: Politics and Pedagogies of Access.* Mahwah, N.J.: Lawrence Erlbaum, 2001.

Recent challenges posed to basic writing instruction demand alternative configurations that attempt to do justice to both students' needs and administrative constraints. Twelve chapters, including the following, address a wide representation on the issue of mainstreaming basic writers at the college level: Gerri McNenny, "Writing Instruction and the Post-Remedial University: Setting the Scene for the Mainstreaming Debate in Basic Writing"; Ira Shor, "Errors and Economics: Inequality Breeds Remediation"; Mary Soliday, "Ideologies of Access and the Politics of Agency"; Eleanor Agnew and Margaret McLaughlin, "Those Crazy Gates and How They Swing: Tracking the System That Tracks African-American Students"; Barbara Gleason, "Returning Adults to the Mainstream: Toward a Curriculum for Diverse Student Writers"; Mark Wiley, "Mainstreaming and Other Experiments in a Learning Community"; Trudy Smoke, "Mainstreaming Writing: What Does This Mean for ESL Students?"

465   Moran, Michael G., and Martin J. Jacobi, eds. *Research in Basic Writing: A Bibliographic Sourcebook.* Westport, Conn.: Greenwood Press, 1990.

Ten extensive bibliographic essays: Andrea Lunsford and Patricia Sullivan, "Who Are Basic Writers?"; Donn Haisty Winchell, "Developmental Psychology and Basic Writers"; Mariolina Salvatori and Glynda Hull, "Literacy Theory and Basic Writing"; Ronald Lunsford, "Modern Grammar and Basic Writers"; Michael Montgomery, "Dialects and Basic Writers"; Sue Render, "TESL Research and Basic Writing"; Michael Hood, "Basic Writing Courses and Programs"; Stephen Bernhardt and Patricia Wojahn, "Computers and Writing Instruction"; Donna Beth Nelson, "Writing Laboratories and Basic Writing"; and Richard Filloy, "Preparing Teachers of Basic Writing."

See: Marie Nelson, *At the Point of Need* [538].

466   Rose, Mike. "The Language of Exclusion: Writing Instruction at the University." *CE* 47 (April 1985): 341–59.

The language used to describe and defend writing programs contributes to the attitude that writing is a secondary part of the university curriculum. "Error" was a convenient object of study for behaviorists, who then recommended drilling as a remedy. Their positivistic defense of writing instruction lingers on, despite its limitations and its degrading connotations. The once-effective defense of writing as a "skill" now relegates it to second-class intellectual status. "Remediation" suggests medical deficiency, or that material should have been learned before and is therefore inappropriate to the college curriculum. "Illiteracy" oversimplifies a complex problem and stigmatizes both students and teachers. Finally, the myth that remediation leads to a final cure persists, despite historical evidence, and further marginalizes writing programs and their students as merely temporary phenomena. We must contest the assumptions of such language and offer instead a more cognitively, historically, and culturally accurate description of writing.

467   Rose, Mike. *Lives on the Boundary: The Struggles and Achievements of America's Underprepared.* New York: Free Press, 1989.

"Deprived" and "deficient" elementary school children, "vocational-track" high-school students, and "remedial" college students have all been judged negatively by teachers, by parents, and often by themselves on the basis of their inability to perform a very small set of intellectual activities. But these students possess knowledge and mental capacities fully representative of the richness of human creativity. Their difficulties should be understood in terms of the intellectual and, especially, the affective dissonances evoked by their experiences of crossing boundaries into school from relatively marginalized social positions. Rose offers poignantly detailed anecdotes from his own life as an "underprepared" student and as a teacher of such students, illustrating how teachers, parents, students, and others can sensitively acknowledge the boundary-crossing experience and avoid treating the boundaries as unbreachable walls. Winner of the Mina P. Shaughnessy Prize and the CCCC Outstanding Book Award.

468   Rose, Mike. "Narrowing the Mind and the Page: Remedial Writers and Cognitive Reductionism." CCC 39 (October 1988): 267–302.

The misguided effort to find a single cognitive explanation for complex and varied student problems — cognitive reductionism — has many avatars: studies of cognitive style characterize people as field-dependent or field-independent, brain research uses hemisphericity to account for logical and verbal abilities, the work of Piaget offers stages of cognitive development and logical thinking, and orality-literacy theorists connect literacy to logic and thinking ability. Applying these theories to student writers is problematic because they tend to level differences between individuals, they describe mental processes that can be linked only inferentially to writing, they deflect attention from student writers' immediate social contexts, and they often reproduce cultural stereotypes that should themselves be questioned — as the overrepresentation of socially marginal students at the low end of every scale suggests. Cognition is too complex to be captured in such schemes.

469   Rose, Mike. "Remedial Writing Courses: A Critique and a Proposal."
        CE 45 (February 1983): 109–28. Rpt. in Enos [449] and in Corbett,
        Myers, and Tate [171].

        The remedial writing course should not assign simple, personal top-
        ics so that errors can be more easily isolated. Rather, it should em-
        phasize connections with other college work by challenging students
        with academic reading and writing and by focusing on strategies for
        coping with these tasks as part of the composing process.

470   Schwalm, David E. "Degree of Difficulty in Basic Writing Courses:
        Insights from the Oral Proficiency Interview Testing Program." CE
        47 (October 1985): 629–40.

        The Foreign Service Institute's Oral Proficiency Interview (OPI) rates
        adults' conversational competence in a second language according
        to "function," or ability to interact at an appropriate level of formal-
        ity; "context/content," or mastery of vocabulary suited to the topic;
        and "accuracy," or ability to speak correctly and intelligibly. On the
        six-level OPI scale, movement from level 2 to level 3 is most signifi-
        cant because here the speaker becomes able to explain and argue
        rather than simply narrate or describe, to employ more abstract and
        formal vocabulary and demonstrate broad cultural awareness, and to
        use more complex grammatical structures. The linguistic resources
        on which basic writers draw in written communication correspond
        to the characteristics of OPI level 2. Basic writing curricula should
        be designed specifically to move students into writing tasks requiring
        the equivalent of OPI level-3 abilities.

471   Shaughnessy, Mina P. "Basic Writing." *Teaching Composition: Twelve
        Bibliographic Essays.* Ed. Gary Tate [40].

        Little work on college-level basic writing had been done when this
        bibliographic essay was written in 1976. It cites work on remedial
        education in general, Black English, social and cultural factors in
        educational success, Standard English grammar, philosophy of lan-
        guage, and composition pedagogy. All are selected according to
        Shaughnessy's sense of what might be useful to the basic-writing
        teacher. The essay thus provides an interesting picture of the devel-
        opment of her thought.

472   Shaughnessy, Mina P. *Errors and Expectations: A Guide for the Teacher
        of Basic Writing.* New York: Oxford Univ. Press, 1977.

        Basic writers' errors in Standard English fall into patterns derived
        from systematic gaps in students' knowledge of the written form and
        from students' own idiosyncratic but regular plans for using unfamil-
        iar writing conventions. Chapters 1 to 5 catalog students' problems
        with handwriting, punctuation, syntax, and spelling. Chapters 6 to 8
        show that basic writers are unfamiliar with the concepts and argu-
        ment forms that are customary in academic writing. To help these
        students learn Standard English and academic discourse, teachers

should not rely on atomized drills. They should instead discuss the grammatical and argumentative principles that inform academic writing. Teachers should remember that basic writers are intelligent adults. This book has had enormous influence on the study of basic writing, not primarily for its ideas on classroom practice, but for its way of understanding the writing that basic writers produce.

473   Smitherman, Geneva. *Talkin' and Testifyin'*. Boston: Houghton Mifflin, 1977.

Black English takes many grammar rules and pronunciation patterns from West African languages. In America, the use of Black English is associated with a culture that values several forms of oral display, such as church oratory, and that holds a worldview different from that associated with Standard English, for example, in its preference for logical structures that are hierarchical or cyclical rather than linear. This book focuses less on Black English than on black culture, which it describes in detail. Smitherman strongly opposes requiring Standard English forms and culture for Black English speakers. For her comments on a court case mandating bilingual instruction for Black English speakers, see " 'What Go Round Come Round': *King in Perspective*," *Harvard Education Review* 51.1 (February 1981), rpt. in Brooks [445].

474   Soliday, Mary. "From the Margins to the Mainstream: Reconceiving Remediation." CCC 47.1 (February 1996): 85–100.

Within a volatile atmosphere for remedial writing programs, FIPSE funded the Enrichment Approach at City College, featuring a two-course, six-credit sequence that bypassed test scores and mainstreamed students into a well-supported curriculum centered on language variety and cultural differences. A close reading of one student's portfolio illustrates the effectiveness of the mainstreamed curriculum. For example, in learning to approximate academic discourse, "Derek" begins to formulate generalizations more sophisticated than simple agreement or disagreement with a topic and uses both subordination and metalanguage. This student's portfolio illustrates "the promise of responsible mainstreaming" when the curriculum emphasizes linguistic self-consciousness, the study of language and culture, and social interactions with readers; however, what remains is to account for the complex institutional politics of remediation.

475   Soliday, Mary. *The Politics of Remediation: Institutional and Student Needs in Higher Education*. Pittsburgh: Univ. of Pittsburgh Press, 2002.

Remediation at the college level exists to serve institutional needs and to resolve social conflicts and cannot be attributed to students' backgrounds or socioeconomic status. A crisis management tool aimed at what are perceived as singular crises in student preparation, remedial English appeared not as a response to student skill levels but only as the dividing lines between institutions — college, university, academy, public high school — were firmly fixed. Historical analyses of remedial English are needed, rather than studies of individual students and classroom pedagogy, to explode the assumption of today's students as anomalous or "always new," to examine the underpinnings of a discourse of student need, and to distinguish the politics of representation from the politics of access. We must challenge the rhetoric of needs that assumes remediation is a "special" need of nontraditional students, and we must disentangle curricular reforms from institutional ones with, for example, translation theory. City University of New York and City College of New York are used throughout to illustrate the broader dynamics of institutional growth in American higher education: how institutions adopt new standards as a management strategy or use remediation to stratify higher education.

476   Soliday, Mary. "Towards a Consciousness of Language: A Language Pedagogy for Multicultural Classrooms." *Journal of Basic Writing* 16.2 (Fall 1997): 62–73.

The Language Research Project was designed as a year-long course to increase students' understanding of the nature of human language and to move them beyond the view that language (merely) conveys information. Beginning with a literacy narrative, students described a language group and kept a field notebook of language samples; they also wrote weekly self-assessments, analytical and interpretive drafts, and a final research paper. The emphasis on the sociolinguistic nature of language asked students to investigate the relationship between their private and public languages and encouraged them to develop a literate attitude toward language.

477   Sternglass, Marilyn S. *Time to Know Them: A Longitudinal Study of Writing and Learning at the College Level.* Mahwah, N.J.: Lawrence Erlbaum Associates, 1997.

In this first longitudinal study dedicated to tracing the same students through their entire college experience, extensive data for nine students at City College provide a full picture of writing development in a multicultural urban population. Interviews and student writing demonstrate the effect of complex social histories on academic performance, but students also showed metacognitive awareness of the relationship between writing and learning, suggesting that engagement with writing moves students to reflect more deeply on materials and ideas. Chapter 4 illustrates the crucial but also limited role that composition instruction has in the development of writing abilities, especially if the instructor ignores content or relies on generic commentary. Other chapters examine institutional testing, instructional settings, case studies of how the writing process changes over time, and implications for instruction and research. Informed by research in basic writing, ESL, feminist pedagogy, and sociocognitive theories, this in-depth study presents "the true complexity of writing development." Winner of the NCTE Outstanding Book Award.

478   Stygall, Gail. "Resisting Privilege: Basic Writing and Foucault's Author Function." CCC 45 (1994): 320–41.

Just as Foucault's author function organizes the curriculum in English studies and defines its proper object for study, the teaching of basic writing, too, is formulated around the educational discursive practices necessary to keep the author function dominant. Designed to increase consciousness of how teachers and institutional practices participate in constructing basic writers, a "letters" project — exchanges between graduate students enrolled in a seminar designed to study basic writing and basic writing students at two other universities — highlighted claims of neutrality, constructions of educational identities, and attempts to resist privilege. Differences in length between the two sets of letters, for example, placed graduate students firmly in the author category and served to reinscribe the basic writers' positions. Reflection on the "success" of the project is included with recommended changes in basic writing pedagogy.

479   Stygall, Gail. "Unraveling at Both Ends: Anti-Undergraduate Education, Anti-Affirmative Action, and Basic Writing at Research Schools." Journal of Basic Writing 18.2 (1999): 4–12.

While they remain an important facet of work and thought in issues of basic writing, when pressed financially, Research 1 universities cut courses deemed less central to their mission. At the same time, recent successful anti-affirmative action ballot initiatives make diverse student populations less likely. These two intertwined movements — cutting courses and shutting doors — foreground the need for rhetoric and composition specialists to act as public intellectuals and to participate in the forums available for debate. In particular, we should analyze public documents on education, administrative reports as well as newspaper stories. For example, just as predictions are made that future growth in the college population is likely to be from underrepresented groups, university "master plans" position all lower division writing courses as remedial or superfluous in an "efficient" system. Ideologies of fairness and quantification, pervasive in education, undercut commitments to diversity yet are the most difficult to counter among the public. The use of critical discourse analysis — with its attention to agency, action, stakes, absence and presence — helps to explain how underrepresented students can be both welcomed and rejected, among other contradictions.

480   Williams, Joseph M. "The Phenomenology of Error." CCC 32 (May 1981): 152–68.

When we read student papers, we define "errors" as discrete entities found on the page. But "error" has a more important, social dimension. Our perception of error on the page signals a flawed social transaction between us and the writer, similar to a breach of etiquette. When we read the work of professional writers, we do not expect to find errors because our social relation to these writers is different from our relation to students. Many highly respected essays on writing breach their own rules, but we tend not to see these errors, although we always find errors when we look for them — in student papers. In guiding students away from error, then, we should redefine it not as structurally deviant but as socially inappropriate in writing situations.

Gender, Race, and Class

481   Ball, Arnetha, and Ted Lardner. "Dispositions Toward Language: Teacher Constructs of Knowledge and the Ann Arbor Black English Case." CCC 48.4 (December 1997): 469–85.

The 1979 Ann Arbor case ruled that teachers' language attitudes impeded children's literacy learning; however, the court's ruling left pedagogical issues unresolved. One strategy, to inform teachers about sociolinguistics, does not necessarily translate into classroom practice. The authors outline three constructs of teacher knowledge that help to explain the gaps between knowledge and practice: teacher as technician, teacher knowledge as lore, and teacher efficacy. Teachers' attitudes toward racially inflected language cannot be addressed adequately by knowledge constructs that emphasize either a technical or lore-based approach. Teacher efficacy, on the other hand, emphasizes affect and the "emotional tone of classroom interactions." Efficacy begins with a knowledge base of linguistic diversity and cultural discourse patterns but must extend into an understanding of pedagogical theory within a wider sociocultural context. Braddock Award winner.

482   Barnett, Timothy. "Reading 'Whiteness' in English Studies." College English 63.1 (September 2000): 9–37.

As leaders in reading, writing, and literacy training, English studies should better historicize its difficulties with multicultural education, and should more vigorously promote the understanding of race as a construct of language and culture rather than as a result of biology. Engaging more fully with the concept of whiteness (in a broader sense, that "whiteness" as an essentialist notion of race) is the first step in this direction. Discourses on whiteness should be read and rewritten in order to foster stronger ties between academic work and social justice. A look at the development of basic and multicultural education at the Universities of Washington and Michigan in the 1960s and 1970s exemplify the type of exploration needed.

483   Bauer, Dale. "The Other 'F' Word: The Feminist in the Classroom." CE 52 (April 1990): 385–96.

Students frequently attack a teacher's feminist perspective as something personal that does not belong in the classroom. Indeed, students do not wish to acknowledge any value contradictions in their academic work. Feminist teachers should recognize that teaching these students will be a form of persuasion, in which they need to adopt an authoritative but not authoritarian position in setting the course's ethical agenda. They should not reject all forms of authority as patriarchal. Moreover, in seeking to persuade students to feminism, teachers should aim to provoke not only resistance to sexism but also identification (in Kenneth Burke's sense) with feminism's egalitarian vision of the social order. In short, feminist teachers should see themselves as rhetors and aim to develop a feminist rhetoric.

See: Linda Brodkey, "On the Subjects of Class and Gender in 'The Literacy Letters' " [444].

See: Miriam Brody, Manly Writing: Gender, Rhetoric, and the Rise of Composition [80].

484   Brueggemann, Brenda Jo et al., "Becoming Visible: Lessons in Disability." CCC 52.3 (Feb. 2001): 368–98.

Increased awareness of disability reveals, for both teachers and students of composition, the harmful constructions of ability, difference, and normalcy that pervade higher education and society in general. Because differences in ability resemble differences in race, class, gender, and ethnicity insofar as they have the potential to generate learning, compositionists are in a unique position to disrupt accepted notions about disability. By introducing disability texts, by allowing for a multi-modal classroom, and by considering disability within a cultural context rather than just a medical one, composition teachers can make disability visible, and can challenge such binaries as normal/not normal and us/them.

485   Canagarajah, A. Suresh. "Safe Houses in the Contact Zone: Coping Strategies of African-American Students in the Academy." CCC 48.2 (May 1997): 173–96.

First-year ethnic minority students construct and use "safe houses" to negotiate between their vernacular discourses and academic conventions. In a networked classroom organized around argumentative writing, African American students began the course by practicing traditional topic-centered argumentation but later used person-centered and topic-associated argumentation to reframe classroom matters, to celebrate their ethnic solidarity, and to practice acts of "fronting" characterized by vernacular discourses, parody, and subtle messages to outsiders. These strategies helped to develop meta-pedagogical awareness and prepared students to move into the public sites of the contact zone. If teachers become ethnographers and examine their own locations, the safe house can become a pedagogically significant site, integral to the contact zone.

486   Catano, James V. "The Rhetoric of Masculinity: Origins, Institutions, and the Myth of the Self-Made Man." CE 52 (April 1990): 421–36.

The myth of self-making is powerful because it provides identities that seem to fit naturally into the requirements of society. The myth errs in equating masculine growth with an escape from origins —

sex, race, and class — and from institutions. In the American tradition of individualism, fulfillment comes from applying the virtues of perseverance, loyalty, and so on, virtues that are supposedly not dependent on origins or institutions. The very egalitarianism of this appeal masks social reality, for it is, of course, easier to gain personal fulfillment when supported by the institutions one supposedly spurns. Twentieth century versions of the myth substitute prowess in corporations for independence from institutions but retain the dichotomy between male identity as self-contained and female identity as interpersonal. In composition pedagogy, the rhetoric of authentic, expressive prose embodies the myth of self-making. Its goal is to free the writer to experience a true self. Ken Macrorie [411], Peter Elbow [175, 397], and William Coles [406], although they reject masculine self-aggression, use traditionally masculine images to define the personae of their self-made teachers and writers, call upon the Emersonian tradition of individualism, and seek freedom from institutions rather than Freirean confrontation with them.

487   Degenaro, William. "Class Consciousness and the Junior College Movement: Creating a Docile Workforce." JAC 21.3 (2001): 499–520.

The archives of the development and growth of two-year colleges in the early twentieth century reveal a rich narrative of contradiction, diversity, and class consciousness that should provide an historical context for understanding, and possibly undoing, problematic educational practices, such as gatekeeping. The elite scholars who led the junior college movement were motivated in part by the desire to rid prestigious American universities of the masses, in order to more closely approximate the German research model of a university. Discipline and assessment (in the form of intelligence and personality tests), as well as training in taste, civics, and lawfulness, were used to transform junior college students into members of the middle-class — though only ideologically, not materially. Movement leaders were also influenced by philosophical trends of the time, such as scientization and social efficiency. Rather than delivering on the promise to prepare students to transfer to four-year colleges and universities (a promise which turned out to be little more than a marketing ploy aimed at students and their parents), junior colleges created poorly respected campuses and a passive working class.

488   Delpit, Lisa. *Other People's Children: Cultural Conflict in the Classroom.* New York: New Press, 1995.

Progressive educational movements, in the name of liberation from oppression, often silence and exclude minority voices. For example, writing process advocates assume that black students need to develop fluency rather than technical skills while many black parents and educators want direct instruction in the "culture of power." White middle-class teachers and parents often use indirect communication in order to deemphasize power; however, not all children have access to the same codes. Children accustomed to more direct instruction and to more authoritative figures will struggle to understand the rules of (white) classroom culture. In this collection of nine articles and essays, Delpit offers ways of appreciating linguistic diversity, shares her research on schooling in multilingual Papua New Guinea, and outlines teacher education for a multicultural society.

489   Enos, Theresa. *Gender Roles and Faculty Lives in Rhetoric and Composition*. Carbondale: Southern Illinois Univ. Press, 1996.

Results of a national study of college writing teachers illustrate the variety of experiences writing faculty have had with gender and disciplinary bias in rhetoric and composition and in English departments. Respondents to a survey were invited to share narrative accounts in addition to statistical data; follow-ups to the questionnaires included informal interviews and campus visits as well as other invited stories. Topics include nontraditional careers, glass ceilings, and tenure cases. Enos argues for broadening the definition of intellectual work in rhetoric and composition and suggests ways in which her study can direct change.

490   Fleckenstein, Kristie S. "Bodysigns: A Biorhetoric for Change." JAC 21.4 (2001): 761–90.

Biorhetoric, or a discourse of bodysigns, can arm one to meet the challenges of transformative teaching and thinking. Transformation must encompass three aspects: a way of seeing that enables recognition of the status quo as constructed through rules and the enactment of those rules, a way of speaking that enables the use of language in ways that surpass representation, and a way of living that enables change. A discourse of bodysigns focuses on the inextricable connection between materiality and semiosis, on the point at which the material and the semiotic blur. Biorhetoric makes transformation possible because it provides a double way of seeing, speaking, and living — a perspective that can recognize the material-semiotic nature of both the status quo and change. The work of feminist writing teachers demonstrates the idea of double vision, while a paradigm shift in science illustrates the effect of double speaking. A teaching and writing narrative serves as the site where double being occurs when the boundaries of the who, what, and how of a student-teacher exchange blur.

491   Flynn, Elizabeth A. "Composing as a Woman." CCC 39 (December 1988): 423–35. Rpt. in Perl [239].

The work of Nancy Chodorow on differences between male and female children's relations to their mothers, of Carol Gilligan on female moral development, and of Mary Field Belenky and her colleagues on female intellectual development all suggest that women value collaboration and organize knowledge in networks, whereas men value individual achievement and organize knowledge hierarchically. These differences are reflected in the writing of first-year college students. Material on gender should be included in the composition course so that women students will be encouraged to compose in ways congenial to their gender rather than in the male ways traditionally followed in the academy.

492   Frank, Francine, and Paula A. Wattman. Treichler, et al. *Language, Gender, and Professional Writing: Theoretical Approaches and Guidelines for Nonsexist Usage*. New York: MLA, 1989.

Six essays on language and sexual equality are followed by a set of guidelines with full analysis and explanation of problems and ambiguities. The essays review work on gender and language, give a history of male-chauvinist influences in linguistics, and call for changing sexist language to foster feminist social goals. Essays include Sally McConnell-Ginet, "The Sexual (Re)Production of Meaning: A Discourse-Based Theory"; Paula Treichler, "From Discourse to Dictionary: How Sexist Meanings Are Authorized"; and Susan Wolfe, "The Reconstruction of Word Meanings: A Review of the Scholarship." Extensive bibliography and annotated list of suggestions for further reading.

493   Gannett, Cinthia. *Gender and the Journal*. Albany: State Univ. of New York Press, 1992.

For centuries, women have written journals and diaries to explore their sense of self and to maintain their social networks, although these texts, unlike many men's journals, were never intended for publication. More recently, journal writing has become an accepted part of composition pedagogy because it is seen as fostering pre-writing processes. Social constructionist theory has also supported journal writing through the idea that discourse is constitutive of identity. Expressive writing in journals thus becomes an important way to learn and grow. Feminist theory supports journal writing as a way for women muted by society to come to voice. Research shows that women students are often more comfortable with journal writing and write more than men. Nevertheless, academics remain uneasy with the expressive, personal aspects of journal writing and tend to emphasize its academic function. Journal writing should be treated more seriously as literature and not marginalized.

494   Gibson, Michelle, Martha Marinara, and Deborah Meem. "Bi, Butch, and Bar-Dyke: Pedagogical Performances of Class, Gender, and Sexuality." CCC 52.1 (September 2000): 69–95.

Compositionists who wish to create classrooms that critique traditional academic power structures must do more than incorporate readings on class, race, gender, and sexuality. The inclusion model does not adequately challenge the centrality of white middle-class male heterosexuality. Academic discussions of race, class, and gender downplay the political aspects of identity performance, and remain informed by essentialist identity politics. Narratives of the ways in which three writing teachers perform gender, class, and sexual identity illustrate how academic assumptions can be disrupted.

495   Gilyard, Keith, ed. *Race, Rhetoric, and Composition*. Portsmouth, N.H.: Boynton/Cook, 1999.

A collection of nine essays that critically examine race and discourses of race and identity in rhetoric and composition. Essays include Malea Powell, "Blood and Scholarship: One Mixed Blood's Story"; Meta G. Carstarphen, "News-Surfing the Race Question: Of Bell Curves, Words, and Rhetorical Metaphors"; Anissa Janine Wardi, "Terrorists, Madmen, and Religious Fanatics?: Revisiting Orientalism and Racist Rhetoric"; Keith Gilyard, "Higher Learning: Composition's Racialized Reflection"; David G. Holmes, "Fighting Back by *Writing* Black: Beyond Racially Reductive Composition Theory"; Amy Goodburn, "Racing (Erasing) White Privilege in Teacher/Research Writing about Race"; Robert D. Murray, Jr., "Power, Conflict, and Contact: Re-Constructing Authority in the Classroom"; Brad Peters, "Coming to Voice: 'Anger Disguised and Complex, not Anger Simple and Open' "; Gail Okawa, "Removing Masks: Confronting Graceful Evasion and Bad Habits in a Graduate English Class."

496   Hesford, Wendy. *Framing Identities: Autobiography and the Politics of Pedagogy*. Minneapolis: Univ. of Minnesota Press, 1999.

More than an expressionistic inquiry into one's hidden, essential, or true self, autobiographical acts — be they written texts, speech acts, visual forms, or symbolic gestures — are social, contradictory, and ideologically encoded acts of self-representation. Historically marginalized groups can use autobiography to refuse the identities imposed upon them by dominant groups. However, autobiography is not automatically an empowering tool. An understanding of the ways in which power is claimed, negotiated, and resisted through autobiography is necessary. In order to justify the attention to the personal in the classroom, and to move beyond naïve politics of identity, self-reflections must be integrated with cultural, material, and rhetorical analysis.

See: Karyn Hollis, "Liberating Voices" [410].

497   hooks, bell. *Talking Back: Thinking Feminist, Thinking Black*. Boston: South End Press, 1989.

hooks describes her experiences challenging race, gender, and class barriers to higher education. She analyzes the intersections of race, gender, and class oppressions and articulates a pedagogy to deal with them.

See: Jennifer Horsman, *Something in My Mind besides the Everyday* [266].

498   Howard, Rebecca Moore. "Sexuality, Textuality: The Cultural Work of Plagiarism." *College English* 62.4 (March 2000): 473–91.

The discourse of plagiarism is laden with gendered, sexualized metaphors of weakness, collaboration, disease, adultery, rape, and property. These metaphors connote a sense of sexual as well as textual violation. The term plagiarism, therefore, does as much (or more) cultural work as pedagogical; it regulates sexuality (insisting on compulsory heterosexuality) and student bodies as well as textuality and student papers. However, the metaphors that construct the term plagiarism are not the real problem; the term itself is, and should therefore be abandoned. Instead, we should concern ourselves with fraud, insufficient citation, and excessive repetition — pedagogical concerns rather than moral or sexual issues.

See: Daphne A. Jameson, "Using a Simulation to Teach Intercultural Communication in Business Communication Courses" [590].

499   Jarratt, Susan C., and Lynn Worsham. *Feminism and Composition Studies: In Other Words.* New York: MLA, 1998.

An introduction and afterword, thirteen essays, and six responses contribute to a growing dialogue between feminism and composition across discourses, pedagogies, alliances, and discontinuities. Essays include Laura Brady, "The Reproduction of Othering"; Shirley Wilson Logan, " 'When and Where I Enter': Race, Gender, and Composition Studies"; Pamela L. Caughie, "Let It Pass: Changing the Subject, Once Again"; Christy Desmet, "Equivalent Students, Equitable Classrooms"; Min-Zhan Lu, "Reading and Writing Differences: The Problematic of Experience"; Gail Stygall, "Women and Language in the Collaborative Writing Classroom"; and Harriet Malinowitz, "A Feminist Critique of Writing in the Disciplines." Response essays by Suzanne Clark, Ellen M. Gil-Gomez, Lisa Ede and Andrea Lunsford, and others.

500   Kirsch, Gesa. *Women Writing in the Academy: Audience, Authority, and Transformation.* Carbondale: Southern Illinois Univ. Press, 1993.

Interviews with thirty-five women (twenty students and fifteen faculty members) in five academic disciplines suggest that even successful academic writers struggle to maintain confidence in their own authorial authority. Authority issues can become more salient for women in the higher academic ranks because these women often feel both greater freedom and greater need to challenge disciplinary boundaries and conventional discourse forms. Women should continue to push for more collaborative academic work and more acceptance of a personal dimension in scholarly writing.

501   Kirsch, Gesa E., and Joy S. Ritchie. "Beyond the Personal: Theorizing a Politics of Location in Composition Research." CCC 46 (February 1995): 7–29.

Feminist scholarship has helped to validate personal experience as a source of knowledge in composition research. It is not enough, though, to locate ourselves in our research. To do so risks creating the kind of master narrative that feminism rejects because it silences other views. Rather, the feminist researcher should trace her personal views to their cultural and ideological sources, recognize her multiple and contradictory locations, and use the positions of others to gain critical insight into her own. Specifically, these ends can be served by research practices in which those being studied collaborate with the researcher in designing and interpreting the research. Even so, the researcher, although she cannot avoid being in a position of power, should be sensitive to abuse of power, such as soliciting overly personal information or editing out testimony that supports values different from her own. Ethical issues are critical in such research.

502   Kraemer, Don J., Jr. "Gender and the Autobiographical Essay: A Critical Extension of the Research." CCC 43 (1992): 323–40.

Much research suggests that men write personal narratives in which they are heroic agents struggling for independent achievement. Women's narratives, in contrast, depict the protagonist as one agent among several struggling to forge connections or sort out competing loyalties. Although student writers cannot set aside these gendered discourses, neither are their narratives wholly determined by them. Rather, most personal narratives show authors shaping a complex identity and negotiating among a range of discourses, the events of personal history, and classroom demands. We should read, and encourage students to read, personal narratives with an eye to the complexities, not just the stereotypes.

503   Lamb, Catherine E. "Beyond Argument in Feminist Composition." CCC 42 (February 1991): 11–24.

Monologic argument, in which an author seeks to establish the correctness of his or her view by knocking down all other views, is the dominant form of scholarly writing, a form uncongenial to women, who value relationships and negotiate responsibilities. But monologic argument cannot simply be replaced by autobiography as a preferred form. Women's very concern for others will motivate them to use persuasive power to rectify injustice, although without violence. More collaborative forms of argument are needed, however, in which the parties negotiate a resolution by exploring each other's needs in detail, brainstorming multiple solutions, and discussing alternatives to find a mutually agreeable resolution. Such forms of dealing with conflict, beneficial to both men and women, can be modeled in the composition class.

See: Andrea Lunsford, ed. *Reclaiming Rhetorica* [116].

504   Lyons, Scott Richard. "Rhetorical Sovereignty: What Do American Indians Want from Writing?" CCC 50 (1999): 447–68.

For American Indians, the end goal of literacy can be described as rhetorical sovereignty — as peoples' inherent right and ability to determine their own communicative needs and desires. While the field of composition and rhetoric has exhibited increased interest in American Indian and Native knowledge and voice, some of the literature expressing that interest has contained Indian stereotypes and cultural appropriations, and has excluded any discourse on sovereignty, a central concept in Indian discourse. Such literature actually hinders rhetorical sovereignty, which demands a radical rethinking of what gets taught as the written word. In the interest of rhetorical sovereignty, canons and curricula need to expand; specifically, graduate and writing programs might start by examining American Indian rhetoric, taking treaties and federal laws as rhetorical texts.

505   Malinowitz, Harriet. *Textual Orientations: Lesbian and Gay Students and the Making of Discourse Communities*. Portsmouth, N.H.: Heinemann-Boynton/Cook, 1994.

Gay, lesbian, and bisexual students continue to face a deeply homophobic environment in writing classes, making assignments to reflect on the self, narrate personal events, or otherwise reveal the writer's subjectivity highly problematic. The field of composition needs to recognize the existence of lesbian and gay discourses and discourse communities and allow these students to explore the social construction of their identities. Lesbian and gay students in gay-themed writing courses find that sexual identity is a significant epistemological context and social location. They discover the history and thematics of their community, analyze the ways that "gay" and "straight" have been constructed and valued in dominant discourses; excavate social meanings that underlie mainstream attitudes, complicating the very idea of sexual identity; and escape the disenfranchising individualism that confines them in mainstream views of sexual identity. The theories of social construction and critical pedagogy facilitate this understanding and allow further investigation of complex cross-cultural community definitions with similarly disabling mainstream constructions.

506   Parks, Steven. *Class Politics: The Movement for the Students' Right to Their Own Language*. Urbana, Ill.: NCTE, 2000.

The CCCC 1974 resolution of the Students' Right to Their Own Language (SRTOL) represents much more than a moment in the history of the discipline. When considered in conjunction with the political and social organizations and movements of the time, such as the civil rights movement, Black Power, and anti-Vietnam protests, the SRTOL brings to light the importance of collective action by academics. The SRTOL exemplifies both the possibilities and difficulties of progressive coalition politics; and its history can be read as a guide for new university-community alliances and community-based pedagogy.

507   Phelps, Louise Wetherbee, and Janet Emig, eds. *Feminine Principles and Women's Experience in American Composition and Rhetoric*. Pittsburgh: Univ. of Pittsburgh Press, 1995.

Fourteen essays explore many aspects of women's work as teachers and writers, including Patricia Bizzell, "Praising Folly: Constructing a Postmodern Rhetorical Authority as a Woman"; Lillian Bridwell-Bowles, "Discourse and Diversity: Experimental Writing within the Academy"; Robert Connors, "Women's Reclamation of Rhetoric in Nineteenth-Century America"; Mary Kay Crouch, with Son Kim Vo, "The Role of Vietnamese Women in Literacy Processes: An Interview"; Janice Hays, "Intellectual Parenting and a Developmental Feminist Pedagogy of Writing"; Sara Dalmas Jonsberg, with Maria Salgado and the Women of the Next Step, "Composing the Multiple Self: Teen Mothers Rewrite Their Roles"; Louise Wetherbee Phelps, "Becoming a Warrior: Lessons of the Feminist Workplace"; and Nancy Sommers, "Between the Drafts." In addition, six essays comment on the previous fourteen, identifying recurring themes, significant omissions, and directions for further study.

508   Prendergast, Catherine. "Race: The Absent Presence in Composition Studies." CCC 50.1 (September 1998): 36–53.

Heath's *Ways with Words* forms a point of departure for this analysis of the ways in which race has been ignored in its relationship to the composing process and how race takes the form of other tropes. Studying the "deliberately dissonant" rhetorical stances of critical race theorists — namely, Patricia Williams and Derrick Bell — can help to foreground race in the discourses of composition studies and to uncover composition's colonial sensibilities. Through a rhetoric of double-consciousness, including features of irrationality and other departures from argumentation, these authors use voices that "refuse to be socialized" to reflect experiences of discrimination. Williams creates allegories, for example, to confront myths of black women — a textual act of double-consciousness that the author contends should not be manufactured in the composition classroom. More important is to track the ways race appears and disappears in "the collective unconscious" of composition, for example, in the discourses of basic writing. Critical race theory teaches us that our rhetoric inscribes students as foreigners and leaves whiteness uninvestigated. Braddock Award winner.

509   Ratcliffe, Krista. "Eavesdropping as Rhetorical Tactic: History, Whiteness, and Rhetoric." JAC 20.1 (2000): 87–119.

Using a composite definition formed in part by Mary Daly's method of gynocentric writing, eavesdropping can be redefined, or reconsidered, as an ethical rhetorical tactic, and as a way to study history, whiteness, and rhetoric. If we deliberately place ourselves at the edges of our own knowledge, we can overhear — without the demeaning, gossip-related connotations — and learn from others and ourselves. Further, if we shift our gaze in historical exploration from origins to usage as the focal point, we can eavesdrop on history in productive ways. Within the usage-directed framework, the past empowers us and leads to accountability. By eavesdropping on historical moments when the trope of whiteness was used in the United States, we can disengage dysfunctional realities of the past and dysfunctional idealizations of the present. Eavesdropping prompts scholars to reflect on the role of whiteness in the field and all its embodiments, and enables teachers to better equip students with a rhetorical tactic for examining the role whiteness plays in their lives.

See: Jacqueline Jones Royster, *Traces of a Stream: Literacy and Social Change Among African American Woman* [130].

See: Jacqueline Jones Royster and Jean C. Williams, "History in the Spaces Left: African American Presence and Narratives of Composition Studies" [129].

See: Donnalee Rubin, *Gender Influences* [361].

510   Schell, Eileen E. *Gypsy Academics and Mother Teachers: Gender, Contingent Labor, and Writing Instruction.* Portsmouth, N.H.: Boynton/ Cook, 1998.

Research methodologies informed by socialist feminism — interviews, published narratives, and survey responses — document the perspectives of women who are disproportionally employed as contingent labor in writing instruction and allow intervention into the debates surrounding the erosion of faculty working conditions. Women seek or end up in nontenure-track positions for complex reasons, some of which date back to nineteenth century gender ideologies and the disciplinary formation of English studies, but none of which can be neatly explained as women's desire for a "psychic income." Critiquing the maternal ethic of care in feminist pedagogy, building coalitions to reform working conditions, and developing professional development programs are all strategies to address women's roles in the academy. Schell ends with an analysis of four proposed solutions to reform working conditions for all contingent faculty; without endorsing any of the four, Schell argues for "academic citizenship" as essential to preserving academic freedom.

511   Severino, Carol, Juan C. Guerra, and Johnnella E. Butler, eds. *Writing in Multicultural Settings.* New York: MLA, 1997.

Twenty essays and four cross-talks engage with the challenges of multiculturalism. Four sections address Cultural and Linguistic Diversity, The Roles of Teachers and Texts, ESL Issues, and Sociocultural and Pedagogical Tensions. Essays include Bonnie Lisle and Sandra Mano, "Embracing a Multicultural Rhetoric"; Michelle Grijalva, "Teaching American Indian Students: Interpreting the Rhetorics of Silence"; Kermit E. Campbell, "Real Niggaz's Don't Die: African American Students Speaking Themselves into Their Writing"; Carol Severino, "Two Approaches to 'Cultural Text': Toward Multicultural Literacy"; Esha Niyogi De and Donna Uthus Gregory,

"Decolonizing the Classroom: Freshman Composition in a Multicultural Setting"; Wendy S. Hesford, "Writing Identities: The Essence of Difference in Multicultural Classrooms"; Muriel Harris, "Cultural Conflicts in the Writing Center: Expectations and Assumptions of ESL Students"; Juan C. Guerra, "The Place of Intercultural Literacy in the Writing Classroom"; Mary Soliday, "The Politics of Difference: Toward a Pedagogy of Reciprocity"; and Kate Mangelsdorf, "Students on the Border."

512   Shepard, Alan, John McMillan, and Gary Tate, eds. *Coming to Class: Pedagogy and the Social Class of Teachers.* Portsmouth, N.H.: Boynton/ Cook, 1998.

Reflective, autobiographical essays about the relationship of socioeconomic class to teaching, or how teachers' social class or experiences with class issues influence their teaching practices. Twenty-one essays, including Jim Daniels, "Class and Classroom: Going to Work"; Louise DeSalvo, "Digging Deep"; Donald Lazere, "Class Conflict in the English Profession"; Cecilia Rodrigues Milanes, "Color and Class"; Beverly J. Moss, "Intersections of Race and Class in the Academy"; Hephzibah Roskelly, "Rising and Converging: Race and Class in the South"; Patricia A. Sullivan, "Passing: A Family Dissemblance"; and Gary Tate, "Halfway Back Home."

See: Ira Shor and Caroline Pari, *Critical Literacy in Action* [387].

See: Lad Tobin. "Car Wrecks, Baseball Caps, and Man-to-Man Defense: The Personal Narratives of Adolescent Males" [415].

513   Wallace, David L., and Annissa Bell. "Being Black at a Predominantly White University." *College English* 61.3 (January 1999): 307–27.

Interviews with three African American men — English or education majors at a university with a 7.1 percent minority enrollment rate — challenge the results of quantitative retention studies and offer a richer understanding of minority students' experiences. The three students resisted the label of "success stories," forcing the researchers to rethink how to tell these stories without being reductive or essentialist and without reproducing the dominant culture. Three critical issues from the literature frame the narratives: an educational system that reproduces inequality; the paradoxical position of "being a victim"; and assimilation and resistance. African American men, in particular, face social adjustment problems on predominantly white college campuses which are unknown to white students, but positive contact with faculty — and opportunities to explore the consequences of assimilation or resistance — may determine which students persevere.

Cultural Studies

514   Berlin, James A. *Rhetorics, Poetics, and Cultures: Refiguring English Studies*. Urbana, Ill.: NCTE, 1996.

For almost three centuries, English studies in America served to secure the hegemony of the dominant social group by valorizing their cultural capital. Until about 1970, this meant educating a professional elite — lawyers, ministers, politicians, and business leaders. But after 1970, the global economy began to change rapidly and radically. The American economy deindustrialized, and social power now devolved upon a managerial class, those who could best communicate, collaborate, and learn new tasks quickly. Moreover, American society changed rapidly as well, with immigrants coming in record numbers in the 1980s, rich and poor suddenly moving much further apart culturally and economically, and families developing models other than the nuclear to organize their lives. The traditional English department simply cannot cope with all of these rapid changes. Literary theorists and cultural studies scholars understand that they need to redesign their profession, but they may not realize that they need to enlist the aid of workers in social-epistemic rhetoric. These rhetoricians can help them because they are already accustomed to dealing with a wide range of texts, visual and musical as well as print; because they deal with texts that exert power in the world (political, legal, ceremonial, etc.) and not merely those that exist to be appreciated aesthetically; because they have always focused on the production rather than the reception of texts; and because they are comfortable crossing disciplinary boundaries. They can help create a new English studies discipline that erases the split between rhetoric and poetic and studies all forms of signifying practices, their genres, ideologies, and supporting social institutions. The new English studies will equip students not only for work in a postindustrial age but also for participatory citizenship in a multicultural democracy. Berlin concludes with detailed descriptions of two cultural studies courses that enact the pedagogy for which he calls, and three English departments that have already reorganized themselves along the lines he recommends.

515   Berlin, James A., and Michael J. Vivion, eds. *Cultural Studies in the English Classroom*. Portsmouth, N.H.: Heinemann-Boynton/Cook, 1992.

Scholars in English studies and composition contribute nine essays that address issues involved in designing literature and/or writing courses with a cultural studies focus, including Michael Blitz and C. Mark Hurlbert, "Cults of Culture"; Philip E. Smith II, "Composing a Cultural Studies Curriculum at Pitt"; Delores K. Schriner, "One Person, Many Worlds: A Multi-Cultural Composition Curriculum"; and Richard Penticoff and Linda Brodkey, " 'Writing about Difference': Hard Cases for Cultural Studies." These essays are followed by ten essays that describe cultural studies courses on such varied topics as the research paper, visual texts, and Shakespeare.

516   Cushman, Ellen. "The Rhetorician as an Agent of Social Change." CCC 47 (February 1996): 7–28.

Academics can be activists for progressive social change if they tear down the barriers, both literal and socioeconomic, between them and the communities surrounding their schools. They can find ways to use their specialized academic knowledge to work with literacy activities already happening in the community. Social change need not be defined in terms of sweeping mass movements; it can happen in people's everyday uses of language as well. Rhetoricians can help bring about such changes by sharing academic resources, such as libraries and computers; by tutoring written and oral language, such as that used in a social-service application or job interview; and by implementing service-learning courses according to Bruce Herzberg's model (see [699]). This activist work is reciprocal, not altruistic, because the academic gains such benefits as interesting research sites. Cushman's appendices make clear that she intends her argument here to stand as a powerful critique of the tendency of some cultural studies scholars and Freirean educators to hold aloof from people whom they regard as unenlightened about the functions of oppressive ideologies. Braddock Award winner.

517   Farmer, Frank. "Dialogue and Critique: Bakhtin and the Cultural Studies Writing Classroom." CCC 49 (May 1998): 187–207.

A besetting problem in cultural studies pedagogy is the cultural studies critic's apparent stance of superiority over consumers of mass culture, who do not, as the critic does, notice and resist its ideological messages. Students usually resent this superior role for their teacher and reject it for themselves. Two concepts from the work of literary theorist Mikhail Bakhtin can help address this difficulty. One is his notion of "anacrisis," or critical questioning. The teacher can use questions to bring out the students' "going truths" or ingrained ideologies and also to reveal his or her own positions. The second is the concept of the "superaddressee," a hypothetical listener or reader who is imagined to understand the speaker or writer perfectly. Bakhtin says that one imagines this audience in order to overcome the fear of being misunderstood or ignored, and thus to be willing to take the risk of uttering or writing. This concept can be used to analyze popular culture artifacts for the vision of a better life that they project. For example, The Cosby Show, attacked by television cultural critic Mark Crispin Miller as racist, can be analyzed as providing with its images of affluence a symbolic corrective to social inequities that make such affluence especially hard for African-Americans to obtain. Such an analysis helps to acknowledge the sources of pleasure in popular culture, which students soon become weary of hearing relentlessly denounced.

518   McComiskey, Bruce. "Social-Process Rhetorical Inquiry: Cultural Studies Methodologies for Critical Writing about Advertisements." *Journal of Advanced Composition* 17 (1997): 381–400.

Classical Marxism focuses on a cycle that begins with the production of material things, which are then distributed for purchase, and finally consumed in such a way as to produce more things, so that the cycle continues. Cultural studies applies this cycle to ideology, focusing first on the production of desires for things. Next, cultural studies looks at distribution not in terms of transportation systems and the like but in terms of cultural institutions, such as workplaces, schools, or organs of the mass media, that provide contexts for the values that produce desires. Consumption, for cultural studies, focuses not on the use of material things but on the use of values to construct identities, a process that, in turn, creates new desires. An adequate cultural studies pedagogy must address all three moments in this cycle. It must ask: How do cultural artifacts (advertisements, in this case) construct their ideal consumers through the values they project? How do media that circulate artifacts and their values create larger contexts for them (e.g., how does a fashion magazine create a context for the perfume ad placed in it)? How do the values thus circulated impact consumers, that is, how do people accept, reject, or modify the subject positions these artifacts offer them? Cultural studies critics are often negative about consumers who accept the subject positions offered to them by mass culture as if these were natural or universal. But this view errs by neglecting the extent to which people negotiate with what's offered and shape it to their own ends. McComiskey concludes with specific examples from his own cultural studies pedagogy to teach all three moments in the cycle.

519   Reynolds, Nedra. "Interrupting Our Way to Agency: Feminist Cultural Studies and Composition." *Feminism and Composition Studies: In Other Words.* Ed. Susan C. Jarratt and Lynn Worsham. New York: MLA, 1998.

Women need an idea of agency that reflects postmodernism's insights into the multiple and competing subjectivities within the self but that still conceptualizes the possibility of individual action amid one's own circumstances. A rhetorical dimension of this notion of agency might draw upon interruption as a deliberate strategy for those who are all too often interrupted or silenced when they try to speak. A cultural-studies analysis of the impact of feminist work on British cultural studies shows just such a strategy of interruption in action. Similarly, American feminists need to interrupt cultural-studies work in composition. Cultural-studies scholars John Trimbur and James Berlin replicate British male chauvinism when they allow their Marxist-inspired focus on labor and class issues to cause them to neglect gender issues and feminist scholarship. Lester Faigley can also be faulted for relying too heavily on the work of French cultural critic Jean-François Lyotard, leading him to deny metanarratives, such as the critique of patriarchy, that are vital to feminism, and to portray academic discourse as unrelentingly agonistic. Feminist writing teachers can encourage students to interrupt the academy's expectations for traditional academic discourse, with its emphasis on clarity, coherence, and linear organization to prove a thesis, and help students to devise forms more congenial to women.

520   Rosteck, Thomas, ed. *At the Intersection: Cultural Studies and Rhetorical Studies*. New York: Guilford, 1999.

Scholars from American Studies, Speech Communication, and English contribute thirteen essays that focus on connections between the theoretical discourses of cultural studies and rhetoric, or that trace such links through analysis of cultural artifacts. Contributors include Carole Blair and Neil Michel, "Commemorating in the Theme Park Zone: Reading the Astronauts Memorial"; Steven Mailloux, "Reading the Culture Wars: Traveling Rhetoric and the Reception of Curricular Reform"; Barry Brummett and Detine L. Bowers, "Subject Positions as a Site of Rhetorical Struggle: Representing African Americans"; Elizabeth Walker Mechling and Jay Mechling, "American Cultural Criticism in the Pragmatic Attitude"; Cary Nelson, "The Linguisticality of Cultural Studies: Rhetoric, Close Reading, and Contextualization"; and Thomas S. Frentz and Janice Hocker Rushing, "Courting Community in Contemporary Culture."

See: Carol Severino, Juan C. Guerra, and Johnella E. Butler, eds., *Writing in Multicultural Settings* [511].

521   Sirc, Geoffrey. "Never Mind the Tagmemics, Where's the Sex Pistols?" CCC 48 (February 1997): 9–29.

Composition teachers were drawn to teaching popular music and encouraging self-exploration and self-expression in the 1960s. But the field returned to more academic materials and goals in the 1970s. Therefore, composition studies ignored the phenomenon of punk music when it emerged in the mid-1970s. Punk's ethos was both nihilistic and playful, unconcerned in either case with success or problem-solving. In the 1980s the neglect of punk continued — its demise as a popular music form around 1980 was ignored — because composition studies wanted irony-free reproduction of academic discourse while punk art abounded in irreverent transformations of familiar images of respect and power. Composition studies favored mastery and control over one's medium, whereas punk artists attempted above all to generate energy and emotion, with musicianship taking a back seat. Composition studies could have benefited from admitting the punk perspective — it would have made writing more fun, put more emphasis on process as opposed to product, and given students permission, too, to hate writing and to fail. Punk's negative perspective is still present, fortunately, and beginning to influence composition studies after all, such as in the work of Richard Miller and Joseph Harris. Sirc's essay exemplifies cultural-studies criticism.

522   Trimbur, John. "Articulation Theory and the Problem of Determination: A Reading of *Lives on the Boundary*." *Journal of Advanced Composition* 13 (Winter 1993): 33–50.

Cultural studies can help explain Mike Rose's *Lives on the Boundary* [467]. In this book, Rose tells the story of his own life according to a familiar American pattern: the poor boy who makes good through his own efforts, especially through acquiring advanced literacy. His moments of resistance to the dominant order — when he just wants to be "average" rather than to excel in school — are mediated by adult mentors, and Rose himself eventually enters adult life successfully and takes a secure place in a profession, teaching. This story could be faulted for undercutting the book's larger purpose by suggesting that the educational reforms Rose advocates would not be necessary if everyone worked as hard as he did. Trimbur argues, however, that the presence of this familiar American narrative in Rose's book should be understood as a "conjuncture," in cultural-studies terms, that is, an historical moment when ideas converge and take their meaning from one another. The meaning of the narrative is changed here by its use in a larger project of education reform. It does not simply celebrate individual effort but rather provides a vehicle for demonstrating the many social constraints on educational success. As in Stuart Hall's "articulation" theory, Rose puts together seemingly contradictory discursive elements in order to make meaning out of his life and to make a persuasive case for reform. We know that he is not simply advocating conformity to traditional literacy as the sole path to success because he also dramatizes the unfairness of traditional standards of evaluation and the richness of nontraditional students' literacy experiences outside of school. Rose's use of a familiar autobiographical trope, therefore, should be understood as a strategy to gain broader popular acceptance for his valuable educational views.

523   Trimbur, John. *Popular Literacy: Studies in Cultural Practices and Poetics*. Pittsburgh: Univ. of Pittsburgh Press, 2001.

Poses the question of how people make literacy popular, using reading and writing for their own ends rather than for official purposes, and offers fourteen essays that explore that question, including: Mariolina Salvatori, "Porque no puedo decir mi cuento: Mexican Ex-votos' Iconographic Literacy"; Cheryl Glenn, "Popular Literacy in the Middle Ages: *The Book of Margery Kempe*"; Todd S. Gernes, "Recasting the Culture of Ephemera"; Patricia Bizzell, "Stolen Literacies in *Iola Leroy*"; Stephanie Almagno, Nedra Reynolds, and John Trimbur, "Italian-American Cookbooks: Authenticity and the Market"; Nicholas Coles, "Joe Shakespeare: The Contemporary British Worker Movement"; Diana George, "Changing the Face of Poverty: Nonprofits and the Problem of Representation"; Lundy Braun and John Trimbur, "Popularizing Science: At the Boundary of Expert and Lay Biomedical Knowledge"; Lester Faigley, "Understanding Popular Digital Literacies: Metaphors for the Internet."

Teaching English as a Second Language

524   Belcher, Diane, and George Braine, eds. *Academic Writing in a Second Language: Essays on Research and Pedagogy*. Norwood, N.J.: Ablex, 1994.

Sixteen essays exploring the social perspective on ESL writing issues. Included are Ilona Leki, "Good Writing: I Know It When I See It"; George Braine, "Writing in the Natural Sciences"; Diane Belcher, "Writing Critically across the Curriculum"; Ulla Connor and Melinda Kramer, "Writing from Sources: Case Studies of Graduate Students in Business Management"; Diane Tedick and Maureen Mathison, "Holistic Scoring on ESL Writing Assessment: What Does an Analysis of Rhetorical Features Reveal?"; Ann Johns, "Teaching Classroom and Authentic Genres: Initiating Students into Academic Cultures and Discourses"; and Sally Jacoby, David Leech, and Christine Holten, "A Genre-Based Developmental Writing Course for Undergraduate ESL Science Majors."

525   Belcher, Diane, and Alan Hirvela, eds. *Linking Literacies: Perspectives on L2 Reading-Writing Connections*. Ann Arbor: The Univ. of Michigan Press, 2001.

Examining a wide range of issues within the general rubrics of L2 reading-writing connections and L2 academic literacy illustrates the many ways in which L2 reading-writing relations can be manifested. Following an introduction by the editors, thirteen chapters in four sections consider the theories, history, and research that influence L2 literacy pedagogy, including: William Grabe, "Reading-Writing Relations: Theoretical Perspectives and Instructional Practices"; Paul Kei Matsuda, "Reexamining Audiolingualism: On the Genesis of Reading and Writing in L2 Studies"; Alan Hirvela, "Connecting Reading and Writing through Literature"; George Newell, Maria C. Garriga, and Susan S. Peterson, "Learning to Assume the Role of Author: A Study of Reading-to-Write One's Own Ideas in an Undergraduate ESL Composition Course"; Barbara Dobson and Christine Feak, "A Cognitive Modeling Approach to Teaching Critique Writing to Nonnative Speakers"; Joel Bloch, "Plagiarism and the ESL Student: From Printed to Electronic Texts"; Debbie Barks and Patricia Watts, "Textual Borrowing Strategies for Graduate-Level ESL Writers"; Georgette Jabbour, "Lexis and Grammar in Second Language Reading and Writing."

526   Carson, Joan G., and Ilona Leki, eds. *Reading in the Composition Classroom: Second Language Perspectives*. Boston: Heinle and Heinle, 1993.

After many years of being taught separately as technical skills, reading and writing are increasingly being taught together in ESL courses that recognize the inextricable links between them. Eighteen essays examine how individual readers process text, how cultural contexts affect understanding, and how reading can be taught in writing classes.

Essays include Ilona Leki, "Reciprocal Themes in ESL Reading and Writing"; Joy Reid, "Historical Perspectives on Writing and Reading in the ESL Classroom"; Barbara Kroll, "Teaching Writing Is Teaching Reading: Training the New Teacher of ESL Composition"; Joan Carson, "Reading for Writing: Cognitive Perspectives"; Douglas Flahive and Nathalie Bailey, "Exploring Reading/Writing Relationships in Adult Second Language Learners"; Ruth Spack, "Student Meets Text, Text Meets Student: Finding a Way into Academic Discourse"; Sarah Benesch, "ESL Authors: Reading and Writing Critical Autobiographies"; and Ann Johns, "Reading and Writing Tasks in English for Academic Purposes Classes: Products, Processes, and Resources."

527   Connor, Ulla. *Contrastive Rhetoric: Cross-Cultural Aspects of Second-Language Writing.* New York: Cambridge Univ. Press, 1996.

Contrastive rhetoric studies the ways that a first language interferes with learning a second language. Contrastive rhetoric has become increasingly complex, moving beyond the analysis of merely negative effects to include, today, insights from rhetoric, composition studies, discourse theory, genre theory, theoretical and applied linguistics, and literacy theory. Moreover, studies of ESL learners from different cultures have produced detailed analyses of cultural and educational differences that influence second-language learning. Connor summarizes the relevant aspects of each set of theories and of the major empirical studies and draws implications for further study of ESL, EFL, and ESP research.

528   Cummins, Jim. "The Sanitized Curriculum: Educational Disempowerment in a Nation at Risk." *Richness in Writing: Empowering ESL Students.* Ed. Donna M. Johnson and Duane H. Roen. White Plains: Longman, 1989. 19–38.

The 1983 report "A Nation at Risk" shifted policy emphasis from equity to "excellence." Subsequent reports focus on raising standards and getting tough. This reform movement threatens to disempower students, particularly minority students, by fostering a "transmission" approach to teaching that ignores students' need to develop a sense of efficacy in their relations with educators. Transmission especially harms ESL students by excluding student experience and suppressing the meaningful communication needed to learn language. Moreover, the reforms reflect an autocratic image of society that is counterdemocratic. In addition, the focus on excellence promotes passivity rather than critical thinking. An alternative conception of reform can be based on a more productive interaction between students and teachers, active use of written and oral language for critical thinking, and use of students' cultural resources that will enrich all students. Our children's generation will need critical skills and intercultural understanding in the future and cannot reach the goals set out in "A Nation at Risk" by following the path of "excellence" laid out there.

529   Ferdman, Bernardo M., Rose-Marie Weber, and Arnulfo G. Ramirez, eds. *Literacy across Languages and Cultures*. Albany: State Univ. of New York Press, 1994.

Meeting the English literacy needs of members of linguistic and cultural minorities in the United States requires rethinking many assumptions about literacy itself, especially because most research concentrates on first-language literacy. The eleven essays in this volume probe the meaning of literacy in a multiethnic context, the processes of second-language and second-culture acquisition, and the application of current research to these concerns. Essays include Stephen Reder, "Practice-Engagement Theory: A Sociocultural Approach to Literacy across Languages and Cultures"; Nancy Hornberger, "Continua of Biliteracy"; Concha Delgado-Gaitan, "Sociocultural Change through Literacy: Toward the Empowerment of Families"; Barbara McCaskill, "Literacy in the Loophole of Retreat: Harriet Jacobs's Nineteenth-Century Narrative"; and Alison d'Anglejan, "Language and Literacy in Quebec."

530   Harklau, Linda. "From the 'Good Kids' to the 'Worst': Representations of English Language Learners Across Educational Settings." *TESOL Quarterly* 34.1 (Spring 2000): 35–67.

Learners' identities affect their experiences in school; the institutional label *ESOL student*, largely accepted as unchanging and self-evident, played a crucial role in three students' transitions from high school to college. Three year-long ethnographic case studies of language minority students, each a U.S. high school graduate, illustrate how educators' representations of ESOL student identity are reproduced in broader institutional discourses and how representations have direct effects on classroom behavior and achievement in both settings — keeping students engaged in high school but turning them away in community college. The representation of what it meant to be an ESOL student in high school (immigrants as model students) facilitated favorable conditions for learning while the dominant representation of ESOL students in their community college (new to the U.S.) led to student resistance. In the context of the high school, images of immigrants informed a representation of ESOL students as hardworking and highly motivated; in the ESOL program of the urban community college, however, the curriculum reflected an image of ESOL students as cultural novices — with goals diametrically opposed to these students' self-perceptions and expectations as seasoned school-goers and residents of the U.S. Labels given to students have consequences for students' classroom behavior and investment in learning; at the same time, institutional representations, in determining how entering students are placed and evaluated, have significant educational implications.

531   Harklau, Linda, Kay M. Losey and Meryl Siegal, eds. *Generation 1.5 Meets College Composition: Issues in the Teaching of Writing to U.S.-Educated Learners of ESL*. Mahwah, N.J.: Lawrence Erlbaum, 1999.

The "1.5 generation" represents the student population of U.S. high school graduates who enter higher education while in the process of learning English; their traits and experiences lie somewhere in between those of first or second generation immigrants. Twelve chapters address instructional issues presented by this group and include Ilona Leki, " 'Pretty Much I Screwed Up': Ill-Served Needs of a Permanent Resident"; Judith Rodby, "Contingent Literacy: The Social Construction of Writing for Nonnative English-Speaking College Freshmen"; Yuet-Sim D. Chiang and Mary Schmida, "Language Identity and Language Ownership: Linguistic Conflicts of First-Year University Writing Students"; Beth Hartman and Elaine Tarone, "Preparation for College Writing: Teachers Talk About Writing Instruction for Southeast Asian American Students in Secondary School"; Dana R. Ferris, "One Size Does Not Fit All: Response and Revision Issues for Immigrant Student Writers"; and Kate Wolfe-Quintero and Gabriela Segade, "University Support for Second-Language Writers Across the Curriculum."

532   Huckin, Thomas, Margot Haynes, and James Coady. *Second Language Reading and Vocabulary Learning*. Norwood, N.J.: Ablex, 1993.

Fourteen essays report on research into the ways that ESL students learn vocabulary, including analyses of L1 vocabulary learning and the efficacy of contextual guessing, investigation of the assumption that reading improves vocabulary acquisition, and evaluation of pedagogical practices for improving vocabulary. Essays include Frederika Stoller and William Grabe, "Implication for L2 Vocabulary Acquisition from L1 Research"; Margot Haynes, "Patterns and Perils of Guessing in Second Language Reading"; Chion-Lan Chern, "Chinese Students' Word-Solving Strategies in Reading in English"; Kate Parry, "Too Many Words: Learning the Vocabulary of an Academic Subject"; Mark Stein, "The Healthy Inadequacy of Contextual Definition"; and Cheryl Brown, "Factors Affecting the Acquisition of Vocabulary: Frequency and Saliency of Words."

533   Kubota, Ryoko. "Japanese Culture Constructed by Discourses: Implications for Applied Linguistics Research and ELT." *TESOL Quarterly* 33.1 (Spring 1999): 9–35.

Conceptions of culture tend to dichotomize Western culture and Eastern culture, drawing boundaries between them in areas of inquiry such as contrastive rhetoric. In the applied linguistic literature, Japanese culture is essentialized, the result of discourse that defines the subordinate group as exotic Other. Another way of understanding cultural differences comes from a critique of cultural representations from the concepts of discourse and power/knowledge, not to dismiss the existence of diversity within a culture but to escape the binary logic of same versus different. In this view, characteristics of the Japanese people and culture are seen as ideological constructs that promote homogeneity and thus serve the interest of the government and corporations, as illustrated through *nihonjinron*. The peda-gogical tension between acculturation and pluralist approaches in teaching ESL students suggests an alternative model, that of critical multiculturalism that supports both cultural pluralism and critical acquisition of the dominant language.

534   Kutz, Eleanor, Suzy Q. Groden, and Vivian Zamel. *The Discovery of Competence: Teaching and Learning with Diverse Student Writers*. Ports-mouth, N.H.: Boynton/Cook, 1993.

Teachers of writing, especially to ESL students, should begin with students' competences and not focus on correcting their deficits. Understanding the complexities of language acquisition allows teach-ers to help students acquire new competencies in academic discourse. The academy is a culture with a discourse and mindsets that are alien to many students, particularly to ESL students. Teachers can, how-ever, make the transition to the new culture less frustrating and alien-ating by designing courses that allow students to discover and build on existing abilities and knowledge as they investigate new condi-tions and expectations. Language learning comes from the desire to make meaning, not from building up incremental linguistic units; so, too, with a second language or dialect. Moreover, intellectual devel-opment and cognitive orientations to learning that characterize ex-tant competencies need to be respected and not forced into academic molds. Teachers can use the classroom as a research site for discover-ing students' abilities and examining their own teaching methods, taking a critical view of their curricular frameworks. The authors in-clude many excerpts from student papers reflecting on their language-learning experiences, describe classroom research practices, suggest ways to assess student competencies, and offer advice about creating multicultural frameworks for curriculum development.

535   Leki, Ilona. "Coping Strategies of ESL Students in Writing Tasks across the Curriculum." *TESOL Quarterly* 29.2 (Summer 1995): 235–60.

A naturalistic study examined five ESL visa students' experiences in disciplinary courses and identified strategies that students both bring with them and develop in response to writing demands. Through interviews, observations, student journals, and various documents, ten categories of strategies were cataloged, including relying on past writing experiences, looking for models, and accommodating (and resisting) teachers' demands. Each student is profiled, and then each of the ten categories is illustrated.

536   Leki, Ilona. *Understanding ESL Writers: A Guide for Teachers*. Ports-mouth, N.H.: Boynton/Cook, 1992.

Although teaching writing to ESL students is not radically different from teaching writing to native speakers, it helps to understand the difficulties of learning to write in an L2. Native speakers must or-chestrate many skills and strategies to write: ESL writers face, in addition, limited vocabulary, cultural and idiomatic complexities, un-familiar style and audience expectations, and the frustration of not being able to express their real thoughts or knowledge. Only slowly has ESL teaching shifted from structure-based language instruction to process-based instruction. Research confirms that the desire to communicate aids language acquisition, whereas knowledge of rules and error-correction does not. Immersion in language, especially reading, is vital for writing. At the same time, social comfort increases the desire to communicate. Leki sensitively discusses the characteristics of ESL students and ways to distinguish ESL students from basic writers in classes where they are mixed, recommends classroom practices for teachers in ESL and mixed classes, analyzes ESL-student writing behavior (concerning personal writing, plagiarism, sophistication, and so on), describes L2 writing processes, surveys findings of contrastive rhetoric for several cultures, discusses sentence-level correction, and offers advice about responding. Includes an extensive, unannotated bibliography.

See: Min-Zhan Lu, "From Silence to Words: Writing as Struggle" [462].

537   Matsuda, Paul Kei and Tony Silva. "Cross-Cultural Composition: Mediated Integration of U.S. and International Students." *Composition Studies* 27.1 (Spring 1999): 15–30.

A cross-cultural composition course, designed to integrate U.S. and international students, provides an alternative placement option for ESL writers and promotes intercultural understanding for both groups of students. Integrating ESL writers into existing writing courses has an economic advantage; however, traditional mainstreaming has several problems when ESL writers are a distinct minority. ESL-friendly courses provide a mediated integration of NES and ESL writers; not conflict-free, such a course foregrounds difference. The cross-cultural aspect of this placement option may be especially valuable at institutions where linguistic and cultural diversity is not prevalent.

538   Nelson, Marie W. *At the Point of Need: Teaching Basic and ESL Writers*. Portsmouth, N.H.: Boynton/Cook, 1991.

Beginning with the premise that attending closely to students' own descriptions of the writing help they need would improve their pedagogy, teams of writing-center tutors over five years carefully recorded their interactions with basic-writing and ESL students — and with one another — as they sought to discover how best to teach writing. The teams discovered significant similarities between ESL and basic writers in writing behaviors, assumptions, and development. Students also had unrecognized skills of invention and language production that could be tapped once they were given permission to use them. Allowing students to be independent of the teacher produced the best results in the long term, a condition accomplished by establishing a safe atmosphere, modeling successful writing behaviors, unteaching misperceptions about how to write, pointing out strengths in student writing, rewarding critical attitudes and risk taking, and so on. The tutors refined the process of working with students and the steps that might be taken to help writers become independent and fluent. Many case studies illustrate the development of students — basic writers and ESL students from many cultures — and of the tutors. Chapters examine longitudinal studies of writers, types of writing assignments, the organization of the writing center, the training of tutors, and research design.

539   Pennycook, Alastair. "Borrowing Others' Words: Text, Ownership, Memory, and Plagiarism." *TESOL Quarterly* 30:2 (Summer 1996): 201–230.

Memorizing the words of others and other acts of language learning differ significantly across cultures, and understanding the complex issues related to textual borrowing makes Western notions of plagiarism confusing and hypocritical. A brief history of authorship and the individual shows that the author is a modern invention and that famous authors have often borrowed from the texts of others. Changing textual practices (through writing technologies) mark yet another shift in notions of originality and authorship and illustrate how different cultural practices (here, Chinese educational practices) represent fundamentally different beliefs about the relationship between language and reality. Informal interviews with ESL students challenge our traditional views of plagiarism and reveal "the extent to which these students feel the English language remains a language of colonialism."

See: Mary Louise Pratt, "Arts of the Contact Zone" [212].

540   Raimes, Ann. "Out of the Woods: Emerging Traditions in the Teaching of Writing." *TESOL Quarterly* 25 (1991): 407–30.

Four approaches characterize ESL teaching since the mid-1960s. At the beginning of this period, the audiolingual method made writing subservient to oral learning. Students wrote only to practice grammatical or rhetorical forms. In the late 1970s, influenced by L1 scholars' research on composing processes, L2 teachers began to think about writers, meaning-making, multiple drafts, and journals, downplaying linguistic accuracy — at least in early drafts. In the late 1980s, some reacted against process, arguing that academic writing was what students would need to do, resulting in the adjunct course model to provide academic content. At the same time, a focus on academic readers' expectations generated English for academic purposes and a concern for socializing students into the academic discourse community. These methods all continue to stir controversy. Should students do personal writing or practice "real" academic writing? When we teach to the academic discourse community, mustn't we beware of simply enforcing submission to a set of rules (as L1 researchers warn)? In this same period, contrastive rhetoric has developed. Although it offers no pedagogical suggestions, contrastive rhetoric raises consciousness about composing conventions in different cultures. This consciousness makes us aware not only of English forms, but of alternate rhetorics from many cultures. The field of ESL teaching must continue to recognize the complexity of composing, the diversity of students and their composing processes, the politics of pedagogy, and the need for classroom-based research.

See: Mike Rose, "The Language of Exclusion: Writing Instruction at the University" [466].

See: Alice Roy, "ESL Concerns for Writing Program Administrators" [613].

541   Silva, Tony, and Paul Kei Matsuda. *Landmark Essays on ESL Writing*. Mahwah, N.J.: Lawrence Erlbaum, 2001.

Sixteen essays, arranged chronologically, (beginning with Anita Pincas, "Structural Linguistics and Systematic Composition Teaching to Students of English as a Foreign Language" (1962)), make available previously-published ESL writing scholarship over the last four decades. Includes Robert B. Kaplan, "Cultural Thought Patterns in Inter-Cultural Education"; Vivian Zamel, "Teaching Composition in the ESL Classroom: What We Can Learn from Research in the Teaching of English"; Ann Raimes, "What Unskilled ESL Students Do as They Write: A Classroom Study of Composing"; Ulla Connor, "Research Frontiers in Writing Analysis"; Ruth Spack, "Initiating ESL Students into the Academic Discourse Community: How Far Should We Go?"; Ann M. Johns, "Interpreting an English Competency Examination: The Frustrations of an ESL Science Student"; Ilona Leki, "Reciprocal Themes in ESL Reading and Writing"; Tony Silva, "Toward an Understanding of the Distinct Nature of L2 Writing: The ESL Research and Its Implications"; and Liz Hamp-Lyons and Barbara Kroll, "Issues in ESL Writing Assessment: An Overview."

542   Silva, Tony, and Paul Kei Matsuda, ed. *On Second Language Writing*. Mahwah, N.J.: Lawrence Erlbaum, 2001.

Second language writing specialists systematically address basic concerns in the field, including theory, research, instruction assessment, politics, and articulation with other disciplines and standards. Fifteen chapters include the following: Ilona Leki, "Hearing Voices: L2 Students' Experiences in L2 Writing Courses"; Diane Belcher, "Does Second Language Writing Theory Have Gender?"; Lynn Goldstein, "For Kyla: What Does the Research Say About Responding to ESL Writers"; Liz Hamp-Lyons, "Fourth Generation Writing Assessment"; Trudy Smoke, "Instructional Strategies for Making ESL Students Integral to the University"; Sarah Benesch, "Critical Pragmatism: A Politics of L2 Composition"; Carol Severino, "Dangerous Liaisons: Problems of Representation and Articulation"; and Alister Cumming, "The Difficulty of Standards, For Example in L2 Writing."

543   Spack, Ruth. "The Acquisition of Academic Literacy in a Second Language: A Longitudinal Case Study." *Written Communication* 14.1 (January 1997): 3–62.

A three-year study of an undergraduate L2 student, "Yuko," combines qualitative methods to understand how this student drew upon multiple resources or developed strategies for reading and writing successfully in a university setting. Beginning with an account of Yuko's acquisition of academic literacy in early childhood, this study follows Yuko through nine courses in English and social science classes. The longitudinal narrative, informed by interviews, observations, writing samples, and other data, attributes Yuko's lack of confidence, despite her strong TOEFL score, to her educational background in Japan. Deliberate avoidance of reading courses and a struggle to analyze rather than summarize were replaced by the third year with her recognition that "acquisition involves being engaged in a process of constructing knowledge."

544   Tucker, Amy. *Decoding ESL: International Students in the American College Classroom.* Portsmouth, N.H.: Boynton/Cook, 1995.

Teaching writing to international students is not training in an isolated skill but in a way of experiencing the world. Contrastive rhetoric shows that the errors of ESL writers can be read not as random mistakes but as patterns that are inevitable in cultural transformation. In our readings of other cultures, we must be students of cultural difference, conscious of the rhetorical limitations placed on both writer and reader (the teacher) by limitations of language, the clash of conventions, deep ideological differences, and current political situations. These are not incapacitating differences but challenges that ultimately deepen cross-cultural understanding. Tucker illustrates with case studies of students from Afghanistan, Russia, Greece, China, and Japan, examining their experience in writing and literature courses.

545   Valdes, Guadalupe. "Bilingual Minorities and Language Issues in Writing." *Written Communication* 9 (January 1992): 85–136.

The teaching of English is divided into segments, with mainstream and basic writers in one group and ESL students in the other. This division fails to take into account the complexity of bilingualism in America. A bilingual individual's ability to function in a second language depends on a large number of social factors such as age, previous language learning, and degree of contact with fluent speakers of the second language. These factors also affect the time it takes to pass through the incipient (nonfluent) bilingual stage. The difficulty of identifying these factors causes confusion about some students' instructional needs in our simple bipartite system. The very same nonnativelike features in their writing can be variously interpreted. Some nonidiomatic forms persist, for example, in the writing of fluent bilinguals who don't need ESL instruction. ESL research has focused on some groups of bilinguals, but the profession as a whole must deal with the entire range of bilinguals. To do so, we must do more research on the kinds of writing bilingual minorities are exposed to, the ways that mainstream teachers respond to the writing of these students, and the linguistic and social factors that affect their writing. To address these pressing issues, we must break out of our current compartmentalization.

546   Zamel, Vivian. "Strangers in Academia: The Experiences of Faculty and ESL Students across the Curriculum." CCC 46.4 (December 1995): 506–21.

Faculty across the disciplines, surveyed about ESL students in their classes, often conflated students' "deficient and inadequate" language use with intellectual ability. When instructors believe in a deficit model of learning, students are not invited to participate in intellectual work. Two faculty responses to working with nonnative speakers of English illustrate very different sets of assumptions about language and knowledge, one rich and complicated, the other static and limited to gatekeeping. At the same time, ESL students enrolled in various courses were asked about how they learn best and what they want faculty to know, and their responses clarify much about ESL students' academic lives. When faculty hold reductive approaches to teaching academic discourse, they need more information about the process of language acquisition and ways to represent the distinct culture of each discipline.

547   Zamel, Vivian. "Writing One's Way into Reading. TESOL Quarterly 26 (1992): 463–85.

Both reading and writing are acts of meaning-making, yet reading continues to be taught by a transmission or information-retrieval model. Reading ought not to be passive, but a transaction between the text and the reader's knowledge and experience. Writing can reveal and enhance this transaction by enabling students to engage the text through their responses. Reading journals or logs are effective for this purpose, as research attests. Sequencing assignments around readings is another way of allowing students to approach a text from different perspectives, avoiding the sense that there is a single meaning to extract. Students can become better readers by becoming better writers.

548   Zamel, Vivian, and Ruth Spack, eds. *Negotiating Academic Literacies: Teaching and Learning across Languages and Cultures.* Mahwah, N.J.: Lawrence Erlbaum Associates, 1998.

Essays from several different fields — composition studies, education, applied linguistics, anthropology, and others — explore how students acquire literacies but also reconsider how academic discourse is typically conceptualized. Essays include Mina Shaughnessy, "Diving In: An Introduction to Basic Writing"; Eleanor Kutz, "Between Students' Language and Academic Discourse: Interlanguage as Middle Ground";

Ruth Spack, "Initiating ESL Students into the Academic Discourse Community: How Far Should We Go?"; Fan Shen, "The Classroom and the Wider Culture: Identity as a Key to Learning English Composition"; Robert E. Land, Jr., and Catherine Whitley, "Evaluating Second Language Essays in Regular Composition Classes: Toward a Pluralistic U.S. Rhetoric"; Linda Lonon Blanton, "Discourse, Artifacts, and the Ozarks: Understanding Academic Literacy"; and Norma Gonzalez, "Blurred Voices: Who Speaks for the Subaltern?"

See also: [371], [374], [166], [539], [546].

Technical Communication

549   Alred, Gerald J. *St. Martin's Bibliography of Business and Technical Communication*. New York: St. Martin's Press, 1997.

An extensively annotated bibliography of 376 items divided into sections on research and history, theory and rhetoric, profession and curriculum, genre studies, technology and visual theory, and interdisciplinary connections, each with several subcategories. Includes complete contact information for journals, professional associations, conferences, and Internet discussion groups, as well as an author index and a subject index.

550   Anderson, Paul V., R. John Brockmann, and Carolyn R. Miller, eds. *New Essays in Technical and Scientific Communication: Research, Theory, Practice*. Farmingdale, N.Y.: Baywood, 1983.

Twelve essays take a serious scholarly approach to empirical research, theory, pedagogy, and historical study in the field of technical communication. Essays include Lee Odell, Dixie Goswami, Anne Herrington, and Doris Quick, "Studying Writing in Non-Academic Settings"; Linda Flower, John Hayes, and Heidi Swarts, "Revising Functional Documents: The Scenario Principle"; Lester Faigley and Stephen Witte, "Topical Focus in Technical Writing"; Jack Selzer, "What Constitutes a 'Readable' Technical Style?"; James Zappen, "A Rhetoric for Research in Sciences and Technologies"; Charles Bazerman, "Scientific Writing as a Social Act: A Review of the Literature of the Sociology of Science"; and David Dobrin, "What's Technical about Technical Writing?" Winner of the NCTE Award in Technical and Scientific Communication.

See: Charles Bazerman and James Paradis, eds., *Textual Dynamics of the Professions: Historical and Contemporary Studies of Writing in Professional Communities* [580].

551   Blakeslee, Ann M. "Bridging the Workplace and the Academy: Teaching Professional Genres Through Classroom-Workplace Collaborations." *Technical Communication* 10.2 (2001): 169–92.

Two case studies of classroom-workplace collaborations in which students solved workplace problems as part of an academic course requirement demonstrate how such collaborations help in the teaching of professional genres. Students in a 300-level class of undergraduates only and students in a 400-level class of both undergraduate and graduate students completed projects that were provided by professionals in industry or academia. The results suggest that classroom-workplace collaborations may have several benefits. The collaborations can prove valuable to the students because they expose them to workplace activities and cultures, introduce them to the genres associated with those activities and cultures, and provide occasion for reflection and application of students' classroom and theoretical knowledge.

See: Nancy Roundy Blyler, "Theory and Curriculum: Reexamining the Curricular Separation of Business and Technical Communication" [583].

552   Blyler, Nancy Roundy and Charlotte Thralls, eds. *Professional Communication: The Social Perspective*. Newbury Park, Calif.: Sage Publications, 1993.

Fourteen essays examine the ways that the social paradigm in the study of writing and rhetoric can contribute to an understanding of professional communication. Essays include Charlotte Thralls and Nancy Roundy Blyler, "The Social Perspective and Professional Communication: Diversity and Directions in Research"; Bruce Herzberg, "Rhetoric Unbound: Discourse, Community, and Knowledge"; Ben Barton and Marthalee Barton, "Ideology and the Map: Toward a Postmodern Visual Design Practice"; Thomas Kent, "Formalism, Social Construction, and the Problem of Interpretive Authority"; Joseph Comprone, "Generic Constraints and Expressive Motives: Rhetorical Perspectives on Textual Dialogues"; James Porter, "The Role of Law, Policy, and Ethics in Corporate Composing: Toward a Practical Ethics for Professional Writing"; Janice Lauer and Patricia Sullivan, "Validity and Reliability as Social Constructions"; and Mary Lay, "Gender Studies: Implications for the Professional Communication Classroom." Winner of the NCTE Award in Technical and Scientific Communication.

553   Brockmann, R. John, ed. *The Case Method in Technical Communication: Theory and Models*. St. Paul, Minn.: Association of Teachers of Technical Writing, 1984.

The case method holds that writing is best learned by performing in situations that specify data, characters, politics, and a writer's role. This collection offers seven essays on using and generating cases, an annotated bibliography on the case method in communication, eight cases for writing, and two cases for graphics. Includes R. John Brockmann, "What Is a Case?"; Marcus Green, "How to Use Case Studies in the Classroom"; and Charles Sides, "Comparing the Case Approach to Five Traditional Approaches to Teaching Technical Communication."

See: Robert L. Brown, Jr., and Carl G. Herndl, "An Ethnographic Study of Corporate Writing: Job Status as Reflected in Written Text" [584].

554   Bryan, John. "Seven Types of Distortion: A Taxonomy of Manipulative Techniques Used in Charts and Graphs." *Journal of Technical Writing and Communication* 25. 2 (1995): 127–79.

Whether distortions in presenting data in graphic form occur inadvertently, through guile, or because of software defaults, the increased use of graphing software requires communicators to be more vigilant about distortions. Seven types of distortion have been well-documented: manipulation of scale ratios (extreme differences between x and y axes); manipulation of the second dimension (fat lines representing what should be one-dimensional lines); manipulation of the third dimension (drop shadows and perspectives that inaccurately suggest volume); color distortion (highlighting or diminishing particular data); manipulation of composition (using design, typography, orientation, or embellishment to distract or overinterpret); manipulation of symbolism (failing to distinguish comparative data or obscuring data with illustrations); and manipulation of affect (using emotionally charged illustrations).

555   Connors, Robert J. "The Rise of Technical Writing Instruction in America." *Journal of Technical Writing and Communication* 12 (1982): 329–52.

The need for technical writing instruction grew in the latter part of the nineteenth century in the United States as engineering education grew and classical education shrank. However, no courses in technical writing were offered before 1900, reflecting the hope that freshman composition would suffice. It did not, as complaints in professional journals about nearly illiterate engineers attest. The first technical writing textbook, in 1908, concerned usage for professionals. The 1911 textbook by Samuel Chandler Earle is the first genuine attempt to address the needs of an advanced undergraduate technical-writing course. It condemned the "two cultures" split, chastising English teachers for regarding engineers as philistines. Earle used the modes of discourse as his pedagogical model. By 1920, though, books using technical-writing formats began to appear, along with a wave of books that attempted to humanize the engineering student by combining literature with writing instruction. World War II dramatically increased the need for technical-writing instruction: technical writing became a distinct job description, and teaching technical writing began to have more professional status, a trend particularly strong since the 1970s, with the appearance of professional societies and journals.

556   Couture, Barbara. "Categorizing Professional Discourse: Engineering, Administrative, and Technical/Professional Writing." *Journal of Business and Technical Communication* 6 (1992): 5–37.

Because knowledge depends on interpretation that is constrained by communal values (see Winsor, "The Construction of Knowledge in Organizations" [577]), scholars of professional writing need to develop an understanding of how discourse is framed and interpreted in organizations. Rhetorical categories can help reveal both textual and contextual elements in interpretive frames. Such categories are not technical labels but indicators of situations, disciplines, and forms that operate in particular contexts. Three rhetorical categories that identify group values and their effect on interpretation appear to have theoretical and empirical validity. The first, engineering writing, responds to the professional values of scientific objectivity, professional judgment, and corporate interests. The second, administrative writing, reflects decision-making authority and promotes institutional identity. The third, technical/professional writing, aims to accommodate the audience by meeting professional readability standards. Defining the characteristics of these types more precisely can help describe writing in ways that are more telling and more usable for those who teach professional writing.

557   Draga, Sam, and Van Doss. "Cruel Pies: The Inhumanity of Technical Illustrations." *Technical Communication* 48.3 (2001): 265–74.

A review of research on the ethics of visual communication reveals that the definition of ethics is almost always associated with deception and distortion. While it is important to incorporate visuals with honesty and accuracy, technical communicators should also expand their understanding of the ethics of visual communication and develop techniques that bring humanity as well as honesty to technical illustrations. Too often, particularly in writing that reports human fatalities, visual images objectify and dehumanize people for purposes of statistical manipulation. However, using pictographs or superimposing bar graphs and line graphs on pictures or drawings of human subjects are two possible ways to humanize the visual display of information.

558   Gelinas, Ulric J., D. V. Rama, and Terrance M. Skelton. "Selection of Technical Communication Concepts for Integration into an Accounting Information Systems Course: A WAC Case Study." *Technical Communication Quarterly* 6 (Fall 1997): 381–401.

In a project to improve communication skills for accounting majors in an accounting information systems course, faculty in accounting and technical communication collaborated to determine the precise discipline-specific forms of communication appropriate for the course and ways to make communication instruction integral to the curriculum. In accounting, as in many technical fields, discourse forms have not been well described. Where discipline-specific communication texts exist, their use is impeded by the mismatch between textbook goals and course goals. In the present project, collaborators first adopted the quality measure of "fitness for use" (in place of traditional measures such as readability). This measure proved applicable to both accounting problem-solving and writing, and was easy to explain to students. Next, a small number of specific forms of communication were chosen for assignments — a "playscript" model for documenting procedures, interviewing, and report writing. A small set of specific skills was then targeted: situational analysis, document planning, and presentation mechanics — all developed in the context of fitness-for-use. Over several semesters, a very successful pedagogy developed. Some specific elements here may be transferable to other disciplines — the fitness-for-use measure and document planning skills — but the general approach may be a helpful model for bringing WAC into fields where little is known about how practitioners function as a discourse community.

559   Harris, John S. *Teaching Technical Writing: A Pragmatic Approach*. St. Paul, Minn.: Association of Teachers of Technical Writing, 1992.

Beginning teachers of technical writing (and more experienced teachers looking for new ideas) can learn much from a book that not only presents materials and methods for teaching the course but also speaks frankly about the career path of such teachers in the academy. In twenty-one chapters, Harris defines technical writing, describes programs and textbooks, and tells how to work within an indifferent English department, design a course, teach special forms (proposals, correspondence, term papers, graphics), grade papers, and get promoted.

See: Thomas N. Huckin, "Technical Writing and Community Service" [701].

See: Johndan Johnson-Eilola and Stuart A. Selber, "Policing Ourselves: Defining the Boundaries of Appropriate Discussions in Online Forums" [681].

560   Hart-Davidson, William. "On Writing, *Technical Communication*, and Information Technology: The Core Competencies of Technical Communication." *Technical Communication* 48.2 (2001): 145–155.

Writing is the core technology that all information technology systems seek to leverage; by extension, then, technical communication plays a central role in all information technology systems. In the development of information technology, technical communicators deal with two critical issues: identity (fixed or fluid) and strategy (situated or flexible). Technical communicators in both the workplace and the academy, however, can take on an even more pivotal role through the construction of theories about their work that expand the core expertise by raising new questions, researching new possibilities, and inventing new information technologies that build on their expertise and that help shape policy. By claiming and cultivating the conceptual spaces where identity and strategy are closely aligned, technical communicators can enter discourses in social, ethical, and political arenas.

561   Johnson, Robert R. *User-Centered Technology: A Rhetorical Theory for Computers and Other Mundane Artifacts*. N.Y.: State University of New York Press, 1998.

Modern technology is for the most part system- or artifact-centered. However, the end of technology should be refigured in terms of the user: the human who interacts with the technology. Based in rhetoric, the user-centered model focuses on the user's situation. User-centered theory classifies user knowledge in terms of practitioners, producers, and citizens. User as practitioner assumes that users are just that — mere users of tools that have already been designed and delivered; user as producer assumes that users not only employ the technological tools available to them, but also are capable of designing and maintaining them. User as citizen envisions users as contributing, responsible members of technological enterprises. The user as citizen produces and participates, rather than just consuming. In addition to user knowledge, human-technology interaction and technological determinism are also central to user-centered theory of technology.

562   Johnson-Eilola, Johndan, and Stuart A. Selber. "Sketching a Framework for Graduate Education in Technical Communication." *Technical Communication Quarterly* 10.4 (2001): 403–437.

Graduate education in technical communication should offer an expansive view of the field. One way to achieve that view is through a three-dimensional framework that places the multiple and varied approaches to technical communication into one coherent structure. Rather than introducing students to the field of technical communication through an historical survey or through the conventional topics, this framework, geared toward a standard entry-level course in technical communication, organizes the field's modes of analysis (in this case, rhetorical, spatial, empirical, and critical modes) into three categories: thinking, doing, and teaching. Such an arrangement highlights and encompasses the diversity of the discipline, and can also provide a space in which the discipline can grow. A sample syllabus is included. Winner of NCTE award in technical communication.

563   Katz, Steven B. "The Ethic of Expediency: Classical Rhetoric, Technology, and the Holocaust." *CE* 54 (March 1992): 255–75.

The ethos of expediency, objectivity, logic, and narrow focus that characterizes technical writing and deliberative rhetoric can become an ethical imperative. This ethos, adopted by the Nazi regime and combined with science and technology, helped create a "moral" basis for Nazi culture, an ethos of the society as a whole. The Holocaust is not an aberration, a breach in the standard of virtue, but a result, in part, of the ethic of expediency. Expediency in deliberative rhetoric traces back to Aristotle, for whom even ethical prudence is an element of praxis and for whom utility is itself a good. The Nazi regime represents an extreme in which the *polis* as a whole adopted a *telos* of expediency. We should not ignore the implications of our own ex-treme adoption of expediency in an individualistic and materialistic technology-driven capitalist society. We should make awareness of the ethical force of the role of expediency in rhetoric part of our teaching of ethics in technical communication.

564   Koerber, Amy. "Toward a Feminist Rhetoric of Technology." *Journal of Business and Technical Communication* 14.1 (January 2000): 58–73.

A rhetoric of technology enables meaning-making about technologi-cal aspects of the world; a feminist rhetoric of technology, therefore, enables meaning-making that reflects feminist concerns about tech-nology. In contemplating what a rhetoric of technology might look like, there are three ways that a feminist approach should differ from a nonfeminist approach. First, a feminist rhetoric of technology should expand the definition of technology into one that addresses the con-cern that current definitions of technology exclude the historical contributions of women. Second, feminist scholars should also ask different research questions; specifically, their questions should aim to account for technologies' role and participation in the construc-tion of gendered meanings. Finally, a feminist rhetoric of technology should move beyond the design and development phases of technol-ogy in order to address the fact that although new technologies are often promoted as liberatory, they rarely meet that potential. These three suggestions are a starting place in the move toward a feminist rhetoric of technology, a rhetoric that will draw from, as well as chal-lenge and contradict, nonfeminist rhetorics of technology.

565   Lay, Mary M., and William M. Karis, eds. *Collaborative Writing in In-dustry: Investigations in Theory and Practice*. Amityville, N.Y.: Baywood, 1991.

The theory and practice of collaborative writing as it applies to work-place writing, along with studies of the implications of this research for the classroom, are the subjects of twelve essays, including David K. Farkas, "Collaborative Writing, Software Development, and the Universe of Collaborative Activity"; Timothy Weiss, "Bruffee, the Bakhtin Circle, and the Concept of Collaboration"; Barbara Cou-ture and Jone Rymer, "Discourse Interaction between Writer and Supervisor: A Primary Collaboration in Workplace Writing"; Will-iam Van Pelt and Alice Gillam, "Peer Collaboration and the Com-puter-Assisted Classroom: Bridging the Gap between Academia and the Workplace"; Dixie Elise Hickman, "Neuro-Linguistic Program-ming Tools for Collaborative Writers"; and Roger Grice, "Verifying Technical Information: Issues in Information-Development Collabo-ration." Winner of the NCTE Award in Technical and Scientific Communication.

566   Locker, Kitty O. "What Do Writers in Industry Write?" *Technical Writing Teacher* 9 (1982): 122–27.

Students in technical writing classes are often surprised to hear that people in business and industry routinely write more than ten pages a week and often much more. Writing is invaluable because it provides a permanent record, it is often more effective than other means of communicating, it is often less expensive than other forms of communicating, it is taken more seriously than oral communication, and so on. Thus, a huge amount of writing goes on in the workplace — far more than could ever be handled by a corps of professional writers. There are innumerable genres of reports, proposals, and letters, external and internal, to be produced regularly. Technical writing teachers should be aware of these forms and include business communication, logic, and audience analysis in their courses.

See: Carolyn B. Matalene, ed., *Worlds of Writing: Teaching and Learning in Discourse Communities of Work* [593].

567   Longo, Bernadette. *Spurious Coin: A History of Science, Management, and Technical Writing.* New York: State University of New York Press, 2000.

Within the framework of the historical tension between scientific knowledge-making and liberal arts knowledge-making, technical writing becomes both a genuine and a counterfeit form of currency of scientific knowledge. The scientific knowledge constructed and communicated by scientists and engineers is taken as true currency in a culture dominated by scientific culture, whereas the scientific knowledge made by technical writers with liberal arts backgrounds is considered spurious. The unscientific language practices that can, and do, make scientific knowledge must be transformed into science before they can become genuine currency of scientific knowledge. Intellectual practices spanning centuries of Western civilization, such as the use of clear, correct English; maximum efficiency of production and operation; the need to contribute to the wealth of scientific knowledge aimed at bettering the human condition; the tension between the role of science and the role of art within a culture; and the urge to purify language and standardize practice, frame this cultural history of technical writing.

568   Markel, Mike. *Ethics in Technical Communication: A Critique and Synthesis.* Westport, Conn.: Ablex, 2001.

The relationship between ethics and technical communication should be considered a practical art rather than an abstract theory. Traditional ethical systems do not offer effective problem-solving techniques, but they do provide necessary insight into values that have long been a part of civilization. In developing new, practical approaches to ethics, the long heritage of philosophical ethics has to be considered. Likewise, business ethics should also be studied in order to understand the relationship between ethics and technical communication, because technical communicators typically face one of business ethics' most common conflicts — the conflict between an organization's utilitarian thinking and an individual's subjective, rights-based thinking. Overall, technical communicators wrestling with issues of truth telling, liability, multicultural communication, intellectual property, and codes of conduct, will benefit from an approach to ethical decision making that involves clearheaded, practical thinking about rights, justice, utility, and care, in a free and open discourse.

569   Miller, Carolyn R. "A Humanistic Rationale for Technical Writing." CE 40 (1979): 610–17.

A pervasive positivist view of science is the source of the erroneous belief that technical writing is a skills course. Believing truth to be a function of perceiving material reality, positivists wish scientific and technical rhetoric to subdue language and transmit bare technical knowledge. Technical-writing textbooks endorse this antirhetorical belief. The shortcomings of the positivist view are evident in the confused definitions of technical writing it produces ("clarity" neither defines nor characterizes technical writing), in its emphasis on form at the expense of invention, and in its tendency to analyze audience in terms of "levels" (which reduces to vocabulary choice). Yet scientists themselves no longer hold a positivist view but understand that knowledge is inseparable from the knower: communal discussion and argument determines knowledge. From this perspective, teaching technical writing is a form of enculturation, not a set of forms and techniques, but an understanding of how to participate in a community, a thoroughly humanistic endeavor.

570   Miller, Carolyn R. "What's Practical about Technical Writing?" *Technical Writing: Theory and Practice.* Ed. Bertie E. Fearing and W. Keats Sparrow. New York: MLA, 1989. 14–24.

Technical writing has long been regarded as practical in the "low" sense of being mundane and untheoretical. This view gives rise to a contradiction in technical writing instruction: that workplace writing is at once imperfect (requiring improvement through instruction) and authoritative (the goal of instruction). This contradiction mirrors the larger conflict between practical and humanistic studies in the recent history of education. Professional education tends to acquiesce in treating common industry or professional practice as useful and therefore good. There is a "high" sense of practicality, though, that can be applied to technical writing and other professional education. Aristotle characterizes rhetoric as *techne* or art, a middle term between theory and practice, "a productive state that is truly reasoned." To this should be added Aristotle's sense of phronesis or prudence: rhetoric in this sense is a form of conduct, like ethics, drawing upon observation of human affairs in order to take socially responsible action. Practical rhetoric of this sort must allow for criticism and judgment, and take responsibility not only for the corporation but for the larger community in which it operates.

571   Odell, Lee, and Dixie Goswami, eds. *Writing in Nonacademic Settings*. New York and London: Guilford Press, 1985.

Fourteen essays describe how to conduct research on writing in the workplace; what such research has found concerning the structure of professional discourse, the use of electronic media, and the social/institutional influences on nonacademic writing; and how such research can influence academic and nonacademic writing instruction. Essays include Stephen Doheny-Farina and Lee Odell, "Ethnographic Research on Writing: Assumptions and Methodology"; Carolyn R. Miller and Jack Selzer, "Special Topics of Argument in Engineering Reports"; Lester Faigley, "Nonacademic Writing: The Social Perspective"; David A. Lauerman, Melvin W. Schroeder, Kenneth Sroka, and E. Roger Stephenson, "Workplace and Classroom: Principles for Designing Writing Courses."

572   Sauer, Beverly. "Embodied Knowledge: The Textual Representation of Embodied Sensory Information in a Dynamic and Uncertain Material Environment." *Written Communication* 15 (1998): 131–69.

The dynamic, uncertain material world of a coal mine raises ethical questions concerning textbook notions of instructions as systematic procedures that can translate expert knowledge to lay audiences or that can prescribe safe behaviors to highly specific, local, and unpredictable environments. While workers in risky environments may in fact follow instructions, they still experience failure and injury. Management and engineering solutions will not suffice unless they reflect embodied sensory information that assesses risk in practice, on-site, rather than just in theory, on paper. Non-textual sources, such as the gestures of experienced miners when recounting work successes and failures, need to be explored and included when experts represent embodied information that is not articulated in written texts.

573   Selber, Stuart A, ed. *Computers and Technical Communication: Pedagogical and Programmatic Perspectives*. Greenwich, Conn.: Ablex, 1997.

Placing computers and computing activities within the cultural context of a technological society, seventeen essays examine the pedagogical and programmatic issues that face technical communication teachers and program directors. The essays, arranged in four sections, address challenges that must be met if humanistic instructional practices at both the undergraduate and graduate levels is a goal of technical communicators. Part One, Broadening Notions of Computer Literacy, focuses on the design and use of computer hardware and software in a variety of contexts, such as social, cultural, political, ethical, and legal. Part Two, Exploring Pedagogical Frameworks for Computers and Technical Communication, considers the ways teachers and program directors might facilitate critical literacies suggested by part one. Part Three, Examining Computer-Supported Communication Facilities from Pedagogical Perspectives, calls attention to the complications and challenges in supporting the computing needs of technical communication programs. Part Four, "Planning for Technological Changes in Technical Communication Programs," offers guidelines for long-term thinking about computers and technical communication in instructional and institutional contexts. Essays include Stuart A. Selber, "Hypertext Spheres of Influence in Technical Communication Instructional Contexts"; James E. Porter, "Legal Realities and Ethical Hyperrealities: A Critical Approach Toward Cyberwriting"; Johndan Johnson-Eilola, "Wild Technologies: Computer Use and Social Possibility"; Ann Hill Duin and Ray Archee, "Distance learning Via the World Wide Web: Information, Engagement, and Community"; Brad Mehlenbacher, "Technologies and Tensions: Designing Online Environments for Teaching Technical Communication"; Richard J. Selfe and Cynthia L. Selfe, "Forces of Conservatism and Change in Computer-Supported Communication Facilities: Progammatic and Institutional Responses to Change"; Tharon Howard, "Designing Computer Classrooms for Technical Communication Programs"; Stephen A. Bernhardt and Carolyn S. Vickrey, "Supporting Faculty Development in Computers and Technical Communication"; Pamela S. Ecker and Katherine Staples, "Collaborative Conflict and the Future: Academic-Industrial Alliances and Adaptations." Winner of NCTE Award in Technical Communication.

574   Smith, Elizabeth O. "Strength in the Technical Communication Journals and Diversity in the Serials Cited." *Journal of Business and Technical Communication* 14.2 (April 2000): 131–84.

A citation analysis of the ninety-nine most frequently cited serials for technical communication scholars over a ten year period demonstrates the strength of five technical communication journals: *IEEE Transactions on Professional Communication*, the *Journal of Business and Technical Communication*, the *Journal of Technical Writing and Communication*, *Technical Communication*, and *Technical Communication Quarterly*. Identifying the journal these serials call on for background and support also demonstrates the diversity of the technical communication discipline. Because of this diversity, technical communication scholars must be skilled in accessing and analyzing information from across the disciplines. The list of serials covered provides newcomers to technical communication with a good starting point for exploring the field, while experienced professionals may encounter new source materials.

575   Spilka, Rachel, ed. *Writing in the Workplace: New Research Perspectives*. Carbondale: Southern Illinois Univ. Press, 1993.

Nineteen essays report on research in workplace communication based on the social-perspective model and examine implications of recent research for teaching and future research. Includes Barbara Couture and Jone Rymer, "Situational Exigence: Composing Processes on the Job by Writer's Role and Task Value"; Jamie MacKinnon, "Becoming a Rhetor: Developing Writing Ability in a Mature, Writing-Intensive Organization"; Judy Segal, "Writing and Medicine: Text and Context"; Jennie Dautermann, "Negotiating Meaning in a Hospital Discourse Community"; Graham Smart, "Genre as Community Invention: A Central Bank's Response to Its Executives' Expectations as Readers"; Rachel Spilka, "Influencing Workplace Practice: A Challenge for Professional Writing Specialists in Academia"; and Stephen Doheny-Farina, "Research as Rhetoric: Confronting the Methodological and Ethical Problems of Research on Writing in Nonacademic Settings."

576   Staples, Katherine, and Cezar Ornatowski. *Foundations for Teaching Technical Communication: Theory, Practice, and Program Design*. Greenwich, Conn.: Ablex, 1997.

This collection includes twenty-two new essays divided into four sections: Theoretical Foundations, Practical Foundations, Professional Roles for Technical Communicators, and Program Design. Each essay is concise and includes a thorough bibliography. Theory topics include an overview, by Mary Coney; organizational context, by Teresa Harrison and Susan Katz; rhetorical theory, by Ornatowski; social construction theory, by Mahalingam Subbiah; and cognitive psychology, by Janice Redish. Topics in the practical section include ethics, by Scott Sanders; gender, by Linda LaDuc; collaboration, by Rebecca Burnett, Christianna White, and Ann Hill Duin; new technology, by Henrietta Shirk; and media design, by Stuart Selber. In the professional roles section are essays on technical writing, by Roger Grice; technical editing, by Elizabeth Turpin and Judith Gunn Bronson; and visual communication, by Kenneth Rainey. Program design includes an overview by M. Jimmie Killingsworth; four-year programs, by Sam Geonetta; two-year programs, by Staples; certificate programs, by Sherry Burgus Little; service courses, by Nell Ann Pickett; research programs, by Billie Wahlstrom; and evaluating programs, by Meg Morgan.

577   Winsor, D. "The Construction of Knowledge in Organizations: Asking the Right Questions about the *Challenger*." *Journal of Business and Technical Communication* 4 (1990): 7–20.

Research on communication failures that led to the *Challenger* explosion asked why those who knew about the faulty O-rings failed to pass the information on to decision makers. This question betrays a simplistic notion of knowledge and a conduit model of communication. Knowledge is, in fact, socially conditioned and does not come about, as is usually imagined, by contemplating evidence. The engineers and managers of the *Challenger* project were using different ideas of what counted as evidence, influenced by factors other than evidence, chiefly by membership in task groups with particular views of the project. Knowledge is not certain. Thus, information — such as that the O-rings were faulty — cannot simply be passed on. Reception of a report does not signify reception of information because information does not convey its own interpretation. The questions to ask in this case concern the rhetorical power to affect communal knowledge, which is the crucial factor. See also Couture [556].

578   Winsor, Dorothy. "Engineering Writing/Writing Engineering." CCC 41 (1990): 58–70.

We accept the idea that knowledge is shaped by language, but engineers tend to see knowledge as coming from physical reality without textual mediation. Textbooks often reinforce the view of language as merely a means of transmitting information. A study of a veteran mechanical engineer's writing showed, though, that most source documents and his own writing were based on other documents rather than direct observation. Writing about a new engine, the engineer referred not to the engine but to documents reporting the results and interpretations of tests, to technical summaries, and to handouts used in oral reports. Moreover, many of the reports were written in such a way as to suggest that decisions were consistently made in an orderly way on the basis of prior information, rather than on hunches or instinct. These reports reflect the engineers as they imagine themselves to be. Engineering writing, like all writing, constructs the world that the writer can bear to inhabit.

Business Communication

579   Alred, Gerald J. " 'We Regret to Inform You': Toward a New Theory of Negative Messages." *Studies in Technical Communication: Selected Papers from the 1992 CCCC and NCTE Meetings.* Ed. Brenda R. Sims. CCCC Committee on Technical Communications. 17–36.

Five factors determine how direct or indirect the communication of a negative message should be: (1) the reader's and writer's stakes in the message; (2) expectations of the discourse community or culture; (3) the ethos or value the writer wishes to project; (4) the writer's anticipation of the reader's response; and (5) the writer's and reader's personality characteristics. Standard advice to "buffer" negative messages is incorrect. Sometimes a buffered message will appear obtuse or insulting, especially to an American. Hence, the five factors should be consulted. However, many other cultures value indirectness, so American business students should learn indirect style options for use when cultural conditions demand it.

580   Bazerman, Charles, and James Paradis, eds. *Textual Dynamics of the Professions: Historical and Contemporary Studies of Writing in Professional Communities.* Madison: Univ. of Wisconsin Press, 1990.

In the workplace, "textual dynamics are a central agency in the social construction of objects, concepts, and institutions" (4). Fifteen essays examine the textual construction of professions, the dynamics of professional discourse communities, and the operational force of texts. Essays include Charles Bazerman, "How Natural Philosophers Can Cooperate: The Literary Technology of Coordinated Investigation in Joseph Priestley's *History and Present State of Electricity* (1767)"; Greg Myers, "Stories and Styles in Two Molecular Biology Review Articles"; James Zappen, "Scientific Rhetoric in the Nineteenth and Early Twentieth Centuries: Herbert Spencer, Thomas N. Huxley, and John Dewey"; Robert Schwegler and Linda Shamoon, "Meaning Attribution in Ambiguous Texts in Sociology"; Carl Herndl, Barbara Fennell, and Carolyn Miller, "Understanding Failures in Organizational Discourse: The Accident at Three Mile Island and the Shuttle Challenger Disaster"; and Amy Devitt, "Intertextuality in Tax Accounting: Generic, Referential, and Functional."

581   Beard, John D., Jone Rymer, and David L. Williams. "An Assessment System for Collaborative Writing Groups: Theory and Empirical Evaluation." *Journal of Business and Technical Communication* 3 (September 1989): 29–51.

Group writing, ever important in business communication courses because of the prevalence of project teams in industry, is difficult to grade and often produces dissatisfaction among students and teachers. A system applying 50 pecent of the grade to the final product (all group members get the same grade), 25 percent to oral interaction (an individual assessment), and 25 percent to the composing process (an individual assessment) proved to be highly satisfactory to students in this study. This system requires informal observation of group meetings, collecting all working papers, assigning a journal focused on interactions and composing behavior, and a peer evaluation form. Participants reported high motivation to contribute to the group, a positive sense of the learning experience, and a belief that the grades were fair.

582   Beason, Larry. "Ethos and Error: How Business People React to Errors." CCC 53 (September 2001): 33–64.

Non-academic readers may not share the notion that errors in written texts are serious only if they impede effective communication. Error must be understood in terms of its *impact* on judgments made about writers who create errors; at the same time, errors must be defined not as the breaking of handbook rules but as mental events or consequences outside the text. Fourteen business people, identified through purposive sampling, responded to questionnaires designed to gauge error gravity, and follow-up semi-structured interviews revealed that all subjects had concerns about the writer's image. While there are no quantitative formulas for anticipating reactions to errors, people's negative reactions to errors in business discourse seem to center on the writer's credibility and how it is jeopardized by errors. Image problems ranged from that of the hasty, careless writer to the faulty thinker, poor oral communicator, or a representative of the company who can be a liability.

583   Blyler, Nancy Roundy. "Theory and Curriculum: Reexamining the Curricular Separation of Business and Technical Communication." *Journal of Business and Technical Communication* 7 (1993): 218–45.

Business and technical communication have conventionally been separated in academe, a separation supported by institutional practices and by a formalist rhetoric that posits business communication as chiefly persuasive and technical writing as chiefly informative. Social-epistemic rhetoric, which links language with knowledge and centers on the social context of discourse rather than taxonomies of finished products, posits that discourse does not reflect reality but presents visions of reality that have been accepted as true. Social-epistemic rhetoric treats both business and technical writing as thoroughly rhetorical, a view confirmed by studies of workplace writing. The curricular division has thus lost its rationale. Teaching that emphasizes the ways that social context influences content and form decisions is superior to labeling and dividing typical forms. Students are better served when they learn about the social construction of knowledge and the ways it illuminates the production and reception of workplace communication.

See: Nancy Roundy Blyler and Charlotte Thralls, eds. *Professional Communication: The Social Perspective* [552].

584   Brown, Robert L., Jr., and Carl G. Herndl. "An Ethnographic Study of Corporate Writing: Job Status as Reflected in Written Text." *Functional Approaches to Writing: Research Perspectives*. Ed. Barbara Couture. London: Francis Pinter, 1986, 11–28.

Despite convincing research, commonsense observation, and direct instruction, some professionals continue to use ineffective techniques such as excessive nominalization and long project narratives in their writing. These features appear to be signs of status and anxiety rather than decisions about effective writing. In a study, nominalization was greater for those whose job position had changed or seemed vulnerable. It was also greater in writing for the eyes of upper management and greater generally for those who worked in a corporation undergoing internal reorganization. Nominalization appears to be an attempt to be hypercorrect and to show sophistication. Inappropriate narration seems to come most from young technical professionals who are maintaining a distance from decision making (which depends on interpretation, not narration) and mirroring scientific method. These and perhaps other instances of less effective writing choices reflect social circumstances in the workplace. Stress tends to reduce fluency; nominalization and narration tend to preserve anonymity; hypercorrection reflects insecurity about status. These forces are more powerful than conscious knowledge about preferred writing conventions.

See: Janis Forman, *New Visions of Collaborative Writing* [398].

585   Cross, Geoffrey A. "The Interrelation of Genre, Context, and Process in the Collaborative Writing of Two Corporate Documents." *Writing in the Workplace: New Research Perspectives* [575].

To consider how textual features are produced in organizational cultures by collaborators, this ethnographic study describes the collaborative writing of an executive letter and planning report for a large insurance corporation. Bakhtinian theory generates a view of group writing based upon the political situation and genre: group writing as cacophony, as monotone, and as symphony. In this study, generic and contextual differences helped create two very different collaborative processes: cacophony occurred in the letter-writing process because writers had different perceptions of the composite audience and of standard English. The subsequent report-writing process, on the other hand, was more monovocal as a result of a more stable corporate culture, a more multivocal genre, and postproduction rerouting. The interaction of genre and context caused a conflictive process with the letter and an accordant process with the report; genre and social forces must be considered together. More real-world studies of group writing of different genres need to be conducted to trace how generic conventions and social forces shape the group-writing process.

586   Geisler, Cheryl, et al. "Itext: Future Directions for Research on the Relationship between Information Technology and Writing." *Journal of Business and Technical Communication* 15.3 (July 2001): 269–309.

Information technology (IT) used in text-centered interactions appears to be altering the very character of texts and the interactions of those who use them. Research on ITexts, (e-mail and the like), brings together and draws from a variety of research traditions that provide foundational understandings of ITexts: rhetorical theory, activity theory, literacy studies, genre theory, usability research, and workplace writing. Because specific issues arise when texts move from print to online, IT research must take into account, for example, the interplay of visual and verbal, credibility, or information overload. ITexts are bound to have an influence on the digital divide, organizational life, education, and everyday life. Building on skills and concepts derived from a rhetorical tradition that is design-oriented, research on IText must acknowledge the complexity of the meaning-making process, the historical forces that shape interactions with texts, and the powerful impact these new electronic environments are having on society.

587   Hagge, John. "The Process Religion and Business Communication." *Journal of Business Communication* 24 (Winter 1987), 89–120.

Process activists argue that rigorous empirical research supports their claim of the superiority of process over product. However, process research suffers from many flaws, such as the assumption of protocol reliability and the tiny number of cases studied. Moreover, some research confirms that writers may prefer linear to recursive processing. Process pedagogy is problematic, even vacuous, often amounting to nothing more than repackaging of standard procedures. Process advocates often use mystical language in their claims for the liberatory effects of the process method. This utopianism arises from misunderstandings of the difference between linguistic competence and performance and from an arguable assumption about the existence of prior mental processes. Aside from its questionable basis in theory, the process method is inappropriate for business writing, which depends upon textual predictability and context-linked effectiveness.

588   Henry, Jim. *Writing Workplace Cultures: An Archaeology of Professional Writing.* Carbondale: Southern Illinois Univ. Press, 2000.

A sea change in theoretical movements and technologies have reshaped the very conceptualization of writing; given this shift, composition must attend to a growing class of professional writers by investigating subjectivity based on empirical findings in workplace cultures. Over a seven-year period, eighty-four writers enrolled in an MA program in professional writing and editing conducted ethnographic analyses of workplace cultures and served as research subjects for this study, based on Foucault's concept of archaeological work. Researchers in a Cultures of Professional Writing class conducted autoethnographic work and engaged in intersubjective research; the results help to bring together academic understandings of subjectivity and lived workplace realities for a greater understanding of subjective work identities. Construing work sites as fieldwork sites gives writers the opportunity to take stock of the organizational structures and processes of workplaces and empowers them as a professional class by helping them to understand cultural production via writing in organizational sites. Composition theory aimed at exploring agency should consider the many workplace subject positions constructed in specific organizational contexts and must revisit theories of authorship. Appendices include researchers' abstracts of workplace ethnographies.

589   Jameson, Daphne. "Telling the Investment Story: A Narrative Analysis of Shareholder Reports." *The Journal of Business Communication* 37.7 (2000): 37–44.

When the situation is complex in terms of ambiguous content, technical subject matter, and challenging writing processes, analyzing such documents as narratives offers a better understanding of writers' options and the implications of their choices. Studies of shareholder reports have rarely drawn on narrative theory; however, two methodological approaches, reading them as narratives and analyzing them as written texts, led to complementary conclusions about a random sample of shareholder reports, including all verbal components but excluding numerical components. Three dimensions create the report's story: level of directness or indirectness, underlying fabula, and the theme. The mixed-return reports were less direct than the top-return reports, with statistically significant differences. The mixed-return reports also develop a variety of themes (e.g., blame) that defy simple categorization as direct or indirect; mixed-return reports encourage readers to participate in constructing the story; offer multiple narrators; embed a variety of subgenres; and develop a nonlinear narrative hyperstructure. Each narrative element has both verbal and visual manifestations that interact with one another. Winner of Outstanding Article for 2000 in *The Journal of Business Communication*.

590   Jameson, Daphne A. "Using a Simulation to Teach Intercultural Communication in Business Communication Courses." *Bulletin of the Association for Business Communication* 56 (March 1993): 3–11.

It is nearly impossible to explain the enormous variety of cultural differences using real cultural information. Moreover, presenting cultural "differences" masks the fact that Western culture is also "different." Simulation games have, however, been successful in sensitizing people to the nature of cultural difference as well as providing concrete suggestions about successful interaction. In simulations, participants assume a role spelled out for them by instructions, then interact in character. Debriefings following the game are reliably lively, revealing a vast range of cultural assumptions and ideas for improving intercultural relations. Jameson describes a successful simulation game in which participants learn to represent three invented cultures coming together in a business venture.

591   Kogen, Myra, ed. *Writing in the Business Professions*. Urbana, Ill.: NCTE, 1989.

Fourteen essays investigate professional and pedagogical concerns in the development of business communication as an academic discipline. Essays include Linda Flower, "Rhetorical Problem Solving: Cognition and Professional Writing"; Jack Selzer, "Arranging Business Prose"; Edward P. J. Corbett, "What Classical Rhetoric Has to Offer the Teacher of Business and Professional Writing"; Janice Redish, "Writing in Organizations"; George Gopen, "The State of Legal Writing: Res Ipsa Loquitur"; John DiGaetani, "Use of the Case Method in Teaching Business Communication"; David Lauerman, "Building Ethos: Field Research in a Business Communication Course"; C. H. Knoblauch, "The Teaching and Practice of 'Professional Writing'"; and John Brereton, "The Professional Writing Program and the English Department."

See: Mary M. Lay and William M. Karis, eds., *Collaborative Writing in Industry: Investigations in Theory and Practice* [565].

See: Kitty O. Locker, "What Do Writers in Industry Write?" [566].

592   Locker, Kitty O. "Factors in Reader Responses to Negative Letters: Experimental Evidence for Changing What We Teach." *Journal of Business and Technical Communication* 13.1 (January 1999): 5–48.

Traditional textbook advice about writing negative messages — a set of six principles, including the use of a buffer — has been contradicted by empirical evidence and various points of critique. Two bodies of evidence suggest that it is time to change what we teach about the content and arrangement of negative messages: a summary of the scholarly debate over the past twenty years, and studies conducted on negative messages in recent years. Most of the quantitative research on negative messages deals with content and arrangement, and the literature provides the most support for the principle "explain why you are refusing." This researcher tested with university students three of the traditional principles — use a buffer, place the reason before the refusal, and end on a positive note — with a credit refusal pretest design and a graduate school rejection experiment design. Pretests and experiments suggest that in negative letters, buffers do not matter, strong resale is counterproductive, and giving a brief reason before refusal makes people more likely to say the decision is fair. Also tested were the effects of gender and situational context, but results suggest that gender is not a factor in readers' responses to negative messages. Implications for writers of negative letters are outlined, along with implications for further research.

593   Matalene, Carolyn B., ed. *Worlds of Writing: Teaching and Learning in Discourse Communities of Work*. New York: Random House, 1989.

Adequate understanding of writing in the workplace cannot be provided by traditional academic analyses of texts and processes. The special concerns of collaborative writing, audience constraints, and the conventions of workplace writing must become part of the undergraduate writing curriculum. Twenty-three essays analyze discourse communities of work, including Kristin Woolever, "Coming to Terms with Different Standards for Excellence for Written Communication"; Stephen Doheny-Farina, "A Case Study of One Adult Writing in Academic and Nonacademic Discourse Communities"; Janette Lewis, "Adaptation: Business Writing as Catalyst in a Liberal Arts Curriculum"; Theresa Enos, "Rhetoric and the Discourse of Technology"; Nancy Wilds, "Writing in the Military: A Different Mission"; Janis Forman, "The Discourse Communities and Group Writing Practices of Management Students"; Carolyn Matalene, "A Writing Teacher in the Newsroom"; Aletha Hendrickson, "How to Appear Reliable without Being Liable: C.P.A. Writing in Its Rhetorical Context"; Philip Rubens, "Writing for an On Line Age: The Influence of Electronic Text on Writing"; John Warnock, "To English Professors: On What to Do with a Lawyer"; and James Raymond, "Rhetoric and Bricolage: Theory and Its Limits in Legal and Other Sorts of Discourse."

See: Lee Odell and Dixie Goswami, eds., *Writing in Nonacademic Settings* [571].

594   Rogers, Priscilla S. "Analytic Measures for Evaluating Managerial Writing." *Journal of Business and Technical Communication* 8 (October 1994): 380–407.

Persuasiveness, not correctness, is the most desirable quality of good managerial writing. But persuasiveness is difficult to judge. Holistic evaluation — widely used for M.B.A. writing assessment — does not provide a useful tool for identifying persuasiveness, and is not useful for teaching or research. Two other assessment tools are superior. One, the Analysis of Argument Measure, assesses writing in terms of Toulmin's argument attributes — claim, data, and warrant. Evaluators were able to reach a high degree of consistency in the tests of this measure. The other tool, the Persuasiveness Adaptiveness Measure, assesses writing in terms of achieving the desired reader response. Higher scores are awarded to writing that is clear about recommendations, deals with potential reader objections, demonstrates the desirability of the recommendation, and so on. Here, too, graders reached a high degree of consistency. While high scores on these two measures do not ensure success, the measures do identify important elements of persuasive writing and can sensitize writers to rhetorical considerations.

See: Rachel Spilka, ed., *Writing in the Workplace: New Research Perspectives* [575].

595   Rogers, Priscilla S. and Jone Rymer. "Analytical Tools to Facilitate Transitions Into New Writing Contexts: A Communicative Perspective." *The Journal of Business Communication* 38.2 (April 2001): 112–50.

How can we help writers move into new writing contexts? What writing skills carry over from context to context? A field study using essays from the Analytical Writing Assessment (AWA) of the GMAT (Graduate Management Admission Test) led to the development of a set of analytical tools for diagnosing students' potential problems in MBA writing assignments. MBA writing experts and students in two contrasting business schools participated in this exploratory field study, designed to explore how to use the AWA to help new graduate students identify deficiencies that might interfere with their development as effective MBA writers. The study identified and described traits for successful performance in MBA writing and developed them into analytical tools for use in consultations with students; these tools were subsequently tested for their appropriateness in bridging discourses.

596   Smart, Graham. "Storytelling in a Central Bank: The Role of Narrative in the Creation and Use of Specialized Economic Knowledge." *Journal of Business and Technical Communication* 13.3 (July 1999): 249–73.

Narrative plays an important role in professional discourse and a central part in the analytic and policy work of Bank of Canada economists. Both genre theory and distributed cognition theory contribute to understanding the collaborative process of narrative construction. A view of genre that encompasses "an organization's drama of interaction" clarifies the nature of the collaboration through which an organizational narrative is constructed and used. Distributed cognition, an extension of activity theory, attends to the symbolic representations that groups employ for reasoning and for accomplishing work. One particular narrative — the *monetary-policy story* — operates as a vehicle of organizational thought, evolving across a number of written genres, and serves several purposes within the institution. Eventually the *monetary-policy story*, presented in one version of the *White Book*, is used by the bank's executives as a shared cognitive and rhetorical resource for conducting and communicating policy. A wide variety of qualitative data, collected over several years, traces how the *monetary-policy story* is constructed in three stages, over time and across a set of written genres and how knowledge-making is constructed within a professional organization.

597   Suchan, Jim. "The Effect of High-Impact Writing on Decision Making within a Public Sector Bureaucracy." *The Journal of Business Communication* 35.3 (July 1998): 299–328.

Readers interpreting reports written in a high-impact style — theoretically more effective — did not make significantly better decisions than readers interpreting the same report written in a bureaucratic, low-impact style, one in keeping with the organization's norm. Organizational context factors — perceived work roles, job design, organizational structure, report genre expectations, and organizational language norms — were more important for readers' assessments of reports than high-impact style. Report Assessors at a medium-size federal government agency make decisions solely on the written reports of Information Gatherers. Seven report characteristics were revised to reflect high-impact writing; however, because they had developed a variety of creative means to sort and organize information, Report Assessors perceived the high-impact treatments as abnormal discourse. Both qualitative and statistical data were used to conclude that the theoretical frameworks and the assumptions that shape teaching in business and managerial writing need to be seriously re-examined.

598   Sullivan, Patricia and Jennie Dautermann. *Electronic Literacies in the Workplace: Technologies of Writing.* Urbana: NCTE, 1996.

Fourteen chapters in four sections address issues of written literacy and electronic literacy in workplace settings and the challenges to traditional views of writing. Chapters include the following: Jennie Dautermann, "Writing with Electronic Tools in Midwestern Businesses"; Brenda R. Sims, "Electronic Mail in Two Corporate Workplaces"; Johndan Johnson-Eilola and Stuart A. Selber, "After Automation: Hypertext and Corporate Structures"; Tharon W. Howard, "Who 'Owns' Electronic Texts?"; Craig J. Hansen, "Networking Technology in the Classroom: Whose Interests Are We Serving?"; Nancy Allen, "Gaining Electronic Literacy: Workplace Simulations in the Classroom"; Robert R. Johnson, "Tales from the Crossing: Professional Communication Internships in the Electronic Workplace"; Cynthia L. Selfe, "Theorizing E-Mail for the Practice, Instruction, and Study of Literacy"; James E. Porter and Patricia Sullivan, "Working across Methodological Interfaces: The Study of Computers and Writing in the Workplace."

599   Tyler, Lisa. "Ecological Disaster and Rhetorical Response: Exxon's Communications in the Wake of the *Valdez* Spill." *Journal of Business and Technical Communication* 6 (April 1992): 149–71.

Following the *Valdez* spill, Exxon contributed to public perceptions of its corporate arrogance through eleven communication practices that damaged its credibility and antagonized the public. These include understating the likelihood of a spill and overstating the company's ability to respond; slow response by corporate leaders following the spill; refusing help by local residents; emphasizing its efforts rather than its accomplishments; excessive optimism; presenting itself as a victim; attempting to control information flow; and anger and rudeness. Exxon fell into a spiral of defensive communication, blaming others, attempting to maintain control, and generally being self-regarding. This is an excellent case for teaching about ethical business practices and crisis communication, for the implications — regarding promises, responsibilities, and post-crisis behavior — are exceptionally clear.

600   Varner, Iris, and Linda Beamer. *Intercultural Communication in the Workplace*. Boston: Irwin McGraw-Hill, 1995.

Both domestic diversity and international commerce demand competence in intercultural communication. Culture is a learned, coherent view of the world that determines what is important, evaluates attitudes, and dictates behavior. High-context cultures rely on complex and implicit messages, value relationships, and avoid giving negative messages. Low-context cultures make messages explicit and value directness. Cultures differ in terms of their assumptions about the source of knowledge (e.g., from received wisdom or from experiment), about the value of doing versus being, about the centrality of the individual or the group, about privacy and authority. Students can learn to use basic differences, and categories of questions to ask. By knowing some of the basic differences among cultures and the implications of interpersonal, group, and written communication when applied to each, students can broaden their repertoire of behaviors and become successful at intercultural communication. Twelve chapters cover these topics plus nonverbal communication, information gathering and decision making, negotiation, legal concerns, and the impact of business structures on relationships.

Writing Programs

Writing Program Administration

601   Bishop, Wendy. *Something Old, Something New: College Writing Teachers and Classroom Change*. Carbondale: Southern Illinois Univ. Press, 1990.

Ethnographic study of five writing teachers' responses to a graduate seminar in basic writing pedagogy shows that each assimilated the recommended collaborative method in a different way, as a function of his or her developing identity. Writing program administrators and teacher trainers seeking to implement curricula with a diverse staff need to be aware of the factors that may lead to change and resistance.

602   Brown, Stuart C., and Theresa Enos, eds. *The Writing Program Administrator's Resource: A Guide to Reflective Institutional Practice*. Mahwah, NJ: Lawrence Erlbaum, 2002.

WPA work is increasingly specialized and professionalized. Thirty chapters address instituting change and instituting practice, including Douglas D. Hesse, "Politics and the WPA: Traveling Through and Past Realms of Expertise"; Gail Stygall, "Certifying the Knowledge of WPAs"; Edward M. White, "Teaching a Graduate Course in Writing Program Administration"; David E. Schwalm, "Writing Program Administration as Preparation for an Administrative Career"; Stuart C. Brown, "Applying Ethics: A Decision-Making Heuristic for Writing Program Administrators"; Eileen E. Schell, "Part-Time/Adjunct Issues: Working Toward Change"; Sharon Crowley, "How the Professional Lives of WPAs Would Change if FYC Were Elective"; Chris M. Anson, "Figuring It Out: Writing Programs in the Context of University Budgets"; Jeanne Gunner, "Collaborative Administration"; Daniel J. Royer and Roger Gilles, "Placement Issues"; Gregory R. Glau, "Hard Work and Hard Data: Using Statistics to Help Your Program"; Anne-Marie Hall, "Expanding the Community: A Comprehensive Look at Outreach and Articulation"; Ken S. McAllister and Cynthia L. Selfe, "Writing Program Administration and Instructional Computing"; Victoria Holmsten, "This Site Under Construction: Negotiating Space for WPA Work in the Community College"; Martha A. Townsend, "Writing Across the Curriculum"; Rebecca Jackson and Patricia Wojahn, "Issues in Writing Program Administration: A Select Annotated Bibliography."

603   Council of Writing Program Administrators. "Evaluating the Intellectual Work of Writing Administration." *WPA: Writing Program Administration* 22 (Fall/Winter 1998): 85–104.

This statement from the council, developed from a draft by Charles Schuster, aims to present a framework by which writing administration can be seen as scholarly work and therefore subject to the same kinds of evaluation as scholarship and teaching. This intellectual work falls into five categories. *Program creation* or reform is work based on disciplinary knowledge, theoretical as well as practical. *Curricular design* draws on the same knowledge base and includes the choice of emphases, selection of textbooks, criteria for evaluation, and so on. *Faculty development* calls on the administrator to develop and implement training programs that reflect disciplinary developments and programmatic goals, to communicate current research to staff, and to provide intellectual leadership in thinking about teaching writing. *Program assessment* requires the development of appropriate measures to evaluate goals, pedagogy, and overall effectiveness and therefore draws on knowledge of scoring, portfolio or other forms of assessment, and descriptive analysis. *Program-related textual production* includes traditional forms of scholarly production, but also such things as innovative model syllabi, funding proposals, statements of program or teaching philosophy, original workshop materials, evaluations of teaching, and resource materials. Evaluation in these categories must consider, of course, whether activities and materials reflect expertise and knowledge and whether they are innovative and effectively disseminated. Finally, peer evaluation — typically by an outside expert — is critical for fair evaluation.

604   Fox, Tom. *Defending Access: A Critique of Standards in Higher Education.* Portsmouth, N.H.: Heinemann-Boynton/Cook, 1999.

Although efforts to improve access to higher education for underrepresented groups, such as African Americans, have produced only very small changes, a strong backlash against them has arisen, emphasizing that improved access leads to lowered academic standards. This kind of anti-access argument has been made since the nineteenth century and becomes especially acute in discussions of basic writing. Fox describes programs that have successfully resisted standards-based anti-access pressure. He advocates for standards that define good writing by its abilities: to analyze and resist inequities based on prejudices against race, gender, social class, and sexual preference; to aim at diverse audiences; and to avoid oversimplifying complex issues. Such good writing can be encouraged in writing courses that highlight the classroom as a contact zone (see Pratt [212]), that encourage students to explore the history of literacy's uses for political resistance in the United States, and that reward efforts at intellectual critique of inequities.

605   George, Diana, ed. *Kitchen Cooks, Plate Twirlers, and Troubadors: Writing Program Administrators Tell Their Stories.* Portsmouth, NH: Boynton/Cook, 1999.

A collection of meaningful stories that offer a portrait of a profession. Sixteen essays include the following: Richard Miller, "Critique's the Easy Part: Choice and the Scale of Relative Oppression"; Doug

Hesse, "The WPA as Father, Husband, Ex"; Mary Pinard, "Surviving the Honeymoon: Bliss and Anxiety in a WPA's First Year, or Appreciating the Plate Twirler's Art"; Alice M. Gillam, "Taking It Personally: Redefining the Role and Work of the WPA"; Ralph Walstrom, "Catching Our Tail: A Writing Center in Transition"; Johanna Atwood Brown, "The Peer Who Isn't a Peer: Authority and the Graduate Student Administrator"; Kathleen Yancey, "The Teaching Circle, the WPA, and the Work of Writing in the University"; Beth Daniell, "Establishing E-Mail in a First-Year Program"; Jeanette Harris (coda), "On Being an Accidental Administrator." Foreword by Patricia Bizzell.

606   Gunner, Jeanne. "Decentering the WPA." *WPA: Writing Program Administration* 18.1–2 (Fall/Winter 1994): 8–15.

Professionalizing the WPA position, as many resolutions have advised, often neglects the larger network that includes writing instructors and often assumes that tenure will secure professional status. The belief that a centralized WPA enhances professionalism, or that a program without a tenured director is in a weakened institutional position, is a delusion that excludes non-tenure-track faculty from the processes of curricular renewal or program development. Decentering the WPA allows for a collaborative structure that reconsiders a faculty's role in a writing program's direction. Faced with a series of acting directors and a crisis of faculty rights, the program at UCLA designed an administrative structure that de-emphasizes the director's position and allows the faculty to share program authority. A structure made up of committees and individually held positions — positions that rotate and result from elections — and reviews of both individuals and the program contributes to a democratic model that gives all instructors a voice in program governance.

607   Hartzog, Carol P. *Composition and the Academy: A Study of Writing Program Administration*. New York: MLA, 1986.

A report on the results of a survey of forty-four writing programs at a variety of colleges and universities, as well as extensive descriptions of the programs at Chapel Hill, University of Pennsylvania, and Harvard. The survey data cover administrative structures, program design, staffing, and campus attitudes toward writing. No single model for success is apparent, but good programs seem to be aided to some degree by writing program alliances within the university, the pedagogical skill and scholarly visibility of the director and staff, and a campus commitment to liberal education. Includes extensive bibliography.

608   Hult, Christine, ed. *Evaluating Teachers of Writing*. Urbana, Ill.: NCTE, 1994.

Evaluating teachers, whether for development or judgment, is a complex and sensitive task for program administrators. Too often, formative evaluation (for improving teaching) and summative evaluation (for judging overall performance) are insufficiently distinguished by the instruments for gathering information and by our use of the information. The thirteen essays here address three main concerns. The first, theoretical and ideological issues, includes Hult's introduction; David Bleich, "Evaluating the Teaching of Writing: Questions of Ideology"; and Jesse Jones's overview of purposes, objects of evaluation, sources of information, and the process of evaluation. The second, evaluation methods, includes essays on peer review by Ellen Strenski; class observation by Anne Marie Flanagan; Peter Elbow, "Making Better Use of Student Evaluations of Teachers"; and Mark A. Baker and Joyce A. Kinkead, "Using Microteaching to Evaluate Teaching Assistants in a Writing Program." The third, evaluating specific faculty groups, includes David E. Schwalm, "Evaluating Adjunct Faculty"; Irwin Weiser, "Teaching Assistants as Collaborators in Their Preparation and Evaluation"; John Bean, "Evaluating Teachers in Writing-across-the-Curriculum Programs"; and Deborah Holdstein, "Evaluating Teachers in Computerized Classrooms."

609   Janangelo, Joseph, and Kristine Hansen. *Resituating Writing: Constructing and Administering Writing Programs*. Portsmouth, N.H.: Heinemann-Boynton/Cook, 1995.

Writing program administration is a significant expression of academic scholarship, as the Portland Resolution strongly states [603]. The eleven essays here extend and substantiate that claim through analysis of the history and current state of the main concerns facing the WPA. Essays include Hansen on part-time teachers; Lester Faigley and Susan Romano on technology; Elizabeth Nist and Helon Raines on two-year college programs; Ellen Strenski on recruitment and retraining; Molly Wingate on writing centers; Susan McLeod on WAC; Christine Hult on the scholarship of administration; and Edward White on program evaluation.

See: Harvey Kail and John Trimbur, "The Politics of Peer Tutoring" [633].

610   Myers-Breslin, Linda, ed. *Administrative Problem-Solving for Writing Programs and Writing Centers: Scenarios in Effective Program Management*. Urbana, Ill.: NCTE, 1999.

Each of the nineteen chapters in three sections (Selection and Training, Program Development, and Professional Issues) presents real-world situations about different aspects of administration; the cases place readers into administrative situations. Chapters include Richard Bullock, "In Pursuit of Competence: Preparing New Graduate Teaching Assistants for the Classroom"; Allene Cooper, et al., "What Happens When Discourse Communities Collide? Portfolio Assessment and Non-Tenure-Track Faculty"; Howard Tinberg, "Examining Our Assumptions as Gatekeepers: A Two-Year College Perspective"; Louise Wetherbee Phelps, "Mobilizing Human Resources to (Re)Form a Writing Program"; Joan A. Mullin, "Writing Across the Curriculum"; Linda S. Houston, "Budgeting and Politics: Keeping the Writing Center Alive"; Deborah H. Holdstein, "From Virtual to Reality: Thinking about Technology and the Composition Program"; Linda Myers-Breslin, "Running a Large Writing Program"; Barry M. Maid, "How WPAs Can Learn to Use Power to Their Own Advantage"; Dave Healy, "Managing the Writing Center/Classroom Relationship"; Lisa Gerrard, "The WPA, the Composition Instructor, and Scholarship."

611   Raines, Helon Howell. "Teaching Writing in the Two-Year College." *WPA: Writing Program Administration* 12 (Winter 1988): 29–37.

A survey of 230 two-year colleges shows that most of their English departments concentrate on teaching writing rather than literature. Writing courses are not in separate programs, there are few program administrators, and course planning is often done by committee, with individual teachers retaining much classroom autonomy. Writing courses often concentrate on basic skills, academic discourse, and technical or business writing. Most teachers have five courses per semester, three of them in composition, and see themselves primarily as teachers, not researchers. Their lack of familiarity with current professional discourse can make them feel excluded, but university-level writing program administrators would do well to bring them into collaborative projects to draw on their rich stores of pedagogical knowledge.

612   Rose, Shirley K. and Irwin Weiser, eds. *The Writing Program Administrator as Researcher: Inquiry in Action and Reflection*. Portsmouth, N.H.: Boynton/Cook, 1999.

WPAs' work as researchers deserves a greater understanding, and both new and experienced WPAs need to learn to identify opportunities for doing significant intellectual work in the context of their programs. Fourteen chapters follow an introduction by the editors; they include Muriel Harris, "Diverse Research Methodologies at Work for Diverse Audiences: Shaping the Writing Center to the Institution"; Betty Bamberg, "Conflicts Between Teaching and Assessing Writing: Using Program-Based Research to Resolve Pedagogical and Ethical Dilemmas"; Mark Schaub, "The Contributions of Sociolinguistic Profiling and Constituents' Expectations to Writing Program Evaluation"; Sarah Liggett, "After the Practicum: Assessing Teacher Preparation Programs"; Irwin Weiser, "Local Research and Curriculum Development: Using Surveys to Learn about Writing Assignments in the Disciplines"; Ruth M. Mirtz, "WPAs as Historians: Discovering a First-Year Writing Program by Researching Its Past"; Tim Peeples, " 'Seeing' the WPA With/Through Postmodern Mapping"; Louise Wetherbee Phelps, "Telling a Writing Program Its Own Story: A Tenth-Anniversary Speech."

613   Roy, Alice. "ESL Concerns for Writing Program Administrators: Problems and Policies." *WPA: Writing Program Administration* 11 (Spring 1988): 17–26.

ESL students may be foreign students planning to return home after college, recent immigrants, or bilingual native students. Current theories of second-language acquisition are similar to current theories of composition for native English speakers, namely, that ESL students need practice in writing to make meaning and to develop strategies for construing meaning rather than grammar drill or audiolingual work. Linguists tend not to be the best writing teachers for ESL students because they are likely to use a grammar-based approach. Specialists in ESL are better because they bring knowledge of cultural diversity and contrastive rhetoric, but often their training has concentrated on oral communication. ESL students may be best served by composition specialists familiar with college-level reading and writing. Mainstreaming ESL students instead of offering a separate ESL course may offer students more sophisticated instruction and oral practice while benefiting native English speakers by providing cultural diversity. Schools should provide support programs for mainstreamed ESL students rather than track them into courses where English competency may not be needed.

See: Robert C. Small, Jr., and Joseph E. Strzepek, *A Casebook for English Teachers: Dilemmas and Decisions* [388].

614   Tinberg, Howard B. *Border Talk: Writing and Knowing in the Two-Year College.* Urbana, Ill.: NCTE, 1997.

Tinberg chronicles a summer workshop comprising a writing lab assistant and nine community college professors who had also worked in the lab. Their disciplines included business, dental hygiene, English, ESL, history, mathematics, nursing, and psychology. Their task was to revise a college policy statement on criteria for good writing so that it reflected disciplinary perspectives. In the process, they addressed issues of professional expertise, the nature of knowledge, student and faculty historical consciousness, and cross-disciplinary methods of assessing and responding to writing. They became "border crossers" who had to abandon narrow disciplinary perspectives, to become comfortable with professional discourse that blurred genres, and to recognize and use their own experiences of education and social-class identity in their community college teaching.

See: Trimbur, John. "The Problem of Freshman English (Only): Towards Programs of Study in Writing." [439]

615   Ward, Irene and William J. Carpenter, eds. *The Allyn & Bacon Sourcebook for Writing Program Administrators.* NY: Addison Wesley, 2002.

Twenty-three essays in five parts, covering teacher training, curriculum design, program assessment, administrative techniques, and professional issues. Includes nine historical documents related to program administration. The eleven essays written specifically for this book are Jeanne Gunner, "Professional Advancement of the WPA: Rhetoric and Politics in Tenure and Promotion"; Doug Hesse, "Understanding Larger Discourses in Higher Education: Practical Advice for WPAs"; Brian A. Huot and Ellen E. Schendel, "A Working Methodology of Assessment for Writing Program Administrators"; Barry M. Maid, "Working Outside of English"; David Schwalm, "The Writing Program (Administrator) in Context: Where Am I, and Can I Still Behave Like a Faculty Member?"; David Smit, "Curriculum Design for First-Year Programs"; Todd Taylor, "Ten Commandments for Computers and Composition"; Martha Townsend, "Writing Across the Curriculum"; Irene Ward and Merry Perry, "A Selection of Strategies for Training Teaching Assistants"; William J. Carpenter, "Professional Development for Writing Program Staff."

616   White, Edward M. *Developing Successful College Writing Programs*. San Francisco: Jossey-Bass, 1989.

Writing program directors seeking to design or redesign a program can plan for organic development by taking a comprehensive view of the many separate activities that constitute a good program. Ten concise chapters examine the campus climate for writing programs (the roles of the English department, the writing program administrator, and the administration), research on existing programs, prevalent teaching methods, course designs, assessment issues and practices, instructor evaluation, administration (setting policies on placement and credit for remedial courses, setting up ESL and writing-across-the-curriculum programs), training and support of faculty, and evaluation of the program.

617   Witte, Stephen P., and Lester Faigley. *Evaluating College Writing Programs*. Carbondale and Edwardsville: Southern Illinois Univ. Press, 1983.

Two models dominate writing program evaluation. The qualitative "expert-opinion approach," used by teams from the Council of Writing Program Administrators, confuses description with evaluation. Moreover, team members sometimes differ greatly in the quality of their "expert" credentials and use disparate evaluation methods. The quantitative approach, used in many pre- and post-test studies (four of which are analyzed here), rests on faulty assumptions about the writing process, does not assess either a program's goals or its administrative structure, and tends to produce data with only local applicability. An adequate theory of program evaluation would allow for both qualitative and quantitative measures in assessing a program's cultural and social context, institutional context, administrative structure, curriculum, and pedagogy. See also Faigley et al. [351].

618   WPA Board of Consultant Evaluators. "Writing Program Evaluation: An Outline for Self-Study." *WPA: Writing Program Administration* 4 (Winter 1980): 23–28.

A list of seventy-six questions based on the guidelines for WPA Consultant Evaluators covers curriculum (subdivided into courses and goals, syllabus, methods, testing, grading), program administration (institutional and program structure, the writing program administrator's job description), faculty development (current conditions, support), and support services (organization, personnel, administration).

Wyoming Resolution

619   Robertson, Linda R., Sharon Crowley, and Frank Lentricchia. "The Wyoming Conference Resolution Opposing Unfair Salaries and Working Conditions for Post-Secondary Teachers of Writing." *CE* 49 (March 1987): 274–80.

CCCC Committee on Professional Standards for Quality Education. "CCCC Initiatives on the Wyoming Conference Resolution: A Draft Report." *CCC* 40 (February 1989): 61–72.

MLA Commission on Writing and Literature. "Report of the Commission on Writing and Literature." *Profession* 88 (1988): 70–76.

At the 1986 University of Wyoming summer conference on composition and literature, a protest was raised against the generally low professional status of composition scholars and the economic exploitation of many writing teachers. The resolution resulting from this protest calls on the CCCC to formulate standards for the working conditions of postsecondary writing teachers and to prescribe grievance and sanction procedures where these standards are not met. The resolution was unanimously endorsed at the Business Meeting of the 1987 CCCC Convention, and, in response, the CCCC Executive Committee created the Committee on Professional Standards for Quality Education, charged with delineating such standards and developing ways for the CCCC to support efforts at reform. The committee's draft report concludes with appendices on professional organizations and accrediting bodies to which teachers might appeal. At the 1989 CCCC Convention, the Executive Committee promulgated an official statement on professional standards. This statement offers guidelines on optimal teaching conditions as well as on the placement and evaluation of writing teachers who are tenure-line faculty, graduate students, part-time faculty, and full-time temporary faculty members. This statement also refers positively to the report of the MLA Commission on Writing and Literature, which provides guidelines for evaluating scholarship and professional activities in composition studies.

Writing Centers

620   Blythe, Stuart. "Networked Computers + Writing Centers = ? Thinking about Networked Computers in Writing Center Practice." *Writing Center Journal* 17.2 (Spring 1997): 89–110.

Writing centers have been rushing to add networked computer technologies to their services, but logistical questions have dominated ("How can this be done?") rather than theoretical questions. The latter are necessary for examining conceptions of technology that underlie discussions of networked writing-center services. Instrumental theories, the idea that technology is neutral, lead to a focus on purely logistical concerns and the belief that a center's basic mission will not change; substantive theories focus on the power of technology and the inevitable changes (for good or bad) that it will bring. Both theories are inadequate for researching theoretical questions; what's needed is a critical theory of technology (Feenberg) that can help to shape the designs of writing-center technologies.

621   Boquet, Elizabeth H. *Noise from the Writing Center*. Logan, UT: Utah State Univ. Press, 2002.

Paying attention to the noise in (and about) the writing center allows for a new representation of writing centers. By embracing, even amplifying, the noise of the writing center — the feedback, distortion, dissonance, harmony, and repetition — we can come to recognize the writing center as a powerful place — a place where people go in search of information that might be excluded in more "efficient" systems, and as a place where teaching and learning are transformed into more performative processes.

622   Boquet, Elizabeth H. " 'Our Little Secret': A History of Writing Centers, Pre- to Post-Open Admissions." CCC 50.3 (February 1999): 463–82.

Some forms of "secrecy" are endemic to the institutional position of writing centers because of the tension enacted there between institutional goals and individual pedagogies. A history of writing centers reveals a tension between time and space: "between the writing center whose identity rests on method and the writing center whose identity rests on site." Early writing centers evolved from a method of instruction but by the 1940s became a site — a place where, for example, students were sent by the institution for remediation. Open admissions writing centers, forced to take a defensive stance within their institutions, began to train peer tutors, furthering the implications of the site-method dichotomy. Boquet is most interested in the "excessive institutional possibilities" of writing centers — the ways in which they exceed their spaces and methods.

623   Brooks, Jeff. "Minimalist Tutoring: Making the Student Do All the Work." *Writing Lab Newsletter* 15 (February 1991): 1–4.

The tutor's job is not to improve papers (tempting though that is) but to improve writers. To avoid the temptation to edit, the tutor should follow simple rules: sit beside the student, keep the paper close to the student, don't hold a pen or pencil, and have the student read the paper aloud at the start of the conference to reinforce the student's authority and engagement. In addition, be sure to praise something in the paper, ask questions rather than give suggestions, and, if possible, have students do some writing. Don't allow students to force you to edit: they will ultimately appreciate your refusal to do so.

624   Carino, Peter. "Open Admissions and the Construction of Writing Center History: A Tale of Three Models." *Writing Center Journal* 17.1 (Fall 1996): 30–48.

A cultural model of writing-center history — drawing upon poststructuralist assumptions, thick descriptions, and untidy versions of progress — challenges both evolutionary and dialectic models, neither of which is adequate to representing center history from 1968 to 1983. Open admissions initiatives did not give birth to writing centers and were not central to debates on remediation. The evolutionary model — the idea that labs "have come a long way" — serves a political and rhetorical purpose but is too seamless as a narrative. The dialectic model offers a "heroic tale of resistance" to the lab as a remedial operation and reinforces the idea of centers as radically innovative. Using the Purdue lab in 1975 as one example, Carino demonstrates the more detailed history of the cultural model.

625   DiPardo, Anne. *A Kind of Passport: A Basic Writing Adjunct Program and the Challenge of Student Diversity.* Urbana, Ill.: NCTE, 1993.

Case studies focus on four basic writers — a Mexican-American woman, a Native American woman, an African-American man, and a recently arrived Salvadoran man — and on the adjuncts assigned to them for tutorial support — two more accomplished undergraduate writers, an African-American woman and a European-American woman. Their struggles and successes suggest that the tensions aroused by campus diversity and educational-opportunity programs should be discussed openly by faculty and students, that basic writers need help finding personal meaning in the academic work in a cultural environment that is often unfamiliar or hostile, and that peer tutors need to establish their role as facilitators without being undermined by student resistance or riding roughshod over it.

626   Grimm, Nancy Maloney. *Good Intentions: Writing Center Work for Postmodern Times.* Portsmouth, N.H.: Heinemann/Boynton-Cook, 1999.

Postmodern theory, particularly because of its emphasis on diversity, subjectivity, and agency, engages writing center practices in a reconsideration of literacy, fairness, and social justice. The good intentions of those who do and do not fully understand writing center work must be disrupted. Given the regulatory nature of literacy and given the fact that writing centers facilitate both literacy and assimilation into academic discourses, writing center work is neither innocent nor ideologically neutral. Writing centers can, however, rise above their normalizing and gatekeeping functions. Writing centers can be not only places where students gain access to literacy, but also places where public and political action occurs. Recipient of the IWCA Outstanding Scholarship Award.

627   Grimm, Nancy. "The Regulatory Role of the Writing Center: Coming to Terms with a Loss of Innocence." *Writing Center Journal* 17.1 (Fall 1996): 5–29.

Writing centers are often implicated in regulatory uses of literacy despite the innocence with which writing-center work is currently theorized. The institutional role of the writing center and its implication in disciplinary forms of power (Foucault) assumes that the problem of literacy has been located in the individual rather than in institutional practices and in academic discourse. The stories of two "successful" students who encountered normalizing practices illustrate how writing-center instruction is tied to an autonomous view of literacy, where individuals must master the code, rather than to an ideological view of literacy, where "proofreading," for example, becomes a complex "normalized cultural belief" that requires critical engagement.

628   Harris, Jeanette, and Joyce Kinkead, eds. *Writing Centers in Context: Twelve Case Studies*. Urbana, Ill.: NCTE, 1993.

Twelve circumstantial descriptions of working writing centers provide concrete details about how centers work. Each description follows the same outline: history, physical description (including a floor plan), chronology of a typical day, clientele, selection and training of tutors, types of services (including tutoring, testing, computers, WAC, etc.), administration (management, staff, budget), evaluation, research, and plans for the future. Centers described are at Purdue, Medgar Evers College, University of Toledo, Lehigh University, University of Southern California, Harvard, University of Puget Sound, Johnson County Community College, University of Washington, Utah State, and Colorado State. A concluding essay by Kinkead examines themes raised in the text. Includes bibliography and index.

629   Harris, Muriel. "Talking in the Middle: Why Writers Need Writing Tutors." CE 57 (1995): 27–42.

Tutoring should not be seen as an extension of other forms of instruction. In the one-to-one experience of working with a tutor, student writers gain knowledge that does not arise in other settings. The tutor is a middleperson mediating between the teacher and the student, a role teachers cannot truly take. The tutorial relationship is, moreover, flexible and conversational and therefore more personal than classroom interaction. Students feel helped rather than instructed by the tutor. Writing-center evaluations show that students prefer to do their own work, to reach their own conclusions — again, a situation not usually available in a class setting. Talking to a teacher, students feel pressured to perform rather than to think freely, as they can with a tutor. In the tutoring experience, students actually write, reread, and revise, gaining practical knowledge in collaboration with the tutor. Students can also express anxiety with a tutor, rarely if at all with a teacher. In their intermediate position, tutors are able to interpret academic language and ease the transition to a new discourse community. In short, writing instruction without a writing center would lack activities essential for students to mature as writers.

See: Muriel Harris, *Teaching One-to-One: The Writing Conference* [355].

630   Healy, Dave. "Countering the Myth on (In)dependence: Developing Life-Long Clients." *Writing Lab Newsletter* 18 (1994): 1–3.

Metaphors of writing centers as clinics and clients as diseased cast the center as a place that should cure and discharge the client. One who returns is not fully cured. Although these metaphors have been thoroughly criticized, we still assume that the goal of the center is to make the client independent, to leave the center and not return. Those who do return signal the center's failure. But this view misrepresents the center's mission. Centers are not storehouses dispensing knowledge, but Burkean parlors where writers can discuss writing and get feedback. Writing, we know, is ongoing collaboration. The image of the solitary writer is a throwback. Why stigmatize those who seek the presence of others? A place where talk about writing occurs should hardly be seen as a place where there is an impoverished understanding of writing.

631   Hobson, Eric H., ed. *Wiring the Writing Center*. Logan: Utah State Univ. Press, 1998.

An introduction by the editor and fourteen chapters discuss the possibilities and limitations of online applications for writing centers. Essays include David Coogan, "Email 'Tutoring' as Collaborative Writing"; Sara Kimball, "WAC on the Web: Writing Center Outreach to Teachers of Writing Intensive Courses"; Stuart Blythe, "Wiring a Usable Center: Usability Research and Writing Center Practice"; Neal Lerner, "Drill Pads, Teaching Machines, and Programmed Texts: Origins of Instructional Technology in Writing Centers"; and Ellen Mohr, "The Community College Mission and the Electronic Writing Center."

632   Hult, Christine, and Joyce Kinkead, eds. *Writing Centers Online*, a special issue of *Computers and Composition* 12.2 (1995).

Twelve essays comprise this special issue, including Jane Nelson and Cynthia Wambeam, "Moving Computers into the Writing Center: The Path to Least Resistance"; Muriel Harris and Michael Pemberton, "Online Writing Labs (OWLS): A Taxonomy of Options and Issues"; David Coogan, "E-Mail Tutoring, a New Way to Do New Work"; Irene Clark, "Information Literacy and the Writing Center"; Gail Wood, "Making the Transition from ASL [American Sign Language] to English: Deaf Students, Computers, and the Writing Center"; and

Cindy Johanek and Rebecca Rickly, "Online Tutor Training: Synchronous Conferencing in a Professional Community."

633   Kail, Harvey, and John Trimbur. "The Politics of Peer Tutoring." *WPA: Writing Program Administration* 11 (Fall 1987): 5–12.

Peer tutoring may be based in the writing center or in the curriculum. The writing-center model makes tutoring voluntary and open with regard to the stage of writing or questions addressed. Its success depends on publicity and image. In the curriculum-based model, tutoring is required of writing students. More students see tutors this way, and the program is easier to administer. But in the curriculum-based model, tutors are part of the institution and share its authority, and this situation inhibits collaboration. The writing-center model is superior in this regard. Writing-center collaboration also challenges institutional authority and may demystify the institution's ideology of knowledge delivery.

634   Konstant, Shoshana Beth. "Multi-Sensory Tutoring for Multi-Sensory Learners." *Writing Lab Newsletter* 16 (May–June 1992): 6–8.

Learning disabled students — who are of average intelligence but have perceptual or processing problems — require a bit more creativity from tutors. First, find the student's strongest perceptual channel — visual, auditory, or kinesthetic. Many LD students know their best learning style or channel, so ask first. For visual learners, use charts, diagrams, colors, and gestures; for auditory learners, read aloud, use the tape recorder, and encourage the student to record classes and assignments; for kinesthetic learners, use physical objects and act out ideas. But don't be formulaic. Try a variety of approaches, use whatever works, and be patient.

635   Lerner, Neal. "Confessions of a First-Time Writing Center Director." *The Writing Center Journal* 21.1 (2000): 29–48.

Despite progress made since the 1981 CCCC resolution and the 1985 NWCA position statement on professional status for writing center directors, the quest for professionalism remains a dilemma. A review of three surveys of writing center directors reveals that the field continues to be split between the haves and the have-nots: those who have full-time or tenure track positions, and those who have part-time, contingent, or staff positions. While tenure track status may not be the goal of all involved in writing center work, and while some argue that the pursuit of professional status may have more risks than benefits, a two-tiered system of writing center directors harms the field as a whole. Ultimately, writing center directors who "make it" to positions of institutional stability and leverage should work not only to transform their own institutions, but also to prevent this "haves and have-nots" structure of writing center directors for the good of writing centers themselves. Winner of the IWCA Outstanding Scholarship Award.

636   Lunsford, Andrea. "Collaboration, Control, and the Idea of a Writing Center." *Writing Center Journal* 12 (1991): 3–10.

The idea of collaboration is based on a view of knowledge as socially constructed. Collaboration threatens the idea of the writing center as a storehouse of knowledge that prescribes skills and strategies to individual learners, given that the storehouse approach incorporates the assumption that knowledge is external and accessible. Collaboration also threatens the idea of the center as a writer's garret because that approach incorporates the assumption that knowledge is interior, within the student. Both kinds of centers do good work, but we must acknowledge the superiority of collaboration as a model of real-world writing, as an aid in problem-solving and to critical thinking, and as a route to excellence. Collaborative centers are difficult to create because they require appropriate tasks and group cooperation. But the need to help students learn to work with others is paramount. Collaborative centers engage students not only in solving problems set by teachers but in identifying problems for themselves, negotiating issues of control, and valuing diversity.

637   Maxwell, Martha, ed. *When Tutor Meets Student.* 2nd ed. Ann Arbor: Univ. of Michigan Press, 1994.

Fifty-four stories of tutoring encounters by student writing tutors at UC Berkeley. The tutors describe tutoring sessions and the process of defining their roles, dealing with cultural diversity and gender difference, and learning from their experiences. The stories, addressed to new tutors, reveal successes and failures, insights, techniques, personal dilemmas, and awkward situations (plagiarism, unwanted advances, problems with a teacher, tutor dependency). Includes, in appendices, descriptions of and paperwork for the UC Berkeley peer-tutoring center.

638   Meyer, Emily, and Louise Z. Smith. *The Practical Tutor.* New York: Oxford Univ. Press, 1987.

Experienced writers who serve as tutors may take for granted the very skills most difficult for inexperienced writers to attain. The fourteen chapters of this textbook lead tutors through sets of problems and strategies for dealing with them: establishing a tutorial dialogue that maintains trust; dealing with anger and frustration; avoiding evaluation; using open-ended questions; promoting fluency through heuristics; deepening critical analysis and concept formation; using teachers' comments productively during revision; reclaiming the writer's authority over the text; addressing sentence-level errors, punctuation, spelling, vocabulary, and dialect-based errors; helping writers to develop reading strategies; and tutoring with computers. Writing assignments, suggestions for class activities, and a bibliography end each chapter.

639   Mullin, Joan, and Ray Wallace, eds. *Intersections: Theory-Practice in the Writing Center.* Urbana, Ill.: NCTE, 1994.

Fifteen essays explore and critique composition theories, particularly those concerning collaboration, as they have been and might be applied to writing-center practices. Included are Eric Hobson, "Writing Center Practice Often Counters Its Theory. So What?"; Sallyanne Fitzgerald, "Collaborative Learning and Whole Language Theory"; Christina Murphy, "The Writing Center and Social Constructionist Theory"; Alice Gillan, "Collaborative Learning Theory and Peer Tutoring Practice"; Julie Neff, "Learning Disabilities and the Writing Center"; Muriel Harris, "Individualized Instruction in Writing Centers: Attending to Cross-Cultural Differences"; Jay Jacoby, " 'The Use of Force': Medical Ethics and Center Practice"; and Mary Abascal-Hildegrand, "Tutor and Student Relations: Applying Gadamer's Notions of Translation."

640   Murphy, Christina, and Joe Law, eds. *Landmark Essays on Writing Centers*. Davis, Calif.: Hermagoras Press, 1995.

Writing centers have had a place in American universities since the 1930s, and their methods have generally followed the theoretical directions of the profession as a whole. Twenty-one previously published essays examine the history, theory, and praxis of writing centers, including Lou Kelly, "One-on-One, Iowa City Style: Fifty Years of Individualized Writing Instruction"; Muriel Harris, "What's Up and What's In: Trends and Traditions in Writing Centers"; Gary Olson and Evelyn Ashton-Jones, "Writing Center Directors: The Search for Professional Status"; Judith Summerfield, "Writing Centers: A Long View"; Stephen North, "The Idea of a Writing Center"; Kenneth Bruffee, "Collaborative Learning and the 'Conversation of Mankind'" (see [164]); Lisa Ede, "Writing as a Social Process: A Theoretical Foundation for Writing Centers?"; Andrea Lunsford, "Collaboration, Control, and the Idea of a Writing Center" (see [636]); Marilyn Cooper, "Really Useful Knowledge: A Cultural Studies Agenda for Writing Centers"; Harvey Kail and John Trimbur, "The Politics of Peer Tutoring"; and Meg Woolbright, "The Politics of Tutoring: Feminism within the Patriarchy."

641   Murphy, Christina, Joe Law, and Steve Sherwood. *Writing Centers: An Annotated Bibliography*. Westport, Conn.: Greenwood Press, 1996.

Part of a series of bibliographies and indexes in Education. Brief annotations accompany more than fourteen hundred entries in such categories as History, Program Descriptions, Professional Concerns, Writing Center Theory, Writing across the Curriculum, and Tutoring.

See: Marie Nelson, *At the Point of Need* [538].

642   Nelson, Jane and Kathy Evertz. *The Politics of Writing Centers*. Portsmouth, N.H.: Heinemann/Boynton-Cook, 2001.

Divided into two parts, "The Politics of Conversation," and "The Politics of Location," this collection of twelve essays examines con-

flict in writing center politics, and points out opportunities and recommendations for change. Included are Peter Carino, "Writing Cen-
ters and Writing Programs: Local and Communal Politics"; Pat
McQueeney, "What's in a Name?"; Carrie Shirley Leverenz, "Graduate Students in the Writing Center: Confronting the Cult of
(Non)Expertise"; Carol Peterson Haviland, Carmen M. Fye, and
Richard Colby, "The Politics of Administrative and Physical Location"; Pamela B. Childers and James K. Upton, "Political Issues in
Secondary School Writing Centers"; Eric Hobson and Kelly Lowe,
"An Audit of the National Writing Centers Association's Growth";
and Christina Murphy and Joe Law, "The Disappearing Writing Center Within the Disappearing Academy: The Challenges and Conse-
quences of Outsourcing in the Twenty-First Century." Winner of the
IWCA Outstanding Scholarship Award.

643   North, Stephen M. "The Idea of a Writing Center." CE 46 (September 1984): 433–46. Rpt. in Graves [376].

English-department faculty have a false sense of what goes on in the
writing center. This makes it difficult to dispel their notion of the
center as a fix-it shop that deals with "special problems" in composition, corrects mechanical errors, and serves only poor writers. Such
ideas created the skill-and-drill model that most writing centers have
battled to escape. Writing centers attempt to produce better writers,
not better writing, through a student-centered, process-oriented approach, which chiefly means talking to writers about writing. Teachers should not send students to the center — students must come
when they are ready to talk about writing. Writing centers are gaining recognition, but institutional and faculty support leave much room
for improvement.

644   Olson, Gary A., ed. *Writing Centers: Theory and Administration*. Urbana, Ill.: NCTE, 1984.

Nineteen essays on theory, administration, and special concerns in-
clude Kenneth A. Bruffee, "Collaborative Learning and the 'Con-
versation of Mankind'" (see [164]); Stephen M. North, "Writing
Center Research: Testing Our Assumptions"; Patrick Hartwell, "The
Writing Center and the Paradoxes of Written-Down Speech"; Linda
Bannister-Wills, "Developing a Peer Tutor Program"; and Alexander
Friedlander, "Meeting the Needs of Foreign Students in the Writing
Center."

645   Pemberton, Michael A. "Rethinking the WAC/Writing Center Connection." *Writing Center Journal* 15.2 (Spring 1995): 116–33.

The relationship between writing-across-the-curriculum programs and
writing centers needs to be reconsidered because, despite the pedagogical focus they share, their epistemologies and assumptions about
rhetorical and textual features differ significantly. The "pedagogy of
the generic" common to writing centers — where tutors apply common principles to all academic texts and genres — may do a disser-

vice to students in WAC programs, where writers are expected to follow discipline-specific practices. "Conscious myopia" and the "myth of disciplinarity" characterize the typical ways that WAC and writing centers work together, both of which allow tutors to sidestep the challenges of disciplinary discourse. Pemberton recommends two roles that writing centers can play to support WAC programs.

646   Rafoth, Ben, ed. *A Tutor's Guide: Helping Writers One to One.* Portsmouth, N.H.: Heinemann/Boynton-Cook, 2000.

Fifteen essays offer experienced perspectives on dealing with problems in tutorial sessions. Each essay describes a particular problem, contextualizes it in writing center theory and practice, offers concrete suggestions for handling the problem, and then discusses counterarguments and complications. Each essay also includes an annotated list of further reading. Selections include William J. Macauley, Jr., "Setting the Agenda for the Next 30 Minutes"; Molly Wingate, "What Line? I Don't See Any Line"; Muriel Harris, "Talk to Me: Engaging Reluctant Writers"; Lea Masiello, "Style in the Writing Center: It's a Matter of Choice and Voice"; Ben Rafoth, "Helping Writers to Write Analytically"; Jennifer J. Ritter, "Recent Developments in Assisting ESL Writers"; Beth Rapp Young, "Can you Proofread This?"; and Mary Mortimore Dossin, "Using Others' Words: Quoting, Summarizing and Documenting Sources." The collection ends with six topics for staff discussion and reflection.

647   Silk, Bobbie Bayliss, ed. *The Writing Center Resource Manual.* Emmitsburg, Md.: National Writing Centers Association Press, 1998.

This collection of practical essays is designed for those starting or managing a writing center. Essays include Jeanne Simpson, "Assessing Needs, Identifying an Institutional Home, and Developing a Proposal"; Clinton Gardner, "Centering the Community College Writing Center"; Stuart Blythe, "Technology in the Writing Center: Strategies for Implementation and Maintenance"; Paula Gillespie and Jon Olson, "Tutor Training"; Anne E. Mullin, "Serving Clients with Learning Disabilities"; Joe Law, "Serving Faculty and Writing across the Curriculum"; and Neal Lerner, "Research in the Writing Center."

648   Simpson, Jeanne. "The Challenge of Innovation: Putting New Approaches into Practice." *Writing Lab Newsletter* 18 (September 1993): 1–3.

Writing centers face, like the rest of the academy, threats of budget cuts and calls for accountability. It would be a mistake to be defensive in this situation. Rather, we should see opportunities here. It is important to participate in the processes of institutional change. The growth of writing centers so far has come from steady work and innovation, not from revolution, a process to be continued in the new era. We must tell our stories better to all academic constituencies, connecting with institutional governance in ways that are presently

not typical. Institutional service has not been seen as part of the career path for center directors, but it is the path of change.

649   Vandenberg, Peter. "Lessons of Inscription: Tutor Training and the
       'Professional Conversation.'" *The Writing Center Journal* 19.2 (1999):
       59–83.

The role of student tutors warrants careful consideration in writing
center work. Because of the nature of writing center work, the "student" status of student tutors, and the view of the interaction between tutors and directors as "education," student tutors run the risk
of perpetuating institutional and professional values in which authority and hierarchy are already inscribed. While student tutors may
come to writing centers already understanding writing practices, they
may not necessarily understand the academic institutional practices
that use literacy to measure competence and establish hierarchy. Those
who work in tutor training should be cautious not to engage student
tutors in the replication of problematic models of professionalism.

650   Wolff, William C. "Annotated Bibliography of Scholarship on Writ-
       ing Centers and Related Topics." *Focuses*, annually.

Comprehensive listing of items, all briefly annotated, on writing-
center issues as well as a wide range of theoretical and pedagogical
concerns. Published annually.

Writing across the Curriculum

651   Anderson, Worth, Cynthia Best, Alycia Black, John Hurst, Brandt
       Miller, and Susan Miller. "Cross-Curricular Underlife: A Collabora-
       tive Report on Ways with Academic Words." CCC 41 (February
       1990): 11–36.

Five students and their teacher observed language use in several
courses, discovering how it differed from the freshman-composition
image of academic discourse. Teachers and students did not seem to
form discourse communities but maintained separate views of their
roles and of appropriate language use. The writing course did prepare
students to analyze and imitate writing in other courses, but its model
of collaborative knowledge-making did not match the practice in
other courses. Recording their motives for taking courses, enrollment
and attendance, and types of writing assigned for each of sixteen
courses, the students describe teachers', students', and their own uses
of language for learning — or, rather, for succeeding in each class.
There were few formal assignments; the audience approach taught in
the writing course did help students decide what was called for in
each class in all language interactions. Note taking was the writing
skill most needed in all courses.

652   Anson, Chris M., John E. Schwiebert, and Michael M. Williamson.
       Writing across the Curriculum: An Annotated Bibliography. Westport,
       Conn.: Greenwood Press, 1993.

A bibliography of 1067 items, with annotations of about 50 words each, in eleven categories. Part One, on scholarship, is subdivided into bibliographies, collections, history and implementation, research studies, and theory. Part Two, on pedagogy, is subdivided into general, arts and humanities, math and science, social science, business and economics, and textbooks.

653   Bazerman, Charles, and David R. Russell, eds. *Landmark Essays on Writing across the Curriculum*. Davis, Calif.: Hermagoras Press, 1994.

Thirteen essays on history, programs, pedagogy, and writing in disciplines include Bazerman and Russell, "The Rhetorical Tradition and Specialized Discourses"; David Russell, "American Origins of the Writing-across-the-Curriculum Movement"; Toby Fulwiler, "How Well Does Writing across the Curriculum Work?" [656]; James Kinneavy, "Writing across the Curriculum" [660]; Susan McLeod, "Writing across the Curriculum: The Second Stage, and Beyond"; Janet Emig, "Writing as a Mode of Learning" [291]; Charles Bazerman, "What Written Knowledge Does" [147]; and Greg Myers, "The Social Construction of Two Biologists' Proposals."

654   Blair, Catherine Pastore. "Only One of the Voices: Dialogic Writing across the Curriculum." *CE* 50 (April 1988): 383–89.

The social theory of knowledge that informs the Writing-across-the-Curriculum Movement suggests that each academic discipline has its own way of using language, which makes sense only in the disciplinary context. The discipline of English studies knows only its own discourse, not all the others, and not some generic academic discourse. There is, therefore, no reason to entrust all writing instruction to the English department. A better Writing-across-the-Curriculum program would be taught by professors from all disciplines, whose dialogues over the common writing curriculum would reveal the discursive properties of each discipline in contrast to the others. Composition specialists could serve as consultants to such programs. See Smith [668].

655   Fulwiler, Toby. "The Argument for Writing across the Curriculum." *Writing across the Disciplines: Research into Practice*. Ed. Art Young and Toby Fulwiler. Upper Montclair, N.J.: Boynton/Cook, 1986.

Three principles that underlie Writing across the Curriculum should be elaborated in faculty workshops: that composing is a complex intellectual process of making choices and making meaning; that writing is a mode of learning that calls for expressive as well as transactional composing; and that writing problems arise from a variety of sources, including attitude, skills, and knowledge. Two pedagogical issues are also at issue in workshops: making good assignments and evaluating or responding to student writing. Good assignment design includes setting up a context, allowing time for the composing process, varying the audience, and giving clear directions. Evaluation should, among other things, be positive and specific and focus on content.

656   Fulwiler, Toby. "How Well Does Writing across the Curriculum Work?" *CE* 46 (February 1984): 113–25. Rpt. in *Writing across the Disciplines*. Ed. Art Young and Toby Fulwiler. Upper Montclair, N.J.: Boynton/Cook, 1986.

The interdisciplinary writing workshops at Michigan Technological University introduced the idea that writing can promote learning in all areas. After six years, the program seems to have enjoyed uneven success. Problems have included misunderstanding of special terminology (chiefly "expressive writing"); resistance by suspicious faculty members; conflicts with some members of the English and philosophy departments about language theory; inability to apply the ideas generated in the workshops to some classes, especially large ones; distrust of the peer-review technique and lack of commitment to methods that require it; and lack of reinforcement by the administration. But benefits have included the growth of a community of scholars, a general sense that the program has helped improve students' ability to communicate, more writing by faculty members in the program, greater sensitivity to pedagogy, development of collaborative projects among participants in the program, and more cohesion in the writing department itself.

657   Fulwiler, Toby, and Art Young, eds. *Language Connections: Writing and Reading across the Curriculum*. Urbana, Ill.: NCTE, 1982.

Twelve essays describe the Writing-across-the-Curriculum program at Michigan Technological University. Essays include Toby Fulwiler, "The Personal Connection: Journal Writing across the Curriculum"; Toby Fulwiler and Robert Jones, "Assigning and Evaluating Transactional Writing"; Peter Schiff, "Responding to Writing: Peer Critiques, Teacher-Student Conferences, and Essay Evaluation"; Diana Freisinger and Jill Burkland, "Talking about Writing: The Role of the Writing Lab"; and Bruce Petersen, "A Select Bibliography" (annotated).

See: Ulric J. Gelinas, D. V. Rama, and Terrance M. Skelton, "Selection of Technical Communication Concepts for Integration into an Accounting Information Systems Course: A WAC Case Study" [558].

658   Griffin, C. Williams, ed. *Teaching Writing in All Disciplines*. San Francisco: Jossey-Bass, 1982.

Ten essays on Writing-across-the-Curriculum programs, teaching writing in disciplines other than English, and teaching techniques for using writing as learning include Toby Fulwiler, "Writing: An Act of Cognition"; Barbara King, "Using Writing in the Mathematics Class: Theory and Practice"; Dean Drenk, "Teaching Finance Through Writing"; and Elaine P. Maimon, "Writing across the Curriculum: Past, Present, and Future" [663].

659   Herrington, Anne, and Charles Moran, eds. *Writing, Teaching, and Learning in the Disciplines*. New York: MLA, 1992.

Fourteen essays examine the history, theoretical coherence, and pedagogical practices of Writing across the Curriculum, including Nancy Martin, "Language across the Curriculum: Where It Began and What It Promises"; David Russell, "American Origins of the Writing-across-the-Curriculum Movement"; James Britton, "Theories of the Disciplines and a Learning Theory"; Charles Bazerman, "From Cultural Criticism to Disciplinary Participation: Living with Powerful Words"; Jacqueline Jones Royster, "From Practice to Theory: Writing across the Disciplines at Spelman College"; Toby Fulwiler, "Writing and Learning American Literature"; Joy Marsella, Thomas Hilgers, and Clemence McLaren, "How Students Handle Writing Assignments: A Study of Eighteen Responses in Six Disciplines"; Louise Dunlap, "Advocacy and Neutrality: A Contradiction in the Discourse of Urban Planners"; and Anne Herrington and Charles Moran, "Writing in the Disciplines: A Prospect."

660   Kinneavy, James L. "Writing across the Curriculum." *ADE Bulletin* 76 (Winter 1983): 14–21.

Writing across the Curriculum responds to concerns about declining literacy and reasserts the importance of rhetoric in the liberal arts curriculum. Writing across the Curriculum takes two forms: writing-intensive courses in all departments, and courses in writing for other disciplines offered by the English or writing department. In the first kind of program, the teacher is an expert in the discipline and knows its vocabulary and genres. Students can thus use highly technical language and discipline-specific forms of writing. But such programs reinforce disciplinary isolation and create a heavy burden of writing instruction for teachers untrained in composition. In the second kind of program, esoteric material, technical vocabulary, subtle methodology, and distinctiveness may be sacrificed, but with gains in writing expertise and an opportunity to open a large academic conversation and perhaps, ultimately, an educated public discourse. A well-designed program benefits from both approaches by offering different kinds of writing courses "vertically" throughout the college experience.

661   Kirscht, Judy, Rhonda Levine, and John Reiff. "Evolving Paradigms: WAC and the Rhetoric of Inquiry." *CCC* 45 (October 1994): 369–80.

The WAC Movement continues to be divided between the writing-to-learn model — in which writing is seen as an integral part of the learning process in all disciplines — and the writing-in-the-disciplines model — which studies the discourse communities of the disciplines and brings that knowledge to the writing class. WAC proponents are deeply divided along these lines. The social-constructionist view of disciplines as rhetorically negotiated territory resolves the conflict by treating writing-to-learn as an inquiry into the ways that knowledge is produced in the disciplines. Disciplinary forms and conventions are not separated from the writing process but are presented as communally accepted ways of looking at a particular subject matter, forms that can then be analyzed to determine how they shape the knowledge they produce.

662   Maimon, Elaine P. "Maps and Genres: Exploring Connections in the Arts and Sciences." *Composition and Literature: Bridging the Gap.* Ed. Winifred Bryan Horner [422].

We need to know the forms and traditions of writing in all disciplines in order to fill in the largely uncharted territory we label "nonfiction prose" on our maps of the genres of writing. Trained in literary criticism, we are well suited to exploring the relation of discipline-specific genres to modes of thought in the discipline. Just as the lyric poet writes within and against the structure of his genre, so too the scientist works through the conventions, rituals, and assumptions of lab reports and other genres. Writing students should understand the concept of genre and practice several academic genres. The "modes of discourse" and "composing process" approaches may obscure questions of audience, purpose, and disciplinary method — questions that concern writing as it is used in the academic community — but these approaches can lead to writing that does enter the academic conversation.

663   Maimon, Elaine P. "Writing across the Curriculum: Past, Present, and Future." *Teaching Writing in All Disciplines.* Ed. C. Williams Griffin [658].

The development of Writing-across-the-Curriculum programs has been an effort to make writing an integral part of the learning process in all courses. This effort reinforced the shift in composition pedagogy from a product to a process orientation because the learning process and the writing process work together. Writing across the Curriculum has also promoted collaborative-learning techniques. Process pedagogy requires many drafts and much feedback, and small groups of students can provide each other with audience feedback that may be even more valuable than the teacher's responses. Writing-across-the-Curriculum programs are helping students find "an authentic voice in the community of educated people."

664   Martin, Nancy, ed. *Writing across the Curriculum Pamphlets: A Selection from the Schools Council and London University Institute of Education Joint Project: Writing across the Curriculum.* 1973, 1974, 1975. Rpt. Upper Montclair, N.J.: Boynton/Cook, 1983.

James Britton's colleagues, who worked with British schoolchildren of elementary- and high-school age, offer assignment suggestions and samples of student writing. Included are Nancy Martin, Peter Medway, and Harold Smith, "From Information to Understanding: What Children Do with New Ideas"; Nancy Martin, Peter Medway, Harold Smith, and Pat D'Arcy, "Why Write?"; Peter Medway, "From Talking to Writing"; Pat D'Arcy, "Keeping Options Open: Writing in the Humanities"; and selections from *Writing in Science* (essays by

Sue Watts and Jeff Shapland) and *Language and Learning in the Humanities* (essays by Bryan Newton, and Peter Medway and Ivor Goodson).

665   McLeod, Susan, and Margot Soven, eds. *Writing across the Curriculum: A Guide to Developing Programs*. Newbury Park, Calif.: Sage, 1992.

Twelve essays on the practical elements of setting up and developing WAC programs include Barbara Walvoord, "Getting Started"; Joyce Neff Magnetto and Barbara Stout, "Faculty Workshops"; Linda Peterson, "Writing across the Curriculum and/in the Freshman English Program"; Christine Farris and Raymond Smith, "Writing-Intensive Courses: Tools for Curricular Change"; Christopher Thaiss, "WAC and General Education Courses"; Muriel Harris, "The Writing Center and Tutoring in WAC Programs"; and Tori Haring-Smith, "Changing Students' Attitudes: Writing Fellows Programs."

666   Reiss, Donna, Dickie Selfe, and Art Young, eds. *Electronic Communication across the Curriculum*. Urbana, Ill.: NCTE, 1998.

Three sections of essays — programs, partnerships, and classrooms — explore the intersections of WAC theory and practice and electronic communication and present a number of strategies for approaching ECAC. Essays include Gail E. Hawisher and Michael A. Pemberton, "Writing across the Curriculum Encounters Asynchronous Learning Networks"; Mary E. Hocks and Daniele Bascelli, "Building a Writing-Intensive Multimedia Curriculum"; Stuart Selber and Bill Karis, "Composing Human-Computer Interfaces across the Curriculum in Engineering Schools"; Todd Taylor, "Teacher Training: A Blueprint for Action Using the World Wide Web"; Teresa M. Redd, "Accommodation and Resistance on (the Color) Line: Black Writers Meet White Artists on the Internet"; Margaret Portillo and Gail Summerskill Cummins, "Creativity, Collaboration, and Computers"; Paula Gillespie, "E-Journals: Writing to Learn in the Literature Classroom"; and Maryanne Felter and Daniel F. Schultz, "Network Discussions for Teaching Western Civilization."

See: David Russell, *Writing in the Academic Disciplines, 1870–1990* [133].

667   Smagorinsky, Peter. "Constructing Meaning in the Disciplines: Reconceptualizing Writing across the Curriculum as Composing across the Curriculum." *American Journal of Education* 103 (February 1995): 160–84.

Writing is only one way to promote thinking across the curriculum; its appropriateness as a medium depends on several factors. Theories based on semiotics and multiple intelligences challenge the privileged status of writing for the development of thought. Instead of embracing writing as a unique mode of learning, "each discipline should endorse the notion that meaning construction is the goal of learning," with the medium dependent on the discipline's values as well as the participants' consensus in the transaction. The author's exploratory research on the production of nonwritten texts suggests that an exclusive focus on writing as a mode of learning limits students' abilities to develop conceptual knowledge. Nonwritten texts are also valuable in English classes, where students should be invited to compose and develop interpretations of literature from a variety of media.

668   Smith, Louise Z. "Why English Departments Should 'House' Writing across the Curriculum." CE 50 (April 1988): 390–95.

Catherine Blair's account [654] of Writing-across-the-Curriculum theory is correct. She errs, however, in asserting that English departments can know only their own discipline-specific discourse. Postmodern literary theory blurs disciplinary boundaries by analyzing the influence of canonical cultural artifacts on the supposedly value-neutral discourse of other academic disciplines and by denying the distinction between literary and nonliterary language. Thus, English departments contain many scholars, including composition specialists, who have expertise in examining the relationship between language and knowledge and how these relationships might be taught. The authoritative influence of compositionists may be necessary to prevent mere editing across the curriculum even as we learn about disciplinary discourses from novice writing teachers from other departments.

669   Walvoord, Barbara E. "The Future of WAC." College English 58.1 (January 1996): 58–79.

The twenty-fifth anniversary of Writing across the Curriculum provides an opportunity for long-range planning and for interpreting WAC's past — both of which can be done through examining WAC as a social movement organization. For example, the literature on "movements" highlights early choices made by WAC to focus on micro, rather than on macro, concerns; to choose strategies that depended on changing behavior by persuasion; and to make workshops the backbone of the movement. Now, WAC must refocus its attention on macro issues, most significantly, the need to work with other organizations and to become active in national debates about educational reform. WAC must also define its relationship to administrations, explore the implications of new technologies, and contribute to debates on assessment. As a mature reform organization, WAC must draw upon the power of community so evident in early workshops.

See: Vivian Zamel, "Strangers in Academia: The Experiences of Faculty and ESL Students across the Curriculum" [546].

Electronic Writing Technologies

670   Blair, Kristine, and Pamela Takayoshi, eds. *Feminist Cyberspaces: Mapping Gendered Academic Space*. Stamford, Conn.: Ablex, 1999.

The complex relationship between women and technology is explored through multiple locations in a feminist cyberscape: the body, online identities, discourse communities, coalitions and collaborations, and the future. Thirteen chapters include Joanne Addison and Susan Hilligoss, "Technological Fronts: Lesbian Lives 'On the Line' "; Barbara Monroe, "Re-Membering Mama: The Female Body in Embodied and Disembodied Communication"; Shannon Wilson, "Pedagogy, Emotion, and the Protocol of Care"; Donna LeCourt, "Writing (Without) the Body: Gender and Power in Networked Discussion Groups"; Dene Grigar, "Over the Line, Online, and Gender Lines: E-mail and Women in the Classroom"; Mary E. Hocks, "Designing Feminist Multimedia for the United Nations Fourth World Conference on Women"; Margaret Daisley and Susan Romano, "Thirteen Ways of Looking at an M-Word"; Lisa Gerrard, "Feminist Research in Computers and Composition." Also featured are interviews with Helen Schwartz, Gail Hawisher, Mary Lay and Elizabeth Tebeaux, and Cynthia Selfe, and an online dialogue with the contributors.

671   Bolter, Jay David. *Writing Space: The Computer, Hypertext, and the History of Writing*. Hillside, N.J.: Lawrence Erlbaum Associates, 1991.

Writing is a technology inseparable from the materials and techniques of writing. Forms of text — scroll, codex book, electronic text — determine the organization and presentation of knowledge. Print books make text seem permanent and widen the gap between text and author. Electronic text does the opposite: the reader organizes, shapes, and adds to text, calls up other texts from databases, and creates a unique text in the process of reading. Print text must impose a hierarchy on ideas, reducing the typically associative writing process to linear form. Hypertext restores associative composing and requires associative reading through the layering of text. It comprises a network of verbal ideas. Electronic text recalls older forms of literacy, using picture writing in its icons, and restoring the formulaic, associative, and dynamic qualities of oral literature. Electronic texts dissolve into parts to be recombined and merge into larger textual structures, disrupting the traditional notion of authorship. Electronic fiction takes advantage of these qualities, offering a multitude of paths for the reader to travel. The plurality of the text and the disappearance of the author, imagined by innovative authors and critical theorists, are realized in electronic texts.

672   Bolter, Jay David and Richard Grusin. *Remediation: Understanding New Media*. Cambridge: MIT Press, 1999.

Two seemingly contradictory logics — immediacy and hypermediacy — are mutually dependent; both old and new media invoke these twin logics to remake themselves and each other, and new digital media oscillate between immediacy and hypermediacy, between transparency and opacity, with a social dimension as important as their formal and technical dimensions. A double logic of remediation, which can function explicitly or implicitly, began with the introduction of digital media and borrows from film, television, and photography. However, no medium today does its cultural work in isolation from other media; all new media emerge from within cultural contexts and refashion other media, and a particular medium is always understood in relation to other past and present media. The kind of borrowing extremely common in popular culture today is very old, but unlike paintings, the digital medium can be more aggressive in its remediation. Such contemporary media as computer games, digital photography, film, virtual reality, and the World Wide Web illustrate the process of remediation. Users or viewers enter into a two-fold relationship with the medium; the reflexive relationship between user and medium results in consequences for our culture's definitions of the self, defined by the perspectives that the subject occupies in the virtual space. New media are fully involved in the struggle to define the self as both embodied and mediated by the body. The remediated self, virtual self, and the networked self illustrate that whenever identity is mediated, it is also remediated.

673   Doheny-Farina, Stephen. *The Wired Neighborhood.* New Haven, Conn.: Yale Univ. Press, 1996.

Networked virtual realities offer gee-whiz experiences, but they cut people off from geophysical communities and increase the "placelessness" of modern life. MediaMOO, for example, is not a public space with the opportunity for public discourse, as advocates of online communities claim. Essentially a collection of private rooms, the MOO requires both complex socialization as well as technical expertise; it also reproduces cultural biases and resembles an airport bar more than a democratic space. Telecommuting, virtual schools, and community nets extend Doheny-Farina's argument that our dissolving communities cannot be "fixed" through technology and that users must become Net savvy without ignoring their cities, towns, and neighborhoods.

See: Lester Faigley, *Fragments of Rationality* [179].

674   Gurak, Laura J. *Persuasion and Privacy in Cyberspace: The Online Protests over Lotus Marketplace and the Clipper Chip.* New Haven, Conn.: Yale Univ. Press, 1997.

Two online protests — both motivated by concerns about privacy — offer different models for community action in cyberspace and illustrate the technological determinism embedded in many views of cyberspace. In this empirical study of life on the Internet, the Marketplace and Clipper cases provide the basis for an analysis of the structures of online communication, where ethos and delivery take on new significance and are critical to rhetorical online communities. Although the two case studies demonstrate the potential of communication technologies for more participation in public discourse, Gurak notes the circulation of inaccurate information and also argues that these technologies reproduce, and may even magnify, gender inequity and sexism.

675   Handa, Carolyn, ed. *Computers and Community: Teaching Composition in the Twenty-First Century.* Portsmouth, N.H.: Boynton/Cook, 1990.

Nine essays, five on teaching and four on theory, describe and explore the changes to pedagogy and classroom structure wrought by computerized classrooms: enhanced collaboration, a stonger sense of community and audience, less focus on the teacher as reader, more fun with writing. Essays include Thomas Barker and Fred Kemp, "Network Theory: A Postmodern Pedagogy for the Writing Classroom"; Carolyn Boiarsky, "Computers in the Classroom: The Instruction, the Mess, the Noise, the Writing"; Kathleen Skubikowski and John Elder, "Computers and the Social Contexts of Writing"; Mary Flores, "Computer Conferencing: Composing a Feminist Community of Writers"; and Carolyn Handa, "Politics, Ideology, and Strange, Slow Death of the Isolated Composer or Why We Need Community in the Writing Classroom."

See: Stuart Blythe, "Networked Computers + Writing Centers = ? Thinking about Networked Computers in Writing Center Practice" [620].

676   Hawisher, Gail E., and Sidney I. Dobrin, eds. *Evolving Perspectives on Computers and Composition Studies: Questions for the 1990s.* Urbana, Ill.: NCTE, 1991.

Fifteen essays divided into sections that address research, classrooms, hypertext, and politics suggest directions for future work. Included are Nancy Kaplan, "Ideology, Technology, and the Future of Writing Instruction"; Patricia Sullivan, "Taking Control of the Page: Electronic Writing and Word Publishing"; Elizabeth Klem and Charles Moran, "Computers and Instructional Strategies in the Teaching of Writing"; Stuart Moulthrop, "The Politics of Hypertext"; Mary Louise Gomez, "The Equitable Teaching of Composition with Computers: A Case for Change"; and Emily Jessup, "Feminism and Computers in Composition Instruction."

677   Hawisher, Gail E., Paul LeBlanc, Charles Moran, and Cynthia L. Selfe. *Computers and the Teaching of Writing in American Higher Education, 1979–1994: A History.* Norwood, N.J.: Ablex, 1996.

Computers and composition has become a coherent subfield within composition studies, growing from early experimental beginnings. Its development is chronicled in five chapters: 1979–1982, focusing on how personal computers were integrated into writing instruction; 1983–1985, described as the period of greatest enthusiasm for computer use; 1986–1988, when computers and composition emerged as a field; 1989–1991, when revisionist critiques of computer use began to appear; and 1992–1994, exploring the sudden impact of the Internet and commercially viable multimedia. Each chapter situates the field of computers and composition within a time period's developments in both composition studies and computer technology; notes then-current trends in the field; and links the field's issues with contemporary social and political developments. All but the first chapter also include interviews with key figures, both pioneers and emerging leaders.

678   Hawisher, Gail E., and Cynthia L. Selfe, eds. *Passions, Pedagogies, and 21st Century Technologies*. Logan: Utah State Univ. Press and NCTE, 1999.

This substantial collection addresses issues of information technologies and the technocultural contexts facing those in the English profession. Each of the four parts contains a response essay. Essays include Doug Hesse, "Saving a Place for Essayistic Literacy"; Gunther Kress, " 'English' at the Crossroads: Rethinking Curricula of Communication in the Context of the Turn to the Visual"; Lester Faigley, "Beyond Imagination: The Internet and Global Digital Literacy"; Marilyn Cooper, "Postmodern Pedagogy in Electronic Conversations"; Charles Moran, "Access: The A Word in Technology Studies"; James Porter, "Liberal Individualism and Internet Policy: A Communitarian Critique"; Gail E. Hawisher and Patricia A. Sullivan, "Fleeting Images: Women Visually Writing the Web"; Cynthia L. Selfe, "Lest We Think the Revolution Is a Revolution: Images of Technology and the Nature of Change"; Anne Frances Wysocki and Johndan Johnson-Eilola, "Blinded by the Letter: Why Are We Using Literacy as a Metaphor for Everything Else?"; and Janet Carey Eldred, "Technology's Strange, Familiar Voices."

679   Hawisher, Gail E., and Cynthia L. Selfe. "The Rhetoric of Technology and the Electronic Writing Class." *College Composition and Communication* 42 (February 1991): 55–65.

Articles on computers and composition are overwhelmingly laudatory, praising the rise of collaboration among students in the networked classroom. Observations in such classrooms show, however, that students often work alone at their computers, interact with peers in nonsubstantive ways, or rigidly follow an agenda set by the teacher. Hence noncollaborative activities are not prevented by computer use. Computer-based pedagogies must be informed by critical perspectives, as well as the usual optimistic enthusiasm, to circumvent such problems. For example, assignments involving electronic conferencing should be informed by Foucault's critique of surveillance strategies.

680   Holdstein, Deborah, and Cynthia L. Selfe, eds. *Computers and Writing: Theory, Research, Practice*. New York: MLA, 1990.

Ten essays address problems associated with computers and writing, such as software selection, staffing, control of equipment and facilities, and courseware development. Helen Schwartz argues in "Ethical Considerations of Educational Computer Use" that the inflexibility of software affects teacher-student interactions, that teachers are responsible for training as well as using software, that student ownership of texts in networks must be protected, that program limitations may cause miseducation, that software piracy must be prevented, and that access to technology must be spread as widely as possible. In "A Limitation on the Use of Computers in Composition," David N. Dobrin maintains that text processors are reliable and make no claims to give advice or analyze meaning, but that style analyzers, idea processors, and invention programs do not live up to their claims and are of little use. Michael Spitzer, in "Local and Global Networking: Implications for the Future," discusses how recognition of the capabilities of different kinds of networks facilitates selection of a variety of opportunities for collaborative writing, such as coauthorship, text swapping, conferencing, teacher coaching, and research.

681   Johnson-Eilola, Johndan, and Stuart A. Selber. "Policing Ourselves: Defining the Boundaries of Appropriate Discussion in Online Forums." *Computers and Composition* 13 (1996): 269–91.

Computers and writing specialists need to consider the mechanisms of language and how discourses "write us." For example, as individuals operate in online forums, they internalize certain discourse laws and then "police" themselves and others. An analysis of one public, nonacademic listserv for technical writers, TECHWR-L, demonstrates the regulating mechanisms that function in online forums and the consequences of violating them. Common messages were strictly on-topic and followed accepted practices, for example, that participants should make their presence known. When threads developed that transgressed the boundaries of conventional discourse in technical communication — such as discussions of racism and sexism — subscribers posted complaints and commands to get back on topic, or they enacted the silent treatment. The authors analyze the debate over appropriate topics and recommend that students learn to recognize discourse regulations.

682   Selfe, Cynthia. *Technology and Literacy in the Twenty-First Century: The Importance of Paying Attention.* Carbondale, Ill.: Southern Illinois University Press, 1999.

The national project to expand technological literacy supports and exacerbates inequities within our culture and the public education system. The Technology Literacy Challenge, a federal literacy project begun in 1996, provides a case study of the failure of such an initiative when it does not address the uneven distribution of technologies along the lines of race and socioeconomic status and the continuing reproduction of both illiteracy and poverty. Government initiatives, educators, businesses, parents, and ideology all play a role in creating a potent configuration for technological literacy that feeds Americans' belief that science + technology = progress, and that disguises the fact that technology is not available to everyone. Discounting the importance of multiple literacies and presenting either/or versions of technology, the dominant brand of technological literacy is defined as "competence with computers" rather than as a complex set of values, practices, and skills. The tendency to construct computers as either bane or boon encourages people to ignore the complicated relationships between technology and literacy, or to assume that the social and financial costs of technological literacy are inevitable. Humanist educators and literacy professionals should work on the local level to construct a larger vision of these issues; then intervene in the national project of expansion; and finally advocate critical technological literacy, which analyzes the technology-literacy link at fundamental levels of both conception and social practice.

683   Selfe, Cynthia L., and Susan Hilligoss. *Literacy and Computers: The Complications of Teaching and Learning with Technology.* New York: MLA, 1994.

While providing a good introduction to the issues involved in using computers in literacy education, this collection also considers philosophical concerns of interest to experienced computer users, concerns that seem unlikely to become dated soon. Three sections explore how computer technology changes literacy instruction; issues for teachers and scholars in using collaborative computer networks and hypertext; and suggestions for further research on literacy and technology. These sections begin with overviews and conclude with critical responses and a fourth section concludes the book. Essays include Paul J. LeBlanc, "The Politics of Literacy and Technology in Secondary School Classrooms"; Gail E. Hawisher, "Blinding Insights: Classification Schemes and Software for Literacy Instruction"; Ann Hill Duin and Craig Hansen, "Reading and Writing on Computer Networks as Social Construction and Social Interaction"; William Goodrich Jones, "Humanist Scholars' Use of Computers in Libraries and Writing"; Billie J. Wahlstrom, "Communication and Technology: Defining a Feminist Presence in Research and Practice"; Stuart Moulthrop and Nancy Kaplan, "They Became What They Beheld: The Futility of Resistance in the Space of Electronic Writing"; Davida Charney, "The Effect of Hypertext on Processes of Reading and Writing"; and Christina Haas and Christine M. Neuwirth, "Writing the Technology that Writes Us: Research on Literacy and the Shape of Technology."

684   Selfe, Cynthia L., and Richard J. Selfe, Jr. "The Politics of the Interface: Power and Its Exercise in Electronic Contact Zones." CCC 45 (December 1994): 480–504.

Limited access is the most obvious political issue related to computers; more serious are the ways in which computer interfaces reproduce racist, sexist, and colonialist attitudes. Mapping computer interfaces illustrates their representation of knowledge as hierarchial, rational, and logical, including the dominance of American corporate culture in the languages and icons. A critically reflective stance toward computers will highlight the effects of domination and colonialism and will require educators and computer specialists to locate themselves on the map of interfaces. One tactic is to teach students to be technology critics, not just technology users; another is to redesign interfaces around different metaphors of work and production.

685   Sibyelle, Gruber. "Technology and Tenure: Creating Oppositional Discourse in an Offline and Online World." *Computers and Composition* 17.1 (2000): 41–56.

Specialists in computers and composition may be positioned as outsiders to the traditional promotion and tenure process, but simple dichotomies don't do justice to the contradictions and multiplicity that characterize the status of technorhetoricians, who can take advantage of the complexity of their status to enact change. Sandoval's idea of differential movement creates an oppositional consciousness that can help to form coalitions. Those faculty working with instructional uses of technology should see their work as an oppositional form of praxis, where current value systems can be used to promote transformation within the academy. Technology-enhanced work does not simply follow accepted norms nor does it undermine those norms. Those who become chimeras, cyborgs, or boundary crossers employ theories of opposition to renegotiate what is marginal.

686   Spooner, Michael, and Kathleen Yancey. "Postings on a Genre of Email." CCC 47.2 (May 1996): 252–78.

Does e-mail differ from other types of writing, or is the only distinctive feature of online writing its transmission via computer? Is e-mail a genre-in-the-making, with parallels to the development of the Victorian novel, or are electronic communications simply reproducing extant genres, rather than creating new ones? How much does the technology change the rhetorical situation? In an essay/dialogue that uses the tropes and codes of the net, two voices discuss whether e-mail constitutes a genre and raise questions about teaching with technology. E-mail can be categorized in at least five ways; none of the categories, as practiced in electronic classrooms, promises innovative pedagogy. What students need is strategies for "how to manage the multi-vocality and at the same time create enough coherence that a spectating conversationalist can enter the fray."

687   Sullivan, Patricia and James E. Porter. *Opening Spaces: Writing Technologies and Critical Research Practices.* Greenwich, Conn.: Ablex, 1997.

Critical research practices in computers and composition, key to the development of knowledge, require a revision of methodology that calls attention to its rhetorical nature as well as to the rhetorical situation of participants, writing technologies, and technology design. Methodology has theoretical dimensions and should be seen as a heuristic rather than as a set of rules; "announcing" a method, for example, does not ground a study in site-specific, situated ways. Postmodern researchers can develop a critical praxis to combat traditional methodological rules or guidelines; methodology in a postmodern sense is local, contingent, malleable, and heuristic, and research becomes a form of political and ethical action. Postmodern mapping serves as an analytic tool for critical framing; mapping relationships and positions visually and spatially helps to achieve methodological reflectiveness and epistemological vigilance in examining issues in the study of computers in the classroom and in the workplace. Critical postmodern theory helps to articulate criteria for determining uses of computers for studying writing with a focus on the politics and ethics of research in terms of both participants and aims. Enacting critical research practices requires a doubling action: an interplay of tensions and tactics not only at the level of overarching concerns but also in terms of specific critical moves. Tactics such as advocacy charting are offered for exploring the tensions between researchers and participants, and an early chapter serves as a glossary.

688   Taylor, Todd and Irene Ward. *Literacy Theory in the Age of the Internet.* New York: Columbia University Press, 1998.

Concerned with the politics of technology and education, the eleven chapters in this volume suggest ways to solve complex issues regarding instructional technology. In three sections, Literacy in the Information Age, Literacy and the Body Electric, and Electronic Pedagogies, the essays include: Lester Faigley, "Literacy After the Revolution: 1996 CCCC Chair's Address"; Johndan Johnson-Eilola, "Negative Spaces: From Production to Connection in Composition"; Cynthia Haynes, "prosthetic rhetorics@writing.loss.technology"; Raul Sanchez, "Our Bodies? Our Selves?: Questions About Teaching in the MUD"; Todd Taylor, "The Persistence of Authority: Coercing the Student Body"; Tim Mayers and Kevin Swafford, "Reading the Networks of Power: Rethinking 'Critical Thinking' in Computerized Classrooms"; Patricia Fitzsimmons-Hunter and Charles Moran, "Writing Teachers, Schools, Access, and Change."

See: Barbara Warnick, "Rhetorical Criticism of Public Discourse on the Internet: Theoretical Implications" [223].

689   Yagelski, Robert P. and Jeffrey T. Grabill, "Computer-Mediated Communication in the Undergraduate Writing Classroom: A Study of the Relationship of Online Discourse and Classroom Discourse in Two Writing Classes." *Computers and Composition* 15 (1998): 11–40.

Online discourse in educational settings is characterized by complex relationships, more complicated than the findings of previous studies on the use of computer-mediated communication (CMC). Benefits are cited routinely in studies of CMC, but little attention has been paid to the ways in which online discussions and conventional in-class discourse may relate to and influence each other. Qualitative and quantitative techniques were employed to collect a variety of data related to the in-class and online discourse of two undergraduate writing courses at Purdue University: field notes of class meetings, interviews, surveys, and monitoring online discussions. Results of content coding were tabulated and then put into context through qualitative analyses. Findings indicated that how instructors set up, assigned, and managed the CMC components seemed to play a key role in shaping students' online participation, also a function of the perceptions about and experiences with CMC in general. Without models of online discussions, for example, students focused on issues that rarely surfaced in class; in addition, students *as students* reproduced in online discussions "normal" in-class discourse. Simply putting students online does not necessarily increases their rates of participation, change the nature of that participation, or provide a more egalitarian space.

Service Learning

690   Adler-Kassner, Linda, Robert Crooks, and Ann Watters, eds. *Writing the Community: Concepts and Models for Service-Learning in Composition.* Washington, D.C.: American Association for Higher Education, 1997.

Thirteen essays and an annotated bibliography on service-learning theories and practices. Included are Tom Deans, "Writing across the Curriculum and Service Learning"; Nora Bacon, "Community Service Writing: Problems, Challenges, Questions"; Bruce Herzberg, "Community Service and Critical Teaching" [699]; David Cooper and Laura Julier, "Democratic Conversations: Civic Literacy and Service-Learning in the American Grains" [695]; Linda Flower, "Partners in Inquiry: A Logic for Community Outreach"; and Chris Anson, "On Reflection: The Role of Logs and Journals in Service-Learning Courses" [691].

691   Anson, Chris. "On Reflection: The Role of Logs and Journals in Service-Learning Courses." *Writing the Community: Concepts and Models for Service-Learning in Composition.* Ed. Linda Adler-Kassner, Robert Crooks, and Ann Watters. Washington, D.C.: American Association for Higher Education, 1997. 167–80. [690]

Service-learning courses require an element of reflection that is typically served by journal writing. The complexity and personal engagement in such courses makes journals an ideal medium for recording events and personal reactions. However, with direction and modeling, journals can become quite sophisticated ways for students to engage in more focused reflection and critical examination of ideas. A direct way to do this is simply to assign students to first record reactions and then reflect on them. The reflection assignment can be enriched by specifying theoretical frameworks — drawn from readings or class presentation — for examining experience. In responding to these journals, teachers have the opportunity to deepen reflection within the framework, to shift to other perhaps more fruitful frames, or to encourage deeper reflection on social practices.

692   Bacon, Nora. "Building a Swan's Nest for Instruction in Rhetoric." *CCC* 51.4 (June 2000): 589–609.

Community-based writing assignments highlight the need for writing instruction that attends to matters of rhetorical variation. Students need to understand the rhetorical function of the texts they are asked to produce; they need to analyze language in a wide range of texts and contexts, academic as well as nonacademic, in order to discover the ways in which form corresponds to rhetorical function. The evolution of one teacher's community-based writing curriculum demonstrates the possibility of rendering the teaching of rhetorical awareness from the classroom a less contradictory and more manageable task.

693   Bacon, Nora. "Setting the Course for Service-Learning Research." *Reflections on Community-Based Writing Instruction* 2.1 (Fall 2000): 1–7.

Pragmatic issues, such as whether or not service learning actually works, have typically dominated service learning research. Responding to a call put forth at the First Annual International Conference on Service-Learning Research, future research will prove more rigorous in terms of both questions and design. An increase in empirical work focused on academics, on students' mastery of course content, will be seen, as will an increase in studies that compare service learning pedagogy to more traditional pedagogy. Further, the impact of service learning on community (in all its multiple meanings) and on faculty, as well as on particular higher education institutions, is also likely to play a significant role in future investigations of service learning. Of most significance for composition studies, however, will be the expanded role of qualitative research. As questions shift from "does service learning work?" to "*how* does service learning work?", methodological approaches will shift and yield new insights into teaching and learning.

694   Ball, Kevin and Amy Goodburn. "Composition Studies and Service Learning: Appealing to Communities?" *Composition Studies* 28.1 (2000): 79–94.

Although much of composition's literature on service learning calls for reciprocity and community empowerment, the value of service learning is still primarily argued to a peer/professional audience, rather than to the community or public being served. Furthermore, neither the learning of community participants, nor the impact such learning has on service learning's value in the classroom, is represented in most professional literature on service learning. Community perspectives as well as all participants' experiences, not just students' and teachers', in service learning endeavors might be integrated more fully into service learning curricula by conducting community problem-solving dialogues, as described by Linda Flower, and by assigning students research projects that ask them not only to study the community contexts in which they will be working but also to include community participants' perspectives in their papers and reflections.

695   Cooper, David D., and Laura Julier. "Democratic Conversations: Civic Literacy and Service-Learning in the American Grains." *Writing the Community: Concepts and Models for Service-Learning in Composition.* Ed. Linda Adler-Kassner, Robert Crooks, and Ann Watters. Washington, D.C.: American Association for Higher Education, 1997. 79–94. [690].

In a service learning composition course called Public Life in America, students examine what it means to be a member of a community and a citizen in a democracy and ask how civic, religious, economic, and social traditions shaped moral life in America. They read works by civic writers such as Jefferson, King, and Dorothy Day, study civic problems such as inequality and prejudice, and analyze the many outlets for political persuasion that flood citizens with information and propaganda. For their service work, students engage in writing projects for nonprofits in the area. Research papers focus on local issues of civic importance such as civil rights cases and include surveys, interviews, and attending public meetings. Quite often, as a result of this work and their growing ability to write for public agencies, students engage in the civic debate on the issues they are studying and thus participate in the search for solutions to problems. In this process, the vocabulary of democracy comes alive, students gain both academic discourse skills and civic literacy, and they begin themselves to participate in the conversation that constitutes democracy.

696   Deans, Thomas. *Writing Partnerships: Service-Learning in Composition.* Urbana: NCTE, 2000.

The works of John Dewey and Paulo Friere provide a theoretical framework for setting up community writing initiatives. Such initiatives can be categorized according to where the primary learning takes place, which literacies (workplace, academic, critical, and hybrid) are privileged, and which discourses (academic, workplace, and hybrid) are most highly valued. Whether writing *for, with,* or *about* the community (the three classifications in the taxonomy of community writing paradigms), community based composition courses emphasize experiential learning, community work paired with academic study, community outreach experiences blended with research and writing projects, and a commitment to investigating social justice and community problems through writing and rhetoric.

697 Ervin, Elizabeth. "Learning to Write with a Civic Tongue." *Blundering for a Change: Errors and Expectations in Critical Pedagogy*. Eds. John Paul Tassoni and William H. Thelin. Portsmouth, N.H.: Boynton/Cook-Heinemann, 2000. 144–57.

Errors can serve useful heuristic functions. When considered as honestly and generously as student errors, teacher/researcher errors can prompt the necessary reflection and action that lead to new understandings. If service learning is to be the micro-revolution many enthuse it can be, those who practice it and record their practices must straightforwardly own up to their blunders. Only by revealing the "messy realities" of pedagogy can teachers truly practice teaching that is both radical and democratic.

698 Flower, Linda and Shirley Brice Heath. "Drawing on the Local: Collaboration and Community Expertise." *Language and Learning Across the Disciplines* 4.3 (October 2000): 43–55.

Service learning initiatives should work toward creating relationships that respect, nurture, and draw on local expertise. In doing so, however, student and faculty participants in service learning face the problem of not only hearing local expertise, but also of constructing an understanding of that expertise that has the power to change the participants themselves and the communities they encounter. The "rival hypotheses" that develop from a community problem-solving dialogue suggest that sustainability in service learning initiatives requires more than good intentions. Sustainability also requires stepping out of one's own discourse and framework as well as off campus; and reciprocity must come in multiple forms: recognition of a community institution's history and contributions, commitment to a relationship beyond the single semester parameter, and a respect for community expertise that shows itself via engaged dialogue.

699 Herzberg, Bruce. "Community Service and Critical Teaching." CCC 45 (October 1994): 307–19. Rpt. in *Writing the Community*. Ed. Linda Adler-Kassner et al. [690]. Rpt. in *Critical Literacy in Action*. Ed. Ira Shor and Caroline Pari [387].

Students in service learning courses who go into the community as volunteers are performing needed work. Moreover, they report a heightened sense of the reality of homelessness and need. But their perceptions of these problems tend to be personal rather than social and systemic. They see illiteracy, for example, as the consequence of not studying hard enough. Band-aid volunteer work thus masks the causes of social problems. Service learning must promote critical analysis and social change: Students must therefore do more than write about their experiences. Studying and writing about social forces and how they operate through institutions like schools challenges their long-held beliefs in meritocracy and individualism, but finally leads to deeper reflection on the nature of the problems they see in their community-service work.

700   Herzberg, Bruce. "Service Learning and Public Discourse." *JAC* 20.2 (Spring 2000): 391–404.

Those who contend that the composition course is truly about rhetoric and civic virtue, and about public discourse as well as academic, need to develop convincing conceptualizations about the connections between society and the academy. One approach in a service-learning course asks students to write research papers that draw on their experiences in service projects. However, while this approach enables a deeper understanding of the issues, it does not lead students into an exploration of the gap between academic research and public policy. Students need both academic discourse and public discourse; they need to practice both and to find a way to bring academic knowledge to bear in public argument. One way students can do this in a service learning course is to identify a number of ways to go public with their community service-related academic research — phone calls, letters, personal appearances, Web postings, interactive Web pages, fliers, demonstrations, tee-shirts, running for office, seeking organizations, and establishing organizations are some ways — and then to examine the rhetorical characteristics of these forms and choose one through which to go public with their arguments. This exercise teaches students to make use of arguments that they develop in academic research papers; it sharpens their awareness of the purposes of different forms, and it enables them to better recognize rhetorical dimensions of both academic and public discourse.

701   Huckin, Thomas N. "Technical Writing and Community Service." *Journal of Business and Technical Communication* 11 (January 1997): 49–59.

Technical-writing courses have long sent students off campus to do projects in businesses, government agencies, and nonprofit organizations. These projects successfully motivate students, help them learn audience awareness and collaboration, and develop project management skills. In addition to these benefits, students in service learning courses develop civic awareness and help the larger community. Agencies with technical writing needs abound. Instructors should, however, work with each agency to define the project clearly, establish goals, and assure agency support. Small groups for each project work well. Students will need to learn on-site consulting skills, such as interviewing. Once projects are under way, students should work independently, producing progress reports and meeting with the instructor, though full-class meetings may not be necessary every week. The instructor should monitor the projects for quality control and maintain contact with the agencies. Civic education, a major benefit, requires classroom reflection periodically and at the end of the semester. Such a course prepares technical writers for a life of active citizenship.

702   Peck, Wayne Campbell, Linda Flower, and Lorraine Higgins. "Community Literacy." CCC 46 (May 1995): 199–222.

The Community Literacy Center, a collaboration between a Pittsburgh settlement house and Carnegie Mellon, seeks to foster literacy as action and reflection. It promotes collaborative, intercultural efforts to write public texts as a form of community action. Unlike cultural literacy, which seeks to build community by minimizing difference, and unlike social critique, which seeks community through ideological struggle, community literacy seeks alternative discourses that promote social change, intercultural conversation, inquiry, and strategic rhetoric. Community literacy approaches difference with the goal of negotiating meanings as a way of responding to conflicts. In the CLC collaboration, CMU student mentors do not work to "improve" community residents' writing or help them "find their own voice." Their approach instead is rhetorical: finding ways to use writing as a tool in a literate transaction. This process, to be successful, requires intercultural conversation, problem-solving, and negotiation. Several examples illustrate the successes of the community literacy approach.

703   Roswell, Barbara. "Service-Learning and Composition: Towards an Engaged Academy." Reflections on Community-Based Writing Instruction 1.3 (Winter 2000): 1–7.

Students should learn that their education is not simply for their own personal growth or gain, that they are members of communities, and that what they do and learn can benefit fellow citizens as well as themselves. Service learning increases students' concepts of the social and personal significance of the skills which composition teaches, and can heighten students' awareness of their own sense of themselves as agents of change. Service learning courses underscore a dual responsibility: to develop effective learning strategies and to promote meaningful, productive change. To live up to both responsibilities, service learning courses should involve long-term partnerships, rather than placements that change from term to term.

704   Schutz, Aaron, and Anne Ruggles Gere. "Service Learning and English Studies: Rethinking 'Public' Service." CE 60 (February 1998): 129–48.

If students in service-learning composition courses are not gaining a critical social perspective from their service work, as some have complained, the problem may be that one-on-one work such as tutoring — a frequent type of project — naturally emphasizes a model of "caring" over a model of public policy advocacy. The "caring" approach focuses on the needs of the individual being served and displaces engagement with larger social dimensions. To gain a more public perspective, tutors would need a connection to the tutee's larger community. Students are, however, already connected to a community that they can serve: the campus. In on-campus service and research projects, students explore social and political forces and are participants in the policy issues they investigate. Writing projects can contribute to the local public debate on the issue. Moreover, in such projects, students are not "experts" serving others; they are, rather, relative equals seeking to define a public space and take social action to benefit a community of which they are a part.

Composition Books from Bedford/St. Martin's

Below you'll find a list of Bedford/St. Martin's titles of interest to composition instructors. We publish a complete line of handbooks, rhetorics, readers, research guides, and professional resources. New titles are listed in bold. Please see our Web page, **bedfordstmartins.com,** for full descriptions and ordering information, or contact your local sales representative.

COMPOSITION TEXTS

Handbooks

Diana Hacker, A Pocket Style Manual, Fourth Edition, 2004

Diana Hacker, Rules for Writers, Fifth Edition, 2004

Larry Beason and Mark Lester, A Commonsense Guide to Grammar and Usage, Third Edition, 2003

Diana Hacker, A Writer's Reference, Fifth Edition, 2003

Andrea A. Lunsford, The St. Martin's Handbook, Fifth Edition, 2003

Andrew Harnack and Eugene Kleppinger, Online! A Reference Guide to Using Internet Sources, 2001 Update

Diana Hacker, The Bedford Handbook, Sixth Edition, 2002

Andrea A. Lunsford, The Everyday Writer, Second Edition, 2001

Andrea A. Lunsford, EasyWriter: A Pocket Guide, Second Edition, 2002

Rhetorics

Rise B. Axelrod and Charles R. Cooper, The St. Martin's Guide to Writing, Sixth Edition, 2004

Lisa Ede, Work in Progress: A Guide to Academic Writing and Revising, Sixth Edition, 2004

Carolyn Handa, Visual Rhetoric in a Digital World, 2004

Rise B. Axelrod and Charles R. Cooper, Axelrod and Cooper's Concise Guide to Writing, Third Edition, 2002

X. J. Kennedy, Dorothy M. Kennedy, and Sylvia A. Holladay, The Bedford Guide for College Writers, Sixth Edition, 2002

Kathleen T. McWhorter, *Successful College Writing: Skills, Strategies, Learning Styles*, Second Edition, 2003

Nancy Huddleston Packer and John Timpane, *Writing Worth Reading: The Critical Process*, Third Edition, 1997

Nedra Reynolds, *Portfolio Keeping: A Guide for Students*, 2000

Mike Rose and Malcolm Kiniry, *Critical Strategies for Academic Thinking and Writing*, Third Edition, 1998

Robert Scholes, Nancy R. Comley, and Janice Peritz, *The Practice of Writing*, Fifth Edition, 2001

Research Guides

Diana Hacker and Barbara Fister, *Research and Documentation in the Electronic Age*, Third Edition, 2002

Jean Johnson, *The Bedford Guide to the Research Process*, Third Edition, 1997

Mike Palmquist, *The Bedford Researcher: An Integrated Text, CD-ROM, and Web Site*, 2003

Brenda Spatt, *Writing from Sources*, Sixth Edition, 2003

Bonnie Stone Sunstein and Elizabeth Chiseri-Strater, *Fieldworking: Reading and Writing Research*, Second Edition, 2002

Stephen Weidenborner and Domenick Caruso, *Writing Research Papers: A Guide to the Process*, Sixth Edition, 2001

COMPOSITION READERS

Rhetorical Readers

Alfred Rosa and Paul Eschholz, Models for Writers: Short Essays for Composition, Eighth Edition, 2004

Laurie G. Kirszner and Stephen R. Mandell, Patterns for College Writing: A Rhetorical Reader and Guide, Ninth Edition, 2004

Jane E. Aaron, *The Compact Reader: Short Essays by Method and Theme*, Seventh Edition, 2003

Rise B. Axelrod and Charles R. Cooper, *Reading Critically, Writing Well: A Reader and Guide*, Sixth Edition, 2002

Lynn Z. Bloom and Louise Z. Smith, *The St. Martin's Custom Reader*, 2002

Charles R. Cooper, *Writing the World: Reading and Writing about Issues of the Day*, 2000

Paul Eschholz and Alfred Rosa, *Subjects/Strategies: A Writer's Reader*, Ninth Edition, 2002

Cheryl Glenn, *Making Sense: A New Rhetorical Reader*, 2002

X. J. Kennedy, Dorothy Kennedy, and Jane E. Aaron, *The Bedford Reader*, Eighth Edition, 2003

X. J. Kennedy, Dorothy Kennedy, and Jane E. Aaron, *The Brief Bedford Reader*, Eighth Edition, 2003

Donald McQuade and Robert Atwan, *The Writer's Presence: A Pool of Readings*, Fourth Edition, 2003

Thematic Readers

Gary Colombo, Robert Cullen, and Bonnie Lisle, *Rereading America: Cultural Contexts for Critical Thinking and Writing*, Fifth Edition, 2004

Andrea Lunsford and John Ruskiewicz, *The Presence of Others: Voices and Images That Call for Response*, Fourth Edition, 2004

Robert Atwan, *America Now: Short Readings from Recent Periodicals*, Fifth Edition, 2003

Robert Atwan, *Convergences: Message, Method, Medium*, 2002

Robert Atwan, *Our Times: Readings from Recent Periodicals*, Fifth Edition, 1998

Robert Atwan, *Ten on Ten: Major Essays on Recurring Themes*, 1992

David Bartholomae and Anthony Petrosky, *Ways of Reading Words and Images*, 2003

Lynn Z. Bloom and Louise Z. Smith, *The Arlington Reader: Canons and Contexts*, 2003

David Cavitch, *Life Studies: An Analytic Reader*, Seventh Edition, 2001

Gary Colombo, *Mind Readings: An Anthology for Writers*, 2002

Charles R. Cooper and Susan Peck MacDonald, *Writing the World: Reading and Writing about Issues of the Day*, 2000

Stephen Dilks, Regina Hansen, and Matthew Parfitt, *Cultural Conversations: The Presence of the Past*, 2001

Paul Eschholz, Alfred Rosa, and Virginia Clark, *Language Awareness: Readings for College Writers*, Eighth Edition, 2001

Sonia Maasik and Jack Solomon, *Signs of Life in the U.S.A.: Readings on Popular Culture for Writers*, Fourth Edition, 2003

Donald McQuade and Christine McQuade, *Seeing & Writing 2*, 2003

Joan T. Mims and Elizabeth M. Nollen, *Mirror on America: Short Essays and Images from Popular Culture*, Second Edition, 2003

Carol J. Verburg, *Ourselves Among Others: Readings from Home and Abroad*, Fourth Edition, 2000

Cross-Curricular Readers

Nancy R. Comley, David Hamilton, Carl H. Klaus, Robert Scholes, Nancy Sommers, *Fields of Reading: Motives for Writing*, Seventh Edition, 2004

Lee A. Jacobus, *A World of Ideas: Essential Readings for College Writers*, Sixth Edition, 2002

Mike Rose and Malcolm Kiniry, *Critical Strategies for Academic Thinking and Writing*, Third Edition, 1998

Cultural Studies Readers

Gary Colombo, Robert Cullen, and Bonnie Lisle, *Rereading America: Cultural Contexts for Critical Thinking and Writing*, Fifth Edition, 2004

Charles R. Cooper, *Writing the World: Reading and Writing about Issues of the Day*, 2000

David Bartholomae and Anthony Petrosky, *Ways of Reading: An Anthology for Writers*, Sixth Edition, 2002

Patricia Bizzell and Bruce Herzberg, *Negotiating Difference: Cultural Case Studies for Composition*, 1996

Stephen Dilks, Regina Hansen, and Matthew Parfitt, *Cultural Conversations: The Presence of the Past*, 2001

Paul Eschholz, Alfred Rosa, and Virginia Clark, *Language Awareness: Readings for College Writers*, Eighth Edition, 2001

Sonia Maasik and Jack Solomon, *California Dreams and Realities: Readings for Critical Thinkers and Writers*, Second Edition, 1999

Sonia Maasik and Jack Solomon, *Signs of Life in the USA: Readings on Popular Culture for Writers*, Fourth Edition, 2003

Donald McQuade and Christine McQuade, *Seeing & Writing 2*, 2003

Mike Rose and Malcolm Kiniry, *Critical Strategies for Academic Thinking and Writing*, Third Edition, 1998

Joan T. Mims and Elizabeth M. Nollen, *Mirror on America: Short Essays and Images from Popular Culture*, Second Edition, 2003

Carol J. Verburg, *Ourselves Among Others: Readings from Home and Abroad*, Fourth Edition, 2000

Short Essay Readers

Alfred Rosa and Paul Eschholz, *Models for Writers: Short Essays for Composition*, Eighth Edition, 2004

Jane E. Aaron, *The Compact Reader: Short Essays by Method and Theme*, Seventh Edition, 2003

Robert Atwan, *America Now: Short Readings from Recent Periodicals*, Fifth Edition, 2003

Joan T. Mims and Elizabeth M. Nollen, *Mirror on America: Short Essays and Images from Popular Culture*, Second Edition, 2003

Mike Rose and Malcolm Kiniry, *Critical Strategies for Academic Thinking and Writing*, Third Edition, 1998

Argument/Critical Thinking Readers

Andrea Lunsford and John Ruszkiewicz, *Everything's an Argument with Readings*, Third Edition, 2004

Rise B. Axelrod and Charles R. Cooper, *Reading Critically, Writing Well: A Reader and a Guide*, Sixth Edition, 2002

Sylvan Barnet and Hugo Bedau, *Current Issues and Enduring Questions: A Guide to Critical Thinking and Argument, with Readings*, Sixth Edition, 2002

Annette T. Rottenberg, *Elements of Argument: A Text and Reader*, Seventh Edition, 2003

Annette T. Rottenberg, *The Structure of Argument*, Fourth Edition, 2003

Readers Arranged Alphabetically

Sam Cohen, *50 Essays: A Portable Anthology*, 2004

Readers Arranged by Author

David Bartholomae and Anthony Petrosky, *Ways of Reading: An Anthology for Writers*, Sixth Edition, 2002

Donald Hall, *The Contemporary Essay*, Third Edition, 1995

Donald McQuade and Robert Atwan, *The Writer's Presence: A Pool of Readings*, Fourth Edition, 2003

William Smart, *Eight Modern Essayists*, Sixth Edition, 1995

INSTRUCTORS' RESOURCES

Keith Hjortshoj and Katerine Gottschalk, *Elements of Teaching Writing*, 2004

Nedra Reynolds, Patricia Bizzell, Bruce Herzberg, *The Bedford Bibliography for Teachers of Writing*, Sixth Edition, 2004

Linda Adler-Kassner and Gregory R. Glau, *The Bedford Bibliography for Teachers of Basic Writing*, 2002

Timothy Barnett, *Teaching Argument in the Composition Course: Background Readings*, 2001

Glenn Blalock, *Background Readings for Instructors Using* The Bedford Handbook, Sixth Edition, 2002

Patricia Bizzell and Bruce Herzberg, *The Rhetorical Tradition: Readings from Classical Times to the Present*, Second Edition, 2001

Richard Bullock, *The St. Martin's Manual for Writing in the Disciplines*, 1999

Ellen Cushman, Eugene R. Kintgen, Barry M. Kroll, and Mike Rose, *Literacy: A Critical Sourcebook*, 2001

Lisa Ede, *On Writing Research: The Braddock Essays 1975–1998*, 1999

Lisa Ede and Andrea A. Lunsford, *Selected Essays of Robert J. Connors*, 2003

Cheryl Glenn and Robert Connors, *The New St. Martin's Guide to Teaching Writing*, Fifth Edition, 2003

T. R. Johnson and Shirley Morahan, *Teaching Composition: Background Readings*, 2002

Gesa E. Kirsch, Faye Spencer Maor, Lance Massey, Lee Nickoson-Massey, and Mary P. Sheridan-Rabideau, *Feminism and Composition: A Critical Sourcebook*, 2003

Christina Murphy and Steve Sherwood, *The St. Martin's Sourcebook for Writing Tutors*, Second Edition, 2003

Nedra Reynolds, *Portfolio Keeping: A Guide for Students*, Fifth Edition, 2002

Nedra Reynolds, *Portfolio Teaching: A Guide for Instructors*, Fourth Edition, 2002

Leigh Ryan, *The Bedford Guide for Writing Tutors*, Third Edition, 2002

Edward W. White, *Assigning, Responding, Evaluating: A Writing Teacher's Guide*, Fourth Edition, 1999

Index of Authors Cited

Numbers refer to entries within the bibliography.

Taylor, Denny, 283
Taylor, Todd, 688
Tenney, Deborah, 302
Thelin, William H., 697
Thompson, Craig R., 56
Thralls, Charlotte, 552
Tinberg, Howard B., 614
Tobin, Lad, 243, 415
Trapp, Robert, 182
Treichler, Paula A., 492
Trimbur, John, 165, 220, 402, 439, 522, 523, 633
Trimmer, Joseph F., 416
Tuana, Nancy, 139
Tucker, Amy, 544
Tuman, Myron C., 284
Tyler, Lisa, 599

Valdes, Guadalupe, 545
Vandenberg, Peter, 36, 649
Varner, Iris, 600
Varnum, Robin, 140
Villanueva, Victor, Jr., 221, 285
Vitanza, Victor, 222
Vivion, Michael J., 515

Wallace, David L., 233, 513
Wallace, Ray, 336, 639
Walvoord, Barbara E. Fassler, 366, 669
Ward, Irene, 615, 688
Warnick, Barbara, 223
Watson, J.S., 52
Watters, Ann, 690, 691, 695
Weathers, Winston, 341
Weaver, Christopher C., 370

Weaver, Purcell, 210
Weaver, Richard M., 224
Weber, Rose-Marie, 529
Weiser, Irwin, 369, 612
Wells, Susan, 225
Wertheimer, Molly Meijer, 141
Whately, Richard, 69
White, Edward M., 160, 367, 616
Wiener, Harvey S., 354, 403
Wilkinson, John, 210
Willard, Frances E., 72
Williams, David L., 581
Williams, James D., 391
Williams, Jean C., 129
Williams, Joseph M., 480
Williamson, Michael M., 652
Winsor, Dorothy, 577, 578
Winterowd, W. Ross, 300
Witherspoon, John, 67
Witte, Stephen P., 301, 317, 617
Wolff, William C., 650
Woodward, William Harrison, 142
Worsham, Lynn, 499, 519
Wozniak, John Michael, 143
WPA Board of Consultant Evaluators, 618

Yagelski, Robert P., 286, 321, 689
Yancey, Kathleen Blake, 362, 368, 369, 417, 686
Young, Art, 655, 656, 657, 666
Young, Richard E., 294, 295

Zak, Frances, 370
Zamel, Vivian, 534, 546, 547, 548